D1712967

Romantic Theory

Romantic Theory

Forms of Reflexivity in the Revolutionary Era

LEON CHAI

The Johns Hopkins University Press

Baltimore

The Johns Hopkins University Press

2715 North Charles Street

Baltimore, Maryland 21218-4363

www.press.jhu.edu

Library of Congress Cataloging-in-Publication Data

Chai, Leon.

Romantic theory : forms of reflexivity in the Revolutionary Era / Leon Chai.

p. cm.

Includes bibliographical references (p.   ) and index.

ISBN 0-8018-8396-2 (alk. paper)

1. Romanticism. I. Title.

PN56.R7C43 2006

809′.9145—dc22

2005055244

A catalog record for this book is available from the British Library.

CONTENTS

In recent years, the fate of theory has given rise to much concern. To see why, it's only necessary to take a quick look at the current scene: since 1990, roughly, no new forms of theory, and, instead, a lot of restatements, with some variation, of earlier viewpoints. Perhaps the most noticeable trend, in fact, has been a tendency to combine some of these. The new eclecticism, you might call it. Yet even the combination of different approaches hasn't quite managed to produce an entirely satisfactory result. Hence our present critical impasse.

A number of possible explanations come to mind. Maybe our present forms of theory simply don't answer the questions we really want to ask. Or maybe the conversation has just turned away from theory. In any case, what no one can deny is a definite shift. Before, it seemed a common belief that all the larger questions could be answered only by theory. And now that belief is no longer there. Yet it isn't as if we've come to feel we no longer need theory because it's already fulfilled its purpose, given us what we want. On the contrary: the reason theory now faces an uncertain future might well be its failure to satisfy a need we still feel. Simply put, what we want from theory is a higher level of conceptual awareness. So if we no longer turn so hopefully to theory as we once did, our reluctance might well imply doubt as to whether theory has that sort of awareness to give.

To understand how we've arrived at the point where we now are, it seems useful to go back to the springtime of hope for theory: the last moment, in recent memory, when theory seemed as if about to answer all our questions. Specifically, I want to revisit Paris structuralism, and most of all (despite his vehement efforts to dissociate himself from that movement) the work of Michel Foucault. *The Order of Things* marks perhaps the last attempt, in recent years, at universal theory. Its ambition was to integrate a history of the human sciences with a theory of those sciences. By his refusal to adopt a teleological perspective, Foucault believed he could produce a better account of the history of the human sciences. At the same time, his account of their history was also supposed to yield a theoretical framework. But the historical account never quite managed to coalesce with the theory, largely because Foucault couldn't find a way to conceptualize the developmental aspect of nineteenth-century theory. So his project broke down after the end of what he termed the era of representation. His failure, of course, has had consequences. One of these is that we now find in more recent work a widespread resistance to universal theory.

The way Foucault proposed to integrate the history of the human sciences with a theory of those sciences was by means of what he called the Classical episteme. For Foucault, the episteme is what makes knowledge possible. It's the discovery that things have the capacity to be ordered. And because such a capacity was universal, we would then have the possibility of universal theory. At the same time, Foucault didn't want development. As a result, he found himself forced to adopt a spatial framework, where all relationships exist simultaneously. Specifically, Foucault chose to highlight the seventeenth-/eighteenth-century belief in a relationship between representations and a relationship between things, both of which pointed to resemblances. These resemblances led Foucault to suggest a "continuum" between being and representation, based on their correspondence. Implied was the notion that representation could encompass existence in its entirety because of a similar structure of internal resemblances within each field. The problem with belief in a correspondence between ontology and representation, however, was that it assumed exactly what you had to prove: that the world out there looks the way you represent it to be. Because of his own commitment to the Classical episteme, moreover, Foucault could only talk about the nineteenth-century shift away from it historically. In the process, he converted nineteenth-century temporal terminology into spatial concepts like analogy and succession. What he left out was any trace of development. But that meant he couldn't talk about the kind of change by which we become what we are.

If the failure of *The Order of Things* and other structuralist attempts at universal theory simply led people to write off the possibility of any such project, the present tendency to combine viewpoints nonetheless hints at a wish to go beyond a field-specific level of theory. It points, I would argue, to a hope that theory might offer more: a means to elucidate what we can't otherwise understand, by recourse to a higher vantage point that can relate our particular inquiry to a matrix of all the other relevant knowledge we have. It suggests, in other words, that what theory is at the present time isn't necessarily all it wants to be.

To get beyond the present theory impasse, I felt we had to retrace the way we got here: to go back to the source or sources of all modern theory. Specifically, it meant we had to look for the moment when theory first began to display the tendency toward self-reflexivity that we identify as the hallmark of the modern. And that meant a need to go back to theory in the Romantic period. But if reflexivity first emerged in the Romantic era, our present theory impasse ought to be traceable to the same source. Nor was it difficult, once I began to think about the inward turn of Romantic theory, to see how it might have happened. As a result of its self-reflexive gaze, Romantic theory had become aware of its power to conceptualize any and all material circumstances. From there, it was bound to arrive at the inevitable corollary: that we can achieve ascendancy over anything material via theory. Hence the dream of universal theory, which would allow us to talk about any field we wanted at a higher level of generality than what was possible to the field itself. Given the circumstances, it can hardly come as a surprise that Romantic theory tried to make its dream a reality. Or that at a later moment Foucault would do the same. From his failure, in turn, we come to our present theory impasse as one of the consequences.

At the same time, it seemed to me that if Romantic theory lay at the source of our present impasse, it might also point to a way out of it. After all, we'd gotten to where we were because of the Romantic dream of universal theory, which was based on an awareness of its own power to conceptualize. But if Romantic theory did in fact possess a virtually limitless capacity to conceptualize, perhaps that same capacity might prove relevant to our impasse. If we could recover the way it conceptualized its own theory scene, perhaps we could see by the same token how its perspective might be applied to our present circumstances. To some extent, the failure of contemporary theory had come about because of its attempt to pursue a goal defined by the Romantic period. Perhaps, then, we had to try to see that goal in terms of the conceptual framework from which it arose. Hence Romantic theory came to seem not only the source of our trouble but equally a source of possibility.

Nonetheless, I also knew that any attempt to see it as a way out of our present theory impasse would at some point have to confront the New Historicist critique of Romantic theory. From a New Historicist perspective, the move toward reflexivity, which led theory in the Romantic era to stress its own formal aspect, was only a form of blindness, perhaps deliberate, by which it tried to deny the hegemony of material circumstances. But if the material base did in fact determine what consciousness in a given period might perceive or feel, any such move away from the material circumstances out of which theory had emerged could only lead to a sort of false consciousness, rather than to any insight relevant to our present scene.

Yet if this was what the New Historicist perspective implied, I couldn't help but feel that some of its own most exemplary instances gave hints of a distinctly different tendency. Yes, Jerome McGann in *The Romantic Ideology* had initially tried to make the hegemony of material circumstances essential to any Romantic New Historicist programme. But in *Wordsworth's Great Period Poems* Marjorie Levinson put a significant spin on that programme in the way she read "Tintern Abbey": the poem is all about what it *doesn't* say rather than what it says, yet the negative twist by which its silence becomes its message is itself expressive of agency. To me, it seemed that Alan Liu took the same process even further. *Wordsworth: The Sense of History* considers how the Romantic mind or consciousness internalizes its experiences, where the result, as in the "imagery" of *The Ruined Cottage* or the effort to repress Napoleon, can even be creative. Finally, a decade later, James Chandler's *England in 1819* explicitly attempts to theorize history. So instead of theory reduced to the material circumstances out of which it arose, we seemed to have material circumstances that gave rise to theory.

At an even deeper level, there was what Marx himself had discovered as he worked out the foundations of his critique of political economy in the *Grundrisse*. Initially, he had tried to describe, as simply as possible, what he took to be the most basic economic process: the production/consumption cycle. Once he got into it, however, he quickly found how difficult it was to avoid Hegelian self-development: not only production/consumption but also the commodity/money cycle seemed to involve a movement into otherness so as to return into oneself. He tried to resist it, by a more general description of the movement from abstract concepts to a complex real. Yet here, too, he found his path blocked by money. Money was odd: its autonomy, as well as its tendency to absorb everything into itself, suggested a movement from the real to the conceptual or abstract. At this point, I suspect, Marx saw he would need to talk about the entire process of economic development, in order to get around the problem posed by money. But once he had embarked on a general analysis of economic development, he couldn't help but feel the way that it, too, seemed to move from the real to the abstract. From the perspective of capital, the goal of economic development was to create a higher exchange value. In order to create that higher exchange value, capital was ready to sacrifice its labor force and its material. But the concept of a higher exchange value was clearly abstract. Nor could Marx deny that capital was the motive force behind economic development, the force that made it happen. As a result, he could only stake his hope on the historical development of economy. Capital, he argued, would eventually result in a universal development of all the productive forces. Yet even this development, if embraced as a goal or end, clearly constituted an ideal. At every level, then, the *Grundrisse* itself seemed to testify to movement from a concrete real to the abstract or conceptual.

Finally, there is the testimony of history. More than any other event, the French Revolution loomed large over the entire Romantic era. Here, then, if anywhere, we ought to be able to discern the hegemony of material circumstances. Yet French Revolutionary scholarship in recent years has had a very different story to tell. It began with Alfred Cobban, who in *The Social Interpretation of the French Revolution* questioned the definability of social classes and their Revolutionary role. But the decisive shift came from the work of François Furet. *Penser la Revolution française* marked a direct attack on the Marxist account of the Revolution as economically or socially transformative. Instead, Furet argued, its primary consequence was a new ideology: democratic political culture. In effect, Furet went back to Tocqueville, who claimed that for the Revolution the political had been cause, rather than effect, of the economic/social. Furet, moreover, saw the Terror not as excess but as an integral part of Revolutionary ideology. An ideology, however, is purely conceptual. Nonetheless, its pull on Revolutionary events has been amply documented by Mona Ozouf, Lynn Hunt, and others. Through their studies, we can now see the force of Revolutionary rhetoric and imagery, and how these took on a life of their own. Lastly, there was the work of Richard Cobb. More than anyone else, he brought the Revolution to life through his portrayal of the acts and beliefs of the *menu peuple:* the shopkeepers and artisans of Paris, who peopled the Revolutionary armies, enforced the decrees, made the Revolution happen. What Cobb showed, above all, was that they didn't do it purely for personal gain, that their commitment often meant significant personal losses. As a result, what we get is a sense of the force of the Revolutionary ideal, its power over material circumstances.

But if the story of Romantic theory isn't about the hegemony of material circumstances, there was a reason why the road from material circumstances to theory still seemed necessary to my story. Simply put, as soon as we try to talk about Romantic theory, we invariably get into the genesis of theory. And the reason we do that is because of the way it talked about itself. Asked to say what theory consists of, Romantic theory would describe how it came to be. If Romantic theory is all about the genesis of theory, however, the particular circumstances of its own actual genesis must have possessed some significance for it. Hence an account of how Romantic theory grew out of those circumstances might likewise be meaningful. Increasingly, then, I began to see the way Romantic theory grew out of particular material circumstances as crucial to its story. Specifically, I wanted to focus on the process by which that came about. To me, it seemed we might even see the move from material circumstances to theory as a way to define the Romantic period itself. Faced with the chaos of Revolutionary circumstances, what the Romantic era did was to assimilate these to theory. For me, the question was how to describe the process by which it got from circumstances to theory. Clearly, any attempt to answer that question would have to take a close look at the relevant factors. Only then could we try to trace the process or sequence by which circumstances had led, subtly and almost imperceptibly, to theory.

Yet even beyond the story of how it came to be, what drew me to Romantic theory was its vision of theory, as more than just knowledge or explanation. In that respect, Romantic theory was never just a heuristic framework for a given field. To be only that would be to say, in effect, that we're no better than our epistemological or cognitive sources. And from the outset, Romantic theory had never professed to be only a means to organize its source material. Instead, what I began to see, as I worked my way into different Romantic theory texts, was how, beyond a given point, they no longer looked to all the factual minutiae for the answers. Not that they became careless or indifferent in their treatment of their sources. But they seemed to have arrived at an unspoken belief that the answers, if discoverable at all, would have to be found elsewhere. At some deeper level, they seemed to say, the reasons we do theory the way we do it come less from our knowledge of a given field than from what we intuitively feel about theory itself. And that, in turn, could point to the possibility of a new kind of autonomy for theory.

Apart from its effort to be more than just explanatory, Romantic theory wanted to go beyond the rational. To a large extent, even at the present time, we still appeal to rational criteria. We believe in a need for consistency. And we respect assertions based on logical inferences. We respect these because we know how hard it is to satisfy the requirements involved. In addition, we've seen instances of what a world without those requirements might be. It wasn't that Romantic theory didn't respect such requirements, or the kind of thought moves that give theory its rational quality. But it believed, at the same time, in other ways to justify our thought moves. And if these went beyond the rational, that wasn't because they somehow lacked rationality but because they tried to get at what gave the rational its necessary quality or aspect. From a Romantic perspective, in other words, the necessary quality of the rational grew out of a more basic level at which thought moved. It was as if you were to feel the essential rightness of some passage from a musical work, and only later to learn of the harmonic principle on which it had all been based. For the Romantic period, then, theory grew out of a deeper necessity than any described by our efforts to specify what was rational. The role of theory was to find out what the sources of that necessity were.

Finally, from a Romantic standpoint, there was the question of what we could say on a more general level about the form and content of any given theory. For years I had been haunted by a remark of Évariste Galois: his hope that mathematical equations would one day become solvable by their form, rather than their content. If theory was in fact governed by a kind of internal necessity, we ought to be able to describe the overall shape of a theory independently of the field to which it pertained. And that in turn suggested we might even be in a position to say what a theory for any given field ought to entail, without a knowledge of that field. But if we could specify the form of a theory independently of its field, we would then presumably gain some insight into the essential nature of all forms of theory. Insight of this kind, I think, was what Galois had dreamed of. For his project was always more than simply a theory of equations, or even just of algebra. In his preface to a planned collection of his papers, he spoke of a knowledge that would apply to all the sciences. But knowledge on that level amounts to metatheory. By its self-reflexivity, then, theory could hope to know more about theory for any given field, which would in turn yield insight into the very nature of theory itself. For thought or theory to come to an awareness of what it is, however, could only mean a greater awareness of its own capacity.

I begin chapter 1 with an image: the tomb of Jean-Jacques Rousseau, on the Isle of Poplars at Ermenonville. A favorite site for the late eighteenth-century Rousseau cult, it typically moved viewers to tears. From the pleasure of emotion at Rousseau's tomb I shift to *La Nouvelle Héloise* and its treatment of what it means to give oneself emotionally, then to Rousseau as tutelary figure for Shelley in "The Triumph of Life." As an alternative to the pleasure of passion, Shelley, I argue, hints at the need for reflexivity, or a perspective characterized by an awareness of itself. Which is to say: theory. Confronted by allegory in the form of a triumphal pageant of Life, the narrator comes to see that the only way we can hope to understand it is by an awareness of our own conceptual framework or perspective. So the ultimate conceptual frame would be the ultimate theory. Significantly, it isn't as if Shelley knows what exactly that theory would entail.

But his figuration of it, as the "shape all light," points to the future of theory in the Romantic era and beyond, by the abstract way it represents its object. Likewise, it looks forward proleptically to my subsequent treatment, in the rest of the book, of theory.

If my first chapter is introductory, my second is about the move from history to theory within Romantic theory. I start with Hadrian's villa, which shows how the nostalgia for Greek antiquity can be traced back to antiquity itself. From there I turn to Friedrich Wolf, whose *Prolegomena to Homer* revolutionized classical studies in 1795. Whereas Hadrian yearned for an antique Greek subjectivity he believed Antinoüs embodied, Wolf hoped at best for Greek antiquity at one remove: the Homeric text as it existed for a cultured, critical late antique subjectivity. Yet even that, for Friedrich Schlegel, can no longer be recovered. As he saw it, the fate of classical scholarship was precisely to yearn for what it knows it can't recover. Instead, he felt, the quest for Greek subjectivity forced classical scholarship to reflect on its own tendency toward nostalgia. As it did that, it became aware of how the antique subjectivity it yearned for was a creation of scholarship. Elevated to the level of an ideal, it had ceased to be history and become, rather, a construct of theory.

I conclude the first section of my book with what might well be the biggest challenge for Romantic theory: how to develop itself out of purely material circumstances. Perhaps the most massive, intractable circumstances are those of war. Here, if anywhere, we ought to find external necessity. And yet, even here, it would be possible for Napoleon at Jena to lift material circumstances to the level of theory. His battle plan displays a constant flow of development, from beginning, to middle, to end. At the same time, it also displays an awareness of its own tendency toward development: hence the *manoeuvre sur les derrières,* a surprise flank or rear attack that actually defers victory but also makes possible what I call the moment of return, the final assault by a reserve force Napoleon termed the *masse de rupture.* And that same tendency toward development and the movement of return would continue upward, to an even more abstract level in the mind of an observer who saw Napoleon at Jena. So I shift to Hegel and the *Phenomenology of Spirit* Preface, with its movement from Substance to otherness, followed by a return to itself as Subject. With Hegel, we get our first look at what will become the dominant *topoi* of high Romantic theory: the spatial treatment of concepts, the primacy of development over concepts, and, finally, the creation of metatheory.

From Hegel I turn to the sciences, and, first of all, the French physiologist Xavier Bichat. His vital theory would exert great influence on a later generation of British physicians: Abernethy, William Lawrence, and others. Through them, in turn, it would have further, wider consequences for the British Romantic scene. But my interest is in the genesis of that theory, as it emerged out of post-Revolutionary Paris hospital circumstances. It was, after all, the experience of death in the Hôtel-Dieu and other Paris hospitals that gave rise to a sense of what life might consist of. And that, in turn, would help to shape vital theory. For Bichat, it began as resistance to a single vital principle: to him, it made more sense to talk about vital properties. Each vital property, however, could be explained by the way different vital functions interact. And each vital function, in turn, could be traced to a single tissue. Yet the quest for vitality doesn't end here, because tissue properties outlast death. So finally Bichat was led to think of vitality as a process, by which the non-vital gets converted to the vital. Hence theory comes to take on the form of a process.

If Bichat is about the need for theory to engage process or development, the work of British chemist Humphry Davy points to the origin of metatheory in the Romantic sciences. From the phlogiston debate, he arrived at the need for theoretical economy, universal explanation, and, ultimately, the creation of objectivity by theory. His own work in the isolation of chemical elements had shown him how few chemical substances there really were, hence how few theoretical constructs were necessary. Theoretical economy led in turn to a desire for universal explanation, a theory that might do explanatory work for all the sciences. Hence his efforts to prove chemical and electrical affinity were identical. The fact that chemical explanation appeared to be based on theoretical preferences, moreover, would finally force him to become aware of how so-called objectivity was actually shaped by theory. Theory engaged factual material via analogy and experiment, but it returned at the end to theory. And his insight into the process by which all that happened places Davy at the origin of metatheory.

The culmination of Romantic metatheory in the sciences comes, for me, in the work of Évariste Galois. If Hegel marks the high point of the first section of my book, Galois represents that of the second. His celebrated memoir on the solvability of equations by radicals had shown it was possible to determine whether any equation (up to degree 5) was solvable without actually solving it. In my account, I give the basic schema of his proof: an equivalence between subfields of an extension K (a splitting field that contains the roots of a polynomial, defined over a field F) and subgroups of the group G(K,F), which consists of all automorphisms of K to itself that leave every element of F fixed. Although what I do with Galois theory may seem more technical than the rest of my book, I felt it was necessary to explore the material in some detail. In effect, it looks forward to much of what appears in the epilogue to my work. Specifically, the notion of a spatial perspective on concepts, the power or capacity of abstraction, and the emergence of metatheory all occur here, but with a specificity that my epilogue couldn't hope to equal because of its greater scope. And, to the extent that it's possible, even a discussion of theory at this level ought to be grounded on specific instances.

The third section of my book, which begins with Coleridge, is about reactions to Romantic theory. Unlike other Romantic theorists, Coleridge didn't try to develop theory for a particular field. Instead, his ambition was to relate different forms of theory to each other. His belief was that virtually all forms of theory lacked perspective. For him, in other words, theory didn't translate into metatheory. On the contrary: if you did theory, your effort to conceptualize data would probably preclude an awareness of your own thought processes, or metatheory. Hence his attempt to provide that awareness, by means of a Reason/Understanding distinction. As Coleridge saw it, philosophy shows what the difference between Reason and Understanding is, the natural sciences subordinate the first to the second, religion strives to do the opposite, and psychology attempts to explain the conflict. For Coleridge, however, theory isn't just about knowledge or explanation. What fascinated him was, rather, its nature as thought or activity. In that respect, you might say, he looked beyond some of the immediate aims of Romantic theory, to a more "natural" perspective that saw it as part of a larger quest to make our experiences meaningful.

To some extent, Mary Shelley reacts to theory in an even more radical way. The dream she describes in her 1831 Introduction to *Frankenstein* largely mirrors that of her protagonist. Both are about the effort we make to impose our own subjectivity on external objectivity. That same process occurs in the novel, when Victor, as creator, tries to impose his subjectivity on his creature, whose desperate efforts to get Victor to recognize his own subjectivity only provoke his creator to more elaborate forms of denial. Once his request for a female companion is dismissed, the only option left to the creature is to assimilate his subjectivity to Victor's, which has destructive consequences. The point of all this, I take it, isn't just a critique of science: the tyranny of subjectivity in the novel is much more pervasive. Nor is it just to recapitulate subjectivity/objectivity. Instead, it seems to me, Shelley sees the impulse to conceptualize the external (i.e., to do theory) as natural: we get into it out of a fear of external forces. At the same time, she seems to feel our only hope is to abandon theory for a completely different kind of relationship to the external: intersubjectivity, or sympathy.

It remains for Friedrich Hölderlin, finally, to reflect on the limits of theory.

Rather than look at any of his theoretical texts, however, I focus on a late poem: "Patmos." Here the nearness of the God, combined with its otherness, is precisely what makes it unrepresentable. So Hölderlin discovers the limit of theory: it can't conceptualize anything too close to itself. The difficulty is briefly overcome at an epiphanic moment of the Passion narrative, which sees relationships from a spatial rather than rational viewpoint. But this viewpoint can't be sustained in the aftertime, which can at best only hope to symbolize what it can't conceive. For Hölderlin, that sort of process was what lay beyond the capacity of theory to represent. Yet if we're somehow aware of it, our awareness might hint at a way to go beyond theory. In his awareness of that possibility, Hölderlin might be said to sum up what Romantic theory was all about. Deeply immersed in the rational, it nonetheless embraced what couldn't be encompassed within a purely rational framework: the spatial, and development. Above all, Hölderlin displays the capacity of Romantic theory to look beyond itself.

In the course of my work on this book, I've had to draw on many people, some with expertise far outside my own field.

My biggest debt is to Bruce Reznick. Through tutorial sessions over a period of several years, he initiated me into all the areas of higher algebra necessary for a comprehension of Galois theory. I can't say enough about his patience, generosity, insight, and kindness throughout the entire process. In addition, he also applied his careful eye more than once to chapter 6: a number of editorial corrections and improvements in it come from him directly. For all that he's done, I'm deeply grateful.

In a different way, I'm also extremely grateful to William M. Calder III, who offered a kind of privileged access to the field of classical scholarship. He, too, not only gave generously from his knowledge of the entire field, but also saved me from error on classical matters in my chapter on Wolf and Schlegel.

A number of friends and colleagues assisted with their expertise on particular chapters as well. Liz Bohls read and commented on chapters 5 and 8, Kerstin Behnke emended my Friedrich Schlegel translations in chapter 2, Laurie Johnson gave me bibliographical guidance for the same, and Laurence Mall supplied some helpful advice for chapter 1.

At an earlier stage, I benefited from the encouragement of Marilyn Butler and the advice of James Chandler. I owe an even more significant debt, however, to Paul Hamilton. His careful and perceptive reading of successive versions of the book led to changes that I hope have brought out its conceptual structure much more clearly. More recently, an anonymous reader for Johns Hopkins University Press prompted improvements of a different kind.

Other people helped in material ways. Ann Gilkerson and Eugene Hill procured much-needed primary sources. Tom Hove transferred an earlier version of the manuscript onto disk. My sister, Jean Chai, collected material for me on the

Hôtel-Dieu in Paris. Jean-Marc Dabadie checked some of my translations from Bichat and Galois. Others helped in ways less material, especially Jonathan Arac. I also owe Cary Nelson for his efforts to assist. At Johns Hopkins University Press, Michael Lonegro gave astute editorial advice and managed the submission process adroitly.

I owe a special debt to Leon Waldoff. His detailed and careful commentary on the entire manuscript compelled me to clarify much that might otherwise have remained unclear, and saved me from multiple errors. Beyond that, his friendly counsel, his faith in the project, and his many kindnesses helped in innumerable ways.

Finally, I want to thank Cara Ryan. For all her work on the book, and for much else I can hardly specify, I'm more grateful than I can say.

Romantic Theory

The Triumph of Theory

Picture the scene to yourself: a tiny island, situated in the middle of a small lake. The stillness of the water furnishes a natural inducement to meditation, or reverie. The foreground, meanwhile, offers an appropriate spot: a bench by the shore, where a seated woman, nursing an infant, gazes on a stone tablet graced by a votive inscription. But the focal point, toward which the spectator's eye is unerringly directed, remains the island itself. Covered by a small grove of poplars whose dark massed foliage rears dramatically upward, it harbors a modest white monument, embellished by various figures in bas-relief. This monument is the tomb of Jean-Jacques Rousseau.

By the end of the eighteenth century, it had become the object of a new, secular veneration: the cult of sensibility. Once in sight of the tomb, the obligatory response was to weep. Sensibility implies, of course, a capacity for intense emotion within the "feeling soul," or *l'âme sensible,* to whom the tomb's epitaph was above all addressed. But a mere capacity for emotion needn't necessitate its release. Instead, we have to ask what could excite sensibility to overflow, to dilate. For late eighteenth-century audiences, sensibility involves not only emotion but awareness or sensitivity as well. But to what? Since sensibility itself consists of a capacity to feel, the highest form of awareness must be the ability to detect the same capacity in others. Accordingly, discovery of a capacity for emotion within another "feeling soul" can itself cause a sudden access of emotion. As a "feeling soul," then, Rousseau becomes worthy of sympathy from anyone of similar sensibility.[1]

To understand more fully the particular psychological dynamic that prompts such an access of emotion, we need to look at *La Nouvelle Héloise,* and, specifically, the scene that forms the climax of this novel.[2] After an absence of more than six years, Saint-Preux returns to see Julie, now married. Their reunion leads to the celebrated "promenade" on Lake Geneva in which their boat nearly capsizes. Afterward, as night begins to fall, they turn homeward. The moonlight, the tranquility of the lake, and the measured sound of the oars all incite Saint-Preux to reverie. Gradually, reminiscences of his past with Julie begin to grow in poignancy, until he finds himself almost unable to bear it. While he can now see her, touch her, speak to her, love her, and almost possess her, he knows equally well that she is lost to him forever. In his despair, he feels tempted to plunge into the water with her, so as to end his existence in her company. By his abrupt withdrawal from her side, however, he manages to regain some self-control. Tenderness, he writes, progressively overcomes despair, and he begins to weep almost uncontrollably. As he does so, he experiences a kind of pleasure. Soothed by this, he can then return to Julie. Significantly, her handkerchief is damp, and when they later disembark, he notices her eyes are reddened and swollen. What he doesn't realize at the time is that her tears have a very different cause. While Saint-Preux grieves for a past irrevocably lost, what affects Julie is the recognition that she still loves Saint-Preux.

Contrary to appearances, though, what induces Saint-Preux to cry isn't the loss of an earlier Julie, the one he loved. Instead, in order to understand his present emotion, we need to turn to an earlier remark by Julie herself as she writes about Saint-Preux to her confidante Claire: "Ce n'est point le présent que je crains; c'est le passé qui me tourmente. Il est des souvenirs aussi redoubtables que le sentiment actuel; on s'attendrit par reminiscence; on a honte de se sentir pleurer, et l'on n'en pleure que davantage" [It's not at all the present that I'm afraid of, it's the past that torments me. There are memories as formidable as present emotion; one becomes tender by reminiscence; one's ashamed to feel oneself cry, and one just cries all the more]. In her description, Julie distinguishes firmly between present and past. It isn't the present that makes her cry: she can bear, her statement suggests, her present relation to Saint-Preux. But if the past is as formidable as any present emotion, that can only be because she relives what she felt then. Her confession goes on to link tenderness with reminiscence. Subsequently, it would seem, crying occurs almost involuntarily. In fact, she doesn't even mark the moment she begins. Instead, she simply says she becomes aware of it (se sentir pleurer), which only emphasizes its involuntary quality. But if she isn't afraid of the present, her tears can't be due to regret for the loss of her relationship to Saint-Preux. Presumably, then, the thought or emotion that prompts her to cry isn't one of regret at all. The fact that she perceives a connection between her sense of shame and her disposition to cry all the more implies that her awareness of her own tears only induces a greater indulgence. All of this would seem to hint at a pleasure produced by the memory of Saint-Preux. But even that doesn't quite suffice to explain her need to weep. After all, she could still enjoy her memory of him without it. So weeping must itself be pleasurable in some way. Since it's linked to a past with Saint-Preux that's distinctly different from their present relationship, it seems natural to infer that she obtains pleasure from *giving herself emotionally* to his memory. If she simply thought of him, her pleasure would then come wholly from the memory itself. But her irresistible urge to cry suggests that the real source of her pleasure isn't merely an image of Saint-Preux but the act by which she surrenders herself emotionally to it.

For Saint-Preux, by contrast, the pleasure of weeping offers even more than what he gets from his reminiscences. We've seen how the process of *attendrissement* is linked for Julie to memory. If we assume a similar link between memory and *attendrissement* for Saint-Preux, we can then associate memory or reminiscence with the "softer emotion" (un sentiment plus doux) that "insinuates" its way into his sensibility after he leaves her side. By itself, nevertheless, such an emotion appears hardly sufficient to provoke the "torrents" of tears he subsequently begins to shed. Nor is it insignificant that he should specify how that gave him pleasure: "I wept strongly, for a long time, and felt relieved" [Je pleurai fortement, longtems, et fus soulagé]. Clearly his relief can't come simply from the memory of Julie. Instead, it seems to emanate from the act of weeping itself, whose intensity visibly overshadows that of the "softer emotion" associated with *attendrissement*. As a result, it ultimately alters his relation to the past: by the time he finishes, he can feel the emotional cycle that began with the memory of a Julie now lost has indeed reached a sort of closure.

Unfortunately, Julie can't rest so easy. Unlike Saint-Preux, she knows she can't simply take refuge in the past. Her awareness that he still loves her makes this impossible. It forces her to recognize that the way her awareness of his love affects her can have only one explanation. When she yields to the impulse to cry, then, she can no longer pretend that her grief is for a past Saint-Preux who can't be recovered. Instead, she knows too well her attraction to him at the present moment. Given that knowledge, she must also realize how dangerous it would be to surrender to her emotions at all. To give herself emotionally to any image of Saint-Preux might easily cause her to yield to the actual person. Nevertheless, she still allows herself to cry. No doubt she's already discovered that she can't extinguish her love for Saint-Preux. In his presence, moreover, there's a distinct possibility she'll somehow betray her emotion. In order to prevent this, what she does, I believe, is to give herself emotionally to *her love for Saint-Preux*. To do that isn't, of course, the same as to give yourself to an actual person. When you give yourself to a particular love, your emotion remains, as it were, within yourself. On some level, then, Julie appears to believe that by giving herself over to her love, she might avoid the problem posed by Saint-Preux himself.

At the same time, she clearly sees the risk involved. As he rejoins her at the stern of the boat, Saint-Preux observes softly, "I see that our hearts have never ceased to understand each other!" She acknowledges his remark to be true, but goes on to warn: "let this be the last time they will have spoken to each other in this way" [mais que ce soit la dernière fois qu'ils auront parlé sur ce ton]. To be sure, Saint-Preux doesn't grasp the real meaning of what she says. He assumes that she, like himself, has given herself emotionally to grief for a love that can't be recovered. Clearly, this isn't what she has in mind. What isn't clear, though, is why she can no longer give herself to her love for Saint-Preux. Perhaps what she feels, on some level, is that to give yourself to your love for someone in that way is to run the risk of emotional exhaustion. We have only so much emotion to give. And when we lavish all of it on what amounts to a form of pure psychological reflexivity, we start to live dangerously.

~

Half a century later, what Rousseau discovered and brought to collective awareness continued to affect new readers with undiminished force. In 1822, a young British poet living in Italy drowned off the Tuscan coast. Among his papers was what appeared to be an unfinished poem in manuscript. The poem, entitled "The Triumph of Life," offers a sequence of interconnected visions, each embedded within the one before it. At one point, Rousseau appears as a sort of tutelary figure. Yet not exactly:

> I turned and knew
> (O Heaven have mercy on such wretchedness!)
>
> That what I thought was an old root which grew
> To strange distortion out of the hill side
> Was indeed one of that deluded crew,
>
> And that the grass which methought hung so wide
> And white, was but his thin discoloured hair,
> And that the holes it vainly sought to hide
>
> Were or had been eyes.   (ll.180–88)

At first glance, it isn't clear why Rousseau should be presented so negatively. Nor why his mortality is emphasized. What he says when asked by the narrator to identify himself only partly answers these questions:

> Before thy memory
>
> I feared, loved, hated, suffered, did, and died,
> And if the spark with which Heaven lit my spirit
> Earth had with purer nutriment supplied
>
> Corruption would not now thus much inherit
> Of what was once Rousseau—nor this disguise
> Stain that within which still disdains to wear it.—   (ll.199–205)

Perhaps the only clue lies in the way Rousseau characterizes his past life: virtually everything he says focuses on his emotions almost exclusively. In addition, the emotions he talks about seem highly suggestive. Taken collectively, they hint at a kind of emotional violence. Apart from the contrast between love and hate, fear and suffering are both quite passionate. Still, it isn't immediately evident why Rousseau's intense emotionality has gotten the censure or blame it's apparently received.

Given these unusual circumstances, we need to know more in order to understand what might have led Shelley to select Rousseau for his tutelary figure.[3] After he introduces himself, Rousseau goes on to identify others chained to the triumphal chariot of Life: Napoleon, Voltaire, Frederick the Great, Kant, Catherine the Great, Leopold II. All of these, Rousseau remarks, are people "Whose name the fresh world thinks already old—/For in the battle Life and they did wage/She remained conqueror" (ll.238–40). By contrast, he was different:

> I was overcome
> By my own heart alone; which neither age
>
> Nor tears nor infamy nor now the tomb
> Could temper to its object.   (ll.240–43)

For the eighteenth century, as we've seen, "heart" had come to mean sensibility. Thus Rousseau's epitaph speaks of "true hearts" and "feeling souls" (*âmes sensibles*) as more or less equivalent. To be "overcome" by one's own heart, then, is to be overcome by one's sensibility. In this respect, Rousseau seems to suggest, what befell him was unique: while others were overcome by external forces, the source of his ruin lay purely in his capacity to feel. Hence his significance for Shelley: while ruin by external forces is easy to understand, it isn't nearly as easy to see why a capacity to feel should prove fatal.

Here the explanation would seem to involve what it means for a heart to be "tempered" to its object. Tradition (which reaches back to Platonic and neoplatonic sources) had endowed the notion of being "tempered" with a musical sense that carried spiritual resonances. Shelley himself appears quite aware of all this: as the poem opens, we're told that "at the birth/Of light, the Ocean's orison arose/To which the birds tempered their matin lay" (ll.6–8). Hence to be "tempered" is to be in "accord" with something else. The implication, then, is that Rousseau's sensibility isn't in accord with its object. Instead, "neither age/Nor tears nor infamy nor now the tomb" appears to have any influence whatsoever.

The failure of all these circumstances to affect what Rousseau felt suggests that the emotion in question must be some form of romantic love. Undeterred by either age, or the grief of an abandoned love, or the infamy associated with a refusal to accept responsibility for the infants produced by love, or, finally, fear of death, an inexhaustible capacity for romantic love might seem undesirable simply because of its larger social or moral consequences. Yet by itself it isn't clear why such a capacity should be harmful to the person who experiences it.

On this point, what Rousseau goes on to observe about Plato proves useful:

> All that is mortal of great Plato there
> Expiates the joy and woe his master knew not;
>   That star that ruled his doom was far too fair—
>
> And Life, where long that flower of Heaven grew not,
>   Conquered the heart by love which gold or pain
> Or age or sloth or slavery could subdue not.—   (ll.254–59)

An allusion to the name of the youth Plato loved ("Aster" = Greek "star" but also the name of a flower, hence "flower of Heaven") reveals the source of his ruin and, indirectly, that of the speaker. Earlier, Rousseau had characterized himself as "overcome/By my own heart alone," in contrast to those vanquished by Life. The present passage, however, shows a more complex relationship between internal and external forces. Even for Rousseau, in other words, the process isn't purely internal. Instead, the example of Plato points to a more complicated causal sequence: by allowing himself to love, Rousseau submits to a situation where his emotions cease to be controlled by his own will, and thereby become subject to an external force or agency. In this fashion, what other external forces (gold, pain, age, slavery) couldn't accomplish is effected by love. Despite the appearance of free will, the only exercise of will performed by either Plato or Rousseau lies in the initial surrender to impulse. All the rest is inevitable, given the kind of emotion involved. The "star" (i.e., Aster) that "ruled" the "doom" of

Plato was "far too fair": too fair, in other words, for Plato not to yield to his own attraction to Aster. From that point on, Plato can only experience whatever "joy and woe" his love for Aster compels him to feel.

By itself, however, the affair with Aster doesn't immediately precipitate Plato's downfall. On the contrary: Rousseau explicitly dissociates him from the deeper source of Plato's corruption (i.e., "Life"), which is said to work "where long that flower of Heaven grew not." The mention of time or duration, moreover, points to the gradual nature of the process. But if Plato's corruption occurs only gradually, its etiology must presumably involve an external cause of some kind. And since the text specifically declares that "Life . . ./Conquered the heart by love," we know it has to do with what happens to the heart (i.e., sensibility) as a result of love. Significantly, the text doesn't indicate a subsequent attachment felt by Plato for anyone else. Yet it seems fairly evident that he does in fact continue to experience love (but not, presumably, for Aster). In Rousseauistic terms, we might say Plato gave himself emotionally to Aster. So if his relationship to Aster helps to bring about his own later conquest by love, to give oneself emotionally would then appear to be responsible for an inability to resist love at a later point, even after the original attachment has ceased to exist. What isn't clear, though, is why giving oneself emotionally to a particular individual at one moment should render one vulnerable to recurrences of the same impulse. For Rousseau, what we obtain from our experience of love is a new form of knowledge. So as a result of his affair with Aster, Plato learns what "his master knew not." Which is to say: "joy and woe." At first glance, this may sound questionable, if not downright false. Surely Socrates had been intimately acquainted with both joy and woe in the course of his long, eventful life. Yet even if that were true, he might nonetheless have missed the sudden alternation between these that characterizes love. What Plato learns, then, is an emotional dynamic that those who have never experienced love possess no knowledge of. Fascinated by it, he (and anyone else who has known love) becomes vulnerable to recurrences of the romantic impulse. Thus what attracts Plato to love isn't the specific qualities of the person he loves or the happiness of romantic possession, but the *emotionality* of love itself. Likewise, what Plato "expiates" is the "joy and woe" that result from his submission to love. But if love offers a richer emotionality than other experiences, why should "expiation" be necessary? The very mention of it suggests a transgression similar to that of Original Sin—in other words, the sort of delinquency whose significance lies primarily in its psychological consequences for the transgressor. Yet we know Shelley had in his own life been an outspoken advocate of free love. . . .

To see why Shelley is so critical of Rousseauistic love, we need to have some idea of what the alternative might be. In a subsequent passage, Rousseau compares his fate to that of others who refused to yield to the romantic impulse:

> See the great bards of old who inly quelled
>
> The passions which they sung, as by their strain
>> May well be known: their living melody
> Tempers its own contagion to the vein
>
>> Of those who are infected with it—I
> Have suffered what I wrote, or viler pain!—
>
>> And so my words were seeds of misery—
> Even as the deeds of others.   (ll.274–81)

Like Rousseau, these poets had felt the desire to give themselves emotionally to someone else. But, unlike Rousseau, they "inly quelled" that desire. Yet since they still write about it, we might ask why their works lack the pernicious effect Rousseau ascribes to his own. The difference, as he sees it, is that their "living melody" (i.e., their verse) "tempers" or adjusts "its own contagion" (i.e., its influence) to those "infected" by a love of poetry, rather than those who crave passion per se. All the same, we might wonder how they manage to do this, given that their verse focuses on the same sort of passion Rousseau himself speaks of. The crucial difference lies in their refusal to yield to the passions to which he surrendered. As a result, what they can't and don't describe is *what it actually feels like to surrender yourself emotionally.* In that respect, their passion remains unspent, destined for some other outlet. According to Rousseau, it finds that outlet in poetry. What poetry does, then, is to sublimate passion that's been repressed. Instead of the release produced by giving oneself emotionally, the passion of poets expresses itself in the "living melody" of verse. Sublimated into formal art, passion thereby relinquishes its capacity to act directly on a sensibility. In the process of its transformation into verse, it "tempers" its influence, subjects itself to a kind of control or restraint.

For Rousseau, by contrast, the relationship between passion and *écriture* is quite different. While the great poets of the past sublimate passion into verse, Rousseau admits that what he wrote fails to transform what he felt in any way. Instead, as he confesses to the narrator, "I/Have suffered what I wrote, or viler pain!" The fact that he can say he's suffered what he describes (or, in some instances, worse) indicates, first of all, a lack of emotional restraint. His hint at

shameful, unspeakable experiences ("viler pain") suggests, moreover, an awareness of the moral obloquy involved. But his refusal to exercise any self-restraint
applies not only to his passion but to his *écriture* as well. For it would have been
perfectly possible for Rousseau to indulge every passion or impulse yet not reveal
what he had experienced. Obviously his lack of emotional self-restraint means
he can't aesthetically sublimate his passion, as did the great poets of the past.
Still, there's a considerable difference between literature that can't quite do that
and an unrestrained disclosure of one's experiences.

Significantly, Rousseau seems fully aware of the harmful consequences his
disclosure is destined to have. As he himself puts it: "And so my words were seeds
of misery—/Even as the deeds of others." His use of the connective "And so . . . "
appears to imply a causal relationship of some kind. In addition, it points to a
prior awareness of the effect his confession is likely to produce. In particular, he
seems to foresee that his willingness to reveal what happened when he surrendered to his passions will lead to others' downfall. His narrative of the consequences produced by his disclosure betrays no surprise. He observes how others
are corrupted by what he wrote, and isn't at all disturbed by that. Instead, he sees
it as inevitable. At the same time, Rousseau even manages subtly to amplify his
own guilt. As "seeds" of misery, his words are ultimately responsible for all the
evils to which they give rise: they plant germs that will corrupt the future. Lastly,
he compares them to the "deeds" of others, which gives them the distinctness
and moral importance of acts. But if Rousseau is fully aware of the likely
consequences of his disclosure, why is he unable to refrain from it?

To understand why, we need to look more closely at what Rousseau says about
his indiscretion. In fact, the logic of his statements is somewhat curious, to say
the least. Summarized, it looks like: I've suffered, and because I described what I
suffered, others have suffered as well. Taken collectively, these statements suggest that if Rousseau had described how someone else had suffered, others (i.e.,
his readers) wouldn't have suffered. His statements also imply that it's his *description* of what he suffered, rather than *what* he suffered, that caused others
misery. But why should a mere *description* cause others misery? Obviously, not
simply because of their empathy with Jean-Jacques or the characters of *La
Nouvelle Héloise*. By specifying that his words were only "seeds" of misery for
others, Rousseau avoids the imputation of having created a purely sensationalist
literature. Utterances that are "seeds" plant the germs of particular ideas in the
minds of his readers, which subsequently lead to their corruption. And clearly all
three events are inextricably linked in his mind. What he neglects to explain is
why they should necessarily be connected.

When Rousseau describes himself as one who's suffered, the context makes it evident that the cause lay in his inability to suppress desire. As a result of his failure, he finds out what it's like to yield to passion, to give oneself emotionally to someone else. Unlike the Rousseau of *La Nouvelle Héloise* or even the *Confessions*, however, the tutelary presence in "The Triumph of Life" doesn't dwell on the pleasure he derived from it. On the contrary, he characterizes his experiences as intensely painful. That doesn't of course categorically exclude the possibility of any enjoyment or pleasure. But it does imply that the end result is undesirable even from his standpoint. Yet if this transaction is, on balance, undesirable, the pleasure of release from all emotional constraints must be outweighed by a negative effect that's even worse. Although Rousseau doesn't specify what it is, he hints that its nature is shameful ("viler pain!"). I submit that what he has in mind is the sort of emotion produced by a characteristically Rousseauistic situation, the violation of one's amour-propre. To give oneself emotionally to someone else is to court the risk of refusal or indifference. Hence the element of shame involved. But the ultimate danger is, obviously, emotional exhaustion, tantamount for Rousseau to a loss of self. From what he says to the narrator, moreover, we can surmise he experienced it all personally. Yet if his purpose isn't to warn the reader (and, from the consequences, it seems pretty evident it isn't), why does he disclose these experiences?

By his disclosure, what Rousseau hopes to obtain is an audience to whom he can give himself emotionally. At first glance, an audience hardly seems like a personal love relationship. Yet we know Rousseau had worked hard to create a very personal and even intimate relation to his readership. A work like *La Nouvelle Héloise* or the *Confessions* invariably begins with an address to the reader, who is assiduously cultivated throughout the text. No doubt enthusiastic readers helped foster belief in such a relationship. At the same time, Rousseau is quite aware that his relation to his audience isn't the same as his liaison with Mme de Warens or Mme d'Houdetot. For one thing, he knows his readers can't refuse his addresses in the same way these women might. And that's precisely what he wants: a relationship where his love can't be easily rejected, if at all. So the risk of emotional exhaustion or loss of self that comes when you give yourself to another is counterbalanced by a new source of fulfillment. Hence the motive for disclosure: by exposure of his experiences, Rousseau establishes the sort of intimacy that allows him to give himself to his readers emotionally.

But if Rousseau's motive for disclosure is now evident, what remains unclear is why his readers felt compelled to accept it. I believe the reason has to do with the particular kind of intimacy Rousseau manages to create. By his disclosure,

Rousseau in effect reawakens his own past emotions. And, since these can no longer be directed at their original objects, they come to be aimed at his audience instead. Now if he were simply to describe what he felt, it would be easier to resist engagement or complicity. But his emotional disclosure is invariably mixed with a narrative. To assimilate his narrative, then, is tacitly to accept his emotions as well. Hence the intimacy that links his audience to him personally.

By itself, nonetheless, the disclosure Rousseau makes to his readers seems hardly sufficient to bring about their corruption. Yet if the audience itself actually experiences a surrender to passion on some level, it then has to find a way to direct its emotion toward a particular object. Hence its desire for a personal relationship to the author. Perhaps the most significant fact about its quest for an emotional outlet, though, is the absence of any real wish for reciprocity. Instead, what Rousseau's readers crave is merely a pretext for their own emotion. As they yield to passion, they discover what it's like to feel passion for its own sake rather than for a particular individual or object. As a result, Rousseau's readers get to taste the pleasure of passion itself. Whereas passion for a particular individual looks for a response from that individual, passion for the sake of passion doesn't really need an external object at all. It relies, rather, on the excitement produced by its own emotion, which sparks a desire for more emotion so as to increase the initial excitement. So passion leads to excitement, which in turn produces a demand for more emotion.

The problem with this sort of cycle, however, is its lack of any foreseeable end. Inevitably, emotion is bound to create excitement. But excitement is a condition that requires incessant stimulation to sustain itself. Hence the need for greater emotional intensity, which in turn translates into more excitement. The process can never come to a definitive end because the real motive for emotion isn't some external object but rather passion itself. With no external object, it can't rely on reciprocity for satisfaction. Consequently, it can only demand ever-higher levels of excitement, which don't really satisfy but only defer gratification by the promise of a greater future payoff. But the excitement produced by emotion is inherently empty: by itself, it can never yield fulfillment, insofar as it's merely an effect of emotion.

And, to a large extent, this is why Shelley is critical of Rousseau: he creates a need that can't be satisfied. By his use of Rousseau as tutelary presence, then, Shelley attempts to expose the problem of emotion for its own sake. His critique of Rousseau emphasizes how emotion for its own sake *precludes* the possibility of any relation to others because of its tendency to produce its own perpetual cycle. Because we give ourselves emotionally to some object or individual, we feel we've performed a distinct act, and thereby created a relation. Only if we examine our gesture more closely do we see how deceptive it is: we believe our emotion creates a relation to something or someone else because we want to believe it, and the reason we want to believe it is because we get to define what that relation consists of. Still, as Shelley himself realizes, we can't escape emotion. The real question, then, is whether any other alternative is possible.[4]

On that point, perhaps what we notice immediately about "The Triumph of Life" is its recessive structure: the initial sequence consists of a dream or vision, which opens into a second dream or vision, one that itself turns out to disclose a further vision. At each transition, moreover, we encounter a sequence whose purpose is to explain the one that precedes it. But each time explanation is deferred to a new visionary disclosure, which promises a deeper, fuller explanation of all the previous material. Yet the fact that explanation is endlessly deferred inevitably leads to questions about whether such an explanation is actually possible. Hence the negative inferences of many readers. Before we can come to any conclusion, however, I feel we need to look at precisely what prompts each new visionary episode. Only after we've examined all of these can we determine whether they reveal a distinct pattern of any kind, and what its significance might be.

The initial sequence portrays the condition or situation of all who live. It begins, quite appropriately, with the motif of dawn. Symbolically, dawn announces the advent of human time: the hour when we awake and prepare for the work by which humanity must struggle to sustain itself. Steeped in a classical tradition that reaches back to Hesiod's *Works and Days,* Shelley knows that work defines the shape of everyday time, and hence of life. In addition, he knows that productive work requires a sense of measure, of each task performed at its appropriate time and place. All that gets expressed in his notion of succession:

And in succession due, did Continent,

    Isle, Ocean, and all things that in them wear
The form and character of mortal mould
    Rise as the Sun their father rose, to bear

Their portion of the toil which he of old
    Took as his own and then imposed on them.   (ll. 15–20)

In many respects, what Shelley says here harks back to an earlier passage from *Adonais,* his elegy on the death of Keats:

He is a portion of the loveliness
Which once he made more lovely: he doth bear
His part, while the one Spirit's plastic stress
Sweeps through the dull dense world, compelling there,
All new successions to the forms they wear.   (ll. 379–83)

At the same time, the present passage hints at a new perspective. Whereas *Adonais* urges us to accept succession, "The Triumph of Life" appears to take it somewhat differently. We've seen that succession implies measure, hence an orderly sequence of some kind. In the phenomenology of human time, however, an orderly sequence merely gives a coherent form to life. Externally imposed (by the Sun, as "father" of humanity), it needn't be intrinsically meaningful. After all, it was the sun who "of old/Took [this toil] as his own" and subsequently "imposed" it on all who "wear the form and character of mortal mould." But the act by which the sun gives light to the world is purely involuntary. Similarly, Shelley seems to suggest, all those who work do so in a purely involuntary way. Work begins with the dawn, and those who assume their portion of the toil "rise as the Sun their father rose"—which is to say: without a conscious act of will. Thus all our work is based on an involuntary impulse. And so our very life is largely defined by a routine we don't create.

For Shelley, however, it's precisely because our life is largely about routine that the initial visionary disclosure in the poem becomes possible. As an orderly sequence, a routine can be grasped conceptually and so seen from an external viewpoint. Since those who work must "rise as the Sun their father rose" (i.e., at dawn), sleep at night is presumably necessary. Not, though, for the narrator, who remains wakeful through the dark hours, as a result of "thoughts which must remain untold." His thoughts lead to a sort of temporal parallax: instead of the normal scene, with night behind him and the day before, he experiences the reverse: "before me fled/The night; behind me rose the day." The effect of that parallax is to make possible a different perspective, one that seems to involve a special kind of clairvoyance:

When a strange trance over my fancy grew
    Which was not slumber, for the shade it spread

Was so transparent that the scene came through
    As clear as when a veil of light is drawn
O'er evening hills they glimmer; and I knew

That I had felt the freshness of that dawn,

Bathed in the same cold dew my brow and hair

And sate as thus upon that slope of lawn

Under the self same bough, and heard as there

The birds, the fountains and the Ocean hold

Sweet talk in music through the enamoured air.   (ll. 29–39)

In contrast to the vivid immediacy of this passage, the triumphal procession or pageant that opens the first visionary episode is described in a self-consciously literary way. The episode begins with a great stream of people "hurrying to and fro/Numerous as gnats upon the evening gleam,/All hastening onward." As it goes on, the description makes use of numerous literary reminiscences: Petrarch's *Trionfi*, Dante's *Inferno*, as well as Homer, Virgil, and Milton. Here the use of Petrarch and Dante seems especially significant. Since both the *Trionfi* and the *Inferno* employ processions in an allegorical fashion, it becomes increasingly difficult to resist the notion that the sort of account Shelley offers of a mysterious figure in a chariot followed by a multitude of attendants must likewise be understood as allegory.[5]

By his use of allegory, I would argue, Shelley forces us to recognize the need for a different kind of perspective. Obviously, allegorical imagery can't be read at the literal level. At that level, it becomes simply opaque. Nor is Shelley unaware of its opacity. In fact, he employs it deliberately. His aim, I believe, is to compel us to focus on that imagery itself, rather than on what it might represent. As allegorical imagery, it involves an abstraction from our experiences. Because of its abstract quality, however, it can be understood only within an abstract framework. But to understand anything that's framed abstractly, we need an awareness of perspective. And that, for Shelley, is precisely the point. His turn to allegory, in other words, isn't about a particular idea or theme but about the abstract quality of all allegory. The motive for the first visionary disclosure, then, is to assert a need for the kind of insight that's made possible precisely by a perspective that's aware of itself as perspective. Which is to say: theory.

If the initial part of the first visionary disclosure is all about a need for perspective that's aware of itself, the rest is about what happens without it. For Shelley, the alternative is emotion or passion. So those who fail to understand what the procession of Life is about are condemned to follow its triumphal chariot to their destruction. As with Rousseau, moreover, the initial surrender to emotion triggers unavoidable consequences. Nor does it seem to me accidental that we should find two motifs unforgettably linked to *La Nouvelle Héloise:* the storm or tempest, and music. Perhaps the emotions most frequently used to typify passion have been fear and desire. Among those inflamed by passion, then, how natural for the narrator to find some "flying from the thing they feared and some/Seeking the object of another's fear." Driven by their passions, they appear completely indifferent to the fountains that symbolize sources of intellectual or imaginative refreshment. Instead, they bask in the splendor of a new crescent moon, a forecast of emotional storm and stress to come. More literally, their passion breaks into "fierce song and maniac dance." But music or dance of this kind is bound to intensify, until it reaches a climax:

> Maidens and youths fling their wild arms in air
>   As their feet twinkle; now recede and now
> Bending within each other's atmosphere
>
>   Kindle invisibly; and as they glow
> Like moths by light attracted and repelled,
>   Oft to new bright destruction come and go:
>
> Till like two clouds into one vale impelled
>   That shake the mountains when their lightnings mingle
> And die in rain—the fiery band which held
>
>   Their natures, snaps . . . the shock may still tingle—
> One falls and then another in the path
>   Senseless.   (ll. 149–60)

Here the twists and turns of erotic passion are expressively figured by those who "bending within each other's atmosphere/Kindle invisibly." At the same time, Shelley points out the dangers involved. Those who yield to passion find themselves equally subject to love and hate, like moths attracted to and repelled by light. To oscillate between these two emotions produces tension. Finally, as the only way that tension can be resolved, those caught within its spell come together, in an act that marks a sexual and emotional climax. But consummation proves fatal, because it exhausts all one's emotional resources. Yet nowhere does the text even hint at any other conceivable outcome. For Shelley, then, no moderation of emotion or passion is really possible. Once we yield to passion at all, we have to go the distance.

From a Shelleyan standpoint, the prime apologist for passion is, of course, Rousseau. Hence his appearance immediately after the demise of those consumed by passion. His dominant presence in the first visionary disclosure allows

Shelley to explore fully the consequences of a complete lack of emotional self-restraint. But perhaps what makes Rousseau as tutelary figure especially poignant is his inability to offer the narrator any real insight into the procession of Life, or even his own experiences. Indeed, at the end of the first visionary episode, he bluntly confesses: "Why this should be my mind can compass not—/ Whither the conqueror hurries me still less./But follow thou, and from spectator turn/Actor or victim in this wretchedness/And what thou wouldst be taught I then may learn/From thee." His admission implies that experience by itself, even if carefully taken note of, isn't quite enough to get us there. After all, Rousseau himself had been both "actor" and "victim" in his own development, without appreciable result. Hence the need for a new disclosure, precisely to show what might make insight possible.

As the second visionary episode opens, Rousseau finds himself in the midst of a supernaturally beautiful scene. The landscape abounds in idyllic detail, and, to cap it off, the grove echoes with a sound "which all who hear must needs forget/ All pleasure and all pain, all hate and love." But the climax of the episode, and of the entire poem, consists of what Rousseau sees next:

> And as I looked the bright omnipresence
> > Of morning through the orient cavern flowed,
> And the Sun's image radiantly intense
>
> > Burned on the waters of the well that glowed
> Like gold, and threaded all the forest maze
> > With winding paths of emerald fire—there stood
>
> Amid the sun, as he amid the blaze
> > Of his own glory, on the vibrating
> Floor of the fountain, paved with flashing rays,
>
> > A shape all light, which with one hand did fling
> Dew on the earth, as if she were the Dawn
> > Whose invisible rain forever seemed to sing
>
> A silver music on the mossy lawn,
> > And still before her on the dusky grass
> Iris her many coloured scarf had drawn.—   (ll. 343–57)

Perhaps the first point to make about the present passage is the way it reflects, within its own arrangement, the poem's overall structure. We've seen how that structure displays the form of disclosure-within-disclosure. The effect is to make us feel, at each disclosure, as if we've gotten closer to some ultimate revelation, some insight that will explain it all. In its own way, the present passage does the same. Start with the "bright omnipresence" of the morning light. In itself, this is already unusual: only in some unearthly existence would we expect to find light everywhere. But its "bright omnipresence" is even intensified within the waters of a well, whose liquid surface "glowed/Like gold, and threaded all the forest maze/With winding paths of emerald fire." Yet even that doesn't quite say it all. Because there is, finally, the sun itself, whose reflected image, "radiantly intense/Burned on the waters of the well." Since these waters thread the forest maze with "emerald fire," it's hard to imagine what could possibly exceed the brilliance of a light that appears to burn fire. Nonetheless, Shelley can say: "there stood/Amid the sun, as he amid the blaze/Of his own glory . . . /A shape all light." At this point, the formal resemblance to disclosure-within-disclosure becomes unmistakable: "*Amid* the sun, as he *amid* the blaze." But anything whose shape can be discerned within the brilliance of sunlight must be, by definition, even brighter. We can only imagine it as symbolically expressive of the ultimate insight the visionary mode of the poem constantly hints at.

Specifically, the "shape all light" might be taken to embody an insight about theory. For Shelley, I would argue, the notion of a framework is precisely what theory consists of. Its abstract perspective amounts to a sense of framework: an awareness of how any attempt we make to understand what our experiences are about has to be conditioned by the conceptual frame of our inquiry. Hence the crucial role of allegory in this poem for Shelley. Because allegory can only be understood by means of an interpretive framework, it forces us into an awareness of the need for framework or perspective. But the "shape all light" is also allegory. Like the triumphal pageant of Life, it can't be understood literally. Unlike the pageant, however, it offers us a clue to insight about itself. Because the "shape all light" isn't just light, but rather light within light. To understand it, then, we need to see it in terms of its framework, of the light that is its frame or background field. Yet it isn't even just light within light, but rather light within light that itself is defined within a larger field of light. And if our initial perception of it as light within light gave us a sense of the need for framework or perspective, our perception of it as light within light within a larger field of light ought to yield a sense of how *any* object or field can be understood if we can only manage to see it within the proper conceptual frame. Hence the ever more intense brightness, as we work our way progressively to the "shape all light" itself. At each transition to a more inward brilliance, Shelley seems to suggest, we get closer to an ultimate source of light that would be the ultimate conceptual frame, the ultimate form of theory. And the sense of that ultimate frame or theory as a possibility gives, for Shelley, a consciousness that might itself be described as radiant. It appears in the poem, admittedly, for only a brief moment. But the brightness or radiance lingers, as if to remind the narrator of its ever-present potential.

At this point, a comment on the silence of the "shape all light" seems useful. If the framework of disclosure-within-disclosure has led us to expect a final word from the "shape," it's all the more remarkable how our expectation doesn't get fulfilled. In fact, the "shape" doesn't even speak to Rousseau. Yet silence, under some circumstances, can be just as significant as what we say. Here, it suggests a belief that theory, ultimately, can only be about theory. At the outset of the first visionary episode, Shelley appears as if about to propose some form of traditional allegory. That, in turn, would mean correspondences of some kind between elements of the allegory and of the world as we know it. The second visionary episode then introduces precisely the sort of figure who ought to reveal what those correspondences are. But since the "shape all light" doesn't speak, we and the narrator and Rousseau are never actually enlightened. The reason why the "shape" doesn't speak, however, isn't merely negative. Instead, the notion of a frame within a frame, which Shelley puts into play with the placement of his "shape" within a field of light, points to the real cause. With each frame, in effect, theory becomes more abstract. In other words, its explanatory field gets larger, but with that comes, simultaneously, a greater difficulty vis-à-vis the minutiae of a given moment or scene. What we finally arrive at, then, is a point where theory has to reflect on its own conceptual frame, or theory itself.

We could, of course, see the "shape all light" simply as a kind of poetic muse. Clearly, the landscape of the second visionary episode is in many ways distinctly poetic or imaginative. Its stream and cavern, for instance, are reminiscent of Coleridge's "Kubla Khan." Likewise, the "gentle trace/Of light diviner than the common Sun" takes us back to Wordsworth's Elegiac Stanzas on Peele Castle: "the gleam/The light that never was, on sea or land,/The consecration, and the Poet's dream." But the synesthesia we find throughout the second visionary episode has, for me, another significance. Like Rimbaud at a later moment, Shelley, I think, sees it as a move toward the "dérèglement de tous les sens" (disordering of all the senses). And that, for him, meant a way to destabilize our sense of framework or perspective. From this standpoint, synesthesia acts as a preliminary to theory: once we've lost our rigid sense of frame or perspective, we're ready to think about perspective itself.

Another aspect of the "shape all light" is the way it works as figuration. As

Rousseau sees it, the "shape" is a fusion of form and pure luminosity. But form, in a larger sense, is all about our effort to impart coherence to our experiences. Certainly Shelley was well aware of how chaotic our experiences can be. On some occasions, he even seems to doubt whether we can ever hope to know the way things really are. At the same time, I think Shelley felt it was meaningful to try to achieve that sort of knowledge. And the way we do that, for him, is by means of theory. Theory, then, is how we represent what we don't yet know. As such, it gives a form or shape to our quest for knowledge. Hence the use of figuration in "The Triumph of Life." Admittedly, Shelley doesn't know what exactly the sort of knowledge the narrator seeks for might entail. Nonetheless, it remains his belief that any kind of ultimate knowledge can only be achieved if we have some sense of what it would involve: in other words, if we have some way to represent it. And that, for him, is what theory is all about.

The final word, however, should be about negativity. We've seen that each section of the poem acts to cancel out what came before. Time and again, a section that seemed to promise some great disclosure gives way to yet another vision from which we expect fulfillment, only to be put off once more. Endlessly postponed in this way, the promise of disclosure comes to haunt the text. The effect of its postponement is to create a powerful pull toward disbelief: a sense that the text will never quite get there, and that the end result will be an awful void, or vacancy. But if the recessive movement of the text appears to lead to disbelief, it's significant that a similar movement should typify the "shape all light," which is in fact light within light, within a larger field of light. The resemblance between these two movements, in turn, suggests that the "shape all light" ought to be considered a symbolic image of negativity. And yet, if we accept that, we still have to explain why Shelley would choose to symbolize negativity by an image whose resonances are so strongly positive.[6]

We can explain it, I believe, if we see Shelleyan negativity as an assertion of the power of mind, its capacity to abolish what we perceive. Even in its negativity, then, the mind is active rather than passive. Not content just to submit to what it experiences, it can alter its perceptual framework at will. And if what we perceive is determined largely by our perceptual framework, to alter that framework would be to alter perception itself. For Shelley, moreover, we know how crucially perception is linked to thought. The whole point of Shelleyan idealism is that we can only think what we've perceived. Power over what we perceive is hence equivalent to power over the thoughts we produce. By its capacity to transform its perceptual framework, then, the mind preserves its own autonomy.

At the same time, Shelley also seems to imply that the recessive movement of the text, its movement of inwardness, is a movement toward essentiality. Every time disclosure is postponed for yet another vision, we get the sense that we come a bit closer to what's really essential. So when a vision is displaced by a new vision, we tend to think the new one must signify at some deeper symbolic level. And that, presumably, will get us closer to the way things really are. So negativity in Shelley amounts to a quest for essentiality. The successive displacement of each vision points to the infinite regress implied in our perception of what's essential: the belief that we can always arrive at an insight that's more essential.[7]

But if the negativity associated with our quest for essentiality meant that we can never quite manage to specify the essential, what Shelley discovered was that we could nevertheless represent it precisely by means of that negativity itself. In other words, the constant displacement of one vision by the next, that describes our quest for the essential, could itself become a way to represent what can't otherwise be specified. After all, the crucial fact about essentiality is just that: our inability to specify what it consists of. Invariably, whenever we seem to be on the verge of specificity, the sense of some as-yet undisclosed aspect of the essential emerges. If what characterizes our perception of the essential is only negative, however, the best way to represent it would then be by an image of that negativity. Clearly, though, we can only represent negativity abstractly: since it involves resistance to specificity, what we represent is the movement by which it resists specificity. To represent negativity abstractly, in turn, amounts to theory. In this fashion, the triumph of Life becomes a triumph of theory. For Shelley, you might say, theory is based on the power of thought to think abstractly, and so to grasp what can't otherwise be specified. His final work, then, is about the power or capacity of theory, typified by its ability to represent negativity itself. From that standpoint, "The Triumph of Life" offers a glimpse not only of what theory meant to Shelley, but of what it might have meant to an entire era.

CHAPTER TWO

Forms of Nostalgia

In many ways, the nostalgia for classical antiquity begins in antiquity itself. Take, for instance, Hadrian's villa at Tivoli, completed sometime around A.D. 135. If you make the journey out to Tivoli from Rome (about seventeen miles), you discover on arrival that the villa doesn't lie anywhere near the center of the town. Instead, you have to find your way to the outskirts, where the town begins to shade off almost imperceptibly into the country. An opportunity, then, to enjoy the charm of rusticity. Cicero's *Tusculan Disputations,* centered around the conversations of a small, intimate group who have withdrawn from public life to reflect on various philosophical topics, hints at the benefits of rustic leisure. Perhaps Hadrian had hoped for a similar retreat. Specifically, his country villa sought to supply an ideal place for reflection, far from worldly disturbances. No doubt in Cicero's time the notion was already a more or less idyllic one. Its literary equivalent was the *locus amoenus,* or "pleasance," an ideal rather than actual landscape created by Virgil and others. Yet even someone like Basil of Caesarea, in the middle of the fourth century, could still yearn for it. And that points to a crucial fact about the pleasance: associated with an Arcadia forever lost, it constituted for the Christian bishop, as for the Roman poet before him, a focal point of nostalgia. So, likewise, the *vita contemplativa* for the Roman emperor and his worldly predecessors, attached as they were to the idyll evoked by Cicero. In the end, the notion of a way of life irrevocably lost merely symbolizes any unattainable object.

Of the numerous motifs at Tivoli, one stands out especially. Near the center of the villa, you find a pool adjacent to the banquet hall. Here an elegant marble colonnade serves to frame a rectangular space, bordered by fine gravel walkways. At one end, the statue of a Greek divinity gazes musingly on the water. Alongside the pool, a row of caryatids reinforces the impression of solemn stillness. Meanwhile the water's surface shimmeringly mirrors the colonnade, as well as some trees that loom just beyond. And finally (was the same true in Hadrian's time?)

swans lend to the spot an aura of elegiac reminiscence. Yet the statue of a Greek divinity remains the focal point.[1]

We know that the cultured elite of the Empire had lost its religious piety. Cicero and Pliny the Elder, especially, had ridiculed traditional belief unsparingly. In addition, all the weight of Greek philosophy was set against it. As a result, the religion that had sustained republican Rome fell out of fashion. Instead, the elite professed a humanism that encouraged conformity to reason. For them, Providence was rather abstract. It had no tangible form. Consequently, no Greek divinity could be connected to the cult of Providence in any way. So when we see the statue of a Greek divinity at Tivoli, we can only infer that it's there for some reason other than a belief in the god whose likeness it portrays.

Increasingly, late antiquity had become preoccupied with images.[2] In many respects, the paganism of the Empire amounts to a cult of images. The massive quantity of statues and painted bas-reliefs at temple sites attests to the primacy of the visual in popular religious practices. At the same time, images of the gods had gradually lost their link to what they signified. We know, for instance, that temple idols were often treated like dolls—objects to be dressed, anointed, and handled.[3] Yet perhaps only the populace for whom rituals were performed would have assumed that acts like these could influence the gods themselves. Overall, the rites simply reveal how late antiquity expressed its most intimate thoughts and wishes. Even the cultured elite, for whom a background in classical rhetoric was *de rigueur,* felt the influence of the visual. Thus Basil, in a letter to Maximus the philosopher: "In truth words are the images of the mind."[4]

What the cult of images doesn't quite explain is the primacy of the image per se for late antiquity. On that, we need to turn to a contemporary of Basil, the fourth-century rhetorician Libanius. A propos of a portrait of Aelius Aristeides (a principal figure in the Second Sophistic), Libanius writes to the sender: "I have the portrait of Aristeides, something I have long desired, and I am almost as grateful to you as if you had resurrected the man himself and sent him to me. And I sit by his portrait, read some book of his and ask him whether he was the one who wrote that. Then I answer my question myself. 'Yes, he did that.'" Libanius goes on to talk about the portrait in some detail. He touches on its authenticity as a likeness, and says how eager he is to obtain another portrait of the same subject. What his letter conveys is an almost personal relationship to the Aristeides portrait.[5] For antiquity, however, we know that the ideal form of attachment was friendship. In the increasingly bitter conflict between paganism and Christianity, it could still bridge differences in religious belief: witness the cordial exchange between Basil and Libanius, marked by remembrance of their past days in Athens together and their shared commitment to classical rhetoric. Even Augustine, writing to a fellow Christian bishop like Paulinus of Nola, will often make friendship the basis of an appeal. From a pagan standpoint, more-over, nothing could be more sacred than the claim of a friend. So when Libanius speaks to a portrait as if to a friend, he displays the sort of emotion antiquity normally reserved for its most cherished relationships. Yet the subject of that portrait had been dead for more than a century.

By its very nature, an image preserves for memory what would otherwise be lost. And whereas what we value most in a friend or acquaintance is obviously some human quality, that very humanness must make it equally subject to change or vicissitude. In light of all this, a letter from Basil to Peter of Alex-andria speaks eloquently: "Eyes are the promoters of bodily friendship, and the intimacy engendered through long association strengthens such friendship. But true love is formed by the gift of the Spirit, which brings together objects separated by a wide space, and causes loved ones to know each other, not through the features of the body, but through the peculiarities of the soul. This indeed the favor of the Lord has wrought in our case also, making it possible for us to see you with the eyes of the soul."[6]

For late antiquity, then, the image itself becomes the primary object of nostal-gia. If communion with a long-lost friend is out of the question, emotion focuses on his or her image. Of course, the image emphasized a friend's most cherished qualities. In that way, it effectively embodied some portion of an individual subjectivity. All this, obviously, meant a very different view of subjectivity from the one we now have. But if we could think of subjectivity as capable of embodi-ment in an object, we might find such a belief easier to accept. Late antiquity didn't share our reluctance on that score. Rather, it felt individuals as presences. As a result, the "presence" of a friend could be strongly felt even in his or her absence. A belief in presences might help to explain the figures of Greek gods at Hadrian's villa. To one for whom the gods themselves were indifferent, these likenesses constituted presences. Above all, there was the presence of Antinoüs, the youth whom Hadrian had lost years before.

Because Antinoüs himself was only an embodiment of Greek consciousness, other objects could point to his presence indirectly. Hence the role of Egyptian deities and other visual reminiscences of Egypt at Tivoli: since Antinoüs had drowned in the Nile, it, too, could now claim a portion of his subjectivity. And likewise for any embodiment of the Nile or Egypt. To dwell in the presence of objects that embody a portion of the subjectivity of Antinoüs is thus to dwell, by extension, in the presence of Antinoüs himself. So the entire villa at Tivoli becomes an expression of nostalgia: the embodiment of a subjectivity one has loved, and, by the same token, a form of its presence. And, since Antinoüs himself had embodied Greek subjectivity from an earlier period, the emperor's attachment to the youth implied a relationship to the past. In that respect, Antinoüs himself turns out to be a symbolic image for nostalgia. The ultimate object of Hadrian's passion, then, isn't just an idealized youth but rather the spirit of Greek antiquity.

As a form of nostalgia, the attempt to recover a classical text obviously differs from Hadrian's quest for a vital embodiment of Greek subjectivity. Instead of material reminiscences of the classical in stone or landscape architecture, there is the quiet, laborious collation of manuscripts, followed by intensive critical analysis of a given text and, subsequently, the slow, patient piecework of deductions and inferences by which the lost archetype is re-created. And yet, despite all the differences, the two forms of nostalgia share a similarity. To be able to remove layers of textual corruption that have gradually accumulated like some sort of fine sediment, to restore a work of great antiquity to its original purity, offers a glimpse of a subjectivity that has since ceased to exist, but nonetheless lies at the origin of the way we now think and feel.

When F. A. Wolf published his *Prolegomena to Homer* in Germany in 1795, it created an immediate sensation. Wilhelm von Humboldt promptly made it the basis for his reform of the humanities in German higher education. Friedrich Schlegel saw it as a model for his own studies in Greek poetry. His brother, August Wilhelm Schlegel, popularized it in a series of well-attended lectures on literature. To Schelling, it even offered a discourse on method for the natural sciences. Meanwhile, Herder appropriated it for his theory of the *Volkgeist* in poetry. And Goethe supposedly hid behind a curtain to hear Wolf lecture on classical literature.[7]

Given its immense impact on classical studies, one naturally expects the *Prolegomena* to show how we might recover the original Homeric text. Certainly the full title of the work would seem to promise that: *Prolegomena to Homer, or Concerning the Original and Genuine Form of the Homeric Works and Their Various Alterations and the Proper Method of Emendation.* So it comes as a real surprise when the promise isn't fulfilled. Early in the work, Wolf candidly admits that an Ur-text of the *Iliad* is impossible: "Once I gave up hope, then, that the original form of the Homeric Poems could ever be laid out save in our minds, and even there only in rough outlines, it seemed appropriate to investigate how far the ancient evidence would take us in polishing these eternal and unique remains of the Greek genius" (*Prolegomena*, p. 47).[8] Subsequently he says what he thinks can be achieved textually: "And indeed, my single primary intention was to correct the text of Homer by the standard of learned antiquity, and to display him in a text the wording, punctuation, and accentuation of which, remade from the recensions that were once considered best, might—if one may properly hope for so much—satisfy some Longinus or other ancient critic who knew how to use the materials of the Alexandrians with skill and tact" (*Prolegomena*, pp. 56–57). By his mention of Longinus, Wolf appears to imply the Homeric text as it would have stood somewhere around the third century A.D. But his use of Longinus as a reference point hardly explains why we can't have the original Homeric text.[9]

In order for Wolf to justify his refusal to pursue the Ur-text, what he needs to demonstrate is its unknowability. To some extent, eighteenth-century interest in Homer grew out of a larger interest in the period. Clearly, though, any knowledge of the Homeric period (ca. 1200 B.C.) must rely at least partly on the Homeric texts. To undermine their value as historical evidence, then, Wolf has to show that they don't actually date from the period they represent. Yet even that needn't imply they don't accurately depict Homeric life. In fact, some texts might even contain authentic Homeric material, passages that date back to the Homeric period itself. The crucial point here is simply that we can't trace the entire work to genuine Homeric sources. Hence, Wolf insists, we can no longer take it as a source for that period.[10]

His argument for this thesis is simple: the age of Homer doesn't know writing. "The word *book* is nowhere, *writing* is nowhere, *reading* is nowhere, *letters* are nowhere; nothing in so many thousands of verses is arranged for reading, everything for hearing; there are no pacts or treaties except face to face; there is no source of report for old times except memory and rumor and monuments without writing; from that comes the diligent and, in the *Iliad*, strenuously repeated invocation of the Muses, the goddesses of memory; there is no inscription on the pillars and tombs that are sometimes mentioned; there is no other inscription of any kind; there is no coin or fabricated money; there is no use of writing in domestic matters or trade; there are no maps; finally there are no letter carriers and no letters. If these had been in normal use in Ulysses' homeland, or if 'folding tablets' had been adequate to the inquiries of the suitors and Telemachus, we would doubtless have an *Odyssey* that was shorter by some books—or, as Rousseau concluded, none at all" (*Prolegomena*, pp. 101–2).

But if the absence of *écriture* in the Homeric period is a result of choice, it makes sense to relate it to other aspects of Homeric culture. His attempt to describe such a culture leads Wolf, in turn, to think about its *mentalité*: "At this point, let us quite forget the bookcases and libraries that nowadays preserve our studies, and be transported to other times and another world, where many of the inventions which we think necessary for the good life were unknown to both wise men and fools. In those days, not even immortality for one's own name was reason enough to make anyone seek it in enduring monuments; and to believe that Homer sought them is wishful thinking rather than convincing argument. For where does he indicate that he is possessed by such an ambition? Where does he utter a declaration of this sort, so frequent among other poets, or cunningly conceal one? Indeed, he often proclaims that wicked and outstanding deeds are bequeathed to fame by means of his song, but he also affirms that the most recent song is most popular among listeners. But, in general, that age, playing as it were under its nurse's eyes and following the impulse of its divine genius, was content simply to experiment with very beautiful things and to offer them for the delectation of others: if it sought any reward, it was the applause and praise of the contemporary audience—the most splendid of prizes, if we may believe the poets, and one more welcome by far than an immortality preserved in papyrus" (*Prolegomena*, p. 104).

Without a written text, however, the Homeric material becomes subject in crucial ways to all the conditions of live performances. Now while a singer or rhapsode would normally tend to rely largely on memory, he might also feel tempted, as Wolf points out, to emend or improve the Homeric text. After all, what version could his audience possibly know, other than the one they heard? And for the rhapsode, highly sensitive to immediate audience response, what more natural than to give them the best version he could, even if this meant altering what he had received from his predecessor. As a result, the reason for a single, definitive form of the Homeric text disappears.

At the same time, as Wolf observes, performance constraints would shape the Homeric material in another way as well. Because of the length limit on a recital, only a portion of the entire narrative could be delivered at any one time. Consequently, no need for a coherent overall shape to the narrative, as different sections came to stand almost independently. So the poem exists, in effect, only as a loosely related group of episodes in no particular sequence. In fact, Wolf asserts, the original *Iliad* and *Odyssey* probably weren't continuous narratives, their continuity merely the fruit of a later effort to connect previously discrete portions of material. Likewise, the artistic structure or unity that we now associate with both works must also originate at a later period. Thus the *telos* that sees the death of Hector as caused by his triumph over Patroclus, or the battle by the ships as brought about by Agamemnon's quarrel with Achilles over Briseus, would only have emerged after the Homeric period itself.

By this point, Wolf would appear to have shown that the Homeric texts don't necessarily give us access to the Homeric period. If we grant his premise that the age of Homer doesn't write, the circumstances of oral performance seem more or less inescapable. In addition, even the text itself can no longer pose as the work of a single author, or even a single period. To a large extent, our notion of a definitive text tacitly assumes a unitary authorial perspective. With the Homeric text as reconstructed by Wolf, however, such a perspective becomes hard to sustain. If at least some of the material goes back to the Homeric period itself, then at no single moment in the history of the text do we get all of it. Instead, the process by which the work gradually achieves completion is simultaneously that of its corruption.

But if a definitive Homeric text is out of the question, what Wolf presents in its place is an account of how the Homeric text comes to be. In other words, the Homeric text as a history of successive efforts to recover the authentic Homeric material. For Wolf, each period in that history (chapter 7 lists six in all) works its way into some portion of the received text. In its present form, then, the text amounts to a palimpsest: not a text in the ordinary sense, but rather the cumulative record of what various periods tried to make of it. From this standpoint, obviously, there can be no definitive Homeric text. What the actual text does offer, as Wolf sees it, is something equally significant: the history of a collective effort to recover the cultural voice of an earlier period. If we can no longer hope to recover the Homeric period itself, we can at least try to recover the attempts at its recovery. For Wolf, what each period brought to its editorial work was its own form of nostalgia for the past. To analyze what it did is thus to arrive at some sense of why it felt a recovery of the Homeric text to be meaningful. In this fashion, what we ultimately hope to gain is an insight into the sources of our own nostalgia.

If the Homeric material was in fact originally oral, the first task for any editor would have been to collect and preserve it in written form. In chapter 34, Wolf sums up the situation: "But if, as the ancients held, no one before Pisistratus thought seriously about gluing the works of Homer together, it is not credible that they could immediately have reached the public complete in all their parts and in the state in which we now see them, even if the gluing had been elaborately worked out in advance. Pisistratus could have thought it enough to put several sections into an appropriate order, leaving to the side those that impeded the general plot, even if inconsistencies and gaps might exist here and there, or scraps remain from the earlier form. One motive among others for seeking out that uninterrupted sequence could have been the very activity of continuous writing, in which each poem had to be assigned its place. But polishing everything and, as it were, making it absolutely smooth might have seemed too toilsome to manage in the first attempt" (*Prolegomena*, p. 142).

Here the magnitude of the task becomes apparent. Quite simply, preservation involves a lot more than mere transcription. What faced Pisistratus was in fact a problem of daunting complexity. To begin with, there are those sections that might have "impeded the general plot": presumably, either because they're purely discursive (i.e., no plot elements at all) or because they even contradict the basic narrative sequence. To leave them out would be one option. But then, as Wolf observes, "inconsistencies and gaps" might result. The possibility of "inconsistencies" is especially significant, insofar as they suggest internal conflicts within the narrative.

Clearly, then, recovery of the text would have meant not just a careful transcription of oral material but a genuine restoration. As Wolf himself points out, if every rhapsode were merely asked to recite and his words recorded, the result would be a plethora of different versions, each supposedly definitive. Nor could they necessarily be reconciled. Instead, someone would have had to act as a supervisor or polisher of the text. Wolf says the ancients themselves clearly distinguished a supervisor or polisher from someone who simply produced a critical recension of the text. And where the differences between various versions loomed too large to be negotiated, decisions would have to be made comparable to those of a stage manager who rearranges a play rather freely to suit the demands of a particular performance. But obviously such rearrangements are often tantamount to a new creation. Wolf even reports that early revisers of the Homeric material were known to have resorted to forgery in order to give a proper arrangement to the text, and that their efforts were judged unworthy by later antiquity, and so removed. Nonetheless, Wolf himself doesn't condemn the work of these revisers in any way. But if his own aim is to recover the authentic Homeric material, it seems odd that he doesn't.

For Wolf, I would argue, forgery is okay because of his perception that a coherent Homeric text necessitates some original creation. For the revisers to produce a text not palpably inconsistent, significant alterations become more or less unavoidable. Furthermore, to simply refuse to eliminate any material at all, to reproduce everything extant without any regard for consistency, would probably lead to a formless and unmanageable text. Nor would it be likely to survive, given its solely antiquarian interest. Instead, what Wolf emphasizes is the revisers' ability to impart a coherent shape to the Homeric material so as to make it a permanent cultural possession for all antiquity. At this distance in time, we may be hard pressed to appreciate fully what they accomplished. Unversed in the tradition of oral performance, we can't properly discern the enormous gap that separates brief, fragmentary oral utterances from the formal structure of a written text. It offers, in effect, a redefinition of what the Homeric material is all about. Thus the real work of nostalgia, as Wolf sees it, isn't simply one of appreciation. Ultimately, it implies a more imaginative act: the sort of transformative process by which a mass of individual narrative episodes becomes an expressive totality.

From the task that faced the reviser, Wolf shifts to the individual or individuals who did it. In particular, he questions whether Pisistratus alone would have had the time, with all the pressures of his position as Athenian tyrant. Given the magnitude of the project, Wolf believes a collaboration of some kind more natural: "A lovely flowering of lyric and ethical poetry occurred in the age of these two men [Pisistratus and his son Hipparchus], together with new additions—namely, tragedy and comedy. Among so many poets there were perhaps some who could help Pisistratus and Hipparchus in this matter, especially since both of them were very well disposed both to the arts and to learned men. It is expressly reported that Orpheus of Croton, the author of an *Argonautica,* Onomacritus of Athens, who was later exiled from the city by Hipparchus, Simonides of Ceos, and Anacreon of Teos lived in the closest friendship with Pisistratus and Hipparchus. I would conjecture that one of these men offered him his help in arranging the poems. Pisistratus himself certainly had his hands full with his own affairs, while the poets had leisure and a considerable familiarity with the ancient works" (*Prolegomena,* pp. 144–45).

Although the Pisistratean recension most likely involved poets (read: some creative resourcefulness in the arrangement of the text), Wolf observes that these poets also had a "considerable familiarity with the ancient works." Such familiarity argues a genuine love of the older poetry for its own sake (since everything of interest would have to be committed to memory). Thus any creative impulse in the arrangement of the text would probably have been counterbalanced by a purely antiquarian tendency. If Pisistratus himself were at all involved in the project, moreover, his own influence would certainly have worked to preserve the Homeric material as an archaic text. In this fashion, the first period of editing emerges as a brilliant fusion of antiquarianism and creativity. And although a creative revision might well come closer to the spirit of the poems than any purely antiquarian labor, it seems clear that what really attracts Wolf is precisely the way the Homeric material gets transformed. For Wolf, then, the true object of nostalgia isn't the original material but rather its rearrangement by Pisistratus and his circle, an arrangement informed by their own nostalgia for the Homeric period.

At this point, we enter into what Wolf sees as the second period of editing. It begins in a somewhat curious way, triggered by the genesis of Homeric interpretation. In particular, Wolf traces its origin to philosophy: "That is why I do not doubt that the most ancient philosophers are to be considered the founders of Homeric interpretation and, at least at the beginning, of a pragmatic interpretation. For there was basically no obscurity in the words of those ages, since each of the best poets normally used the same diction. But when the philosophers saw that the poems were considered sacred and were celebrated by the whole populace, and that the precepts for governing one's life rightly were drawn from them, and when they nevertheless also noticed in them many false, ridiculous, and unseemly fictions concerning the nature of the gods and the world, they began to correct the fables by interpreting them and to accommodate them to the physical and ethical beliefs of their own age, and finally to reduce the stories and almost everything else to wrappings for an elaborate philosophy" (*Prolegomena*, p. 149).

By itself, the interpretation of poetic texts needn't necessarily imply their being edited. Later, however, Wolf attempts to relate the two activities: "For it is the nature of reason that we insert almost all our own opinions and those of our age into the books with which we have been continuously familiar since early youth; and if those books have long since been consecrated by popular usage, then veneration also hinders us from believing that they contain absurd and ridiculous things. Hence we soften and adorn by interpretation whatever does not seem tolerable in its literal sense" (*Prolegomena*, p. 150). From here it's only a small step to alter sacred or poetic texts, so as to make the literal accord with our sense of what it should be. Subsequently, we even get a few examples (*Prolegomena*, pp. 153–54). Yet, despite the fact that changes of this kind obviously lead to textual corruption, Wolf adamantly professes to find "nothing reprehensible" in it (*Prolegomena*, p. 151).

To understand the motive for his apparent leniency, we need to look at Wolf on the process that brought about a gradual corruption of the Homeric text after Pisistratus: "For suppose (what history does not permit us to imagine in any other way) that ten or twenty copies had been made by private men—for example, by rhapsodes—after that first attempt at writing: a number of variations would necessarily have been introduced into them at once, partly because of the various modes of recitation, partly because of the ingenious caprice of the scribes. . . . Now if new copies were continuously being made from these, then unless an ignorant scribe faithfully transcribed whatever he seized upon next, those who were concerned with these matters, once they had compared several texts, could only have approached the problem by judging and choosing what seemed most appropriate to each passage. They would thus produce a very different version of the text. . . . As the number of manuscripts gradually increased in this way, that Pisistratean source, if indeed it was one source, was soon divided into several streams with different flavors, so to speak, and impeded the attempt to arrive at an accurate reading. Hence if some intelligent person . . . had compared the best manuscripts which he had heard were preserved anywhere in order to prepare for himself and for his friends a new copy, he would quite often have found it extremely difficult to judge what might really be the genuine reading, and would have had no readier and better aid than his own talent" (*Prolegomena*, pp. 156–57).

Hence the need for a developed critical faculty, so as to be able to discriminate between different versions of the text. Here historical scholarship really doesn't help. What we have, Wolf says, are several manuscripts of equal value, all derived independently from the same Pisistratean source. From a historical standpoint, then, they're equally good: philological criteria won't give precedence to one over the rest. Nor is there any question, in historical terms, of inferiority. Thus any judgment between these manuscripts would have to be based on other criteria. Yet the content of one isn't the same as what we get from a second. Now philosophy becomes useful. What it does is to subject that content to the test of rationality. We've seen that all the early copies of the Pisistratus text would probably have undergone variation not only because of different recitation modes but also because of what Wolf refers to as the "ingenious caprice of the scribes." But "ingenious caprice" typically leads to the excessively fanciful. Thus the need for rationality as a corrective. The result would presumably be a text purified of the excessively fanciful or arbitrary. At the same time, it wouldn't simply represent a return to what Pisistratus and his circle had originally produced. Instead, it would most likely also try to accommodate the "physical and ethical beliefs" of a later, more rational age. Nor would this mean the loss of those beliefs that typify the religion of a more archaic period, since it was probably already difficult (if not impossible) to tell what might embody authentic Homeric belief from the "ingenious caprice" of a copyist. In fact, subjection of the Homeric text to philosophical rationality might even yield what's really essential to the ethos of that period.

The notion of a text that preserves what's essential to the ethos of the Homeric period gives rise to the possibility of a single, ideal recension. In chapter 40, Wolf allows himself to speculate about it: "But we see a memorable object lesson about the role of blind chance in the preservation of these bits and scraps, in the fact that our scholia do not mention even once the recension generally attributed to Aristotle, 'the one from the unguent casket.' . . . Nor does any other source offer more certain knowledge of that very celebrated monument which, according to Plutarch, contained only the *Iliad.* Furthermore, when Plutarch and Strabo are compared, it becomes clear that many scholars, and Alexander the Great himself, took a hand in emending it. If each of these writers followed reliable sources, Alexander first received that book from his Stagirite teacher, then brought it with him into Asia as a comrade on his expedition, read it together with Callisthenes and Anaxarchus in spare moments, annotated it with his own hand, and deposited it as *the most precious work of the human mind* in a very elaborate Persian chest" (*Prolegomena*, pp. 163–64).

As a symbolic object, it seems almost perfect: a fusion of what was best from the archaic period with all the editorial intelligence of Greek rationality. Yet it's also indicative of what Wolf values most in the Homeric text. Not simply the Homeric period itself, but how that period was seen by the cultural zenith of antiquity. From his standpoint, "the most precious work of the human mind" is highly appropriate: it refers not only to the achievement of the Homeric poet and all his early successors, but also to the collective insight of the finest critical intelligences of Greek antiquity. That such a recension should have been passed on to Alexander the Great, that he himself should have taken it with him on his expedition into Asia, even that he chose to deposit it in a "very elaborate Persian chest," exemplify what the process of cultural transmission is all about. Indeed, nostalgia might well focus on this, Alexander's copy of the Aristotelian recension of the *Iliad*, as a material embodiment of "the most precious work of the human mind."

After the zenith of Greek antiquity, it's only natural for the next period of Homeric editing to involve a decline. Wolf himself is quick to admit it: "In place of the agora, the speaker's platform, the stage, and the public festival appeared museums and libraries; in place of genius rich in its own resources appeared timid imitation, which undertook only modest tasks; in place of a very elevated spirit of poetry and eloquence appeared sober and sometimes chill erudition, reading spread over all areas of learning; in place of original ideas appeared thoroughness, care, and a certain polish of arrangement and poetic diction; in place, finally, of the magnificent native bloom of all the arts appeared garlands composed of the blossoms from everywhere" (*Prolegomena*, p. 167). Still, an age of erudition can display qualities of another kind: as Keats observes of autumn in his famous ode, "thou hast thy music too.—" For Wolf, the primary achievement of what he sees as the third period of Homeric editing is imme-diately evident: "*a text more consistent in form* was introduced" (*Prolegomena*, p. 167). Nor is the establishment of textual consistency purely accidental. Instead, Wolf sees it as a natural result of the development of a new field or discipline: the "*art of interpretation and emendation*" (*Prolegomena*, p. 167). More broadly, it points to the emergence of historical scholarship. From that standpoint, the third period of editorial work on Homer has, for Wolf, a special poignancy. In the work and aspirations of these Homeric specialists of later antiquity, all modern scholars must inevitably recognize an anticipation of their own. By virtue of its historical perspective, such a period will presumably feel the same sort of nostal-gia for the past as all those who seek to recover some remnant of the culture of classical antiquity.

Of the three specialists who typify the third period of Homeric editing, the first, Zenodotus, serves as an object lesson on the significance of grammar. Ultimately, grammar is about the extent of our passion for detail. By means of grammar, we submit to antiquity rather than trying to impose on it. Grammar gives us a perspective on the primary defects of Zenodotus. Essentially, they amount to rashness and excess: wildly improbable readings, deletions so exces-sive that we no longer recognize Homer, a notorious lack of taste, and a tendency to treat the *Iliad* "as if it were his own composition" (*Prolegomena*, p. 174). Yet Zenodotus is, as Wolf sees it, merely representative of an entire period. Thus his final verdict tempers criticism with leniency. At the same time, Wolf stresses the importance of grammar for any meaningful attempt at textual improvement: "In an age before the language had begun to be minutely examined in accor-dance with precise rules, even a talented man could slip, or be inconsistent in an area which is subject less to talent than to rules. No one of intelligence, moreover, can fail to recognize how much the art of grammar itself, in its early stages, falters in details and how prone it is, in attempting to adjudicate between the custom of the authors and the logic of rules, to wander unawares from either standard" (*Prolegomena*, p. 176).

The difficulties of editing and, more broadly, of any effort to recover the past, point toward one conclusion: the necessity for study. Hence the significance of

Aristophanes of Byzantium. In chapter 44 of the *Prolegomena* Wolf calls him "the leader in embracing with the greatest zeal the study of the poets and all literature of antiquity" (p. 182). To Aristophanes tradition ascribes the foundation of a school of grammar on the philosophical/rhetorical model. The list of his achievements emphasizes the role of study: first to investigate the authenticity of past remains, first to pay close attention to Greek grammar, first to invent a system of punctuation and accents to improve the readability of ancient texts. He won renown as the author of commentaries on various classical authors. Above all there is his work on his namesake Aristophanes, whose plays he discussed in terms of general significance, artistry, and chronology (*Prolegomena*, pp. 183–84). Here, then, we have the necessary groundwork for a more accurate knowledge of Greek antiquity. It imparts a coherence to the subject that is indispensable to scholarly inquiry. And, most important, it conveys a lesson in method.

Nevertheless, mere study of the relevant material isn't sufficient to yield a definitive text of the principal works of Greek antiquity. After all, as Wolf points out, knowledge of Greek grammar was at the time still in its infancy. So a simple use of grammatical analysis to eliminate spurious additions to the text doesn't spell authenticity. Even a sophisticated knowledge of grammar could hardly be the sole requirement: some additions, after all, would presumably date back to the Homeric period itself. In addition, then, an editor would need a feel for the stylistic nuances of authentic Homeric material, a sense of imagery and ways of expression that distinguish the work of an early, more archaic period from a later one. Finally, we might ask if it's even possible to separate authentic but stylistically weak Homeric material from inspired additions by later rhapsodes.

Given these conditions, the recension of Homer produced by Aristarchus represents a remarkable achievement. For we have to assume that what Aristarchus wanted to produce wasn't necessarily the most authentic Homer text, but simply the best in terms of artistic quality. As Wolf puts it: "To that generation of Greeks, moreover, even though they were highly involved in the details of grammar, it would necessarily have seemed unworthy of the talents of a serious and learned man to be concerned with [whatever] belongs to the task of the *grammatista*. *Grammarians* ... differed greatly from these, and particularly ... the *critics*, whose duty it was to inquire into ... ancient works, to assign them to their proper author, and especially to review their virtues and vices so that their hearers might learn what in them was to be imitated, and what was contrary to the laws of true writing. ... It is by this sort of emendation, or rather criticism, that all critics once were rivals in Homer, or rather with Homer. They were driven by the very supremacy of the poems to omit nothing by which it might be increased and by which the most perfect polish of language and poetic art might be contrived. And in this area the more ingenious each was, the more immoderately he seems to have behaved, and often to have corrupted the text in correcting it. Certainly he who could emend the greatest poet by his own ability was thought to be supreme in critical judgment" (*Prolegomena*, p. 192).

If this was the way Aristarchus approached his task, however, what remains to be explained is how he managed to produce the most authentic Homer text. Wolf carefully considers all the relevant circumstances: the "beginnings of all subtlety in grammar" (*Prolegomena*, p. 199), which he credits to Aristarchus, use of the most ancient and best manuscripts, and a refusal to add anything to what was already in the text, so that any improvements would have to be by deletion only. Yet even collectively, these still fall short of an adequate explanation. After all, in its original form the poem was probably a pastiche. No matter how scrupulously edited, then, it could hardly avoid the appearance of heterogeneity. And yet there is the undeniable impression of the work. As described by Wolf: "But the bard himself seems to contradict history, and the sense of the reader bears witness against it. Nor indeed are the poems so deformed and reshaped that they seem excessively unlike their own original form in individual details. Indeed, almost everything in them seems to affirm the same mind, the same customs, the same manner of thinking and speaking. Everyone who reads carefully and sensitively feels this sharply; and to know the reason for it rather than merely to sense it, you must switch from these poems to Apollonius of Rhodes, to the other Alexandrians, and to Quintus of Smyrna, who is commonly thought the image of Homer" (*Prolegomena*, p. 210). Finally, Wolf can only say: "Does it matter if we owe the restoration of that miraculous harmony above all to the exquisite talent and learning of Aristarchus?"

So it comes down, in the end, to this: the learning, but perhaps more than anything else, the talent and taste of Aristarchus. The capacity, in other words, to see which episodes, which passages, which details of imagery or turns of phrase might interweave to form a seamless whole. Thus our perception of the text and, ultimately, of the entire Homeric world is based on that of Aristarchus. So the nostalgia for Greek antiquity comes to rest for Wolf not on the Homeric period itself nor even, at last, on the fusion of that period with the outlook of the last and greatest representative of Greek rationality. Instead, it has to do with the textual work of a Homeric specialist from the second century B.C. All our effort to recover the Homeric world can be summed up as an effort to see that world as he saw it. To know, in other words, not just the text he finally established, but the indefinable yet palpable impression he received of an earlier period, which had led to the text he produced because it gave to what he felt the richest, fullest expression.

Nostalgia takes on different forms in different contexts. With Hadrian, it wants to become one with the subjectivity of an earlier period. With Wolf, it yearns for Greek antiquity as filtered through the perception of a Hellenistic observer. With Friedrich Schlegel, finally, the connection to antiquity becomes even more distant. Now early Greek subjectivity is perceived purely as the embodiment of an ideal. No doubt he had recognized the impossibility of a genuine recovery of the Homeric period as a result of Wolf's *Prolegomena*. Nevertheless, what his own youthful essay "Über das Studium der Griechischen Poesie" (1795–97) gives us is something else: a meditation on the very nature of nostalgia.[11] Instead of a desire for some concrete aspect of the past, what Schlegel has in mind assumes the form of an ideal. But an ideal is obviously subjective. Significantly, the very definition of objectivity in the "Studium" essay makes it essentially subjective as well. On a more general level, what Schlegel's discussion of Greek antiquity would seem to imply is that for any theory of nostalgia, resolution can come only out of its relation to itself.

For Friedrich Schlegel, nostalgia for Greek antiquity began from one of those luminous experiences that shape a mind forever after. Decades later, he himself vividly recalled his visit to Dresden in 1789: "[I] was equally happy and astonished to see actually before me the long yearned-for likenesses of the antique gods, among which I often lingered and wandered around for hours, especially in the incomparable collection of casts by Mengs, which at that time could be found, as yet barely arranged, in Brühl's garden, where I often let myself be locked in, so as to remain the more undisturbed. It wasn't however solely the high beauty of the form, which fulfilled and exceeded my silently nourished expectations, but rather the life and movement about these Olympian marble statues that amazed me even more; for these in my solitary meditations I hadn't been able to represent in that way to myself, nor think them possible. These unforgettable first impressions remained the firm, enduring foundation for my studies of classical antiquity" (*KA* IV, p. 4).

Here what catches the eye is the fact that, from the very outset, appreciation for Greek antiquity in Friedrich Schlegel is deeply connected to his own subjectivity. Note, first of all, that what astonishes him most isn't the "high beauty of the form" but rather the "life and movement" of the statues. And that because "these in my solitary meditations [shades of Rousseau's *promeneur solitaire*] I hadn't been able to represent in that way to myself, nor think them possible." So the impression of vivid life or movement is based on whether we can represent or visualize it beforehand. In those instances where we can't, the shock is all the greater. Thus for Friedrich Schlegel the sense of vitality communicated by a statue results as much from his own subjective state at the time as from any intrinsic quality of the statue itself. Nonetheless, Schlegel doesn't praise these antique works just for their vitality. He also lavishes a lot of praise on their form as well, whose "high beauty" not only "fulfilled" but even "exceeded" his "silently nourished expectations." Presumably, his classical education had already prepared him to expect a distinct formal beauty. Yet somehow the actual works exceed all expectation. And because they go beyond expectation, they leave a deep impression. As with vitality, then, the perception of formal beauty seems to depend largely on what you expect. So once again, the sense of what antiquity is all about comes to be defined by the particular condition of an individual subjectivity.

Apart from the effect produced by the initial impression in Brühl's sculpture garden, a special poignancy attaches to the very act of memory itself. For what led Friedrich Schlegel to recall his early visit to Dresden had no relation to his study of classical antiquity. Instead, his reminiscence appeared in a preface to a collection of his art criticism, assembled for the *Sämmtliche Werke* in 1823, and entitled *Ansichten und Ideen von der christlichen Kunst* [Views and Ideas on Christian Art]. In his preface, Schlegel had urged that criticism ought to specify the personal circumstances under which a work of art had been viewed. Given the context, it seems all the more odd that his one example should focus on classical antiquity. We can only suppose that the Greek statuary he saw in Brühl's garden embodied an aesthetic to which he felt particularly attracted, one he didn't find anywhere else. In light of the widespread imitation of classical antiquity in Renaissance and neoclassical art, this comes as a bit of a surprise. The absence of a desired element in more recent art suggests that what Schlegel found in Greek statuary wasn't purely formal, that it ultimately embraced the entire consciousness of an earlier period.

But if what attracted Friedrich Schlegel to Greek art was its expression of period consciousness, he must have felt, on some level, a nostalgia for that consciousness as one irrevocably lost. To believe an earlier consciousness is no longer possible for you, however, you need to have some notion of consciousness from a historical perspective. For a sense of where that might have come from, we need to turn, as the young Schlegel himself did, to Friedrich Schiller, and specifically his "Über naive und sentimentalische Dichtung":

So long as man isn't quite, be it understood, raw nature, he acts as undivided sensuous unity, and as a harmonious whole. Sense and reason, receptive and self-active capacity, have in their activity not yet become separate, rather stand in opposition to each other. His sensations are not the formless play of chance, his thoughts not the contentless play of imagination; out of the law of *necessity* comes that, out of *reality* comes this. When man has entered into the state of culture, and art has laid its hand on him, that sensuous harmony in him is cancelled out [*aufgehoben*], and he can now only express himself as moral unity, i.e., as striving for unity. The harmony between his sensations and thoughts, which in his initial condition could *actually* be found, exists now only *ideally;* it is no more in him, but outside him; as a thought, that would first need to be realized, no more as a fact of his life. (*Schillers Werke* 20: 436–37)

Here what's crucial is the shift from a state of mind where sensation and thought are in harmony to one where that harmony has ceased to exist. Schiller says the loss of harmony is due to culture. Yet he doesn't really explain why. To understand how such a shift could come about, we need to look at what produces sensation and thought in a mind characterized by sensuous unity. If sensation is produced by a law of necessity and thought by reality, we can infer that all mental activity is externally determined. But once we enter a state of culture, our thoughts no longer come from external nature but rather from the mind itself. Hence the disruption of harmony. Specifically, Schiller observes that from now on this harmony can only exist externally. In other words, once the mind becomes aware of its own capacity, it can no longer be externally determined. As a result, the only way we could hope to recover the harmony we've lost would be to make nature conform to the mind, or the external like the internal. But for that to happen, thought (as Schiller says) would have to be realized or imposed on external reality, which is impossible.

In addition, Schiller remarks that a harmony that can't actually exist can become an ideal. In a later passage, he works out this notion more fully:

Wholly otherwise is it with the sentimental poet. This one *reflects* on the impression that things make on him, and only on that reflection is the emotion grounded, to which he himself is transported, and transports us. The thing is here connected to an idea, and only from this connection gets its poetic force. The sentimental poet has therefore always to do with two conflicting representations and sensations, with reality as limit and with his idea as the infinite, and the mixed feeling that he excites will always be produced from these two sources. (*Schillers Werke* 20: 441)

For Schiller, the passage from actual to ideal comes about by means of reflection. We reflect on an earlier blissful condition we no longer enjoy, and in the process we transform that condition into an ideal. Specifically, the sentimental poet reflects "on the impression that things make on him." In this way, Schiller manages to achieve the crucial move from objective to subjective: from the thing itself we pass over to the impression it produces. And if our emotion is grounded entirely on that reflection, the reason for it, presumably, is that our reflection is all about what we've lost. But loss leads to an ideal. As Schiller puts it, "the thing is here connected to an idea," and the idea is that what we've lost can be recovered. So our position, like that of the sentimental poet, is one of mixed emotion: we see the limit defined by the reality of where we now are, but we also see the infinite possibility of our ideal. And that mixed emotion, you might say, is what characterizes the modern condition.

With Schiller in mind, we can now turn to what Friedrich Schlegel has to say about the genesis of modern subjectivity.[12] In "Über das Studium der Griechischen Poesie" he attempts to offer a narrative: "After the completed natural formation of the ancients had decidedly gone into decline and had degenerated beyond rescue, the loss of finite reality and the shattering of perfected form induced a *striving for infinite reality,* which soon became the general tone of the age. One and the same principle produced the colossal excesses of the Romans, and, after seeing its hopes deceived in the sense-world, [produced] the strange phenomenon of Neoplatonic philosophy, and the general tendency of that curious period, where the human spirit appeared to reel toward a universal and metaphysical religion. The decisive moment in the history of Roman *moeurs,* when the sense for beautiful appearances and moral play had become wholly lost, and the human race sank down to naked reality, has not gone unnoticed by perceptive historians . . . that artificial aesthetic formation, which can only follow upon a fully dissolved natural formation, and which must begin where the other has left off, namely with the interesting, would have to go through many steps, before it could arrive by the laws of an objective theory and the example of classical poetry at the objective and the beautiful" (*KA* I, pp. 213–14).

We might begin here with the question of what Friedrich Schlegel means by the "loss of finite reality." Given the context, a destruction of material objects by wars or conquest hardly seems likely. Instead, careful scrutiny of the text makes it clear that the ancients whom he has in mind don't amount to all of antiquity but merely its Greek element. Since the decline of Greek culture doesn't involve massive physical devastation, however, the finite reality he speaks of must refer to a concept or notion of some kind. If we think of finite reality in terms of the mental rather than the concrete or physical, it suggests an effort to frame what presents itself to perception. The text reinforces this when it goes on to speak of a "derangement of perfect form." After all, "perfect form" is purely a matter of perception: material objects have form, of course, but the notion of "perfect form" exists only in the mind. Moreover, the very idea of form inevitably implies an attempt to impose a coherent framework on what would otherwise remain a chaos of sensory data. But because of the mental effort involved, such an enterprise can't be sustained indefinitely. Hence the eventual loss of this capacity to give aesthetic shape to what we perceive.

The "loss of finite reality" leads us quite naturally to ask what the subsequent "striving for infinite reality" is all about. Since the text speaks of striving but never fulfillment, it seems safe to assume the "infinite reality" in question is never reached. The narrative, moreover, hints at a causal relationship: loss of finite reality produces a striving for infinite reality, as if by way of compensation. And if finite reality is somehow associated with perfect form, its derangement would seem to imply infinite reality is essentially formless. We've seen that the quest for finite reality indicated an effort to frame what we receive from our perceptual faculty. Presumably, then, the striving for infinite reality must also revolve around an effort to apprehend perceptual data as well, but without any attempt to impose an aesthetic shape on what we perceive.

But if infinite reality is merely finite reality without form, its unattainability seems prima facie hard to explain. The text observes that the striving for infinite reality begins with the "colossal excesses" of Rome. Since we're told that its hopes are deceived in the sense-world, the "colossal excesses" that occur would appear to indicate various forms of sensual indulgence. After its disillusionment with sensuality, the Empire then turns to what Friedrich Schlegel terms the "strange phenomenon of Neoplatonic philosophy." Yet, paradoxically, it doesn't even find satisfaction here. Instead, Neoplatonism only reflects the "general tendency" of its period, when "the human spirit seemed to reel toward a universal and metaphysical religion." Yet if sensual indulgence, which sought to immerse itself in purely physical pleasure, proved a failure, it seems only natural to expect that its diametrical opposite, Neoplatonic philosophy, would be more successful. Without any effort to shape perception, sensual indulgence had merely surrendered to the formlessness of sensory experiences. On the other hand, Neoplatonic philosophy simply avoids the sphere of our experiences altogether. Hence both approaches, by their refusal to impart a shape of some kind to what we perceive, fail to address the real issue.

The failure of sensual indulgence as well as Neoplatonic philosophy clearly hints at the need for a new strategy. On that point, Friedrich Schlegel observes that the "decisive moment" in the history of Roman *moeurs* occurred when "the sense for beautiful appearances and moral play had become wholly lost, and the human race sank down to naked reality." Finite reality, we recall, had implied an effort to shape perception. Naked reality, by contrast, apparently involved no such effort. Unlike finite reality, it lacked any belief in the plenitude of the external word. What we have, then, is purely passive perception, without even the desire to immerse oneself in what is perceived. Which is to say: the absolute nadir, the lowest possible condition in the history of a culture. To Friedrich Schlegel, however, such a decline was in fact necessary. Specifically, he asserts that artistic/aesthetic development "can only follow upon a fully dissolved natural formation," and "must begin where the other has left off." The new tendency, as Schlegel saw it, was toward the interesting (*das Interessante*). But that meant a radical departure from the goal of classical poetry, and hence from any sort of antique ideal.

At a later point in his essay, Friedrich Schlegel tries to specify more fully what *das Interessante* consists of: "*Interesting*, namely, is any original individual that contains a greater amount of intellectual content or aesthetic energy. I deliberately said: a *greater*. A greater namely than what the receiving individual already possesses: for the interesting demands an individual receptivity, indeed not infrequently a momentary mood of the same. Since all quantities can be increased to infinity, it becomes clear why complete satisfaction can never be attained in this way; why there is no *highest form of the interesting* [kein *höchstes Interessantes*]. Under the most varied forms and directions, with all degrees of power, what expresses itself throughout in the entire mass of modern poetry is the *need for complete satisfaction,* and an equal striving for an *absolute maximum of art*" (*KA* I, pp. 252–53).

Here we note, first of all, the emphasis on the "greater amount of intellectual content or aesthetic energy" possessed by the "interesting" individual. Schlegel then goes on to qualify: greater, as compared to what the "receiving individual" already possesses. If even a purely passive receptivity already calls for a minimal amount of energy, any higher level of interest in what is perceived must naturally require a greater amount of energy. And specifically, as Schlegel says, "intellectual content or aesthetic energy." Because these have to be superadded to what would otherwise amount to little more than mere sensory data. Thus the interest of the material comes, ultimately, from individual subjectivity.

Since interest appears to depend specifically on receptivity, moreover, it seems useful to look at that more closely as well. And, as Schlegel points out: "indeed not infrequently a momentary mood of the same." Clearly the notion of "mood" (*Stimmung*) is of crucial importance. It emphasizes how subjective receptivity is. To remove any doubt on that score, Schlegel even qualifies it further as "momentary." So our ability to find what is of interest in any given material depends less on any intrinsic property of that material than it does on the energy level of our own subjectivity at the moment we receive a particular impression. In that respect, the kind of interest Friedrich Schlegel has in mind comes extremely close to the purely arbitrary. After all, we know that a sudden flood of emotion, a heightened mood, can be caused by a variety of internal or external circumstances. Yet Schlegel apparently even wants to insist on that aspect of interest.

The fact that interest comes wholly from the energy associated with mood or emotion explains why we can't specify a highest form of the interesting, a *höchstes Interesssantes*. By way of explanation, Friedrich Schlegel simply says: "since all quantities [Grössen] can be increased to infinity, it becomes clear why complete satisfaction can never be attained in this way; why there is no *highest form of the interesting*." Because the amount of interest we feel in a given object depends wholly on our own subjectivity, in other words, we can always endow some other object with even more emotion. While the objects themselves may be finite in number and magnitude, our capacity for emotion about them isn't. And because it isn't, we can never say no object could possibly be of more interest than the one we're now focused on. Our inability to say that means we can never find an object whose capacity to attract interest will absorb all the interest we could ever hope to feel. Our capacity for interest, then, will always be greater than any object to which we could apply it.

The impossibility of a highest object of interest leads the quest for one to take on a different form. As Friedrich Schlegel puts it: "What theory promised, what one sought in Nature, what one hoped to find in each individual idol; what is it other than a *highest form of the aesthetic* [ein *ästhetisches Höchstes*]? The more often the innately human longing for complete satisfaction was deceived by the particular and the changeable (toward whose representation art has thus far been exclusively directed), the more intense and restless it became. Only the universally valid, the abiding, the necessary—the *objective*—can fill this immense gap; only the beautiful can still this ardent yearning. The *beautiful* . . . is the universally valid object of a disinterested pleasure, which is equally independent of the pressure of needs and laws, free and yet necessary, wholly purposeless and yet unconditionally purposive. The excess of the individual leads therefore of itself to the objective, the interesting is the preparation for the beautiful, and the final aim of modern poetry can be nothing other than the *highest form of the beautiful* [das *höchste Schöne*], a maximum of objective aesthetic perfection" (*KA* I, p. 253).

The crucial question here is precisely how we get from the quest for an object of interest to the quest for objectivity. If any given object of interest can invariably be supplanted by an object of greater interest, then obviously our quest for the interesting can never really be satisfied. The source of the problem, as Schlegel sees it, lies in the plenitude or excess (*Übermass*, lit. overflowing) of the individual. Which is to say: the superabundance of our subjective energy, which constantly discovers new objects of interest. But because none of these can permanently satisfy, we put all the more energy into our quest. Hence its "intense and restless" quality, its hunger that can't be appeased. The only solution is to opt out of the game entirely. To do that, however, we need the objective, or objectivity: "the universally valid object of a disinterested pleasure." By its disinterested aspect, such a viewpoint bypasses the whole issue of interest completely. At the same time, as universally valid, it avoids the extremes of individual subjectivity. In that way it becomes "free and yet necessary": free because it doesn't simply respond to a psychological demand, necessary because of its universality.

For Friedrich Schlegel, only one form of art can possibly satisfy all of these criteria. What he has in mind is Greek art, particularly at its highest phase of development.[13] After a discussion of the autonomy of beauty or art in Greek culture, he goes on to talk about what attracts him to it specifically: "One such Greek trait is the *completeness* of its view of the whole of human nature, which, occurring in the happiest *harmony* [Ebenmass], in the most perfect *balance* [Gleichgewicht], is far removed from the one-sided limitation of an errant disposition, and from the perversity of artificial misdevelopment.—The *sphere* of its poetic production is as unlimited as the sphere of the whole of human nature itself. The most extreme ends of the most divergent tendencies, whose original seeds already lay concealed in universal human nature, associate here in a friendly way, as in unconstrained childlike play. Its cheerful and pure representation unites sweeping power with profound tranquility, the sharpest definition with the softest delicacy of outline" (*KA* I, p. 279).

By his focus on the harmony or balance of Greek art, Friedrich Schlegel clearly wants to make it into an ideal that he can set against *das Interessante*, with its extreme reliance on receptivity. Receptivity to a particular object of interest tends to engage a specific mental faculty. Thus the aesthetic of interest translates into an appeal to a specific faculty, to the exclusion of all the rest.

Moreover, the nature of the appeal can only lead to an increased development of that faculty: since no object of interest can really satisfy it, the intensity of its quest, and hence its predominance over the other faculties, only becomes greater. As a result, subjectivity gets to be one-sided. To Friedrich Schlegel, this amounts to a limitation. Because he sees the quest for an object of highest interest as a dead end, the only viable goal from his perspective has to be the development of subjectivity itself. But for that the overdevelopment of a particular faculty merely displays the "perversity of artificial misdevelopment." Hence the need for a different kind of aesthetic ideal.

In contrast to *das Interessante*, what Greek art offers isn't an object of interest but rather the power that comes from self-knowledge. Thus, after his portrayal of the balance or harmony of Greek art, Friedrich Schlegel observes: "The *sphere* of its poetic production is as unlimited as the sphere of the whole of human nature itself." But if the sphere of Greek art is indeed as unlimited as that of human nature, its effort to represent human nature should presumably yield a full picture of what we are. The completeness of Greek art suggests in turn that we don't go to it merely to gratify interest. Instead, we look to it for self-knowledge, or a greater awareness of our own potential. In that way, it plays a role in our journey toward self-consciousness, and hence in the development of our subjectivity.[14]

Greek art doesn't just reproduce human nature, however. For Friedrich Schlegel, it exerts a transformative influence as well. Specifically, he affirms that "the most extreme ends of the most divergent tendencies, whose original seeds already lie concealed in universal human nature, associate here in a friendly way, as in unconstrained childlike play." To expose divergent tendencies of human nature is, of course, useful for self-knowledge. But the particular kind of representation Schlegel has in mind also permits other forms of transaction to take place. Thus besides exposure, the divergent tendencies "associate" as well (gesellen sich zueinander). In other words, Schlegel posits an interaction of some sort, albeit one that appears only rarely if at all in our everyday life because of social pressures or constraints. The text likens that interaction to "unconstrained childlike play." But play, from a Romantic standpoint, is creative. So the interaction between different tendencies facilitated by representation leads to the expression of what might otherwise remain repressed. At the same time, the "friendly" manner of association shows how representation works to effect a harmonious reciprocity between potentially opposed forces.

Although the complete view of human nature that Friedrich Schlegel attributes to Greek art applies most of all to its highest phase, it appears in other periods as well. Perhaps one of the most noteworthy, in fact, is the final phase of its maturity, just before the onset of its decline—a poignant moment in many respects. In his "Studium" essay, Schlegel characterizes it briefly: "Even in the age where its entire mass split in several clearly determined directions—like so many branches of a common trunk—and its sphere thereby became as restricted as its power was raised: even in the lyrical genre, whose proper object is *beautiful peculiarity* [*schöne Eigentümlichkeit*], it nevertheless preserves its constant tendency toward the objective through the mode and the spirit of its representation, which, to the extent permitted by the specific limits of its peculiar direction and its subject matter, approximates the purely human, elevates the particular itself to the universal, and, properly speaking, represents within the peculiar only what is universally valid [das Allgemeingültige]" (*KA* I, p. 283).

The aesthetic of beautiful peculiarity (*schöne Eigentümlichkeit*) that Schlegel adumbrates here is significant because it displays the Greek tendency toward objectivity in a somewhat unusual manner. In his description, Schlegel points to several means by which a lyrical treatment of beautiful peculiarity can still achieve objectivity: (1) it approximates the purely human, (2) it elevates the particular to the level of the universal, (3) it represents within the peculiar only what is universally valid.

To see how peculiarity can approximate the purely human, we need to keep in mind that Greek art preserves its tendency toward objectivity by "the mode and the spirit of its representation." In other words, we shouldn't equate the purely human solely with what gets represented. For Friedrich Schlegel, the representation itself matters equally. To some extent, the purely human element of a representation is discernible in the emotion that colors it. Sympathy, for instance, is purely human. It expresses an attitude toward what is represented that is easily understandable by anyone. Similarly, appreciation. What we recognize as purely human in these instances, then, is the attitude or viewpoint expressed. And since the same attitude gets expressed elsewhere, we can readily dissociate it from the peculiarity it addresses here.

By means of its intensity, the lyrical treatment of beautiful peculiarity in late Greek art also manages to elevate the particular to the level of the universal. Because Greek poetry had turned into a highly specialized concern, its sphere, Schlegel says, "became as restricted as its power was raised." So what the lyric gave up in scope, it gained in intensity. Thus where the ordinary tends to go unnoticed or, if noticed, to have little impact, an unexpected emphasis could give it a special poignancy. An example comes to mind: Anacreon, who reproaches a young boy with the remark that "You have cut off the perfect flower of your soft hair," or who, supposedly infatuated with Sappho, laments that she "finds fault with my hair because it is white, and gapes after another—girl."[15] By the intensity of his lament, the poet forces others to feel his passion, and thereby confers on it a universal quality.

Finally, Friedrich Schlegel shows how the very way late Greek lyric chose to be selective helped to give it a universal appeal. Specifically, the text tells us that in the peculiar the lyric actually represents "only what is universally valid." If we take Anacreon once again as our example, the line "You have cut off the perfect flower of your soft hair" assimilates a trivial act to one whose sense of loss can be more universally felt. Or consider Anacreon's lament that the girl or woman in whom he's interested "finds fault with my hair because it is white, and gapes after another—girl." Here the surprise at being rejected for a lesbian spills over into a scene of wider scope, that of all older lovers who can no longer attract younger partners. Even this, moreover, extends still further to include everyone unable to gain the affection of those they love. In all these instances, Greek lyric focuses on the universal element within the peculiarity it portrays. Thus the tendency of Greek art to seek universality even in peculiarity points once more to its essential characteristic: a desire for objectivity.

For Friedrich Schlegel, the quest for objectivity in Greek art reaches, at a given moment, its highest point: "Once freedom has the preponderance over Nature, then free formation, left to itself, must continue in the selected direction, and climb ever higher, until its course is hindered by an external power, or until the relationship between freedom and Nature changes anew through purely internal development. When the *entire* composite human drive is not only the moving but also the *guiding principle of formation*, when formation is *natural* and not artificial, when the original disposition is the happiest and external support is complete: then will all the elements of the striving power of self-forming humanity develop, grow, and perfect themselves *equably*, until progress has reached the moment where the fullness cannot be increased without dividing and destroying the *harmony of the whole*. If the highest level in the formation of the most perfect genre of the most excellent art happily coincides with the most favorable moment within the current of public taste; if a great artist earns the favor of fate, and knows how to fill in worthily the indeterminate outlines necessity has sketched; then will the utmost goal of beautiful art be achieved, which becomes attainable through the freest development of the happiest disposition. This *final limit of the natural formation* of art and taste, this *highest summit of free beauty* Greek poetry actually achieved. *Perfection* is the state of formation, when the inner striving power has fully developed itself, when the aim has been wholly attained, and when in the equable completeness of the whole no expectation remains unsatisfied. This state is called a *golden age* when it comes to an entire multitude of artwork simultaneously. The pleasure which the works of the golden age of Greek art afford is indeed capable of a supplement, yet is itself without any trouble or need—it is *complete* and *self-sufficient.* I know of no more suitable name for this height than the *highest form of the beautiful* [das *höchste Schöne*]. Not, perhaps, a beauty beyond which nothing more beautiful would be conceivable; but the perfect example of the unattainable idea, which here, as it were, becomes wholly visible: *the archetype of art and of taste*" (*KA* I, pp. 286–88).

What emerges immediately from this description of the highest phase of Greek art is the crucial role played by subjectivity. Elsewhere in the essay it comes out quite clearly, in a passage where Friedrich Schlegel discusses the tension between freedom and Nature more fully: "With this decisive step, by which freedom obtained a preponderance over Nature, man entered into a wholly new order of things; a new level of development began. He now determines, directs, and arranges his powers himself, forms his disposition according to the inner laws of his temperament [Gemüt]. The beauty of art is now no more the gift of a benevolent Nature, but rather his own work, the property of his soul [Gemüt]. The intellectual obtains a preponderance over the sensuous, he independently determines the direction of his taste, and arranges representation. Man not merely appropriates the given, but spontaneously brings forth the beautiful" (*KA* I, p. 285). Although Schlegel would strongly oppose any notion of Greek art as subjective in the same way as modern art, he distinctly wants to emphasize its reliance on subjectivity. His position becomes especially evident when he asserts that the Greek artist "now determines, directs, and arranges his powers himself, forms his disposition according to the inner laws of his temperament." To speak of temperament (*Gemüt*) is, obviously, to speak of subjectivity. Here we have "inner" laws, rather than those of external Nature. Thus the "preponderance" of freedom over Nature would seem to imply the absence of any external deterministic forces. But not only that. Instead, Schlegel goes on to say that for the Greek artist "the beauty of art is now no more the gift of a benevolent Nature, but rather his own work, the property of his soul [Gemüt]." And, subsequently: "Man not merely appropriates the given, but spontaneously brings forth the beautiful." If "the gift" or "the given" (*das Gegebne*) points to what we experience passively, the assertion that Greek art "spontaneously brings forth the beautiful" must mean that it doesn't merely reproduce what it perceives, but that, at the most basic level, what comes out of it amounts to a genuine creative act, a free creation from its own subjectivity.

At the same time, it seems equally apparent that any creation produced by subjectivity must depend on a delicate balance between its different elements or faculties. Under the ideal conditions envisioned by Friedrich Schlegel, "all the elements of the striving power, of self-forming humanity" would "develop, grow, and perfect themselves *equably*." Yet even if they were able to do this, the development of humanity could hardly be expected to go on forever. Instead, as Schlegel sees it, the self-development of humanity would eventually come to a point "where the fullness cannot be increased without dividing and destroying the *harmony of the whole*." Nevertheless, the continued growth of the different subjective elements beyond that point seems more or less unavoidable. After all, by the fact that they continue to grow and evolve, these elements merely adhere to a law of life, a natural principle.[16] And since their evolution is wholly natural, its elements would be unlikely to evolve further at exactly the same pace. Yet if balance or harmony marks the crucial condition of development, no further development is really possible once that balance has been achieved. It follows, then, that the optimal moment of development, if attainable at all, can come only once.

This once-only quality of the highest moment in Greek art is reinforced by what Friedrich Schlegel has to say about the relation between art and public taste. Specifically, he insists on the necessity that "the highest level in the formation of the most perfect genre of the most excellent art happily coincides with the most favorable moment in the current of public taste." Earlier in the same work, he had described how Greek art and taste coincide in more detail: "Greek beauty was the common property of public taste, *the spirit of the entire mass*. Even those poems that betray little artistic wisdom and meager power of invention are conceived, outlined, and executed in the same spirit as those whose traits we in Homer and other poets of the first rank only read more distinctly and clearly. Like the best [poetry], they distinguish themselves by these same peculiarities from all non-Greek poems" (*KA* I, p. 282). But if the creation of those particular forms of the beautiful that typify the highest phase of Greek art necessitates a sympathetic public taste, the possibility of another artistic golden age looks even less likely. At the same time, what Schlegel says about the relation of art to public taste can also serve to redefine the very concept of "golden age" itself. Instead of a notion that focuses purely on artistic expression, what he seems to have in mind when he talks about the congruence of art and public taste is, in effect, the consciousness or sensibility of an entire period.

Yet even if we could somehow manage to re-create historically all the conditions both internal and external that typify the golden age of Greek art, it would still be different from any period of equal achievement. Temporally, after all, the Greek zenith would still be first. For any later period, then, there would always be the awareness that, at best, it could only hope to equal what had already been achieved. No doubt its art would be stylistically quite different. But the crucial condition of art at its finest is, as we've seen, the balance between its different elements. And the balance of Greek art in its maturity was perfect. For that reason, it presents an image of perfection for any future era that yearns to achieve the same. Perhaps this was what Friedrich Schlegel meant to convey when he described it as "the archetype [Urbild] of art and of taste." As *Urbild*, however, it isn't just the archetype but, in another sense of that same word, an ideal. It figures as the image that haunts the mind whenever it tries to imagine what a golden age of art might look like. Moreover, it symbolizes the ideal precisely because it is the archetype. And because it forms both archetype and ideal, it epitomizes the very concept of a golden age of art. By its transformation into a concept, finally, it becomes the supreme object of nostalgia: the purely inward, purely subjective expression of nostalgia itself.

What the concept of a golden age gave Friedrich Schlegel, ultimately, was a way to assimilate history to theory.[17] His portrayal of the golden age of Greek art had placed it beyond any possibility of repetition. As he saw it, the whole point of classical Greece was its unrecoverability. Because it came about from a perfect convergence of internal and external circumstances, it couldn't be reproduced. That was what defined its uniqueness as a historical moment. But if the whole point of golden age Greece was its unrecoverability, what we have here, in effect, is a new level of inwardness in the nostalgia for Greek subjectivity. Hadrian had yearned for an antique subjectivity that he believed Antinoüs embodied. Wolf tried to recover a subjectivity (Aristarchus) already at one remove from the Homeric or classical one. Yet even he believed he could still recover that subjectivity by means of historical scholarship. For Friedrich Schlegel, however, nostalgia has become completely inward: if the subjectivity of classical Greece has simply disappeared, then the fate of historical scholarship is precisely to yearn for what it knows it can't recover. From that standpoint, the quest for Greek subjectivity is one that ultimately forces classical scholarship to reflect on its own activity.

In his treatment of Greek subjectivity in the "Studium" essay, what Friedrich Schlegel tried to address was the problem of how to recover a past era.[18] Like Wolf, he immediately saw that the essential aspect of any earlier era was its subjectivity. Unlike Wolf, however, he also saw how difficult it would be to try to recover that subjectivity. Simply put, we can't know exactly how someone from a past era might have felt because we haven't experienced the same historical conditions or circumstances. So forget about any attempt to inhabit a subjectivity from an earlier period. For Schlegel, it isn't necessary to know exactly what classical Greek subjectivity consists of. Instead, the crucial issue is how we perceive that subjectivity. If our goal is to recover classical Greek subjectivity, what we're after, presumably, is the "feel" of that subjectivity. But the only way to get the "feel" of a subjectivity is to experience it subjectively.

Precisely because he couldn't hope for unmediated access to an earlier historical moment, Friedrich Schlegel found himself compelled to turn to theory. His study of Greek poetry had shown him how difficult it was to recover classical Greek subjectivity: all we get, at best, is Greek subjectivity mediated by our own. For nostalgia, however, only the actual subjectivity of a past era could possibly satisfy. So if we can't hope to recover Greek subjectivity itself, the only other option for nostalgia would be to elevate that subjectivity to the level of an ideal. As an ideal, a subjectivity that can't be recovered historically could still be pursued sentimentally by nostalgia. Hence the kind of treatment Schlegel gives to Greek subjectivity in the "Studium" essay, where the notion of a perfect equality between all internal elements or forces, as well as of a perfect harmony between internal and external, point to the definition of an ideal rather than of the subjectivity of a given historical moment. And clearly neither the sense of a perfection in its development nor of its unattainability by any future era could be said to pertain to Greek subjectivity intrinsically. Put in that way, Greek subjectivity in Schlegel is, in effect, purely a creation of theory. Its source, in other words, has less to do with his knowledge of Greek subjectivity than it does with his reflection on the tendency of classical scholarship. Given the inescapable fact of our own subjectivity, Schlegel seems to imply, what we choose to say about Greek subjectivity comes back, in the end, to what we believe classical scholarship to be capable of, by way of historical recovery. And so we move, ineluctably, from history to theory.

For Friedrich Schlegel, what makes the move from history to theory possible in the "Studium" essay is reflexivity. Reflexivity is why the quest for Greek subjectivity doesn't end once we've found it can't be recovered. By means of reflexivity, we become aware of why Greek subjectivity is unknowable: how its unknowability is due to the discrepancy between its consciousness and ours. And if we don't stop there, it must be because of reflexivity: a tacit belief that the source of that discrepancy, and hence of the unknowability of Greek subjectivity, can be traced to the very outlook of classical scholarship itself. In effect, then, reflexivity suggests that the solution to any problem can be found in the way we frame it. Or, at the deepest level, you might say reflexivity avers that the solution to any problem can be found in the very way we are what we are. So when faced with the unknowability of Greek subjectivity, Friedrich Schlegel turned to the classical scholarship that had discovered it. What he didn't do, however, was to make the process by which he came to trace the unknowability of Greek subjectivity to classical scholarship a part of his response. To do that would be to take the tendency toward inwardness exemplified by reflexivity to its ultimate extreme. But for that we would need to turn to a different form of Romantic theory, one we find in Hegel.

CHAPTER THREE

The Movement of Return

When dawn came to the outskirts of Jena on October 14, 1806, it brought only a slight improvement in visibility. The previous night had begun clear and cold, tinged by frost. But as the hours passed, a dense fog had gradually settled over the entire area. By 6 a.m., daylight was barely discernible. Nevertheless, some 46,000 French troops lay massed in position on the heights of the Landgrafenberg (a steep ridge just beyond the town) and in the adjacent valleys. All through the night, they had worked feverishly to drag their artillery up the heavily wooded slope. Now, as dawn came to Jena, they prepared to attack the Prussian forces hidden in the mist.

Finally, at about 6 a.m., the attack got underway, led by two divisions under Marshal Lannes. Almost immediately, the advance columns ran into several battalions under the Prussian commander Tauenzien. Both sides now unleashed their artillery at almost point-blank range into the mist. Although neither could actually see the other, the flashes produced by gunfire served to indicate positions. As a result, casualties were heavy. Because of the fog and enemy artillery, the French pushed forward only slowly. So it wasn't until 7:30 a.m. that Suchet's lead brigade on the right could make out the ghostly forms of trees, which marked a wood near the village of Closwitz. Once oriented, however, Suchet's forces quickly took Closwitz despite heavy losses, as the light infantry swept away all opposition. On the French left, meanwhile, Gazan ran into more serious trouble. His first attack was repulsed, and only heavy artillery fire enabled his troops to advance and eventually take the village of Cospeda. At this point, Tauenzien ordered his men to fall back on the more distant village of Vierzehnheiligen, where his Saxon reserves were stationed. From here, having rallied the 5,000 who had fled from the French advance, he counter-attacked. Stunned by his assault, the French reeled back in confusion. But Tauenzien was unable to exploit his opportunity, because another French division (under Marshal Augereau) had pushed up the Mühlbach/Mühltal valley and now posed a threat to his southern flank. So Tauenzien withdrew once more, to rejoin the main Prussian force under Prince Hohenlohe. As a result, Lannes was able to reoccupy the ground necessary for the deployment of the *Grande Armée*, a movement critical to Napoleon's battle plan.

Meanwhile, on the French right, Marshal Soult found his forces pitted against 5,000 men under Holtzendorff. Shortly after 10 a.m., having run into enemy forces in the fog, Prussian skirmishers opened fire on one of Soult's divisions (under St. Hilaire). Alerted by the sound of musketry, the rest of the Prussian force swung into echelon formation for a major assault. Hidden behind a reverse slope near Rodigen, however, St. Hilaire's division was able to maneuver undetected around to the left of Holtzendorff, who suddenly had to face an unexpected onset against his left flank as French troops poured out from their concealed position. Under pressure, the Prussians fell back behind a stream near the village of Nerkwitz. At first, Prussian cavalry managed to cover their retreat, until Soult's own cavalry burst upon it in the fog and overwhelmed it. Pursued by Soult's hussars and chasseurs, the Prussian cavalry was driven upon the unprepared Prussian infantry. Carnage then ensued as one of the columns was massacred. Holtzendorff now threw all his energy into a stand behind Nerkwitz. Once more, however, French forces worked around to his left and launched a second cavalry attack. Faced with Soult's thundering horsemen once more, the Prussian line collapsed and disintegrated. Remnants fled toward the distant village of Apolda. At this moment, only events elsewhere on the field kept Soult from the chance for a complete massacre.

In fact, the French center had been compromised by a rash attack under the fiery Marshal Ney, whose impatience to get into action had finally overcome all sense of restraint. At first, the Prussian line crumpled before his unexpected assault. But once over their initial surprise, the Prussians re-formed and attacked him with cavalry. Their attack compelled Ney to arrange his troops in square formation, which left them in an awkward, exposed position. Seeing the danger, Napoleon immediately rushed all available cavalry to the spot. In addition, he ordered Augereau and Lannes to support Ney.

But as Lannes's troops pressed forward through Vierzehnheiligen, they collided with a substantial Prussian force under Gräuwert, drawn up in oblique formation. In response to the well-known command, "Advance in echelon from the left," Gräuwert's troops stepped smartly into position. Brought to a halt within short range of the French line, the Prussian formation now opened fire in measured volleys. After heavy losses on both sides, the French finally fell back on Vierzehnheiligen. Some houses in the village were already aflame, thanks to a

Prussian howitzer battery. Faced with the opportunity offered by the French retreat, however, Prince Hohenlohe now made a fatal mistake. Without the "Freisehaaren" normally used to storm a village, he ordered Gräuwert to draw up his troops in formation just outside Vierzehnheiligen, there to await reinforcements from Weimar. Exposed in this way for two hours to withering enemy fire from behind stone walls and garden fences, Gräuwert's line was brutally decimated. By the end, it presented a poignant spectacle: while all around their comrades lay dead or dying, isolated remnants of companies continued to load and fire mechanically.

It was now time, Lannes thought, to resolve the impasse. Against Hohenlohe's main force he launched frontal and left flank attacks simultaneously. In response, Hohenlohe immediately drew back his left into a defensive posture. Nonetheless, by sheer weight of numbers, the French gradually began to push the Prussians back, until a counter-attack by fresh Saxon squadrons reversed the tide. Once more, Lannes's troops fell back on Vierzehnheiligen, in some confusion. For the second time, Hohenlohe looked at a critical opportunity. But by now Ney's infantry and part of Lannes's force had pushed through Isserstadt wood onto the main road to Weimar, a move that cut off three Saxon brigades from the Prussian center. More ominously, as he looked toward Jena, Hohenlohe could discern the dark blue masses of new French formations on the move. Under these circumstances, he thought it best to reinforce rather than advance. Thus by 1 p.m. every body of Prussian troops had been committed.

With his own massive reserve of 42,000 in readiness, Napoleon could feel the moment had come. His plan was to attack the entire Prussian line: St. Hilaire against the remnants of Holtzendorff's troops on the right, Augereau against the Saxons on the left. Ney and Lannes would assault the Prussian center, supported by Murat's cavalry. Augereau was already engaged by 11:30 a.m., but it took St. Hilaire until 1 p.m. to get his troops into position. At that moment, Napoleon ordered his center to advance.

As formation after formation of the *Grande Armée* swept forward, the pressure on the Prussian line became unbearable. Officers screamed at and threatened their men, but slowly, inexorably, the regiments began to yield under fire. As waves of French infantry swirled around segments of Prussian cavalry and infantry that had come forward to meet their assault, they penetrated into gaps in the Prussian line. Hohenlohe's entire formation now began to disintegrate. Reluctantly, the Prussian command gave the signal for retreat. At first it was orderly, despite the deafening artillery barrage ordered by Lannes to harass the Prussian withdrawal. But as Murat's huge cavalry force thundered forward, the

Prussian formations finally collapsed. Immediately behind Murat with the combined light cavalry of Augereau, Lannes, and Ney, the heavy cavalry plus two dragoon regiments flew over the ground in pursuit. Panic now spread rapidly among what was left of the Prussian forces. Abandoning guns and equipment, they fled in different directions. Many took the road to Weimar.

As pursuers and pursued moved in one confused torrent toward Weimar, however, they abruptly encountered a fresh contingent of 15,000 Prussian troops under Rüchel. These were the reinforcements Hohenlohe had so desperately summoned at 9 a.m. as he realized the magnitude of the French forces he had engaged. While the broken remnants of Hohenlohe's command poured down the slope beyond Gröss-Romstedt into the Capellendorf valley, Rüchel deployed his men in attack formation, then turned over his command to Hohenlohe. Aided by some Saxon cavalry, they beat off Soult's light cavalry, which had been in hot pursuit. Closely packed together, as if on parade-ground drill, Rüchel's corps now marched in measured time up the hill from Capellendorf toward Gröss-Romstedt. As it neared the crest, artillery rushed up by Napoleon from various French corps began to tear wide gaps in the Prussian ranks. Nevertheless, Rüchel's troops stood firm, and a French dragoon regiment that had charged downhill was driven off by Saxon cavalry. Similarly, French skirmishers were also pushed back. So it was only when Rüchel's men reached the crest of the hill that they discovered a solid line of French infantry, stretching as far as the eye could see. For fifteen minutes the two sides engaged in a fierce firefight, marked by volley after volley of lethal flame. Then the French infantry charged, with irresistible force. At that moment the Prussian line wavered and finally broke. Once more a confused mass flowed down the hill, toward Capellendorf. And once more Murat's cavalry began its assault, breaking up what remained of Rüchel's corps. It was now 3 p.m. By 4 p.m., Murat had organized the pursuit of all detachments still left, and at around 5 p.m. the dashing cavalry chief rode into Weimar, "contemptuously wielding a riding whip instead of a saber."[1]

By common consent, Jena counts as a classic example of Napoleonic strategy. It displays the Emperor's favorite tactic: the so-called advance of envelopment, or what Napoleon himself termed the *manoeuvre sur les derrières*. Napoleon had always preferred a flank attack to a straightforward frontal assault: "It is by turning the enemy, by attacking his flank, that battles are won." From his standpoint, a flank attack brings about a breach in the enemy line that ultimately leads to its collapse. This, then, is the critical moment of a conflict: "the breach once made, the equilibrium is broken and everything else is useless."[2]

It all begins once the cavalry has sighted the enemy. As soon as he was informed of its position, Napoleon would order his nearest corps to engage and pin down the force opposed to it. His object: to establish a fixed point around which to maneuver. The flexibility of his own individual corps made such a move possible. Since each corps had its own complement of infantry, guns, and cavalry, it resembled a miniature army. Its balance allowed it to engage a much larger force for some time: its artillery would hinder any assault by the enemy, while its cavalry could easily force enemy troops into a defensive square formation. Meanwhile the corps's infantry protected the other two contingents from being isolated or overwhelmed by superior forces. At the same time, a single, apparently isolated corps would also lure an enemy to attack by the prospect of an easy victory.

Once underway, the initial engagement would quickly escalate into a larger conflict. As soon as a single corps had managed to get involved, others would be rushed up by forced marches to its support. At the outset, these other troops would seem too far away to intervene decisively. Initially, only one corps might come to the aid of the first. As it moved into position, it would cause the enemy to extend its own line to avoid being outflanked. Subsequently, the arrival of other French corps would compel the enemy to extend its line farther. At this point, the enemy commander would probably feel some pressure to resolve the situation quickly, before any further French reinforcements could arrive. And that would mean the use of his own reserves to force a decision.

As the conflict continued to escalate at his front, Napoleon would meanwhile have dispatched another force to attack the enemy flank or rear. Hidden by cavalry and perhaps natural obstacles as well (at Jena, the reverse slope near Rodigen that concealed St. Hilaire's division from Holtzendorff), its movement would be difficult to detect. Here speed was essential: the force must get into position before the enemy could alter its own disposition. Hence the peculiar composition of the corps involved, with a large complement of cavalry. Besides speed, timing was crucial as well: the corps must intervene at just the right moment for decisive effect. For Napoleon, that moment would come when the enemy had committed most or all of its reserve to the conflict at its front.

At the crucial moment, then, the *attaque débordante* would suddenly begin. The enemy commander would immediately feel the threat it posed, since any attack on an unprotected flank or rear could quickly sever his line of communication. He would now have only two options: (1) a general retreat, or (2) withdrawal of troops from his front line to create a new line at a right angle to the original one, so as to protect against the unexpected flank assault. But retreat wouldn't be easy. As his hitherto-concealed troops burst on the enemy flank, Napoleon would also order a general frontal attack against the entire enemy army. Under these circumstances, withdrawal would expose the enemy force to heavy artillery fire, as well as confusion and even possible collapse in the event of a French assault. To create a new line at a right angle to his original one, however, would compel a commander to thin his formation at some point, since all reserve troops would already have been committed.

While the enemy thinned its front line to protect the flank under attack, Napoleon would prepare to assault the weakened "hinge" of its new formation. Earlier, in fact, he would already have secretly massed a reserve. It consisted of picked troops from all services, usually in square formation: artillery in front, infantry on either side, cavalry in the rear. Described by Napoleon as the *masse de décision* or *masse de rupture*, its function was to force a breakthrough at the weakened "hinge" and so split the enemy line.

When the right moment had arrived, the assembled artillery of the Guard Reserve would gallop forward to within 500 yards of the enemy and unleash a devastating barrage of case or cannister shot. Simultaneously, the infantry would press forward at the *pas de charge*. Meanwhile the cavalry would execute a series of assaults against the enemy infantry, so as to force it into square formation and thereby reduce the amount of musketry fire it could oppose to the French advance. As the infantry moved forward, the artillery would likewise push its guns closer and closer to the enemy. Together, the combined effect of all these measures on the enemy line would typically result in a wide gap. Napoleon would now throw unit after unit of infantry into the gap, in an effort to widen it as much as possible. At the same time, his heavy cavalry would thunder forward through the gap to break what was left of the enemy line, until the entire formation collapsed. With its collapse, victory per se had been achieved. What remained was merely to exploit that victory by relentless cavalry pursuit until all remnants of enemy resistance had been annihilated.

At the level of theory, the new autonomy of tactics becomes apparent in its ability to create its own narrative. From his *Correspondence*, we get this remark by Napoleon himself: "A battle is a theatrical piece, with a beginning, a middle and an end." In tactical terms, then, Jena might be described as a story. It begins with an initial conflict on a relatively small scale that expands quickly as more forces become engaged and thereby extend a linear front. Its middle phase involves the surprise attack by St. Hilaire on the Prussian rear. Its end comes about when the massed French reserve splits the Prussian line in half at its most vulnerable point and so forces its collapse. The success of this story, at Jena and elsewhere, would depend on the extent to which Napoleon could draw the enemy into it. From a tactical standpoint, however, what stands out is the way he would invariably try, on each occasion, to re-create the same story, regardless of particular circumstances. It points to a belief in the story itself as somehow sufficient to ensure victory. And that would imply that tactics has managed to raise itself above the level of an analysis of the particular formations and circumstances of a given battlefield: as if it were possible to specify on a higher level of generality the conditions necessary to produce victory. And that, in turn, would suggest the kind of autonomy tactics had now achieved.[3]

But if tactics had in fact arrived at a new kind of autonomy with Napoleon, the extent of that autonomy would still ultimately depend on the internal logic of its narrative. Essentially, the story Napoleon wants to tell is one of extension and consequent return. More specifically, an initially extended enemy line becomes, at a crucial point, overextended. And the deployment of his own massed reserve against its weakest spot would cause its rupture, or what might be described as its movement of return. The logic of this sequence comes from the tactical necessity of what happens at each phase of the story. Once the conflict begins, the enemy commander can't help but extend his own line as Napoleon himself introduces more corps into the fray. Likewise, once attacked on its flank or rear, the enemy simply has to pull troops from elsewhere in its own line so as to form a new front to meet the attack. And, finally, once its line has been thinned out to meet the attack on its flank or rear, the success of an assault by a massed reserve against its weakened line is bound to seem inevitable. Significantly, in the years after Jena Napoleon no longer even bothered to give his *manoeuvre sur les derrières* the element of surprise. We might attribute this to a decline in the quality of his troops. But it also reflects a belief that the intrinsic force of the move itself ought to yield the desired result.

At the same time, his belief in the force of a flank or rear attack shows how Napoleon saw tactics as a kind of "physics." Earlier, I mentioned his tendency to speak of his reserve as a *masse de décision* or a *masse de rupture*. The terminological flavor is significant. It suggests that the capacity of an assault force to achieve a rupture in the enemy line has less to do with its cohesion than with its density, or mass. So we move from an emphasis on the strictness or tautness of line formations to a concern with mass, weight, massive force. But if the pressure a formation can exert is proportional to its density, presumably the amount of pressure exerted by a formation of vast numerical superiority must be more or less irresistible. To sum up, then, we might say that for Napoleon mass $\Rightarrow$ rupture. Likewise, it seems useful to consider his remark about the effect of that rupture: "the breach once made, the equilibrium is broken and everything else is useless." In other words, the cohesion of a line or formation is purely a matter of equilibrium. Obviously, an equilibrium can stand some amount of strain. As Napoleon realized, linear formations can in fact resist a significant amount of pressure from an attack. The trick, then, would be to increase the pressure until that equilibrium can no longer be sustained. And to determine when the crucial point is reached becomes the concern of a tactical "physics."[4]

This description of tactics in terms of a "physics" points to an effort by Napoleon to look at tactical theory from a new perspective. It differed from earlier approaches insofar as it was less rational. In other words, it didn't depend on a close analysis of the potential weaknesses of a specific enemy formation. Instead, its aim was to bring an irresistible force to bear on a given point in that formation. Under these circumstances, it wouldn't matter how the enemy chose to dispose its troops. "Physics" or the weight of numbers plus firepower would overcome any possible artifice of rational disposition. At Jena, Napoleon had also relied on the element of surprise: the maneuver against the Prussian rear executed by St. Hilaire had benefited from the concealment of a reverse slope. To some extent, then, the tactical plan Napoleon employed in that conflict still displayed traces of a more traditional, rational style. It attempted to exploit a perceived weakness in the particular linear formation adopted by the Prussian command. But increasingly, in the years after Jena, his tendency would be to rely more and more exclusively on what might be described as the pure weight or mass of his own forces. It conveys, you might say, a desire to base his objective less on an external arrangement or disposition of troops than on what he perceived as internal to the very nature of the forces he sought to deploy.

What Napoleonic tactics did above all, however, was to sublimate individual moments of the sequence to a higher principle of development. In the initial phase, as we've seen, Napoleon reinforces an isolated corps once it's managed to engage the enemy. Since his reinforcements come up by forced marches, he could easily have deployed a sufficient number to overcome the enemy on this front. But he doesn't. Instead, he introduces his reinforcements only gradually, so that they merely extend the enemy line, rather than overwhelm it. At this stage, then, victory is deferred. In the next phase, he sends a corps on a wide sweep around to the enemy's flank or rear. Carried out with sufficient force, its attack, helped by the element of surprise, could well have been made decisive. The kind of confusion such a move would have produced in the enemy's ranks, the immediate losses, and the force of a determined charge on a weakened formation had proved their ability to resolve a conflict under other circumstances. Yet even here, Napoleon prefers to postpone the climax. It comes about only by means of the subsequent attack by his massed reserve. Thus, at all these earlier moments, a potential for victory is declined in favor of the final phase. In other words, the potential of each moment is subordinated to its role in a larger scheme where the result is achieved by an entire process or development.

For Napoleon, development is all about fulfillment, or fruition. From his standpoint, the sort of movement that marks tactical development is movement toward an end. If the initial phase defers victory by not rushing up distant corps too quickly, it's only so that the final attack by the massed reserve will have an even more decisive effect. The gradual arrival of reinforcements on the initial front locks all the enemy troops on that front in place, so that they can't be moved to support anyone else. Likewise, the attack on the enemy flank or rear acts to overextend a section of the enemy's front line, so that it becomes even more vulnerable to the massed reserve. Because the enemy front line is thinned out in this fashion, because of the weight of the reserve in numbers and artillery, the success of the attack is virtually assured. And, because it can concentrate an irresistible force on the enemy's weakest point, its success will be all the more complete, or total. As a result, it has the capacity to bring the entire process to fulfillment, or fruition. It takes up, you might say, the effects of every earlier phase of the conflict, and advances these to a decisive end.

The day before the battle of Jena, Napoleon was in the city itself. He must have passed through it rather quickly, on his way to the heights beyond, where he spent the hours just before dawn. Nonetheless, he was seen by at least one observer who thought the moment warranted a brief description in a letter to a friend. We don't know much about how or why the observer happened to see the Emperor. No doubt there was some confusion in the city, as invariably happens when a place is occupied by an enemy army. And perhaps the disturbances might have prompted the observer to go out and have a look for himself. Most likely other people were out as well, many probably impelled by a desire to see the Emperor, who by this time had created quite a stir throughout Germany. Nor would the crowd have felt any particular loyalty to Prussia or, on the other hand, hostility either to the Emperor or to France. So we can imagine our observer as part of a crowd that might have gathered somewhere in the city to see the Emperor as he rode by. But if we don't know much about the particular motive that might have induced our observer to try to catch a glimpse of the Emperor, we do at least know his name. He was G.W.F. Hegel, an assistant professor of philosophy at the University of Jena.

His letter to his friend Niethammer, written that same day, is curious in a number of ways. It begins with a very detailed specification of time and place: "*Jena.* Monday, 13 Oct. 1806, on the day Jena was occupied by the French, and the Emperor Napoleon arrived within its walls." Given that Niethammer was a very good friend, and that Hegel had in fact written to him just five days before, it would hardly have been necessary to give him all this information. It's as if Hegel really has some other audience in mind. Or perhaps the description is meant as a kind of memo to himself, to remember precisely the circumstances of what he sees as an event of historical significance. Interestingly, though, the crucial battle that will decide the campaign hasn't yet taken place. Nor does Hegel necessarily know it will happen the next day, or even shortly thereafter. Yet he writes as if it's already happened, and the outcome already known. Hegel then goes on to give a brief narrative of what he himself witnessed: "Yesterday evening toward sundown I saw the shots fired by the French patrols from both Gempenbachtal and Winzerla; the Prussians were driven from the latter in the night, the shots lasted until 12 o'clock, and today between 8 and 9 o'clock the French Tirailleurs [skirmishers] forced their way in [to the city]—and an hour later the regular troops . . . the Emperor—this world-soul—I saw riding through the city to reconnoiter;—it is indeed a wonderful feeling to see such an individual, who here concentrated in a single point, sitting on a horse, reaches out over the world and dominates it" (*Briefe* I: 119–20).

Within this description, one motif seems to me especially suggestive. Hegel says it's wonderful to see someone like Napoleon who "reaches out over the world and dominates it." A movement, then, that passes over things and yet rules or governs (*beherrscht*) them at the same time. In the original, the sense that the movement is somehow over or above what it affects comes out even more explicitly: "über die Welt übergreift." It looks almost like a paradox, really: we wonder how a movement can appear to pass over things and yet affect them in a way that's absolutely central to their existence. Unless it were somehow present within them simultaneously. Hence, perhaps, the term "world-soul." But the essence of this "world-soul" is a movement: it begins at a single point, from which it reaches out or extends itself over the entire world. And, in the process, dominates or governs it.

The fact that Hegel should see in Napoleon an example of a movement that reaches out over the world and yet dominates it might also point to his own concerns at that moment as well. We know that, at the very moment Napoleon was about the engage the Prussian army at Jena, Hegel himself was engaged in an effort to bring his own first book-length work to a close. And that meant the necessity of a preface of some kind.[5] So it would be significant if, in the Preface to the *Phenomenology of Spirit,* we could discern some trace of a similar movement. But for that we need to look at the Preface in detail.

> In my view, which must justify itself through the exhibition of the system itself, everything depends on grasping and expressing the True not as *Substance,* but rather equally as *Subject.* At the same time, it is to be remarked that substantiality encompasses the universal, or the *immediacy of knowing,* just as much as that which is *being* or immediacy *for* knowing.—If to grasp God as the one Substance shocked the age in which this definition was proclaimed, the ground for it lay on the one hand in an instinctive feeling that therein self-consciousness was only submerged [or lost] and not preserved. On the other hand, the opposite view, which holds fast to thought as thought, to *universality* as such, is the same simplicity, is undifferentiated, unmoved substantiality. And if, thirdly, thought does unite itself with the being of Substance, and apprehends immediacy or intuition as thinking, the question is still whether this intellectual intuition does not again fall back into inert simplicity, and represent actuality itself in a non-actual manner. (18. 3–17)

We might wonder, first of all, about the emphasis: why so much should depend on our capacity to grasp and express the True not as Substance but rather equally as Subject. Other questions arise as well. Why the need, for instance, to both "grasp" and "express"—why the first isn't sufficient by itself. And, finally, what the difference between Substance and Subject really is.

We get some sense of why both Substance and Subject are necessary from Hegel's remark that what he says can only be justified by an exposition of the system itself. Substance and Subject, then, are only parts of a larger totality, one whose exposition will justify all its individual elements. Moreover, the rhetoric of the passage ("not as Substance, but rather equally as Subject") hints at Substance as a point of departure and Subject as endpoint. So the Hegelian system would seem to consist of a movement from Substance to Subject.

Even if we admit the necessity for a movement from Substance to Subject, however, it isn't immediately clear why we also need to worry about its expression. To put it another way, we might ask why we should need to express what we've grasped or understood. Yet Hegel distinctly considers the act of expression crucial to comprehension. Elsewhere in the *Phenomenology,* he says the same statement will take on a very different meaning when uttered by an older person as opposed to a child. For the older person, no doubt, the statement will evoke a host of experiences the child presumably doesn't yet have. So expression leads to

self-awareness, which Hegel seems to feel is necessary for the kind of philosophical enterprise he wants to propose.

Finally, we come to the question of what the difference between Substance
and Subject really is. The fact that the text speaks of the "being of Substance"
shows that Substance definitely has being as a property. But Hegel also talks
about thought as united to the being of Substance. So Substance consists not only
of being but thought as well. That in turn might lead one to ask how it could
possibly differ in any fundamental way from Subject. After all, at the most basic
level, everything is either being or thought. Thus if Subject differs from Substance, it can't be in terms of composition. Presumably, then, it must be in terms
of development: Subject presents a more developed version of what Substance
displays in a less developed guise.

In this fashion, at the very outset, we get a glimpse of the movement that will
govern our entire discussion of Hegel. Specifically, it will be a movement from
Substance to Subject. Or, to put it another way, from a condition where being has
the ascendancy to one where that ascendancy has passed over to thought. But if
Substance is somehow supposed to become Subject, the movement by which it
does that will inevitably have to involve its passage over to otherness, to a
condition where it's no longer itself. And that, presumably, will necessitate some
sort of negativity. By means of negativity, as we've seen from Shelley, you deny
what you were before. At the same time, if Subject isn't entirely different from
Substance, the movement from Substance to Subject will also be for Substance a
return to itself. In order to come back to yourself from otherness, however, you
need some sort of reflexivity, or movement of return. That, too, we've seen
before, in Friedrich Schlegel. From Schlegel, moreover, we know that reflexivity
doesn't just involve a movement of return, that it's also one of awareness. But
now the awareness isn't just of our own consciousness. Instead, since we observe
our passage into otherness via negativity and our return to self, you might call it
an awareness of narrative.[6]

Although we've now ascertained that both being and thought can be found in
Substance, the specifics remain to be defined. On this point Hegel observes that
"substantiality encompasses the universal, or the *immediacy of knowing,* just as
much as that which is *being* or immediacy *for* knowing." But what exactly does
the "universal" mean, as a category in Hegel? As he sees it, the "universal" can
apply equally to anything. Consequently, it lacks definition: only a category that
doesn't apply universally can give definition to a particular object. Its lack of
definition makes the universal equivalent for Hegel to immediacy of knowing.

Conceptually, the universal is where we begin, the broad base of generality from which we start in our quest to define specificity. Its immediacy comes precisely from the fact that we begin with it. Associated with knowledge, it takes on a conceptual quality. What the universal encompasses, then, isn't the generality of things but rather that of a conceptual category. It is, you might say, thought at its vaguest, most undeveloped level, without internal content of any kind. But the universal is only one aspect of substantiality. The other is being, or "immediacy *for* knowing." Since Hegel also associates it with immediacy, the sort of being he has in mind here must be the ontological equivalent of the universal: in other words, being in all its undeveloped generality, or the existential property itself. Being of this kind possesses immediacy for knowing since thought in its initial, undeveloped phase can only apprehend what's equally undeveloped. So Substance has both conceptual and ontological aspects, but only in the most indefinite, undeveloped way.

As a comment on this situation, Hegel begins with a remark about why Spinoza's system ultimately proved inadequate. He says it "shocked the age in which this definition was proclaimed" because it failed to notice an omission in its definition of the one Substance: "self-consciousness was only submerged and not preserved." Earlier, Descartes had shown self-consciousness to be connected to thought: to think implied a capacity to recognize thought activity in oneself, and that capacity is a form of self-consciousness. Conversely, absence of self-consciousness would imply a lack of thought capacity, which it seemed unacceptable to attribute to divinity. What the God of Spinoza lacked, then, was the element of thought. As Substance, it seemed devoid of any thought capacity.

On the other hand, Hegel is equally concerned to expose the inadequacy of thought by itself. To him, thought by itself is equivalent to universality. Thus he characterizes it as "the same simplicity," as "undifferentiated, unmoved substantiality." Since he speaks of it as "unmoved," he presumably thinks it has the capacity to move but hasn't exercised it. And the reason it hasn't is that it lacks an object to apprehend. When a capacity to apprehend attempts to apprehend its own apprehensive capacity, it finds only an empty potentiality, one that makes it perfectly "transparent" to itself. Hence its "undifferentiated" quality. In other words, it can't find any way to differentiate itself from itself. And since it has only itself to apprehend, the result is a complete absence of distinction. So thought by itself turns out to exhibit the same sort of inadequacy being had shown before.

Despite the inadequacy of either element by itself, the mere notion of the two as combined doesn't automatically yield what we want. Indeed, as Hegel points out, even if we supposed being and thought to be united, so that thought could apprehend immediacy or intuition as thinking, "the question is still whether this intellectual intuition does not again fall back into inert simplicity." To say that intuition, as immediacy of knowing, is related to thought in some way doesn't necessarily mean they're identical. By its very nature, intuition (as immediacy) is bound to lack development. What it can convey is an immediate perception (*Anschauen*). As immediacy of knowing, perceptions of this kind act as a point of departure for the sort of intellectual development we associate with thought. To claim that intuition *is* thought, however, would be to short-circuit the development this assertion ought to involve. Because it embodies the immediacy of knowing (and so is related to thought in some way), and because it acts as a point of departure for thought, the assertion that intuition is thought can't be dismissed as untrue. On the other hand, it clearly isn't true in any immediate or self-evident way. Nor does it lend itself to further development. Instead, if we take it literally, it actually abolishes the possibility of any development at all. Since intuition is devoid of development, its identity with thought would imply that thought, too, needn't entail any development. Moreover, if intuition = thought, any statement about thought must itself be purely intuitive, and hence incapable of either development or proof. Thus the only way to verify such statements would require that we perceive them as true intuitively. But even here the very nature of intuition gets in the way. Purely apprehensive, it resists any efforts to apprehend it intuitively. And, precisely because any effort to apprehend intuition comes up empty, it falls back into what Hegel terms "inert simplicity": "simplicity" because of a lack of anything to apprehend, "inert" because such a condition can't lead to anything else.

In addition to its inert simplicity, the notion that intuition is equivalent to thought displays another drawback as well: its tendency to "represent actuality itself in a non-actual manner." If the non-actual is associated in the *Phenomenology* with "inert simplicity," the actual must presumably involve a development of some kind. Since thought begins from simplicity, however, the existence of simplicity, at least, seems beyond dispute. Nevertheless, actuality and existence needn't be exactly the same. Thus if actuality is connected to development, conditions that exist but that don't involve any development could presumably figure as non-actual. In this way, we can explain how thought defined as intuition might appear to Hegel a case of actuality depicted "in a non-actual manner." So the movement from Substance to Subject is for him a movement toward actuality. And development is the means by which he expects to get there.

The living Substance is furthermore being, which is in truth *Subject*, or, what is the same, is in truth actual only insofar as it is the movement of positing itself, or the mediation of its becoming-other with itself. It is as Subject pure *simple Negativity*, and even thereby the splitting into two [Entzweyung] of the simple, or the opposition-establishing doubling, which is, again, the negation of this indifferent disparity and its opposite; only this self-reestablishing sameness, or the reflection into otherness within oneself—not an *original* unity as such, or *immediate* as such—is the True. It is the becoming itself, the circle that presupposes its end as its goal and that has its end as its beginning; and only through its being worked out and its end is it actual. (18.18−28)

"Living Substance": face to face with this odd phrase, so manifestly unphilosophical, it seems only natural to ask what might be meant by it. Hegel says, first of all, that living Substance is being, and subsequently, that being is Subject. But we know being isn't Subject straightaway, that it only becomes so by means of development. And the text remarks that the living Substance that is being or Subject "is in truth actual only insofar as it is the movement of positing itself." So movement is necessary to living Substance. Moreover, movement of a particular kind: the movement of positing oneself. Anything, however, that posits itself (sich selbst Setzen) must have within itself a capacity for movement. It's always possible, of course, to posit something else (A, for instance, or A = A). To posit oneself, on the other hand, requires a capacity for movement by what's posited, since to posit oneself is ultimately a form of self-assertion. Living Substance, then, is defined by its capacity to posit itself by its own self-movement.

For Hegel, the capacity of Substance to move itself is crucial to his entire enterprise. From an Enlightenment standpoint, the essential problem for any theory lay in the knowability of external objects. Romantic philosophy (i.e., Kant's immediate successors) tried to solve this by a bold stroke: assert that thought and the being of external objects are identical. Since being and thought in their pure forms are equally undefined, however, the assertion that they're identical couldn't really be demonstrated. Hence the need for a development of some kind. But not just of thought itself. A development of thought by itself would merely amount to analysis: it wouldn't affect the being of external objects in any way, and as a result would be purely external. To avoid that pitfall, then, *being itself must move as well.* And so we come to the need for Substance, the fusion of being and thought, to move.

But if Substance moves, we want to know about the form of its movement. On this point, the text speaks of "the mediation of its becoming-other with itself." So we have several significant "moments" in the process by which Substance posits itself: the moment of immediacy, becoming-other, and, finally, its mediation with Substance. Essentially, the movement is a circular one: it begins with immediacy, goes out to otherness, and then, by a sort of mediation, effects a "return" to the point where it began. Since the entire sequence is one of self-assertion, moreover, we need to understand its "moments" in a special way. When Substance becomes something other than itself, it would be a mistake to regard its new condition as wholly independent of what it originally was. Since its becoming-other is ultimately only a moment in its self-assertion, it obviously can't lose all relation to what it was—otherwise it would no longer be self-assertion. Similarly, mediation between its becoming-other and itself shouldn't be construed in an ordinary way either. Simply put, any mediation between these conditions can't result merely in their "reconciliation" or synthesis. Likewise, mediation is part of the process by which Substance asserts itself. When it connects otherness to Substance, then, what mediation needs to show is how otherness can be perceived within a framework of self-assertion.

Given the sequence just described, the next step for Hegel is to talk about what makes it possible. The answer is negativity. The text tells us that Substance "is as Subject pure *simple Negativity,* and is even thereby the splitting into two [Entzweyung] of the simple, or the opposition-establishing doubling, which is, again, the negation of this indifferent disparity and its opposite." Before we get into any specifics, a quick comment: what we have here amounts to the equivalent of a prolepsis. We know Substance eventually becomes Subject, but only by means of a long, drawn-out process. So if we try to posit Substance as Subject, the natural response would simply be: it isn't. Substance is immediacy. Subject implies development. If we begin with Substance, the only way to arrive at Subject is by a denial of everything Substance is. From the standpoint of immediacy, Subject, as development, can't exist. Similarly, from the standpoint of Subject, Substance in its immediacy marks a moment that can no longer exist if Subject is to be itself. The only way, then, to get from Substance to Subject must be via negativity.

For Hegel, negativity isn't a rational principle. Pure negativity denies everything, even itself. Simple negativity can't include the complexity of exceptions. It begins as negation of the simple, of Substance in its immediacy. Hegel employs the term *Entzweyung* (= *Entzweiung*), which "bifurcation" renders quite nicely, but without the sheerly destructive overtone present in the original. This sort of negativity wants to create dissension, or a breakup. Its breakup of the simple, or Substance in its immediacy, produces something double: Substance and what it isn't. Yet Hegel speaks of the result as an "indifferent" disparity, by which he means one that doesn't demand a resolution of some kind. Nevertheless, this "indifferent" disparity is itself swept away, by the negativity that created it in the first place. Because negativity isn't rational, however, the negation of disparity doesn't preclude the negation of its opposite. On the contrary: since pure negativity implies constant negation, it could only lead initially to a negation of Substance and, subsequently, to negation of the disparity between Substance and what it isn't that the initial negation produces.

To some extent, we might describe negativity as the ultimate risk for Romantic theory. Inevitably, as we've seen from Shelley, the effect of any recessive movement is to create a powerful pull toward disbelief. The risk, then, is that once you introduce negativity into theory you won't be able to stop it. For Shelley, the only way to stop it had been to frame negativity as a movement of inwardness, by which we get closer to what's essential. But Shelley could only see how to retrieve negativity abstractly: the process of endless regress becomes a way to represent what we can't otherwise specify. With Hegel, however, we arrive at a new insight. Negativity, as a movement of thought, was bound to remain purely negative. We know we can always negate whatever we posit, and that this process can go on endlessly. For that matter, we can even negate the very possibility of an end. What Hegel saw was how the situation would change if negativity were to come not from thought but from being or the existential. In other words, if negativity were to be equivalent to the process by which being or the existential becomes what it is, the very movement of negation by which existence is opposed would then be merely the means by which it would draw closer to what it's finally supposed to be.

Yet the ultimate result of pure negativity isn't indefinite negation but a "return" to the point where we began. In fact, Hegel doesn't quite believe you can literally go home again. A "return" to immediacy would imply a lack of development. But to negate what is itself negative simply amounts to a negation of its negativity. It needn't imply affirmation of what was originally negated. Thus Hegel speaks of negativity as "self-reestablishing sameness." For sameness to reestablish itself (wiederherstellende Gleichheit) obviously isn't the same as a simple return to itself. Its need to reestablish itself seems to imply that it's no longer what it was previously. Hegel emphasizes the point when he says the present sameness is "not an *original* unity as such, or *immediate*." Instead, self-reestablishing sameness is equivalent to "the reflection into otherness within oneself." What's crucial here is the fact that "reflection into otherness" occurs within oneself. If the move to what Substance isn't takes place within a larger framework of self-assertion, then no matter what Substance does it will still remain itself.

Finally, what matters most isn't any given moment but the entire process of development. After all, each "moment" of that development is already implied in its initial condition. As Hegel says, it is "the circle that presupposes its end as its goal." Nevertheless, it isn't enough just to have in mind a vague notion of development. Instead, the text insists that "only through its being worked out and its end is it actual." Because it gets worked out, development becomes actual. And because development is crucial to self-definition, the effect must be to give primacy not to individual moments but to the development they exemplify.

> Thus the life of God and divine cognition may well be expressed as a disporting [or play] of Love with itself; but this idea sinks into mere edification and even insipid-ity, if it lacks the seriousness, the suffering, the patience, and the labor of the negative. *In itself* that life is indeed untroubled equality and unity with itself, for which otherness and alienation, as well as the overcoming of this alienation, are not serious matters. But this *in itself* is abstract universality, in which the nature of the divine life *to be for itself,* and thereby above all the self-movement of the form, are neglected. If the form is declared to be the same as the essence, it is even for that very reason a mistake to suppose that cognition can be satisfied with the in-itself or the essence, but can do without the form;—that the absolute principle or absolute intuition makes the working-out of the first or the development of the latter superfluous. Precisely because the form is as essential to the essence as the essence is to itself, the essence is not to be grasped and expressed merely as essence, i.e., as immediate substance, or as the pure self-contemplation of the divine, but equally as *form,* and in the whole wealth of the developed form; only thereby is it first grasped and expressed as an actuality. (18.29–19.11)

Here we have, quite simply, the entire movement of the *Phenomenology.* It goes from *in itself* to *for itself.* In between, there is "the seriousness, the suffering, the patience, and the labor of the negative." To explain the movement, then, we need to know what each condition involves. We need to know why we begin from *in itself,* and why it isn't sufficient for Substance or God to stay there. Next, we need to know why negativity has to be expressed as the "self-movement of the form." We need to find out what form really means here, and why its movement has to be self-movement rather than by means of some other agency. Finally, we need to know what *for itself* is all about: how it differs from *in itself,* and why it (rather than anything else) should be the necessary outcome of *in itself.* Only then can we begin to consider other questions the passage goes on to raise: what makes form and essence identical in the movement from *in itself* to *for itself*, and why form alone should be equivalent to actuality.

If not merely redundant, "untroubled" equality would seem to imply the possibility of a "troubled" equality. Later, the text goes on to mention "otherness and alienation, as well as the overcoming of this alienation." The fact that alienation can be overcome hints at a return to some former condition, like that of equality. From this standpoint, "untroubled" equality would presumably indicate a relation that had never suffered alienation—in other words, one that had never known inequality. For alienation to be overcome, on the other hand, points to a development of some kind. So "troubled" equality implies development, "untroubled" equality the absence of any development.

The distinction between "troubled" and "untroubled" equality also helps to explain why the text has to specify equality as opposed to unity. In fact, it's distinctly possible for a thing to be unequal to itself. That's precisely what happens when it becomes something else. At that point, we no longer speak of it as equal to itself, which simply means it isn't what it was. From its own standpoint, however, a thing is always the same. It is what it is, as we say. For it, to exist is to be itself. And what it was, presently considered, amounts only to what it isn't. As it sees it, then, a thing always is, and hence always is itself. From that we get what Hegel terms its "unity with itself." Unity: literally, oneness (*Einheit*). The fact that it invariably is itself precludes any lapse from that unity.

The capacity of a thing to be itself also shows why otherness, alienation, and the overcoming of alienation seem unnecessary. To be, after all, seems sufficient: nothing about it points to any kind of tangible lack or deficiency. Change doesn't add to it, it merely alters it. Moreover, if to be what one is counts as equivalent to a direct or unmediated relation to oneself, anything that exists must invariably have this sort of self-relation, since to be is to be itself. For that reason, it seems at best dubious why it should ever become involved in otherness and/or alienation.

In fact, whether it actually does so turns out to depend largely on its initial condition. Of that condition, Hegel remarks: "this *in itself* is abstract universality." What we have here, then, is a complete lack of definition of any kind, the sort of condition the existential property produces when considered by itself. Nevertheless, Hegel sees it as an unstable condition. Its instability is due to the element of thought associated with the existential property. While the existential property itself is to some extent inert, thought displays a tendency to activity. Every act of thought is, in effect, an act of creation. As such, it necessitates a development of some kind. But *in itself*, as a condition, offers no possibility for development, because of the lack of any object to apprehend. Ultimately, its lack of object comes from a lack of self-awareness: *in itself* has no sense of itself specifically, nor of anything else. What thought needs, then, is a different kind of relation to itself.

For Hegel, thought is equivalent to development. That's why it would be a mistake "to suppose that cognition can be satisfied with the in-itself or the essence, but can do without the form;—that the absolute principle or absolute intuition makes the working-out of the first or the development of the latter superfluous." To be satisfied with the in-itself or the essence is to care only about the final result. And if we focused on that exclusively, we wouldn't know the particular form of alienation or otherness that had been assumed, nor how it was overcome. We wouldn't know, in other words, the sequence of moments by which thought came to be. But the process by which thought comes to be is crucial to its present condition, and hence to any attempt we might make to understand it. Thus the emphasis the text gives to form. Here the form Hegel speaks of is simply that of development. If thought is a process, the only form it can possibly have is that of the sequence by which it comes to be. By the same token, we arrive at the reason for the self-movement of the form. If the form of thought is that of its development, the only source from which that form could come would have to be thought itself.

To give form to its own development, thought has to enter into a different kind of relation to itself, one whereby it adopts the standpoint Hegel terms *for itself*. The standpoint from which it began, the *in itself*, is merely the standpoint of what is. But thought can't be simply about that. Because what is contains no provision for any possibility, no anticipation of the future, no sense of how things come to be. To get beyond the standpoint of what merely is, thought has to see itself in a different way, as a kind of project rather than an inert fact. For that, however, it needs the perspective of *for itself*. *For itself* doesn't take what thought is at the present moment as everything it will ever be. It looks beyond that, to a moment when that which now exists only as possibility will have become actual. At the same time, it also knows it won't get there simply by awareness of its own possibility. In that respect, *for itself* is also the expression of volition, of intentionality, of purposive will. Thought becomes actual, in other words, because it wants to become actual. And *for itself* is what gives it the capacity to move from possibility to actuality.

> The True is the whole. But the whole is only essence that consummates itself through its development. It must be said of the Absolute that it is essentially a *result*, that it only at the *end* is what it truly is; and that herein even rests its nature,

to be actual, subject, or self-becoming. Though it may seem contradictory that the Absolute should be grasped essentially as a result, a little deliberation sets this appearance of contradiction right. The beginning, the principle, or the Absolute, as it is initially and immediately expressed, is only the universal. Just as when I say "all animals," this expression cannot pass for a zoology, so it is just as noticeable that the words "the Divine," "the Absolute," "the Eternal," etc., do not express what is contained in them;—and only such words in fact express the intuition as something immediate. Whatever is more than such a word, even the transition to a mere proposition, is a *becoming-other* that has to be taken back, that is a mediation. But this is what is rejected with horror, as if thereby more were being made of it [mediation] than just this, that it is not absolute and is not in the Absolute at all, and that absolute cognition were thereby being surrendered. (19.12–27)

At best, we might construe what Hegel says here as a glimpse of what he later does, more fully, at 20.26–21.15. Essentially, the present passage tries to prove just one point: that the Absolute should be seen as a result, rather than as the sort of insight that might be arrived at purely intuitively. In fact, the only really new material has to do with what he terms the transition (*Uebergang*, lit., a going-over) from a single word to a proposition, which he describes as a "becoming-other" (*Anderswerden*). This "becoming-other," he says, has to be "taken back" (*zurückgenommen*). Hegel calls it a mediation. Rather than explain what he means by that, however, he then goes on to remark that the notion of the Absolute as one that involves mediation is rejected with horror, presumably by those who feel that if mediation is allowed to enter into the Absolute at all, the prospect of absolute cognition must be relinquished. But then, rather than try to prove otherwise, Hegel breaks off abruptly. Here at least two possible explanations arise. First, consider the compositional circumstances. Even if Hegel didn't literally finish his Preface the night before the Jena conflict, he obviously had to work under pressure. Pressure leads to haste and, often, oversight. So maybe Hegel started to prove his point, got distracted over a parenthetical remark, later returned to his original point and managed to address it more fully, but then forgot to delete his earlier discussion of it (no word processor). Maybe, too, he felt some reservation about examples, which can be risky when taken too literally. A second explanation. We've seen that the Preface repeatedly insists that the Absolute as end or result is already implicit in Substance. So the apparently abortive effort to prove that the Absolute is essentially a result might simply anticipate the later treatment of this issue (20.26–21.15). To a large extent, these anticipations are typical of the *Phenomenology*. To motivate the transition from each moment to the next, there has to be some sense of insufficiency. By its abortive quality, then, Hegel's initial effort to prove his point reveals its own inadequacy. At the same time, it thereby helps to justify the direction the Preface will later take.

> But this abhorrence [of mediation] stems in fact from ignorance of the nature of mediation and of absolute cognition itself. For mediation is nothing else than self-moving equality to oneself, or is reflection into itself, the moment of the I that is for itself, pure negativity, or, reduced to its pure abstraction, *simple becoming*. The I, or becoming in general, this mediation, on account of its simplicity, is just immediacy in the process of becoming, and is the immediate itself.—It is therefore a misunderstanding of Reason when reflection is excluded from the True and is not grasped as a positive moment of the Absolute. It [reflection] is that which makes the True a result, but it equally sublates this opposition to its becoming, for this becoming is just as simple and therefore not different from the form of the True which shows itself as *simple* in its result; it is rather just this return [Zurück-gegangenseyn, lit., having returned] into simplicity.—Though the embryo is indeed *in itself* a human being, it is not so *for itself*; for itself it is only that as cultivated Reason, which has *made* itself into what it is *in itself*. Only then is it actual. But this result is itself simple immediacy, for it is self-conscious freedom at peace with itself, which has not set the opposition aside and left it lying there, but has been reconciled with it. (19.28–20.10)

At this stage, Hegel introduces the notion of reflection or, more precisely, reflection into oneself. Almost immediately, we encounter an ambiguity. In effect, "reflection" might mean either (1) to be thrown or turned back (i.e., reflected) from a point, which would amount to some form of return, or (2) thought, especially the kind that involves self-awareness. Nor does the German text decisively favor either: "Reflexion" = reflection. So we might want to look at it in the context of mediation. We've seen that what's mediated doesn't have to differ from what it is to achieve equality with itself. At the same time, it ultimately becomes itself when reflected on (hence its reflection into itself). But if reflection was necessary for that, it couldn't simply have been itself already. Instead, it must really have differed from itself in some way, so that when it became itself by reflection it actually did "return" into itself. In sum, both definitions of reflection seem to apply. Still, the mere notion of reflection doesn't quite suffice to explain what happens when a mediated entity is reflected on. It doesn't, in other words, sufficiently motivate a "return" into oneself.

For that, we need "the moment of the I that is for itself." Because the I is associated with reflection, it seems only natural to see it as related to the kind of thought that produces self-awareness. Indeed, the very notion of the I is based on self-awareness. But self-awareness, after all, is itself a process. So suppose a sequence of moments, by which the I comes to exist. Among these, one is especially important to Hegel: the "moment of the I that is for itself." At that moment, the I perceives how it has to become itself. From then on, it turns into what Hegel terms pure negativity or simple becoming, for which the existential property is only another name for development. This connection to the I helps to explain why development has to consist of a movement of reflection into oneself. Because the I can only recognize *what it already is.* Otherwise, it would no longer be the notion of identity it supposedly is. Specifically, I come to a notion of identity by means of reflection, whereby I discover that my perception of my own transformation is precisely what my I consists of.

The key here is simplicity. A remark about the I shows why Hegel considers simplicity crucial to his position: "The I, or becoming in general, this mediation, on account of its simplicity, is just immediacy in the process of becoming [die werdende Unmittelbarkeit], and is the immediate itself." What Hegel wants to maintain, then, is that the I can be an entire transformational cycle, as well as a given moment in that cycle. In order for this to be true, however, the I in its development would have to remain essentially what it was in its immediacy. Only in that way could we still describe it as simple: its fully developed form doesn't differ at the essential level from what it was initially. But for that to be the case, we need a scenario whereby what the I does is to make manifest by its development what it already implicitly was. Under these circumstances Hegel can then say: "It is therefore a misunderstanding of Reason when reflection is excluded from the True and is not grasped as a positive moment of the Absolute." From his standpoint, we misconstrue the Absolute when we suppose that anything by which its development is protracted must be opposed to it. Implied is a belief that delay points to an intrusion of otherness. So what Hegel has to show is that otherness or difference isn't involved at any point.

The real issue here is whether we can equate a development with its end result. Presumably the end result must differ in some way from every earlier phase: otherwise, it couldn't mark an end to development. But if distinct from the process that produces it, we might wonder how Hegel can equate it with that process. On this question the text observes: "It [reflection] is that which makes the True a result, but it equally sublates this opposition to its becoming, for this becoming is just as simple and therefore not different from the form of the True which shows itself as *simple* in its result; it is rather just this return [lit., having returned] into simplicity." Development overcomes its antithesis (i.e., the result), then, by being just as simple. But how can it be just as simple, if it involves a movement into otherness of some kind? According to Hegel, by its return into simplicity. To speak of it, literally, as having returned into simplicity emphasizes a point: there never was a moment when it hadn't returned into simplicity. But simplicity means that Substance or the I doesn't cease to be what it was, so that as it passes over into otherness it remains itself, as it were. So a return to simplicity = a return into oneself. In this way, Hegel tries to overcome the opposition between development and its end result: if development is to become what one already is, the process of development is no different from the end result precisely because it already is that result.

The return into oneself that Hegel speaks of is produced by means of self-awareness. Although it always *is* itself, the I isn't necessarily aware of itself. To pass over into otherness leads to self-awareness, because it forces the I to confront what it isn't. Forced to face that, the I is then reflected back onto what it is. But in its return from a perception of what it isn't, it also becomes aware of its own movement of return. And this awareness of its movement of return means it can't go back to square one. Instead, its awareness pushes it on to a new concept, that of the I. In fact, what the I consists of is its return into itself and its simultaneous awareness of the movement of its return.

The example Hegel gives aptly conveys all of these points. The fact that the embryo is a human being in itself but not for itself shows the I in its immediacy, yet as about to become what it implicitly is. And since it only comes to be what it already is, otherness or difference doesn't define it at any moment. So simplicity is preserved. When the embryo becomes in actuality what it was implicitly, moreover, we can say it really only returns into itself. Meanwhile, Hegel can also speak of its return into simplicity, because the fully developed human being isn't opposed to the one about to become fully developed. Instead, Hegel terms the end result "self-conscious freedom at peace with itself, which has not set the opposition aside and left it lying there, but has been reconciled with it." The opposition comes, of course, from the effort of the self to become fully developed. Yet the fully developed self is reconciled with it, because the effort to be for itself is precisely what leads to development. Thus Hegel's remark about cultivated Reason, that is has "*made* itself into what it is *in itself.*" The effort to become developed also implies an awareness of the entire process of development. But this awareness of its own development is just what describes the fully developed self. In order to be fully developed, the self needs that awareness, since only by a knowledge of its own development, of how it has become what it is, can it ultimately arrive at the freedom to fulfill its own potentiality.

What Hegelian reflection does is to take Romantic reflexivity to a new level. For Shelley, reflexivity had been purely intuitive: a sense that if we could just manage to get outside our own narrative frame we might be able to understand what that narrative was all about. Friedrich Schlegel took it one step further, when he tried to direct attention to consciousness itself: in order to get outside the narrative frame, you need to trace it to its source. Where Hegel differed from his predecessors was in his perception of how reflexivity could simultaneously be aware of itself as a movement of return. What we have in Hegel, then, is a moment of pure transparency: a movement by which we become aware of what we are that's aware of its own movement of awareness. As a result, we get what might be described as a whole new level of narrative. Instead of just the narrative itself, we now also have the narrative of how we've arrived at that narrative. For Hegel, moreover, the narrative of how we've arrived at our narrative not only lets us get outside the original narrative frame, but even lights up the significance of our narrative by its perception of how the process by which we construct a narrative has the same sequential quality as that of our narrative itself.

> What has just been said can also be expressed by saying that Reason is *purposive activity*. The exaltation of a supposed Nature over a misconceived thinking, and especially the banishment of external teleology, has brought the form of purpose in general into discredit. Yet, in the sense in which Aristotle, too, defined Nature as purposive activity, purpose is immediate, *at rest*, the unmoved which is *self-moving*, and so is *Subject*. Its power to move, taken abstractly, is *being-for-self* or pure negativity. The result is therefore the same as the beginning, only because the beginning is the *purpose;*—or the actual is therefore the same as its Concept, only because the immediate, as purpose, contains the self or pure actuality within itself. Realized purpose or the existing actual is movement and unfolded becoming; but just this *unrest* is the self; and the self is therefore like that immediacy and simplicity of the beginning because it is the result, that which has returned into itself,—but that which has returned into itself is just the self, and the self is self-relating equality and simplicity. (20.11—25)

If the text so far has focused largely on how we get from Substance to Subject, what Hegel wants to talk about now is the agency behind it, the reason why it happens at all. Clearly, a movement whose end is implied in its origin must be in some sense teleological. At the same time, Hegel is well aware of the tendency to resist any kind of external teleology. The solution would seem to be an internal teleology. To describe an internal teleology, however, is difficult. Normally, we talk about teleology from a rational perspective. But the movement from Substance to Subject is one of development. An internal teleology, then, should presumably fuse the rational and the developmental. And the only way to do that would be to show that the movement or development from Substance to Subject is rational. Prima facie, nevertheless, it isn't clear what a rational development ought to involve. For Hegel, to say that a development is rational means that every moment of it has come to be in a necessary fashion. So what we find at the heart of internal teleology is a belief about the necessity of development.

Given this basic position, what Hegel initially says about purpose comes as a bit of a surprise. Since purpose is normally linked to movement of some kind, we might wonder why he considers it as at rest. His statement that purpose is immediate furnishes a clue. We know that immediacy is typical of Substance before its development. As such, immediacy pertains to Substance by its very nature, rather than simply by circumstances. But the nature of Substance in its immediacy is to be at rest. Similarly, the assertion that purpose is at rest looks like an attempt to assimilate it to Substance by analogy. Fully assimilated to Substance, purpose can't then be dismissed merely as a consequence of rational analysis.

At the same time, Hegel says, purpose is Subject as well. Specifically, purpose is "the unmoved which is self-moving, and so is Subject." Here it isn't fully apparent why purpose should be "unmoved." Since Hegel goes on to call it "self-moving," he presumably means it isn't moved by any external agency. Nor should it be: otherwise, it would lack the capacity to determine itself. And if it does in fact determine itself, it obviously will be self-moved. Still, there remains the question of how these conditions define purpose as Subject. Earlier, we saw that for Hegel self-movement and development are equivalent. Thus if purpose is self-moved, its movement would then be equivalent to its own development. In that way, since Subject is simply the end result of development, purpose ultimately comes to be Subject.

But perhaps the most important effect of purpose is to give us a whole new take on negativity as a means of development. Up to now, we've seen the downside of negativity, its purely destructive aspect. So far, negativity has meant the breakdown of Substance, its inability to remain what it is. The implication is that such an inability points to a deficiency of some kind. Negativity simply produces the exposure of that deficiency. But the treatment of negativity as purpose would imply that its breakdown is actually intentional. Substance breaks down, in other words, because it wants to break down. And the fact that its breakdown is intentional means that the negativity by which we perceive its deficiency isn't just some sort of rational principle but rather an internal tendency.

Subsequently, Hegel takes this one step further. He asserts that the actual is the same as its Concept "only because the immediate, as purpose, contains the self or pure actuality within itself." For pure actuality, read the end or result of development. So the immediate, as purpose, already contains the end or result of its own development within itself. Yet not just because it has some idea as to what that end will be. The mere fact that it has a notion doesn't necessitate any particular outcome. Purpose, then, isn't simply ideational. Instead, Hegel seems to think of it as an internal tendency within the immediate, which is thereby disposed to a particular end. As a result, Hegel can say that the actual is the same as its Concept. Because purpose, as internal tendency, links the Concept to the actual, the Concept of what is about to be already encompasses its own actuality.

A second consequence of the new take on negativity is that we get unrest as the very definition of what the self is. Before negativity was described as purpose, this wouldn't have been possible. Prior to that moment, unrest evoked instability, prelude to a breakdown of some kind. Purpose, however, changes all that. From now on, unrest is only a tendency to movement, which in turn produces the actual. But Hegel doesn't just want the actual, or even simply the movement that leads to the actual. He admits that "realized purpose or the existing actual is movement and unfolded becoming." What he wants, though, is the *tendency* to movement, by which movement itself comes to be. Hence his assertion that "*unrest* is the self." Unrest doesn't stay anywhere. And the reason it doesn't is that it isn't movement, which comes to an end, but the tendency that produces it.

Finally, purpose shows why movement amounts to a return to oneself, why that which returns is already the self, and why the entire movement is one of self-relating equality and simplicity. Because the internal tendency of an entity is to be itself, the movement by which it comes to be can only comprise a return to itself. Because of its internal tendency to be itself, an entity that returns to itself is itself already. And if the internal tendency of an entity to be itself means that it only returns to what it already is, the movement by which it comes to be is one of self-relating equality because the tendency by which an entity comes to be is brought to actuality as itself. So it becomes related to itself, by its own movement. And that relation is one of equality because in the internal tendency by which it comes to be, it already is itself, which makes the two conditions equal.

The need to represent the Absolute as *Subject* makes use of the propositions: *God* is the eternal, or the moral world-order, or love, and so on. In such propositions the True is only posited straightforwardly as Subject, but not represented as the movement of that which reflects itself into itself. In a proposition of this kind one begins with the word "God." This by itself is a meaningless sound, a mere name; it is only the predicate that says *what he is*, gives his content and meaning; only in this end does the empty beginning become actual knowing. To that extent it is not clear why one does not simply speak of the eternal, of the moral world-order, and so on, or as the ancients did, of pure concepts like Being, the One, and so on—in other words, of that which is the meaning, without adding the *meaningless* sound as well. But through this word it is precisely shown that what is posited is not a being or an essence or a universal above all, but rather something that is reflected into itself, a Subject. But at the same time this is only anticipated. The Subject is taken as a fixed point, to which, as their support, the predicates are affixed, by a movement belonging to the knower of this Subject, and which is not therefore regarded as belonging to the fixed point itself; yet it is only through this movement that the content could be represented as Subject. The way this movement has been brought about, it cannot belong to the fixed point; but after the presupposition of that point, it [the movement] cannot be constituted otherwise, it can only be external. The anticipation that the Absolute is Subject is therefore not only not the actuality of this Concept, but it even makes the actuality impossible, for it posits the subject as an inert point, whereas the actuality is self-movement. (20.26–21.15)

Here "is eternal" functions as a form of negativity: it says what Substance isn't (since "God" doesn't intrinsically contain the predicate "is eternal"). But "is eternal" is insufficient by itself. We have no idea what it's supposed to describe. What we lack, then, is a Subject. But if "is eternal" can't be the Subject itself, we need to apply it to one. Hence the "return" of "is eternal" to the "meaningless name" (i.e., "God"), to which, as Subject, it can now be applied. Yet initially "God" wasn't the Subject at all, and became so only because "is eternal" was affixed to it. Likewise, "is eternal" wasn't really a predicate until it was attached. Thus each becomes what it is only by the attachment of predicate to Subject.

Although the expression "God is eternal" has the form of a Hegelian return, it differs from the movement of Substance to Subject in one crucial respect. As Hegel himself points out, "God is eternal" merely posits the True as Subject in a simple, straightforward way (i.e., it makes a simple statement about the Subject). In other words, it doesn't really exemplify the sort of movement by which Substance returns into itself. So we need to distinguish between that movement and those expressions where the Subject is simply described. For Hegel, only the movement of Substance itself is internal, or self-produced. But the same needn't be true of those expressions that simply describe the Subject. After all, the term "God" that begins the proposition "God is eternal" has, by itself, no content whatsoever. The only way, then, for it to gain any is to have a predicate affixed to it. As a mere name, however, it can't do that by itself. Hence the need for a knower of the Subject, who makes the requisite connection. The fact that this is done by a knower, rather than the Subject itself, is crucial. As Hegel puts it: "but after the presupposition of that point [i.e., the term "God"], it [the movement] cannot be constituted otherwise, it can only be external." The movement is external, in other words, because it doesn't arise from the Subject itself. And that hints at a deficiency.

Finally, Hegel complains about statements that say the Absolute is Subject without any effort to specify how it comes to be that. The problem with these, he seems to feel, is that they offer no capacity for development. Their bland assertion that the Absolute is Subject "is therefore not only not the actuality of this Concept, but it even makes the actuality impossible." What this sort of assertion does, he says, is to posit the subject as an inert point. It simply equates the subject with the Absolute, or some other condition. But the actuality, Hegel goes on to insist, is self-movement. Thus we ought to be able to observe how the Absolute, or some other condition, becomes the subject by its own self-movement. What Hegel wants, then, is to specify the kind of self-movement or development by which the Concept gradually comes to be actual.

> Among various consequences that flow from what has been said, this can be stressed, that knowledge is only actual, and can only be represented, as Science or as *system*. That furthermore a so-called basic thesis or principle of philosophy, if true, is therefore already false, to the extent that it is only a basic thesis or principle. It is for that reason easy to refute it. The refutation consists in showing its deficiency: but it is deficient because it is only the universal or principle, the beginning. If the refutation is fundamental, it is taken and developed from the principle itself—not achieved by counter-affirmations and random thoughts from outside. The refutation would thus properly be the development of the principle and the completion of its deficiency, if it doesn't misunderstand itself by paying attention solely to its *negative* action, without being also aware of its progress and result on their *positive* side.—The genuinely *positive* exposition of the beginning is at the same time conversely just as much a negative attitude toward it, namely against its one-sided form of being initially *immediate* or *purpose*. It can accord-

ingly be taken just as much as a refutation of the principle that constitutes the *ground* of the system, but better, as a demonstration that the *ground* or the principle of the system is in fact only its *beginning.* (21.16–22.2)

For Hegel, system or Science is equivalent to development. The text speaks of a point at which knowledge becomes actual. But that implies a time when it wasn't yet actual, when it hadn't yet come to be. So knowledge involves development. Hegel then goes on to talk about how knowledge gets represented. Yet if knowledge itself involves a development of some kind, we can hardly expect to convey it adequately by means of a form that's purely propositional. Instead, any attempt to represent knowledge must show how that knowledge came to be. Which is to say: it has to show its development. Science or system, then, is all about development, the conceptual development by which knowledge becomes actual.

Subsequently, Hegel shows why Science or system has to be about development. Inevitably, philosophy begins with a number of basic principles. From a Hegelian standpoint, however, any basic thesis or principle (*Grundsatz*) is necessarily false. Nor does the text admit of any exceptions. So it isn't about the specific content of a given thesis or principle. Its falseness comes, rather, from a more general deficiency. As Hegel puts it: "it is deficient because it is only the universal or principle, the beginning." In other words, it isn't that the thesis or principle isn't true. But its converse is also true. Significantly, though, the fact that its converse is true doesn't make the initial thesis or principle any less true. For that reason, it can't be refuted by "counter-affirmations and random thoughts from outside." The only way it can be refuted, then, is by exposure of its deficiency. But if the exposure of its deficiency doesn't make it any less true, what this suggests is that we should consider it merely as our initial premise. And that points to a need for further elaboration. Or, to give it another name: development.

Even when viewed negatively, development still comes out as development rather than negativity. As Hegel points out, if we perceived the assertion of a thesis or principle negatively, our perception could be interpreted as "a refutation of the principle that constitutes the *ground* of the system." Our perception would show that the thesis or principle taken as a ground of the system wasn't in fact a ground at all. As a form of negativity, moreover, it would show only that. Because the refutation of a principle *qua* ground is purely negative: it makes no claim about any other principle, and might even militate against the validity of any principle whatsoever as ground. In fact, though, our perception doesn't just show that a given thesis or principle can't be taken as ground. It also shows that the thesis or principle that supposedly formed a ground is actually a beginning. But to show that, it has to go beyond negativity. And to do that, it has to have in mind a whole conception of how the development of a thesis or principle will turn out.

> That the True is only actual as system, or that Substance is essentially Subject, is expressed in the representation which gives the Absolute as *Spirit*—the most sublime Concept, and that which belongs to the modern age and its religion. The spiritual alone is the *actual;* it is essence, or the *being-in-itself,* —the self-*relating* and determinate, the *being-other* and *being-for-itself*—and in this determinateness or being external to itself remaining within itself; —in other words, it is *in and for itself.* —But this being-in-and-for-itself is initially only for us or *in itself,* it is spiritual *Substance.* It must also be this *for itself,* —it must be the knowledge of the spiritual and the knowledge of itself as Spirit; i.e., it must be an *object* to itself, but just as immediately a sublated object, reflected into itself. It is *for itself* only for us insofar as its spiritual content is produced by itself; but insofar as it is also for itself for its own self, so is this self-producing, the pure Concept, the objective element in which it has its existence; and it is in this way in its existence for itself an object reflected into itself. —The Spirit that, so developed, knows itself as Spirit, is *Science.* Science is its actuality and the realm it builds for itself in its own element. (22.3–20)

And so we come, at the end, to Spirit, by which Hegel means development that has become aware of itself. If system is equivalent to development, the perception that the True is actual only as system can itself only come from a development that knows how it came to be, and hence that what counts as True or essential about it is precisely its own development. Likewise, a Substance that is essentially Subject has of course undergone development. But, as Subject, it's also aware of its own development, and its awareness of its development is exactly what makes it Subject. Hegel then retraces the moments by which Spirit comes to be: its being-in-itself or immediacy, its being-other by which it passes into otherness, and finally its being-for-itself. Throughout all the moments by which Spirit comes to be, however, Hegel insists that it invariably remains within itself. Yet the only way it can do so is by its awareness of its own development. Because of that awareness, it knows that the moment it passes into otherness is only a moment of its own development, and hence one that remains within itself. And because of its awareness of itself, finally, Spirit can also be for-itself, and by that means embrace its own development.

Clearly, the pivotal point of the entire development is the shift from in-itself to for-itself. Hegel makes the crucial role of that shift quite apparent when he says: "But this being-in-and-for-itself is initially only for us or *in itself*, it is spiritual *Substance*. It must also be this *for itself*." If the spiritual is about development that has become aware of itself, presumably spiritual Substance must refer to a capacity for such awareness. As in-itself, however, it remains merely a capacity. From our external viewpoint, we see that capacity. But the development, as in-itself, doesn't. So the shift from in-itself to for-itself marks a move to awareness. For-itself comes about when the development has become aware of itself.

Immediately after, Hegel goes on to specify what "for itself" consists of: "it must be the knowledge of the spiritual and the knowledge of itself as Spirit; i.e., it must be an *object* to itself." Now to become an object to itself, Spirit has to find something within itself to externalize or objectify. Furthermore, the objectified element has to be essential to Spirit: otherwise, that element would no longer be Spirit itself, and so the relation (Spirit to itself) would lose its self-reflexive quality. What counts, though, as essential to Spirit? Above all, the act by which it posits itself: without that, it couldn't exist. So the act by which it posits itself becomes an object for Spirit.

The sublation of Spirit as object, or, equivalently, of its self-positing act, necessitates a slightly different viewpoint. Although Spirit becomes an object to itself by focusing on its own self-positing act, it seems equally evident that in another respect the act isn't really any different from Spirit itself. If it were, we should be able to formulate a description of what Spirit is that didn't include its self-positing act. In fact, though, Spirit wouldn't be what it is if it didn't posit itself. So the sublation of the act by which Spirit posits itself comes about because that act is essentially identical to what Spirit is. For Spirit to sublate its own act, then, it simply has to perceive its act as equivalent to what Spirit itself is.

The process by which Spirit does that is one by which it becomes for itself. Hegel goes into all this in some detail: "It [Spirit] is *for itself* only for us insofar as its spiritual content is produced by itself; but insofar as it is also for itself for its own self, so is this self-producing, the pure Concept, the objective element in which it has its existence; and it is in this way in its existence for itself an object reflected into itself." Here the "spiritual content" that Spirit produces consists of the act by which Spirit posits itself. Because it produces its own development, then, Spirit gets defined as for itself. At first, Hegel speaks of it as for itself for us only, since we alone perceive that Spirit produces its own development. Thus Spirit initially produces its own development without any self-awareness. When it finally does perceive its own development, however, Spirit becomes, as Hegel says, "for itself for its own self." At that moment, Spirit focuses on its self-producing as an act distinct from itself. Hence Hegel's description of its perception of itself as a pure Concept or objective element: it is, simply, the perception Spirit has of its own activity. But because Spirit is development that has become aware of itself, the objective element whereby it perceives itself is also that by which it comes to be. Finally, Hegel asserts that the perception of how it produces its own development is reflected back into Spirit itself. Until Spirit reflects the perception that it produces its own development back into itself, in other words, it doesn't know that this is what it is. The perception remains purely objective, or external to its conception of itself. But once it sees how its very nature or identity is defined by the fact that it has produced itself, Spirit at last comes to recognize that its self-production is itself.

And so we come, finally, to metatheory, or theory that has become aware of itself as theory. Hegel called it Science: "The Spirit that, so developed, knows itself as Spirit." But if the end result of its development consists of what the text refers to as pure Concept, the process by which we get there can only be one of theory. For Hegel, the moment at which Spirit or development becomes aware of itself was the moment it became actual. At the same time, he also speaks of its self-awareness as "the realm it builds for itself in its own element." In this fashion, he appears to express a hope that the self-awareness of theory might ultimately form the basis for all theory. And if that were to occur, it would be because in its awareness of itself as metatheory, theory had at last recognized fully its capacity to create itself.

From here, we can go on to talk about the larger tendency apparent in the whole Hegelian trajectory we've just traced: the tendency toward what I would call a movement of return. For Hegel's predecessors, it began as a movement of inwardness. Its form was that of reflexivity. To resolve a conceptual impasse, you turn back to the way by which you came to it. And that meant, ultimately, that you turned back into yourself. But if this was equivalent to a movement of inwardness, Hegel took it to its ultimate extreme, when he made the very process by which we turned back to the way we came to the impasse the source of our response. As a result, extreme inwardness becomes extreme outwardness or externality. Or, equivalently, extreme subjectivity = extreme objectivity. Yet Hegel didn't just let it go at that. On some level, I suspect, he must have felt that this sort of inward movement by which we turn back on our own reflective process was one that possessed more than just subjective importance. Instead, I would argue, he probably felt how it might well apply to all forms of theory. And the reason was that all of these involved a theoretical development of some kind.

But after development, there had to be some sort of reflection on that development, by which we become clear about what we've done. Which is to say: a movement of return. No doubt Hegel even saw how it might apply at the most fundamental, ontological level. After all, we become what we are. When he first introduced development, it was as if Hegel had deprived ontology of its primacy. But if we initially seem to move away from ontology by means of development, it's only so that we can come back to it more richly, via his movement of return, at the end.

⁓

And so we return, after the *Phenomenology* Preface, to the observer who watched Napoleon pass through Jena, and to what that observer might have seen in his mind's eye as he witnessed this event. (1) He might have seen the triumph of theory over material circumstances. Somehow the Napoleonic will had managed to prevail in virtually every recent conflict. At Ulm, only a year before, the unfortunate General Mack had been forced to surrender an entire army without the chance to fire even a shot. Such had been the speed and brilliance of French tactical maneuvers that rendered his position hopeless. The newspapers were constantly full of the last Napoleonic advances. From his letters, moreover, we know that Hegel entirely expected Napoleon to prevail once again. But that presumably meant he had felt on some level the presence of a mind that understood how material circumstances could be made to yield a particular result, if employed rightly.

(2) The observer might have perceived traces of a development of some sort. Typically, the Napoleonic plan involved a sequence of tactical maneuvers. Probably the observer himself didn't know exactly what they were. In fact, even experienced officers like Jomini or Clausewitz had failed to grasp exactly how the *manoeuvre sur les derrières* worked. So we can hardly expect more of a noncombatant. Yet the observer knew, from his own theoretical work, how powerful development was: that it offered a way to take up material circumstances, to assimilate these into itself. And the way it did that was to make them part of a story. Narrative had that kind of effect. Once you made material circumstances part of a story, people no longer thought of them as inert, unmovable facts. Instead, they came to pertain to a particular moment, to play a role in how a given sequence of events had come about. And once they became associated with a sequence of events, the typical question would no longer be what these circumstances were, but what role they had played in that sequence of events.

(3) In addition, the observer might have felt an awareness of development. Time and time again, Napoleon had *deferred* victory, passed up the easier win in

order to make it more complete. The observer knew what a Napoleonic victory looked like. It wasn't just victory by attrition. Instead, it usually involved the complete collapse of an enemy army. Such a collapse could only be engineered by a sequence of tactical moves, rather than a simple assault. The astute use of tactical maneuvers, however, would probably offer multiple chances to win. So if victory was deferred, its deferral pointed to an awareness of development within the tactical plan. In other words, Napoleon didn't just take the first good opportunity that offered: he knew he had better stuff up his sleeve. Of course his observer couldn't have known what was in the Emperor's mind. Yet the evidence provided by victory after victory suggested that Napoleonic tactics didn't simply display a development. Instead, there had to be a constant awareness of development at each phase of the plan. Informed by that sort of awareness, every phase would then be defined or shaped by the thought of how the affair should end. That was why the Emperor could look to his observer like the embodiment of the world-soul: his confidence seemed to come from a higher level of awareness, as if he literally saw tactics from a different vantage point than his opponent. To Hegel, that was the mark of objectivity. Objectivity meant you had reached a position where you could objectify your own thought movement, see it from an external perspective. If the tactical plan that had led to victory in a given conflict involved development of some kind, objectivity meant the capacity to perceive development, rather than any mere tactical consideration, as the essence of the plan.

For Hegel, awareness of our own thought movement led to (4) metatheory. Metatheory grew out of that sort of awareness within a given field. To Napoleon, metatheory lay in the perception that every battle or conflict could be compared to a drama or theatrical piece, composed as it was of a beginning, middle, and end. By means of that insight, he could look at a conflict without the need to attend to all of its material circumstances. Instead, he could see it solely for the way it enacted a particular sort of development. To see it in that way, however, was to see it purely as a formal construct. And once you see it as a formal construct, your perception itself takes on a distinct autonomy. Its autonomy comes from the fact that you can always define the shape of a conflict formally even if you don't know its material circumstances. And that in turn meant that even if you didn't know the relevant material circumstances, you could still know what was perhaps most important about any given conflict: how it would end. Made possible by a formal perspective on tactics, this autonomy was what marked metatheory. We arrive at metatheory as a result of our awareness of our own thought movement. But that awareness becomes metatheory only when we begin to see theory itself from a formal viewpoint.

Because of metatheory, Hegel could say (5) that theory has the capacity to create itself. In Napoleonic terms, this meant: because it could see battle as a theatrical piece, Napoleonic theory could create victory. More broadly, once you reach the point where you can see the formal element of theory, you've arrived at the capacity to create theory. In itself, theory is essentially formal. We know that because we know we can always define a theory formally, even if we don't know what it's about. But if the formal element of theory is likewise its essential element, it presumably also has to be the formative matrix of any new theory. To create theory, in other words, all we need is the formal perspective of metatheory. Once we arrive at the level of metatheory, theory is no longer primarily about material circumstances. What the observer saw, then, as he watched Napoleon ride by, was that theory had the capacity to create a world out of itself.

CHAPTER FOUR

The House of Life

A portal, flanked by two arched window-spaces. Above the portal, a stone plaque with the inscription Hôtel-Dieu. Below this inscription, on the portal itself, the Revolutionary motto: Liberté, Egalité, Fraternité. And finally, on a plain white placard at street level: Assistance publique. Hôpitaux de Paris. The name Hôtel-Dieu dates back to the seventh century, when the bishop of Paris founded the hospital. The Revolutionary motto announces the moment when reform of the hospital began, a reform inextricably linked to the origins of modern medicine. Assistance publique: quite literally, the Hôtel-Dieu gave medical aid to anyone in Paris, with the poor (the largest part of its clientele) treated at no cost. Similarly, physicians frequently served at the hospital without pay. Their service reflected a firm belief in medical assistance as a right (rather than privilege) of every city resident. The designation Hôpitaux de Paris points to the administrative nexus that connects the Hôtel-Dieu to other hospitals in the city. In the eighteenth century, it was already associated with the Hôpital St.-Louis and the Hôpital de la Santé, as well as the hospitals of the so-called Hôpital Général de Paris: Notre Dame de la Pitié, La Salpêtrière, the Hospice de Bicêtre, and the Hospice de Vaugirard.

Today the Hôtel-Dieu is situated at the northwest corner of the cathedral of Notre Dame, in the very heart of Paris. A massive structure, it completely fills the space between the Rue d'Arcole and the Rue de la Cité, its shape essentially that of a quadrangle whose principle entrance faces the open square in front of the cathedral. The facade enjoys discreet shade from a row of trees whose foliage takes on a warm russet tint in autumn. The main entrance hall offers a well-lit, spacious foyer enhanced by a studied arrangement of pediments and arches. Meanwhile the inner courtyard displays another Gothic motif, a row of arched windows surmounted by a similar row of arches. The effect is that of a cathedral clerestory. Overall, the architectural eclecticism (a mix of classical and medieval) betrays the taste of the nineteenth century. So it should come as no surprise to learn that the original Hôtel-Dieu had been gradually destroyed by a succession of fires the century before. Thus the enormous complex between the Rue d'Arcole and the Rue de la Cité can yield no clue about the original Hôtel-Dieu. Here the faint but persistent resonances of the past, typical of every edifice that has endured and witnessed, have been reduced to silence.

From a variety of sources, we can arrive at some sense of the original Hôtel-Dieu. We at least know its location: unlike the present Hôtel-Dieu, its predecessor had been built on the opposite side of Notre Dame, adjacent to the southwest corner. In fact, the earlier structure even partly blocked access to the cathedral itself. A motley collection of buildings thrown together largely at the time of François Ier, the old Hôtel-Dieu meandered haphazardly along the bank of the Ile de la Cité from the Pont-au Double to just above the Petit Pont. Meanwhile a secondary wing arose on the opposite bank of the Seine, at the present-day quai de Montebello. An arrangement of corridors and wards that straddled the Seine via the Pont-au Double and a second juncture linked this secondary wing to the principal one. What we have, then, is roughly a hollow square built over the river. The interior was in many respects equally haphazard. With its first floor reserved for administrative offices, storage of food, wood, oil, wax, and other combustibles had to be relegated to the basement. In addition, candlemaking carried out there added to the danger of fire. As for the floors reserved for patients, a Byzantine scheme of badly designed stairways and corridors connected the different wards to each other, while an endless array of small, cramped rooms only intensified the awkwardness. Clearly, all these circumstances were bound to impede hospital staff efficiency.

When we turn to the quality of patient care, however, the situation took on the semblance of a genuine nightmare. The Hôtel-Dieu contained 486 single beds and 733 slightly larger, for a total of 1,219. With these it would normally accommodate 2,500 patients. But in unhealthy seasons, that number could quickly escalate to 3,500 and, in the event of an epidemic, 4,800. Moreover, many single beds would be occupied by orderlies, who had nowhere else to sleep. The normal complement for a larger bed was four patients. But with even a slight increase in admissions, this easily became five or six. In the smallpox ward as many as eight children might be found in a single bed. With patients crammed together so that the feet of one lay beside the head of the next, blankets became impossible: to warm the feet of one person would suffocate others. Instead the patients' only source of warmth came from fellow patients afflicted with fever. Nor could they even move. Restricted to eight and a half inches of bed space per patient, they suffered constantly from stiffness. Sleep was absolutely out of the question. Often, babies assigned to beds with their mothers were overlaid and smothered.

Overcrowding, though, was just a minor problem. A bigger one was infection. Within a single bed, patients with different illnesses were indiscriminately mixed together. Even more horrifying, those who had died often weren't removed for hours or even days. Scabies and vermin were universal, and went completely untreated. And beds were almost never changed despite the fact that sweat, pus, and secretions from the sick inevitably soaked through the mattresses. Likewise, unwashed linen would pass from one patient to the next. Even the air was a source of contagion: small, cramped rooms made the atmosphere humid and close, and in hot months especially, with almost no ventilation, patients could only inhale air already breathed many times by others. Lack of space also meant everything had to be done in the wards themselves: bandages changed, infections drained, veins bled, and operations performed (trepanning almost always proved fatal because the air infected the dura mater).

If it's hard these days to imagine operations without anesthesia, those of the Hôtel-Dieu almost surpass belief. For lack of anesthesia was just one difficulty surgical patients there had to face. Situated next to the Rue de la Boucherie, the surgical ward was subject by day to a constant rumble from heavy carts passing by. Night was no better: the screams, convulsions, and fights of the mental patients in the adjacent ward completely destroyed any hope of rest. While the ratio of three surgical patients per bed made even minimal physical comfort hard to come by, the constant presence of attendants with carts of food or linen and outpatients who hovered beside each bed to consult a surgeon only made matters worse. Meanwhile other conditions rendered the plight of those destined for surgery almost unbearable. Since operations were invariably performed in the same room where all surgical patients were kept, anyone not yet operated on could clearly see all the horrors to come. And of course for anyone who'd already undergone the ordeal, the screams and agony of those currently engaged would only revivify the memory of past torment. Next to the surgical ward, moreover, the autopsy room with its unavoidable smell intimated the frequent outcome. At the Hôtel-Dieu, even simple operations were risky. Those of a more complicated kind usually proved fatal. Here statistics tell the tale: of every four patients admitted to the Hôtel-Dieu, one was fated to die there.

Perhaps the most poignant losses concerned those involved in the inception of new life. For every fifteen mothers who entered the Hôtel-Dieu for childbirth, one would lose her own life. The problems were manifold. Typically, three or four mothers at all stages of delivery would be crammed together in a single bed.

Healthy and sick lay together, with expectant mothers often next to patients afflicted by smallpox or syphilis. Of course infections spread. In particular, puerperal fever in the maternity ward (endemic there for twelve years by 1787) went unchecked. On average, maternity patients spent roughly thirty-five days at the Hôtel-Dieu—mostly for recovery from secondary infections. Still, those who lived could count themselves lucky. For anyone who developed complications during pregnancy, the outcome was likely to be worse. Operations almost always proved unsuccessful. Fewer than one out of thirty-five mothers who underwent Caesarian sections survived surgery. Delivery by forceps was similarly fraught with risk. These, then, were the conditions at the Hôtel-Dieu in 1787, as described by the renowned physician Jacques Tenon in his Academy of Science report for the minister Jean-Sylvain Bailly. Taken collectively they suggest: a house of death, not life.[1]

Nonetheless, the Revolution would make matters worse. Almost immediately, institutions became suspect, tainted by their association with the Old Regime. Ideological purity now counted for more than expertise. As the political situation worsened, the polemics increased. The result: a loss of public confidence. Finally, in August 1792, the blow fell: all university faculties and medical schools in France were abolished. With these went the Paris Faculty of Medicine. No more legal requirements for medical practice, no more exams to prove competence. Suddenly the field became wide open to anyone and everyone. Some legislators even voiced the hope that medicine could now return to a more natural mode, and perhaps eventually to that of ancient Greece. A picturesque idyll. It's only too easy to imagine the consequences for helpless patients at hospitals like the Hôtel-Dieu. With the collapse of professional medical care, chaos ensued, marked by the eruption of a flood of untrained medical practitioners onto the scene. Quackery and charlatanism now abounded everywhere. War, meanwhile, only intensified an already desperate situation: between September 1793 and the end of 1794, over 600 doctors were lost, casualties of service in the armies of the Republic. The Paris Académie de Chirurgie lingered out its last days, to be abolished in 1794. Clearly, any sense of the need for medical knowledge had disappeared.

Out of the chaos, however, a new discipline gradually emerged. As the consequences of charlatanism and incompetence began to be felt, public opinion shifted toward support for a radical reform of the medical profession. At the heart of the reform effort was Pierre-Joseph Desault. As chief surgeon of the Hôtel-Dieu, he had himself created the surgical clinic there. A contemporary prospectus conveys an idea of what his course was like. Between 6 and 8:30 a.m., Desault made the rounds of all hospital patients, accompanied by his students. Patient examination included comments by Desault on important aspects of each malady and medical attention either from himself personally or under his direct supervision. The practical surgical lesson (9 to 11 a.m., in the hospital amphitheater) formed the core of the course. Here operations would be performed and observed, accompanied by discussion and possibly prior demonstration on a cadaver by Desault. Also featured were anatomical examination of deceased patients, reports, and intensive scrutiny of a particular disease. At 3 p.m., an anatomy lesson, with questions. At 4:30, visits to patients, with Desault himself present by 5 o'clock. At 6 p.m., further outpatient consultations in the amphitheater. Then, until 8 p.m., more practical preparation: dissections, operations on cadavers, equipment assembly, bandages. Throughout we see constant exposure to the body, dead and alive. By means of such instruction, the house of death began its transformation into a house of life.

Enter, at this moment, a young medical student named Xavier Bichat. With his native Lyon inflamed by Revolutionary disturbances, he had found himself forced to look elsewhere to complete his medical studies. In June 1794 (barely a month before 9 Thermidor, which brought the fall of Robespierre and an end to the Terror) Bichat arrived in Paris. Enrolled in Desault's course, he quickly became the favorite pupil, assistant, and subsequently successor to the great surgeon. In each capacity, he witnessed the struggle between life and death in countless instances. But not only as observer: in the last years of his own brief life, he felt its imminent end. As a result, his research pace became more frenetic. During the winter of 1801–2 he supposedly dissected 600 cadavers. Then the end: on July 22, 1802, shortly after a fall from a staircase at the Hôtel-Dieu, Bichat died in the arms of his friends Roux, Esparron, and Mme Desault, his last days marked by acute illness. His physicians, Corvisart and Lepreux, had tried desperately to save him, but in vain. The celebrated Corvisart then wrote to Napoleon: "Bichat just died at thirty. He fell on a battleground that demands courage too and counts more than one victim. He has enriched medical science. Nobody at his age has done so much so well." His funeral service at the cathedral of Notre Dame next to the hospital where he worked drew almost all the elite of the Paris medical faculty as well as the entire body of medical students in the city. Napoleon ordered a monument to be placed in the main hall of the Hôtel-Dieu. Its inscription is typical of the language and emotion of its period: "This monument, dedicated to the memory of citizens Desault and Bichat, is testimony to the gratitude of their contemporaries for services the former rendered to French surgery as its restorer, and that the latter rendered to French medicine, which he enriched by several works whose realm he would have extended if pitiless death hadn't struck him in his thirty-first year."[2]

Here, one might say, life circumstances seem to form a natural prelude to the work. All around him, in the wards of the Hôtel-Dieu, Bichat had seen patients whose vital flame had flickered under the pressure of illness or infection and often gone out. In some instances, a sudden shock would have been sufficient to arrest vitality in an otherwise healthy individual. In other instances, internal examination or autopsy would have revealed a pathological condition in the patient. But what all these examples shared was evidence of the struggle of vitality against adverse conditions or forces. Because of circumstances at the Hôtel-Dieu, moreover, the fragile thread of vitality was more apparent than elsewhere. In addition, Desault's commitment to careful observation and records of illnesses made it possible to track the vital trajectory of a patient very closely. The autopsy was another source of abundant data about vital processes. Here the high mortality rate of Hôtel-Dieu patients meant a constant supply of new material for study. Finally Bichat had his own condition to think of. If anything, it might give questions about the nature of life a greater urgency. But despite the ample inducement for reflection offered by all these circumstances, they don't quite suffice to dictate the particular form a vital theory ought to take. For that, we need to turn to Bichat's work.

Perhaps the first point to make about Bichat's vital theory is that it doesn't adhere to the notion of a single vital principle. About this the *Anatomie générale* is quite explicit:

> La doctrine générale de cet ouvrage ne porte précisément l'empreinte d'aucune de celles qui règnent en médecine et en physiologie. Opposée à celle de Boerhaave, elle differe, et de celle de Stahl, et de celle des auteurs qui, comme lui, ont tout rapporté, dans l'économie vivante, à une principe unique, principe abstrait, idéal et purement imaginaire, quel que soit le nom d'*ame*, de *principe vital*, d'*archée*, etc., sous lequel on le désigne.
>
> [The general doctrine of this work doesn't exactly carry the stamp of those that reign in medicine and in physiology. Opposed to that of Boerhaave, it differs from that of Stahl and the authors who, like him, have attributed everything in the vital economy to a single principle, an abstract principle, ideal and purely imaginary, whether the name be *soul*, *vital principle*, *first principle*, etc., under which one designates it.] (*Anatomie générale* I: vj–vij)

Subsequently Bichat reiterates his point. About the notion of a unitary vital principle he specifically remarks: "Ce principe appelé vital par Barthez, archée par Van-Helmont, etc., est une abstraction qui n'a pas plus de réalité, qu'en auroit un principe également unique qu'on supposeroit présider aux phénomènes physiques" [This principle termed vital by Barthez, primordial by Van-Helmont, etc., is an abstraction that has no more reality than would an equally unique principle that one might suppose to preside over all physical phenomena] (*Anatomie générale* I: xxxviij–xxxix).

Although Bichat is clearly critical of a single vital principle, the reason isn't immediately evident. After all, the capacity to encompass a wide range of phenomena is precisely what gives a general principle its explanatory value. And while the notion of a single principle for all physical phenomena might seem far-fetched, the same needn't necessarily be true for a single vital principle. Consider: whereas physical events have different sources, all vital phenomena occur within any given individual. From that standpoint, for vital phenomena to originate from different sources could even seem counter-intuitive.

The fact that Bichat doesn't buy the notion of a unitary vital principle points to what counts for him as explanation. Here his rejection of an equivalent principle for physics seems to me highly instructive. It shows his resistance to a unique vital principle isn't based on any perspective peculiar to the life sciences. Instead, his dislike of a unique vital principle would seem akin to his dismissal of an equivalent physical principle. To understand what it involves, we might look at what he considers valid physical principles. Elsewhere in the same passage, he gives attraction and impulsion as examples. Each of these refers to an activity of some kind. Attraction is about the movement by which particles draw toward each other, while impulsion has to do with motion that can be communicated to others. What characterizes both is a high degree of specificity. In each case, we know exactly what's involved. By contrast, it would be extremely hard to specify a content for soul, vital principle, or first principle. Thus "abstraction" is equivalent for Bichat to generality. As we move to higher levels of generality, we become progressively more abstract until at the highest level we arrive at pure abstraction. Obviously, the higher the level of generality, the more phenomena we can cover under a single principle. At the same time, we clearly lose specificity: at each level, it's harder to say what exactly our principle consists of. For Bichat, then, generality always comes at the cost of specificity. And without specificity, there can be for him no explanatory force.

To a significant extent, Bichat's desire for specificity seems to me to reflect the influence of Desault. The outlook of the new surgical school had emphasized observation. Here we need only recall the routine of the surgical course at the Hôtel-Dieu. Significantly, Desault almost never talks about the ultimate cause of a disease or illness, or the broad links between various vital phenomena. Instead, what we get is almost purely observational: an exact record of the minutiae of each patient's illness, postoperative reports on patients, anatomical examination of deceased patients, remarks on illnesses prevalent in the hospital at the time. Even the way Desault tests his students reflects this observational tendency: oral rather than written, and only on material covered in the last ten days. The entire routine clearly expresses a deep suspicion of, and resistance to, the hypothetical or speculative. In that respect, Desault was emphatically a minimalist. His objective might even be described as a replacement of theory by practice, a practice dominated by observation without any trace of the speculative. Given his own immersion in Desault's routine, it's only natural Bichat would have found the notion of a single vital principle, with its implied element of the hypothetical, untenable. If you start with the physiological minutiae that emerge from the daily round of hospital work, to arrive at a general doctrine of vitality would require theory to be buttressed by a massive quantity of inferences. And that, from a purely observational standpoint, could hardly be thought of.[5]

To guard against the dangers of the hypothetical or speculative, then, an explanatory principle has to be endowed with the sort of specificity we obtain from a purely observational standpoint. For Bichat, the best way to achieve that is by properties:

> En donnant l'existence à chaque corps, la nature lui imprima donc un certain nombre de propriétés qui le caractérisent specialement, et en vertu desquelles il concourt, à sa manière, à tous les phenomenes qui se développent, se succèdent et s'enchaînent sans cesse dans l'univers. . . .
>
> Ces propriétés sont tellement inhérentes aux uns et aux autres, qu'on ne peut concevoir ces corps sans elles. Elles en constituent l'essence et l'attribut. Exister et en jouir sont deux choses inséparables pour eux. Supposez qu'ils en soient tout à coup privés; à l'instant tous les phénomènes de la nature cessent, et la matière seule existe. Le chaos n'étoit que la matière sans propriétés: pour créer l'univers, Dieu la doua de gravité, d'élasticité, d'affinité, etc., et de plus, une portion eut en partage la sensibilité et la contractilité.
>
> [In giving existence to each body, nature thus imprinted on it a certain number of properties that specially characterize it, and by virtue of which it concurs in its way with all the phenomena that develop, succeed each other, and connect endlessly in the universe. . . .
>
> These properties are so inherent in one or another [body] that one can't conceive of those bodies without them. They constitute their essence and attribute. To exist and to possess [such properties] are for them two inseparables. Suppose they were suddenly deprived of these; instantly all natural phenomena would cease, and

matter alone would exist. Chaos is only matter without properties: to create the universe, God endowed it with gravity, elasticity, affinity, etc., and, in addition, one portion received as part of its share sensibility and contractility.] (*Anatomie géné-rale* I: xxxvj–xxxvij)

While he clearly wants to emphasize the importance of properties, what isn't clear is why Bichat should want to define these simultaneously as "the essence and attribute" of all material bodies. Typically, essence is supposed to be the base of attributes or qualities. Essence, in other words, is fundamental, while attributes are merely phenomenal or modificational. Yet Bichat obviously wants to make them equally fundamental. To do that, he begins with the remark that "these properties are so inherent in one or another [body] that one can't conceive of those bodies without them." But perhaps our tendency to associate the two is simply the result of our experiences. As if to rule out such a possibility, Bichat goes on: "To exist and to possess [such properties] are for them two inseparables." From his standpoint, then, existence isn't even ontologically prior. All the same, we can easily conceive of it without material properties. The fact that we can do so, more-over, might well imply actual ontological precedence (note that we can't imagine the reverse: properties or qualities without existence). Thus the burden of proof falls on the text: it has to explain why properties are ontologically necessary.

Subsequently Bichat tries to explain just that. What he says points to an awareness of our ability to think material existence without properties: "Suppose they [material bodies] were suddenly deprived of these; instantly all natural phenomena would cease, and matter alone would exist." Significantly, Bichat doesn't try to claim there would be no matter at all. Instead, he seems to recognize that our ability to think material existence without properties does imply real ontological precedence of some kind. What he does claim, however, is that material existence without properties isn't matter as we know it: that its lack of properties or qualities means we couldn't have any perception of it, and hence no knowledge of its existence. Under these circumstances, the result would be simply chaos: "Chaos is only matter without properties: to create the universe, God endowed it with gravity, elasticity, affinity." His description of chaos shows Bichat as clearly concerned about his admission of matter without properties. Despite our inability to perceive it, any admission of its existence could signify that its ontological precedence is real, which would make properties merely modificational. To avoid this undesirable consequence, the text tries a sort of desperate backdoor move: it posits the "creation" of matter as equivalent to God's endowment of it with properties. The problem here is that matter would then exist before it gets endowed with properties, and so conceivably coexist with God. Thus even if we think of creation as the endowment of matter with properties, we still don't arrive at their inseparability from matter.

The reason why this issue is crucial for Bichat has to do with his desire to make properties a kind of ultimate explanatory principle. Immediately after the passage just discussed, he explicitly says:

> Cette manière d'énoncer les propriétés vitales et physiques, annonce assez qu'il ne faut point remonter au-delà dans nos explications, qu'elles offrent les principes, et que ces explications doivent en être déduites comme autant de conséquences.
> [This way of stating vital and physical properties sufficiently announces that there's no need at all to go back any further in our explanations, that they [properties] offer principles, and that these explanations should be deduced from them as so many consequences.] (*Anatomie générale* I: xxxvij)

Here the statement "they [properties] offer principles" shows how far Bichat will go in his effort to make properties the basis of theory. Despite a fundamental category difference, he even tries to equate properties with principles. In addition, he clearly wants to believe properties have explanatory value. Thus his expressed hope that "explanations should be deduced from them as so many consequences." What's at stake for Bichat in the discussion of properties is the role of observation in the formation of theory. From his standpoint, admission of the ontological precedence of material substance over properties or qualities opens the door, in effect, to various forms of theory that hardly take account of observation at all. Hence the need to make observation central via a doctrine of properties, so that the basis of theory will remain observational rather than purely speculative.[4]

While his discussion of properties has so far been more or less general, it's important for Bichat at this point to distinguish vital properties from the merely physical. In fact, he attempts to do so in various ways. Because it epitomizes the rest, his first distinction is particularly significant:

> Lorsqu'on met d'un côté les phénomènes dont les sciences physiques sont l'objet, que, de l'autre, on place ceux dont s'occupent les sciences physiologiques, on voit qu'un espace presque immense en sépare la nature et l'essence. Or, cet intervalle naît de celui qui existe entre les lois des uns et des autres.
> Les lois physiques sont constantes, invariables; elles ne sont sujettes ni à augmenter ni à diminuer. . . . Au contraire, à chaque instant la sensibilité, la contractilité s'exaltent, s'abaissent et s'altèrent: elles ne sont presque jamais les mêmes.

Il suit de là que tous les phénomènes physiques sont constamment invariables, qu'à toutes les époques, sous toutes les influences, ils sont les mêmes; que l'on peut, par conséquent, les prévoir, les prédire, les calculer. . . . Au contraire, toutes les fonctions vitales sont susceptibles d'une foule de variétés. Elles sortent fréquemment de leur degré naturel; elles échappent à toute espèce de calcul; il faudroit presque autant de formules que de cas qui se présentent. On ne peut rien prévoir, rien prédire, rien calculer dans leurs phénomènes: nous n'avons sur eux que des approximations, le plus souvent même incertaines.

[When one sets on one side the phenomena of which the physical sciences are the object, while on the other one places those with which the physiological sciences occupy themselves, one sees that an almost immense space separates the nature and essence [of these sciences]. Now this space grows out of that which exists between the laws of one group and the other.

Physical laws are constant, invariable; they're not subject either to augmentation or diminution. On the contrary, at each instant sensibility, contractility rise, fall, and are altered: they're almost never the same.

It follows from this that all physical phenomena are constantly invariable, that at every epoch, under every influence, they're always the same; that one can consequently foresee them, predict them, calculate them. . . . On the contrary, all the vital functions are susceptible of a host of varieties. They frequently depart from their natural degree; they escape every sort of calculation; it's necessary to have almost as many formulas as cases that present themselves. One can foresee nothing, predict nothing, calculate nothing in their phenomena: we have on them only approximations, most often even uncertain.] (*Anatomie générale* I: lij–liij)

Despite the temptation to assimilate vital to physical properties, Bichat doesn't go that way. To some extent, he seems to have felt pressure (from the Academy of Science and elsewhere) to make the life sciences conform to the paradigm of exactness favored by the physical sciences. Yet his rhetoric expresses an emphatic refusal to yield to that pressure. Hence the "almost immense space" between the life sciences and the physical sciences. As Bichat sees it, the physical sciences simply can't grasp what's essential to vital properties. Specifically, sensibility and contractility "rise, fall, and are altered: they're almost never the same." But if these properties don't remain the same, and if their exact variation is unpredictable, what matters is the kind of movement or activity they embody.

Elsewhere Bichat attempts to define exactly the movement or activity associated with each vital property. His analysis leads him to organize these in a particular fashion:

1^0. La sensibilité organique et la contractilité insensible ont évidemment sous leur dépendance, dans l'état de santé, tous les phénomènes de la circulation capillaire des secrétions, des absorptions, des exhalations, de la nutrition, etc. Aussi en traitant de ces fonctions, faut-il toujours remonter à ces propriétés. . . .

2^0. La contractilité organique sensible, qui, comme la précédente, ne se sépare pas de la sensibilité de même nature, préside surtout dans l'état de santé aux mouvemens que nécessite la digestion, à ceux qu'exige la circulation des gros vaisseaux, au moins pour le sang rouge et pour le sang noir du système général. . . .

3^0. De la sensibilité animale dérivent, dans l'état de santé, toutes les sensations extérieures, la vue, l'ouïe, l'odorat, le goût, le toucher; toutes les sensations intérieures, la soif, la faim. . . .

4^0. La contractilité animale est le principe de la locomotion volontaire et de la voix.

[1^0. Organic sensibility and insensible contractility evidently have under them, in a healthy state, all the phenomena of the capillary circulation of secretions, absorptions, exhalations, nutrition, etc. Thus in treating these functions it's necessary to go back to these properties. . . .

2^0. Organic sensible contractility which, like the preceding, isn't separable from sensibility of the same nature [i.e., organic sensibility], presides especially in a healthy state over movements necessitated by digestion, over those required by circulation in the large vessels, at least for red blood and for the black blood of the general system. . . .

3^0. From animal sensibility derive, in a healthy state, all exterior sensations, sight, hearing, smell, taste, touch; all interior sensations, thirst, hunger. . . .

4^0. Animal contractility is the principle of voluntary locomotion and of the voice.] (*Anatomie générale* I: xliij–xlv)

Perhaps the most helpful comment on what Bichat says here is his own schema from the *Recherches physiologiques sur la vie et la mort*:

Genera	Species	Varieties
Vital Properties:		
Sensibility	Animal Organic	
Contractility	Animal Organic	Sensible Insensible

(p. 130)

What becomes immediately evident is the classificational tendency in Bichat's definition of vital properties. Essentially, sensibility is passive, receptive. Its faculties have to do more or less with what we "feel." Contractility, meanwhile, is active. Collectively, its motions embody our response to what we feel. The further subdivision into animal and organic plays a similar role. Animal life "nous met en rapport avec les corps extérieurs" [places us in relation to exterior bodies], while organic life "sert à la composition et à la décomposition habituelles de nos parties" [serves in the habitual composition and decomposition of our parts] (*Anatomie générale* I: cij). So once again we have, on a different level, the distinction between voluntary and involuntary. Obviously it would be easy for Bichat to continue to apply distinctions of this kind to his schema. At some point, he might accordingly hope to have achieved a detailed enumeration of all vital properties, which would at the same time be exhaustive. Yet even if exhaustive, a detailed, complete enumeration of vital properties would still fail to yield a full knowledge of the essential nature of vitality. As Bichat himself points out, vital properties like sensibility or contractility "rise, fall, and are altered." In that respect, we might say they're ultimately defined by their activity. A classificational scheme, however, can't really explain activity. Instead, its viewpoint is purely descriptive. It allows us, in other words, to specify various forms of sensibility, by which we register external impressions, or contractility, by which we act. What it can't do is to explain precisely how either perception or voluntary motion takes place. Hence the need for a study of function. If the essence of life is activity, any attempt to understand its basic nature has to involve an analysis of vital functions.

It's here that the study of tissues becomes crucial for Bichat. If specification of vital properties turns out to depend on an analysis of vital functions, the real question then is how each function gets performed. But a function almost always implies coordinated activity by different individual elements. So the question becomes: what are the elements by which the vital functions get performed? With his description of tissues, Bichat offers an answer to this question:

> Tous les animaux sont un assemblage de divers organes qui, éxecutant chacun une fonction, concourent, chacun à sa manière, à la conservation du tout. Ce sont autant de machines particulières dans la machine générale qui constitue l'individu. Or ces machines particulières sont elles-mêmes formées par plusieurs tissus de nature très-differente, et qui forment véritablement les élémens de ces organes. La chimie a ses corps simples, qui forment, par les combinaisons diverses dont ils sont susceptibles, les corps composés: tels sont le calorique, la lumière, l'hydrogène,

l'oxigène, le carbone, l'azote, le phosphore, etc. De même l'anatomie a ses tissus simples, qui, par leurs combinaisons quatre à quatre, six à six, huit à huit, etc., forment les organes. [Bichat then enumerates what he considers the twenty-one basic types of tissue.]

Voilà les véritables élémens organisés de nos parties. Quelles que soient celles où ils se rencontrent, leur nature est constamment la même, comme en chimie les corps simples ne varient point, quels que soient les composés qu'ils concourent à former.

[All animals are an assemblage of divers organs that, each executing a function, concur, each in its own way, in the conservation of the whole. These are so many particular machines in the general machine that constitutes the individual. Thus these particular machines are themselves formed by many tissues of a very diverse nature, which actually form the elements of these organs. Chemistry has its simple bodies, which by the diverse combinations of which they're susceptible form composite bodies: such are caloric, light, hydrogen, oxygen, carbon, azote, phosphorus, etc. Similarly, anatomy has its simple tissues, which by their combinations of four by four, six by six, eight by eight, etc., form the organs. . . .

Here, then, are the true organized elements of our parts. Regardless of where they're found, their nature is constantly the same, just as in chemistry the simple bodies don't vary at all, regardless of the composite bodies they concur to form.]
(*Anatomie générale* I: lxxix–lxxx)

For Bichat to arrive at tissues as the basic vital elements by means of the machine concept points to an emphasis on function in his perspective. He begins with every animal as an assemblage of organs, each responsible for a particular function. Now because it's composed of different organs, each in itself functional, the body must by definition be a machine, or a functional totality. In addition, though, each organ has its own function. Hence it, too, must presumably consist of parts that contribute individually to the performance of its function. So it, too, becomes a machine, by definition. As a result Bichat can say: "These are so many particular machines in the general machine that constitutes the individual." But if responsible for a function, each organ must in turn consist of elements by which that function is performed. Thus we arrive at tissues as the basic vital elements from a functionalist perspective.

This functionalist perspective can help to explain why Bichat doesn't see the need to pursue his quest for the basic vital elements any further (and specifically why he refused to employ the microscope, already available in his time). His use of the machine concept showed his perception of tissues as the basic vital elements was determined by function rather than purely empirical inquiry. He knows, in other words, that the body is a functional totality because its existence as a vital entity is based on its capacity to perform various functions, each necessary to survival. Moreover, he knows every necessary vital function is performed by a particular organ. Accordingly, he can infer each organ must itself consist of different elements that collectively perform a function. Beyond that, however, he has no reason to assume the different elements are themselves each associated with individual functions. Hence he has no reason to suppose the breakdown into functional elements need go any further. On the contrary: at some point, the cohesion of matter as organic substance is even likely to disappear (so that, on a truly microscopic level, we no longer have any distinction between organic and inorganic substances). At the level of tissue, then, organic substance still has some relation to function. Beyond that, the link to function can no longer be assured.

Finally, the appeal to chemistry points to Bichat's functionalist perspective in yet another way. In chemistry, our interest is in how substances combine with each other. As Bichat himself observes, "chemistry has its simple bodies, which by the diverse combinations of which they're susceptible form composite bodies." By comparison, we feel less concerned about what they themselves consist of. Bichat adopts a similar stance toward tissues: "regardless of where they're found, their nature is consistently the same, just as in chemistry the simple bodies don't vary at all, regardless of the composite bodies they concur to form." But if the nature or composition of tissues is invariably the same, a detailed compositional examination of these can hardly seem very meaningful. Instead, our interest will presumably be in their function. Which is to say: on how they interact with each other.

One crucial effect of a functionalist perspective is to revise our holistic notion of vitality for a more complex picture, one based on the interaction between different vital properties. Up to this point, the life sciences had simply credited each organ with its own life. But if we see every organ as a machine composed of different tissues, each involved in the function performed by that organ, the picture of its vitality alters somewhat:

> On a beaucoup parlé, depuis Bordeu, de la vie propre de chaque organe, laquelle
> n'est autre chose que le caractère particulier qui distingue l'ensemble des pro-
> priétés vitales d'un organe, de l'ensemble des propriétés vitales d'un autre. Avant
> que ces propriétés eussent été analysées avec rigueur et précision, il étoit visible-
> ment impossible de se former une idée rigoureuse de cette vie propre. Or, d'après

l'idée que je viens d'en donner, il est évident que la plupart des organes étant composés de tissus simples très-différens, l'idée de la vie propre ne peut s'appliquer qu'à ces tissus simples, et non aux organes eux-mêmes.

[There has been much talk, since Bordeu, of the proper life of each organ, which is nothing else than the particular character that distinguishes the ensemble of vital properties of one organ from the ensemble of vital properties of another. Before these properties had been analyzed with rigor and precision, it was visibly impossible to form a rigorous idea of this proper life. Now, according to the idea I've just proposed, it is evident that, the majority of organs being composed of widely different simple tissues, the idea of a proper life can only apply to these simple tissues, and not to the organs themselves.] (*Anatomie générale* I: lxxxiij–lxxxiv)

Although it might seem that Bichat merely shifts the concept of a proper life to a more elementary level, the actual result of his emphasis on tissue is somewhat different. While each organ can be equated with a particular function, the same can't be said for the tissues concerned. For these contribute to perform a vital function only collectively. Consequently, we can't quite talk about the proper life of a tissue in the same way. If the notion of vitality involves the performance of a function, a given tissue, taken by itself, remains incomplete. Yes, it's alive, and yes, it forms the most basic level of life in Bichat's scheme. Nonetheless, it doesn't have its own life in the same way as an organ, simply because it must depend on other tissues to help it perform a vital function. So the emphasis on tissues comes back in the end to an emphasis on function.[5]

Since the discussion of tissue has so far been almost wholly analytical, it's important for Bichat to have some concrete evidence for his claim that tissues constitute the basic vital elements. Subsequently, he appeals to data obtained from pathology:

Puisque les maladies ne sont que des altérations des propriétés vitales, et que chaque tissu est différent des autres sous le rapport de ces propriétés, il est évident qu'il doit en différer aussi par ses maladies. Donc dans tout organe composé de différens tissus, l'un peut être malade, les autres restant intacts: or c'est ce qui arrive dans le plus grand nombre de cas.

[Since diseases are only alterations of vital properties, and since each tissue is different from others with regard to these properties, it's evident that it [the tissue] must also differ in terms of its diseases. Thus in every organ composed of different tissues one can be diseased while the others remain intact: and this is what happens in the majority of instances.] (*Anatomie générale* I: lxxxv)

Here the crucial point is that in a given organ one tissue can be diseased while the rest remain unaffected. Since disease is simply an alteration of vital properties, Bichat can argue for its attachment to one tissue exclusively as significant. Were vitality the same in every tissue, we would have no way to explain why only one tissue was affected. From this, Bichat infers vitality must be different for each tissue. In other words, vitality is tissue-specific. Thus pathology offers support for tissues as the basic vital elements.[6]

Given the close link between tissues and vital properties, it's odd for Bichat not to try to relate vitality to tissue substance directly. Instead, in a section of the *Anatomie* entitled "Des propriétés indépendantes de la vie" [On properties independent of life] he points out that

Ces propriétés sont celles que j'appelle de tissu. Etrangères aux corps inertes, inherentes aux organes des corps vivans, elles dépendent de leur texture, de l'arrangement de leurs molécules, mais non de la vie qui les anime. Aussi la mort ne les détruit-elle pas. Elles restent aux organes quand la vie leur manque; cependent celle-ci accroît beaucoup leur énergie. La putréfaction seule et la décomposition des organes les anéantissent.

[These properties I term those of the tissue. Foreign to inert bodies, inherent in the organs of living bodies, they [tissue properties] depend on the texture, on the arrangement of molecules of those tissues, but not on the life that animates them. Moreover, death doesn't destroy these tissue properties. They remain in organs that no longer have life; however, life greatly enhances their energy. Only putrefaction and the decomposition of organs annihilate these properties.] (*Anatomie générale* I: lxxij)

Because of the peculiar nature of tissue properties, the link between tissues and vitality becomes somewhat complicated. We've already seen how close tissues and vital properties are. Still, this isn't the whole story. Insofar as they depend on its texture and molecular arrangement, the properties of a tissue must be more or less inseparable from its very nature. And since these properties survive death (a point Bichat makes in the *Recherches physiologiques* as well), they obviously can't be identical to the vital properties of a tissue. Thus, to the extent that tissue properties represent what's essential to a tissue, they show that its nature and vital properties can't really be equivalent. Consequently, Bichat can't quite get at the nature of vitality simply by a specification of tissue properties. As a result, he has to go beyond tissue substance in his effort to define vitality. His emphasis on tissue had come about from a desire to isolate the material basis of life. But the failure of tissue substance to answer all the pertinent questions suggests a need to look elsewhere.

In particular, his failure to resolve matters merely by an analysis of tissue substance might well have prompted Bichat to examine the nature of vital activity more closely. The failure of tissue analysis in this respect points to a crucial fact about vitality: it doesn't exist in particular substances simply by virtue of what they are. Instead, vitality would seem to be somewhat independent of substances, even if based on specific functions they fulfill. Its complex relationship to these implies that in order to define vitality properly, Bichat needs to explore its relation to substances in general. And above all, to know how vitality acts on substances. By an analysis of the process involved, he might then hope to arrive at some insight into the nature of vitality itself. Perhaps one of the best means we have to study the process by which vitality acts on substances can be found in nutrition. On that, Bichat observes:

> La nutrition faisant passer sans cesse les molécules de matière, des corps bruts aux corps vivans, et réciproquement, on peut évidemment concevoir la matière comme constamment pénétrée, dans l'immense série des siècles, des propriétés physiques. Ces propriétés s'en emparèrent à la création, si je puis m'exprimer ainsi; elles ne la quitteront que quand le monde cessera d'exister. Eh bien, en passant de temps à autre par les corps vivans, pendant l'espace qui sépare ces deux époques, espace que l'immensité mesure, en passant, dis-je, par les corps vivans, la matière s'y pénètre, par intervalles, des propriétés vitales qui se trouvent alors unies aux propriétés physiques. Voilà donc une grande différence dans la matière, par rapport à ces deux espèces de propriétés: elle ne jouit des unes que par intermittence; elle possède les autres d'une manière continue.

> [With nutrition making molecules of matter pass ceaselessly from undeveloped bodies to living bodies and vice versa, one can evidently conceive of matter as constantly penetrated, in the immense span of centuries, by physical properties. These properties took hold of it from the creation, if I may so express myself; nor will they quit it until the world no longer exists. Well, in passing from time to time through living bodies, during the interval that separates these two epochs, an interval measured by immensity, in passing, I say, through living bodies, matter is penetrated at intervals by vital properties that accordingly find themselves united to physical properties. Here then is a big difference in matter, with respect to these two types of properties: it enjoys the one only intermittently; it possesses the other in a continuous manner.] (*Anatomie générale* I: lvij)

Note, first of all, the mode by which vitality acts on substances. Bichat says that in the course of its existence, matter is "penetrated" at intervals by vital properties. The fact that it happens only intermittently is highly significant. It suggests the properties described are by no means intrinsic to matter by virtue of its nature as a substance. The same must be true even for organic substances: if vital properties pertained to these intrinsically, there would be no way for inert matter to become vital. Obviously matter can't alter its basic nature. So when matter is "penetrated" by vital properties, we have to imagine an external agency. But if vital properties can act on matter only externally, they presumably need to overcome some sort of inertial resistance within matter itself. To do that, however, demands active exertion by vitality.

Equally important to the question of how vitality acts on substances is its relationship to the purely physical. Since matter is "penetrated" by vital properties as well as physical properties, we have to assume vital properties act on substances in the same way as do the purely physical. In addition, Bichat even says vital properties that penetrate matter "find themselves united to physical properties." His inference would seem to be that since physical properties "took hold of [matter] from the creation," any vital properties that now try to do the same must deal with a ground already fully occupied. And since purely physical matter displays no tendency to instability, we have to suppose it has no real need for more properties. In other words, it's completely defined by its physical properties. So when penetrated by additional properties, vital and physical will inevitably interact.

To some extent, this interaction between vital and physical can help to explain why vitality acts on substances only intermittently. Here the earlier penetration of matter by physical properties is relevant. Even if we allow for some inertial resistance by matter to physical properties, the extent is likely to be minimal (after all, resistance itself is a sort of quality, and matter before its penetration by physical properties has no qualities). By contrast, to endow matter with vitality, a considerable amount of energy might well be required to overcome its disposition to remain purely physical. But the need for a constant expenditure of energy to sustain the predominance of vital over physical properties is ultimately bound to exhaust the vital forces. Hence the merely "intermittent" penetration of matter by vital properties.

Subsequently, Bichat attempts to ascertain how vitality manages to overcome the disposition of matter to remain purely physical. In particular, he looks at the role blood plays in the transmission of vitality to physical substances:

Le sang jouit, pour ainsi dire, des rudimens de la sensibilité organique. Suivant que la vie dont il jouit le met plus ou moins en rapport avec les fluides qui y pénètrent, il est plus ou moins disposé à se combiner avec eux, et à les pénétrer de cette vie qui l'anime. Quelquefois il repousse, pour ainsi dire, long-temps les substances qui lui sont hétérogènes. Je suis persuadé qu'un grand nombre de phénomènes que nous éprouvons après le repas, apres ceux surtout où des alimens âcres, des boissons spiritueuses, ont été pris en abondance, dérivent en partie du trouble général qu'éprouve le sang quand sa vitalité commence à se communiquer à ces substances étrangères, de l'espèce de lutte qui s'établit, pour ainsi dire, dans les vaisseaux, entre le fluide vivant et celui qui ne vit pas. Ainsi voyons-nous tous les solides se crisper, se soulever pour ainsi dire contre un excitant qui est nouveau pour eux. Qui ne sait si la vitalité des fluides n'influe pas sur leurs mouvemens? Je le crois très-probable. Je doute que les fluides purement inertes pussent, s'ils se trouvoient seuls dans des vaisseaux animés par la vie, y circuler comme des fluides vivans. De même les fluides animés par la vie ne pourroient point se mouvoir d'eux-mêmes dans des vaisseaux qui en seroient privés. La vie est donc également nécessaire dans les uns et les autres.

[Blood enjoys, so to speak, the rudiments of organic sensibility. According to whether the life it enjoys places it more or less in rapport with the fluids that penetrate it, it's more or less disposed to combine itself with them, and to penetrate them with the life that animates it. Sometimes it repels, so to speak, for a long time the substances heterogeneous to it. I'm persuaded that a greater number of the phenomena we experience after a meal, especially those where piquant food or alcoholic drinks are consumed in abundance, derive in part from the general disturbance blood experiences when its vitality begins to communicate itself to these foreign substances, from the sort of struggle that establishes itself, so to speak, in the vessels, between the vital fluid and the non-vital. Thus we see solids contract, rise up so to speak against an excitant that's new for them. Who knows whether the vitality of fluids doesn't influence their movements? I believe it very likely. I doubt that purely inert fluids can, if they find themselves in vessels animated by life, circulate there like vital fluids. Similarly, fluids animated by life can't move by themselves at all in vessels deprived of it. Life is hence equally necessary in the one and the other.] (*Anatomie générale* I: lxxj–lxxij)

In the process by which vitality attempts to overcome the disposition of matter to remain purely physical, the first phase is one of intermixture. By its very nature, blood is especially well suited to its role: as a liquid, it simply can't avoid mixture with non-vital fluid substances. At first glance, the passage seems to say their mixture will depend on the extent to which it's "disposed." And that, in turn, will depend on its "rapport" with those substances. Looked at more closely, however, we find it's already mixed with these: "in rapport with the fluids that penetrate it." Just as matter is "penetrated" by physical or vital properties, blood is already penetrated by non-vital fluid substances. In other words, it has no choice. Except in one respect: it can decide whether "to penetrate them with the life that animates it." So we have a give-and-take here: blood is penetrated by non-vital fluid substances, but can penetrate them in return with its own life. And what makes the whole process possible is the fluid nature of all the substances involved.

The second phase of the interaction between vital and non-vital involves repulsion. Specifically, blood repels "the substances heterogeneous to it." In fact, however, the process is more complicated. Note, first of all, the apparently involuntary motion by which the vitality of blood gets conveyed: "when its vitality begins to communicate itself to these foreign substances . . . ." While earlier in the passage Bichat seems to maintain that whether blood will "penetrate [non-vital substances] with the life that animates it" would depend on how it's "disposed," the text now gives a distinctly different inflection. Second, note the effect on blood itself of its own communication of vitality: "the general disturbance blood experiences . . . ." So the reaction, too, is more or less involuntary. Finally, note the way Bichat portrays the interaction between vital and non-vital: "the sort of struggle that establishes itself, so to speak, in the vessels, between the vital fluid and the non-vital." As if that struggle had somehow achieved a kind of autonomy and, at the same time, a sort of necessity.

The final phase in the interaction between vital and non-vital is one of assimilation. Simply put, precisely because blood can't repel non-vital substances indefinitely, it has to animate them with its own vitality. Hence the hint of the involuntary or unavoidable in the movement by which blood communicates its vitality to non-vital substances. By its very nature as a fluid, by its location in the body, blood simply can't avoid mixture with non-vital substances. For that reason, it has to engage with them in a perpetual struggle. We've seen that vitality has no relation to matter intrinsically. Even within vital substances like blood, then, it can sustain its hold only by constant exertion. So its intermixture with non-vital substances forces it to even greater exertion. Since vital and non-vital compete for possession of the same material substance, any introduction of the non-vital into a substance animated by vitality introduces a new danger: the threat of dispossession. Invariably, then, introduction of the non-vital is bound to provoke opposition of some kind. But for vitality, opposition alone isn't sufficient.

Because of the constant pressure exerted by the non-vital, vitality must either overcome it or, even better, assimilate it into itself. In terms of its own vital economy, it can't afford to engage in a constant struggle with the non-vital, whose tendency to penetrate and hence possess material substances is potentially inexhaustible. In order for vitality to sustain itself, it must find some way to renew its own vital energy. Hence the logic of assimilation: by the absorption of new substances, it hopes to expand and thereby increase (rather than just maintain) its vital resources.

At this juncture, it seems useful to return to our point of departure: the house of life. For it was, after all, his observation of the struggle for life at the Hôtel-Dieu that probably led Bichat on to his quest to define the nature of vitality. And because the development of a thought often returns it to its source, perhaps it isn't accidental that the most innovative aspect of his work in terms of theory should center on its treatment of the struggle between vital and non-vital forces. Anyone who has studied the history of French medicine knows the famous dictum about life from the *Recherches:* "la vie est l'ensemble des fonctions qui résistent à la mort" [life is the ensemble of functions that resist death] (*Recherches physiologiques*, p. 1). Less well known is the discussion of digestion from the *Anatomie générale* that we've just seen, in which Bichat explores in detail the struggle between vital and non-vital that takes place whenever we assimilate food. Yet it's here that what he says is of most interest. Specifically, Bichat recognizes that in the course of digestion the non-vital (i.e., inert solid or liquid) *becomes* vital, through the action of vital fluid (i.e., blood) upon it. This transformation of non-vital into vital leads to a number of significant consequences for theory.

To begin with, it radically destabilizes the very concept of vitality, by blurring the boundaries between vital and non-vital. Typically, vital properties tend to be associated with a particular substance. Various forms of vital tissue, for example, exhibit traits we identify as characteristic of life. Consequently it seems unclear how we should deal with non-vital matter that gets transformed into a vital substance of some kind. At what point does it become genuinely vital? Can we distinctly separate its non-vital from its vital phase? If the transformation is a gradual one, any attempt to specify the exact moment at which the non-vital becomes vital is bound to seem artificial. In the case of a non-vital fluid, for instance, we need only visualize its intermixture with our blood: each, as Bichat puts it, would penetrate the other, so as to make it almost immediately impossible to distinguish vital from non-vital. Instead, the liquid mixture would simply seethe in a sort of ferment as the blood attempted to infuse the inert fluid with its own life. Nor does Bichat make any attempt to discern the exact moment at which the non-vital fluid is chemically altered into a vital one. And similarly with a non-vital solid: surrounded by and immersed in blood, it contracts, as if in response to an excitant. But if capable of such a reaction, hasn't the solid already become in effect a vital substance? In all these instances, then, our inability to specify the status of a particular substance at a given moment points to a latent instability in our concepts of the vital and non-vital.

A second consequence of the transformation of non-vital into vital is to shift the primacy away from concepts, toward the activity by which substances become either vital or non-vital. And here, I believe, is where Bichat thinks the emphasis ought to be. In order to preserve its own vitality, the vital must convert or assimilate the non-vital into itself. If it fails, it will eventually succumb to non-vital inertia. So the activity by which blood transforms a non-vital fluid or solid into a vital substance is ineluctably necessary. Carefully considered, it might even be the essential condition of life. Because of the constant attrition caused by its interaction with the non-vital, the vital element must renew its own resources. Yet in that very process of renewal, it must engage and transform the non-vital into the vital. Hence the *lutte,* or struggle, Bichat speaks of. We observe its various stages or moments: the initial contact between vital and non-vital, the resistance of inert solids or fluids as the vital element begins to break them down, the moment of crisis at which the resistance of inert substances forces the digestive system to intensify its own activity, the consequent internal strain, and finally the pivotal moment when resistance is at last overcome. In the process, as we've seen, the definability of vital and non-vital as concepts breaks down as well. What remains is the transformative activity of life itself. This, then, is what Bichat must somehow manage to describe. But to describe an activity whose very nature is to be constantly transformative would unquestionably lead to nothing less than a brave new world for theory.

To talk about development, Bichat felt, could only imply a completely different notion of theory. Simply put, theory could no longer be representative. Here we see the paradigm shift away from Bichat's eighteenth-century predecessors. Their effort had all been for some concept to represent vitality. Yet that was precisely what Bichat's hospital experiences had called into question. For nearly a century, the surgical perspective Bichat had absorbed from his mentor Desault at the Hôtel-Dieu had taught that a vital principle of this sort was impossible and, in fact, unnecessary. On a more general level, moreover, surgery was anti-theory. Nonetheless, its anti-theory stance didn't reflect a conservative tendency. On the contrary: to be anti-theory was perhaps, in context, the most radical move possible. What it did was to question the possibility of theory (which is to say: representability) from a standpoint that was itself fully informed by theory.

Once Bichat realized vitality was all about physiological process or development, he knew theory would have to change its posture radically. His study of vital processes like digestion had shown him that traditional theory couldn't adequately represent what was essential to these processes. Here a non-vital element or material *becomes* vital. And that meant you couldn't identify vitality with any particular organ or tissue. It also meant you couldn't really characterize vitality as a vital force or principle, because the static quality of such a principle didn't explain how non-vital material could *become* vital. So you had to find some other way to describe the process or transition from non-vital to vital. If static concepts like vital force or principle didn't work, theory would have to shift its focus to vital activity. So vital theory, for Bichat, has to be about activity. Hence his move from vitality to vital functions to tissues to physiological process. What Bichat came to realize was that the quest for a way to represent vitality would have to find a more fluid conceptual repertory. How exactly it would do that was a problem he never quite managed, in his brief lifetime, to solve. But he had, at least, arrived at an awareness of it.

His awareness of the problem that vitality posed for theory also places Bichat on the threshold of a new era for the sciences. If theory can't represent what it wants to describe, its only hope is to immerse itself completely in pure materiality so as to reproduce what it experiences, at a later point, on the level of theory. For that, however, it would first need to throw out all its theoretical constructs, surrender itself wholly to the sheer materiality, the purely physiological quality of the vital process. Which is to say: observe the entire process, study the transition from each moment or phase to the next down to the minutest detail. So we find Bichat in his last year, dissecting one cadaver after another, always in the hope that he might get a bit closer to the elusive source or sources of vitality. This, then, was what the brave new world of theory looked like: you immerse yourself completely in materiality, you give up any hope of trying to render process directly into theory. And as you do that, you become aware of how much you can afford to concede to materiality, of the easy give-and-take that exists between theory and materiality. You realize, on some level, how objectivity is really permeated by theory, once theory surrenders itself to process, so that the final result of an immersion in materiality would be a return to theory. What we then get, as Bichat realized, would be a new kind of theory: not the sort that simply says what vitality is, but one based on a constant back-and-forth between observation and theory, experiment and theory.[7] That, of course, would itself necessitate a process of some kind. So theory ultimately becomes, for Bichat, a process by which we gradually work out a new form of objectivity. And in that process, he felt, lay the future of the sciences.

Because of his minimalist posture, Bichat is for Romantic theory in the sciences less a climax than a point of departure. In effect, he marks for the Romantic sciences the dawn of a new theoretical awareness. He comes, you might say, at that magical moment when all the old, static concepts no longer seem adequate to describe what we want to talk about, when the essential no longer looks either stable or solid, when all that's solid melts into air. Precisely because he appears on the medical scene at a time when the role of experiment hadn't yet been fully worked out, however, Bichat lacks the sort of reflexivity in theory that would characterize his successors. Out of the fruitful tension between observation and experiment, they would forge a fuller, more developed vital theory. But if the relative newness of medical experiments hindered Bichat from a greater reflexivity in theory, we might look to a different field, where the existence of a longer experimental tradition could help to foster a more developed theoretical awareness.

CHAPTER FIVE

Beyond Radical Empiricism

From 1801 to 1812, the lecture theater of the Royal Institution figured as one of the most fashionable meeting places for London society. In our effort to reconstruct the scene, it's only natural to begin with the room itself. Here, then, you would have steeply banked rows of seats arranged in a semicircle so as to converge on an open space. Above, a gallery supported by posts over the ground floor. At night, lamps attached to these posts would help to light the scene. In the middle of the open space where all eyes converged, a large table with a portion of its rear hollowed out held all the lecturer's equipment. Behind the lecturer, a decorative pediment. And, on either side of that pediment, doors that opened into another room, one whose shelves and apparatus clearly marked it as a laboratory.

Next, we have a description of what the lecturer's equipment would typically consist of: "a sand bath ["a vessel of heated sand used as an equable heater for retorts, etc. in various chemical processes," *OED*], for chemical purposes, and for heating the room; a powerful blast furnace; a moveable iron forge, with a double bellows; a blow-pipe apparatus, attached to a table, with double bellows underneath; a large mercurial trough, and two or three water pneumatic troughs, and various galvanic troughs; not to mention gasometers, filtering stands, and the common necessaries of a laboratory" (Davy, *CW* I, p. 94).

Then we have the lecturer.[1] A contemporary journal offered this impression: "Mr. Davy, who appears to be very young, acquitted himself admirably well. From the sparkling intelligence of his eye, his animated manner, and the *tout ensemble*, we have no doubt of his attaining distinguished excellence" (Davy, *CW* I, p. 88; variant in Paris I, p. 141). His brother John Davy, in the *Memoirs*, gives his appearance in detail: his eyes a light hazel color, "wonderfully bright, and seemed almost to emit a soft light when animated," his voice equally memorable, with a richness of tone that he modulated expressively (*CW* I, pp. 441–44). Another early biographer, John Paris, observes: "So rapid were all his movements, that, while a spectator imagined he was merely making preparations for an experiment, he was actually obtaining the results, which were just as accurate as if a much longer time had been expended" (Paris I, pp. 144–45).

We also know the amount of care bestowed on these lectures—as if they were theatrical performances, with each lecture fully written out, especially the sections designed for rhetorical effect. And how carefully they were rehearsed: "It was almost an invariable rule with him, the evening before, to rehearse his lecture in the presence of his assistants, the preparations having been made and everything in readiness for the experiments; and this he did, not only with a view to the success of the experiments, and the dexterity of his assistants, but also in regard to his own discourse, the effect of which, he knew, depended upon the manner in which it was delivered. He used, I remember, at this recital, to mark the words which required emphasis, and study the effect of intonation; often repeating a passage two or three different times, to witness the difference of effect of variations in the voice" (*CW* I, p. 92).

Finally, the audience. On April 25, 1801, Humphry Davy gave his inaugural address on chemistry to a packed house. Over time, his audience would gradually increase, until it numbered, in his last years, nearly a thousand people. A survey of the crowd would have shown the *beau monde* of London: the duchess of Gordon and all the other prominent ladies of fashion, plus numerous other members of the aristocracy. But the crowd would also have included many of the best and the brightest: Coleridge, Sir Joseph Banks (longtime president of the Royal Society), the notorious Count Rumford, and other founders of the Royal Institution. And a number of people simply curious or eager to learn, like Samuel Purkis (a practical tanner). We also know from various sources about the sort of adulation lavished on Davy: of the literary lady who addressed him anonymously in a verse panegyric, accompanied by a splendid watch ornament that she asked him to wear at his next lecture, of the "general and repeated applause" after each performance, and the constant invitations to the soirees of the high and mighty, who considered his presence indispensable.

To some extent, the interest Davy aroused was due partly to unusual circumstances. Once Napoleon's blockade had closed off continental Europe, the upper class found itself nearly desperate for new sources of entertainment. The intense excitement produced by the French Revolution had been followed by a period of despondency. While reaction to the Revolution itself was mixed, opinion about the Directory and, subsequently, Napoleon, was almost unequivocal. Virtually a decade and a half of war was interrupted only by the brief, uneasy Peace of

Amiens (1802). Grain shortages and the loss of foreign markets brought the national economy dangerously close to collapse. Uncertain finances led in turn to social unrest. Besides the prolonged anxiety fostered by political and economic instability, Napoleon's so-called Continental System or blockade spelled the cultural isolation of England. From now on, it would have to turn inward, to its own resources.[2]

Behind any interest felt by the audience, moreover, lay the pressure exerted by the ideology of the Royal Institution itself.[3] Only recently founded, it represented a joint effort by the aristocracy and some distinguished names from the sciences. Its joint sponsorship reflected a specific programme, based on a belief that science should apply itself to the problems of everyday life. In particular, the Royal Institution wanted to employ the fruits of research to improve conditions for the lower classes. Backed by money from wealthy landowners, it hoped in this way to stave off social unrest. Specifically, it looked to the possibility of a breakthrough in agricultural chemistry or some of the other practical sciences for massive social improvement. In that respect, its emphasis was distinctly empirical.

From the kind of research programme sponsored by the Royal Institution, we can get some sense of how radically the status of chemistry had changed since the eighteenth century.[4] Although work by Cavendish, Priestley, and Lavoisier had elevated Enlightenment chemistry to a new level, the amount of knowledge required to understand current research hadn't yet passed beyond the scope of those outside the field. In part this was because the laboratory equipment used remained relatively simple. Likewise, the experiments performed were the kind of stuff any person of leisure could easily do at home. Henry Cavendish, in particular, had made his fame on experimentation for which the necessary equipment was both small and minimal: in some instances, just a heat source and a bit of glassware.

By contrast, the kind of research work sponsored by the Royal Institution was different. From the list supplied by Davy's brother, we can already form some idea of how it differed: pieces like the "powerful blast furnace" or the "moveable iron forge" or gasometers or filtration devices were hardly available to just anybody. Perhaps the most remarkable, though, was the 2,000-plate battery employed by Davy for his work on electrochemistry. Here was a massive, new kind of apparatus, constructed at a cost that could only be borne by an institution. From equipment of this kind, the Royal Institution expected research results of a different order from what you might obtain from merely private sources. In other words, the new, institutionally funded science ought to yield knowledge that would revolutionize the sciences and lead to a significant payoff on the practical level.

Given this sort of pressure, it seems fairly clear that the only way for Davy to pursue a pure research programme would have to entail experimental results powerful enough to redefine the entire field. As he saw it, the way to do this would have to involve the discovery of new elements, or an isolation of the most basic chemical substances. Nonetheless, the simple discovery of new elements wouldn't suffice by itself to redefine chemistry as a field. Instead, as Davy realized, the importance of any such discovery would become apparent only if it were able to produce a transformative effect on theory. In other words, the discovery of new elements would have to lead to a new and radically different theory of matter. But for that to happen, something more than experimentation would be required. Specifically, he would need a rationale to revise chemical theory, one derived from theory itself.

One of the easiest ways to get there would be to revisit the question of phlogiston. The most intensely debated issue in eighteenth-century chemistry, it had become a focal point in the conflict between different approaches. Hence its usefulness as an index of the dominant trend. Supported by some of the most celebrated chemists at the time (Priestley and Cavendish, among others), the phlogiston doctrine fixes a pivotal moment in the history of chemistry. And the early nineteenth-century revival of phlogiston theory shows that the debate couldn't be resolved simply by an appeal to experimental data. Obviously, the issue carried broader theoretical consequences.[5]

Essentially, phlogiston represents an attempt to describe what happens in combustion. When mercury is gently heated in the presence of air, a red powder gradually spreads over its surface. A similar treatment of copper produces a black film on the metal. In both instances, what we have is a calx (pl. calxes or calces), the product of a metal heated in the presence of air (i.e., what we now term an oxide). G. E. Stahl (1660–1734) explained its formation in the following way:

$$\overbrace{\text{calx } + \text{ phlogiston}}^{\text{METAL}} = \text{calx } + \text{ phlogiston}$$

Heating the metal caused the phlogiston to escape, while the calx remained. The problem here was that the calx turned out to be *heavier* than the original metal, despite a supposed loss of phlogiston (for Stahl, the principle of inflammability).

But if phlogiston lent some weight to the metal, the result of its loss from heat seemed contradictory.

The discrepancy led to a slightly modified explanation:

METAL   CALX

$$\overbrace{X \ + \ phlogiston} \ + \ something \ = \ \overbrace{X \ + \ something} \ + \ phlogiston$$

Here the metal gets defined as X + phlogiston (instead of calx + phlogiston), where X and the calx aren't identical. As heat forces phlogiston to escape, the X unites with "something" to form the calx. Unlike Stahl's version, the modified one avoids any discrepancy because the "something" united with X in the calx is heavier than the phlogiston it replaces. Meanwhile, attention shifts from phlogiston to the "something" whose combination with a metal forms the calx. Since the calx is distinctly heavier than the original metal, the "something" that makes it heavier must weigh more than phlogiston.

Another way to get around the problem was to assume phlogiston didn't escape in combustion. Instead, you might argue it remained in the metal, where it would attract gaseous matter from the air. In that way, you could explain why the calx was heavier than the original metal. What you couldn't explain was what the gaseous matter involved in the formation of a calx consisted of. Still, you could at least offer a more complex picture of that formation. In both of these explanations, phlogiston plays a very diminished role. Yes, it still represents inflammation, but otherwise has largely ceased to figure in the chemistry of the reaction. Whether it remains within the metal or escapes no longer matters. At this point, its presence has become purely perfunctory. The suggestion that it might still be in the metal shows its original function has now been lost sight of entirely.

To this general description, the great French chemist Lavoisier contributed two important points. First, he established (ca. 1774) that the "something" in the modified explanation was oxygen. Second, he showed that the weight of the calx was exactly equal to the weight of the original metal plus the oxygen with which it combined. Collectively, his two points demonstrate the untenability of the modified explanation, where, if we substitute oxygen for the unidentified "something," we get

METAL   CALX

$$\overbrace{X \ + \ phlogiston} \ + \ oxygen \ = \ \overbrace{X \ + \ oxygen} \ + \ phlogiston$$

Such a scheme violated his second point: if the combined weight of the original metal plus the oxygen was *exactly* equal to the weight of the resultant calx, any phlogiston would obviously be extra. Lavoisier then proposed to simplify the modified explanation:

CALX

$$\text{metal} + \text{oxygen} = \overbrace{\text{metal} + \text{oxygen}}$$

In effect, his proposal represented a move to eliminate phlogiston.

Nevertheless, you could still save phlogiston by an ad hoc adjustment:

METAL

$$\overbrace{X + \text{phlogiston}} + \text{oxygen} = X + (\text{phlogiston} + \text{oxygen})$$

CALX

$$= X + \overbrace{(\text{phlogiston} + \text{oxygen})}$$

Here phlogiston escapes from the metal to unite with oxygen. Then, phlogiston plus oxygen combine with the X of the original metal to form a calx. Essentially, this was equivalent to what Lavoisier had proposed, *if* we define the original metal as composed of X + phlogiston. It preserved the weight ratio he had established: the combined weights of metal + oxygen are exactly equal to that of the calx. The complication, of course, was that you had to posit a two-phase process. Still, phlogiston + oxygen on the right-hand side of the equation could have explanatory value under other circumstances. Cavendish's discovery of water = hydrogen + oxygen in 1781 meant that if you identified phlogiston with hydrogen, the presence of water or moisture in various chemical reactions could be readily explained.

From here we can go to Davy, and, specifically, his *Elements of Chemical Philosophy*:

> It has been mentioned that almost all cases of vivid chemical action are connected with the increase of temperature of the acting bodies, and a greater radiation of heat from them; and in a number of instances, light is also produced. . . . The strength of the attraction of the acting bodies determines the rapidity of combination, and in proportion as this is greater, so likewise is there more intensity of heat and light. In the phlogistic doctrine of chemistry, all changes in which heat and light are manifested, were explained by supposing that the acting bodies contained the principle of inflammability; in the anti-phlogistic doctrine, most of them have been accounted for by imagining the position or transfer of oxygen: but all the later researches seem to shew that no *peculiar* substance, or form of matter is necessary for the effect; that it is a *general* result of the actions of any substances

possessed of strong chemical attractions, or different electrical relations, and that it takes place in all cases in which an intense and violent motion can be conceived to be communicated to the corpuscles of bodies. (*CW* IV, pp. 165–66)

If what Davy says in this passage about phlogiston is of interest in itself, it becomes yet more so if we look at it for what it tells us about his entire theoretical perspective. To be sure, his discussion is ostensibly about phlogiston. But his arguments against it have finally less to do with phlogiston than with chemistry in general. In other words, he saw that the phlogiston issue wasn't really just about how you might want to explain a particular kind of chemical reaction. Instead, he realized that what was at stake, ultimately, was the whole way you did chemistry: what counted from your standpoint as explanation, and how you arrived at it. In that respect, I would argue, his remarks point to a meta-theory rather than simply a chemical theory. Looked at closely, they reveal an awareness of what lies behind the theoretical choices we make. At the same time, they also convey a sense of what Davy considered the essential theoretical requirements. For him, the paramount criteria for any theory appear to be:

(a)   theoretical economy
(b)   universal explanation
(c)   creation of objectivity

To see how Davy arrives at these criteria, we need to look at what he says about the history of phlogiston theory elsewhere in *Elements of Chemical Philosophy* (*CW* IV, pp. 28–29). In 1774, Bayen had shown that mercury converted into a calx or oxide by the absorption of air could be restored to its initial state "without the addition of any inflammable substance." His discovery flatly contradicted what phlogiston theory believed ought to happen: if mercury gave off phlogiston (i.e., an inflammable substance) when it became a calx or oxide, it presumably would need to get it back in order to return to its initial state. The fact that this didn't happen allowed Bayen to conclude "that there was no necessity for supposing the existence of any peculiar principle of inflammability." Davy then goes on to discuss Lavoisier, who studied the air given off by the calx of mercury (mercuric oxide), which he found to consist of a gas he named oxygen. But if oxygen were actually given off by the calx of mercury when it reverted to pure mercury, it must have been *acquired* by mercury when it became a calx. So calcination amounts to *gain* (i.e., of oxygen) rather than *loss* (of phlogiston). Davy then sums up all these results with a general remark by Lavoisier himself: "There is no necessity . . . to suppose any phlogiston, any peculiar principle of inflammability: for all the phenomena may be accounted for without this imaginary existence." Subsequently, Davy comments on the methodological principle behind Lavoisier's scheme: "The most important part of the theory of Lavoisier was merely an arrangement of the facts relating to the combinations of oxygen: the principle of reasoning which the French school professed to adopt was, that every body which was not yet decompounded, should be considered as simple; and though mistakes were made with respect to the results of experiments on the nature of bodies, yet this logical and truly philosophical principle was not violated; and the systematic manner in which it was enforced, was of the greatest use in promoting the progress of the science" (*CW* IV, p. 31).

One reason why Davy liked the way Lavoisier treated the phlogiston issue is that it preserves theoretical economy. Obviously, some substances "not yet decompounded" will later prove to consist of more than one element. Yet Davy clearly prefers to define these substances provisionally as simple. Specifically, he speaks of the decision to treat them that way as a "logical and truly philosophical principle." The "philosophical" quality of such a move doesn't necessarily mean it's more accurate in its assessment of individual substances than a theory that sees these as complex. On the contrary: he even admits the French school made "mistakes . . . with respect to the results of experiments on the nature of bodies." What marks the French treatment of undecompounded substances as philosophical, however, is the "systematic manner in which it was enforced." In other words, the payoff for a theory that sees undecompounded substances as simple comes at the level of theory. As long as you stick to the notion that all such substances are simple, you don't have to posit any peculiar substance or principle of inflammability. And that means: no superfluous constructs. It might turn out that you're ultimately forced to admit the existence of some additional substance. But at least you can be sure you'll never posit an element or substance that doesn't exist. Significantly, Davy doesn't even want to rely too heavily on oxygen as a principle of inflammability. So while the antiphlogistic theory wants to account for heat and light by the position or transfer of oxygen, he himself clearly prefers to assert that "no *peculiar* substance, or form of matter is necessary for the effect." What we have here, then, is theoretical economy at its most extreme.

Another reason why Davy liked Lavoisier's treatment of the phlogiston issue is because of its tendency toward universal explanation. Lavoisier had focused primarily on chemical reactions that involved oxygen. As Davy points out, "The most important part of the theory of Lavoisier was merely an arrangement of the facts relating to the combinations of oxygen." But while his experimental data were largely about oxygen, Lavoisier didn't restrict his theory to chemical reactions of a particular class or group. Instead, he generalized his conclusion, so as to embrace all chemical substances: "the principle of reasoning which the French school professed to adopt was, that *every body* which was not yet decompounded, should be considered as simple." In this fashion, what we find out about a particular class or group of substances could potentially be made to apply universally. Like Davy, Lavoisier could then say about his discovery of what happened in a particular set of chemical reactions involving heat and light: "it is a *general* result of the actions of any substances possessed of strong chemical attractions." From a specific body of chemical data, in other words, he moved toward universal explanation.

Finally, the particular way Davy chose to describe what Lavoisier professed allows us a glimpse of how theory could lead to the creation of objectivity. As Davy puts it, the French school maintained that "every body which was not yet decompounded, *should be considered* as simple." Not that it necessarily *was* simple: experimental data, in fact, would often prove otherwise. But what Davy ascribes to Lavoisier here is the insight that because of how the sciences are, it can be useful and even necessary to assert a theory for which we don't have decisive evidence, so that we can eventually arrive at some sort of objectivity. Hence the adherence of the French school to its theory of undecompounded substances as simple "was of the greatest use in promoting the progress of the science." Because of its adherence to that theory, it forced experimental inquiry to move in a particular direction. And out of the interplay between experiment and theory emerged what we term objectivity. But it all begins with theory. As Davy observes, chemical reactions that involve heat and light take place "in all cases in which an intense and violent motion *can be conceived* to be communicated to the corpuscles of bodies." If the objectivity at which we finally arrive has its source in what we can conceive, however, it clearly amounts to an objectivity defined by theory.

If we turn now to the research topics Davy himself pursued, we find an excellent example of his drive toward theoretical economy in his effort to isolate new elements by means of a Voltaic apparatus or pile. An arrangement of metal discs (one zinc or tin, the other silver or copper) stacked on top of each other in pairs, with brine-soaked cardboard in between (e.g., zinc-copper/cardboard/zinc-copper/cardboard, and so on), the Voltaic pile could easily be made more powerful by the addition of more discs and cardboard pieces. With metal strips attached at either end and placed in separate bowls of water, the pile induced a shock in anyone who placed his or her hands in both bowls simultaneously. Shortly after Alessandro Volta communicated this discovery to two correspondents in England, two British scientists accidentally decomposed water into oxygen and hydrogen by means of a Voltaic pile. When they attached two platina wires inserted at opposite ends of a stoppered, water-filled glass tube to the two ends of a pile, they found that oxygen and hydrogen streamed away from the wires. This experiment set the stage for what followed. By means of more powerful devices (the ultimate: a battery of 2,000 double plates, constructed for the Royal Institution), Davy managed to break down a variety of substances. His work led to the discovery of new elements: sodium, potassium, calcium, magnesium, barium, and strontium, among others. At the same time, the proliferation of new elements posed a problem Davy hadn't anticipated. Would the list continue to expand indefinitely? And if so, how could one possibly organize anything that extensive?

Hence the need for a simplification of some kind. In his discussion of how an element ought to be defined, Davy observes:

> The term *element* is used as synonymous with *undecompounded* body; but in modern chemistry its application is limited to the results of experiments. The improvements taking place in the methods of examining bodies, are constantly changing the opinions of chemists with respect to their nature, and there is no reason to suppose that any real *indestructible principle* has been yet discovered. Matter may ultimately be found to be the same in essence, differing only in the arrangements of its particles; or two or three *simple* substances may produce all the varieties of compound bodies. The results of our operations must be considered as offering at best approximations only to the true knowledge of things, and should never be exalted as a standard to estimate the resources of nature. (*CW* IV, p. 132)

Here the emphasis on experiment as a means of definition can be read as an attempt to reduce the list of substances that qualify as elements. Earlier, in his treatment of undecompounded substances as simple, Davy had been quite generous in his admission policy: *any* substance not yet decompounded was allowed in. But even though an element is, in principle, equivalent to an undecompounded substance, the standard for admission is now much tighter: only those substances shown to be undecompoundable by experiment can qualify. In fact, however, the emphasis on experiment as a criterion for admission is even tighter than it might appear to be. After all, the result of any given experiment can always be superseded by a subsequent experiment. So even if the result of a given experiment would seem to suggest that some substance can't be broken down, the result of a subsequent experiment could easily prove otherwise. Potentially, then, the emphasis on experiment as a criterion destabilizes the entire list of elements. Obviously, any so-called element that we manage to break down is categorically eliminated from the list. But because any substance not yet decompounded might be broken down by a subsequent experiment, the present list of elements could conceivably always be further reduced.

In his desire for theoretical economy, moreover, Davy even appears inclined to go beyond what might be ascertained within the field of chemistry. As he himself points out, "The improvements taking place in the methods of examining bodies, are constantly changing the opinions of chemists with respect to their nature." Yet the inference he draws from that may come as somewhat of a surprise: "and there is no reason to suppose that any real *indestructible principle* has been yet discovered." Chemistry is all about relationships between different substances. But if we have no reason to speak of any indestructible principle, any notions we might have about relationships between substances would likewise be radically destabilized. Since any substance could presumably be broken down into multiple constituents, we could no longer talk about the elements out of which these substances were composed. And without some sense of what the elements or primary substances were, any attempt to explain combinations or reactions between substances would also cease to be meaningful: simply put, we'd no longer know what was responsible for a given relationship or combination. In this fashion, what Davy says by way of an argument for theoretical economy appears to look beyond the limits of chemistry itself.

The fact that Davy doesn't seem especially concerned about whether matter turns out to be essentially the same or composed of two or three simple substances also points to how theoretical economy is the real issue. Davy merely observes that "matter may ultimately be found to be the same in essence, differing only in the arrangements of its particles; or two or three *simple* substances may produce all the varieties of compound bodies." In fact, the two scenarios would yield very different consequences. If all of matter turns out to be essentially the same, we need to look to physics for an explanation of why a given combination or reaction ultimately occurs. But if all of matter reduces to two or three simple substances rather than just one, emphasis would then fall on precisely how and why they combine. And that would give the primacy, in effect, to chemistry. Yet Davy doesn't seem to care particularly about which scenario turns out to be true. We can explain his indifference, I would argue, if we see theoretical economy as his central concern. From that perspective, it doesn't matter whether matter is uniform or composed of several elemental substances. In either case, theoretical economy is preserved.

For Davy, the corollary to theoretical economy is universal explanation. You restrict the number of theoretical constructs you use precisely because they yield a universal explanation for all phenomena. But a universal explanation necessitates some sort of explanatory model. Toward the end of *Elements,* Davy attempts to offer one:

> There is, however, no impossibility in the supposition that the same ponderable matter in different electrical states, or in different arrangements, may constitute substances chemically different: there are parallel cases in the different states in which bodies are found, connected with their different relations to temperature. Thus steam, ice, and water, are the same ponderable matter; and certain quantities of ice and steam mixed together produce ice-cold water. Even if it should be ultimately found that oxygen and hydrogen are the same matter in different states of electricity, or that two or three elements in different proportions constitute all bodies, the great doctrines of chemistry, the theory of definite proportions, and the specific attractions of bodies must remain immutable; the causes of the differences of form of the bodies supposed to be elementary, if such a step were made, must be ascertained, and the only change in the science would be, that those substances now considered as primary elements must be considered as secondary; but the numbers representing them would be the same, and they would probably be all found to be produced by the additions of multiples of some simple numbers or fractional parts. (*CW* IV, p. 364)

Clearly, the challenge to any attempt at universal explanation is to be able to explain away differences. Specifically, what Davy wants to show is how we might have essential sameness despite apparent differences. In order to demonstrate that, he has to prove that differences aren't absolute, that they don't carry ontological significance, that they don't define what substances are. His example of ice-cold water produced by a mixture of steam and ice allows him to make his point. Normally, we think of steam and ice as representative of different states of matter. The fact that they can mix to form ice-cold water attests to the lack of any rigid or absolute link between what they are and the states of matter they supposedly represent. In addition, the existence of ice-cold water also blurs the definiteness of any given state of matter. The effect of all this is to erode the significance of physical differences. If physical differences don't invariably indicate different states of matter, they needn't militate against sameness on some more essential level. And if physical differences have no effect on chemical identity (water as chemically the same, whether it's liquid, steam, or ice), the same might presumably be equally true of chemical differences vis-à-vis some more essential definition of substances.

The way to arrive at a universal explanation, as Davy sees it, is by means of a shift from qualitative to quantitative. Steam, water, and ice describe a substance from a qualitative standpoint. But it would be equally appropriate to consider the same substance from a quantitative standpoint, in terms of temperature. And if we did that, what we would discover is the relation between conditions that appear to be completely different on a qualitative level. Instead of differences, then, we get continuity from a quantitative (temperature) standpoint. And the fact that we can describe all substances from a temperature standpoint offers a clue as to how we might arrive at some sort of universal explanation. For Davy, quantitative description isn't just another perspective. Rather, its role is to explain the qualitative. When we ascribe numbers to different substances, our motive isn't merely descriptive. By means of numerical assignments, what we hope to understand is how and why we get the chemical reactions produced by particular substances. We understand these reactions and the substances they involve numerically: "by the additions of multiples of some simple numbers or fractional parts." In this fashion, as a mode of description that can be applied to all substances, the quantitative presents a way to explain how we arrive at the qualitative.[6]

At the same time, the framework of a universal explanation forces Davy to think about the relation of the different sciences to each other. On that point, he observes: "Even if it should be ultimately found that oxygen and hydrogen are the same matter in different states of electricity, or that two or three elements in different proportions constitute all bodies, the great doctrines of chemistry, the theory of definite proportions, and the specific attractions of bodies must remain immutable." So it isn't as if chemistry would disappear if we were able to arrive at some sort of universal explanation. All the same, its position would be altered: "and the only change in the science would be, that those substances now considered as primary elements must be considered as secondary." In other words, chemistry would lose its primacy. The substances now considered primary would become secondary because we could explain their composition in terms of the different electrical states of a few simple substances. And that would be to give the primacy to physics. Yet Davy doesn't seem to care. For him, what's more important is that universal explanation allows us to see a relation between the different sciences.

To a large extent, any attempt at a universal explanation has to be based on a claim that the different forces we observe are either rigorously connected or identical. If that were true, then all the diverse explanations of their activity produced by the different sciences become variants of a single story. In order to substantiate his own version of a universal explanation, Davy specifically needs to show that electrical = chemical forces.[7] His first Bakerian lecture (November 20, 1806) tries to do just that:

> Amongst the substances that combine chemically, all those, the electrical energies of which are well known, exhibit opposite states . . . and supposing perfect freedom of motion in their particles or elementary matter, they ought, according to the principles laid down, to attract each other in consequence of their electrical powers. In the present state of our knowledge, it would be useless to attempt to speculate on the remote cause of the electrical energy, or the reason why different bodies, after being brought into contact, should be found differently electrified; its relation to chemical affinity is, however, sufficiently evident. May it not be identical with it, and an essential property of matter? (*CW* V, pp. 39–40)

At this point, Davy can only advance his claim that electrical = chemical forces as a hypothesis. By way of support, he mentions a simple experimental fact: "Amongst the substances that combine chemically, all those, the electrical energies of which are well known, exhibit opposite states." Since the electrical condition of many other substances is still unknown, however, his evidence remains inconclusive. After all, it might turn out that substances strongly attracted but identically rather than oppositely charged evade notice precisely because an absence of opposite charges is hard to detect. The fact that we don't know the electrical status of many substances that combine might even work *against* the notion that electrical and chemical forces are identical. Furthermore, Davy is fully aware that our ignorance about electricity makes it hard to demonstrate any claim about electrical and chemical forces persuasively. Hence his admission that "in the present state of our knowledge, it would be useless to attempt to speculate on the remote cause of the electrical energy, or the reason why different bodies, after being brought into contact, should be found differently electrified." Conceivably, the fact that we don't know how bodies become differently electrified might even make it difficult to prove the identity of electrical and chemical forces. Given all this, Davy can only say of electricity in substances that "its relation to chemical affinity is . . . sufficiently evident." As a result, his hypothesis that electrical = chemical forces remains initially tentative.

Nonetheless, any evidence of a closely proportional relationship between the degree to which a substance is electrified and the extent of its chemical affinity to other substances would certainly make the hypothesis more plausible. Subsequently, Davy tries to specify a proportionality of this kind:

> But different substances have different degrees of the same electrical energy in relation to the same body: thus the different acids and alkalies are possessed of different energies with regard to the same metal; sulphuric acid, for instance, is more powerful with lead than muriatic acid, and solution of potash is more active with tin than solution of soda. (*CW* V, p. 40)

Here the phrase "different degrees of the same electrical energy" implies that the attractive force in different substances is essentially the same. This sameness of the attractive force allows Davy to explain how one substance can attract a body more strongly than another substance does. In other words, electrical energy is easily quantifiable, whereas affinity (which has to do with qualities) isn't.

Still, the mere fact that one substance exerts a stronger attraction than another needn't imply the attractive force is electrical. Clearly, other physical forces such as heat can easily do the same. To demonstrate that the attractive force is electrical, Davy should be able to point to qualities that apply to it uniquely:

> When two bodies repellent of each other act upon the same body with different degrees of the same electrical attracting energy, the combination would be determined by the degree; and the substance possessing the weakest energy would be repelled; and this principle would afford an expression of the causes of elective affinity, and the decompositions produced in consequence. (*CW* V, p. 41)

Now if the attraction of two bodies to a third were purely chemical, it isn't clear why the first two bodies would mutually repel. Instead, we ought to have either a partial combination of the first and third bodies with a lesser amount of the second and third, or perhaps some combination of all three bodies. What marks the attractive force as electrical, then, is the mutual repulsion between the first two bodies. We can account for it by an exclusively electrical principle: that similarly charged bodies repel.

Davy also puts forward other evidence to support his claim that electrical = chemical forces. For example, he points out that similar consequences accompany intense electrical and chemical activity:

> Whenever bodies brought by artificial means into a high state of opposite electricities are made to restore the equilibrium, heat and light are the common

consequences. It is perhaps an additional circumstance, in favour of the theory to state, that heat and light are likewise the result of all intense chemical action. (*CW* V, p. 43)

Such an observation encourages us to think about electricity and chemical affinity within a larger framework. If heat and light are the common consequences of intense electrical and chemical activity, the fact that they consistently accompany both forms of activity hints at a possible identity of electrical and chemical forces. But it also implies some sort of deeper relation between all these forces, as a way to explain why heat and light *invariably* occur whenever we have intense electrical or chemical activity.

Meanwhile, the notion of an electrical equilibrium serves to link electrical and chemical forces in yet another way. By means of a Voltaic apparatus, Davy found he could elevate bodies to the "high state of opposite electricities" he describes. The process by which that tension is restored to equilibrium gives further evidence of an intimate relation between electrical and chemical forces:

> The great tendency of the attraction of the different chemical agents, by the positive and negative surfaces in the Voltaic apparatus, seems to be to restore the electrical equilibrium. . . . The electrical energies of the metals with regard to each other, or the substances dissolved in the water, in the Voltaic and other analogous instruments, seem to be the causes that disturb the equilibrium, and the chemical changes the causes that tend to restore the equilibrium; and the phenomena most probably depend on their joint agency. (*CW* V, pp. 44–45)

If the chemical changes mentioned by Davy can restore the equilibrium disturbed by electrical forces, it seems natural to suppose these changes result from chemical forces sufficient to counteract the electrical forces he speaks of. But in order for chemical forces to counteract electrical forces, they must be similar in kind.

Despite all the evidence Davy has amassed to demonstrate his claim about electrical and chemical forces, it's still possible to argue they aren't necessarily identical. For instance, they might be involved in a causal relationship of some sort. Superficially, such a relationship could look quite similar to one in which they're identical. After all, forces causally related always occur together. In fact, however, identity and causal relationships are ultimately quite different. If causally related, one element or force should invariably produce the second. But if the two are identical, we might see one without the other (under some circumstances, electrical forces might not manifest themselves chemically, and vice versa). To demonstrate that electrical and chemical forces are identical, then, what Davy needs to specify are instances of electrical energy without chemical alteration and, conversely, of chemical change without electricity (*CW* V, pp. 49–51). By means of these examples, he can then eliminate the possibility of a causal relationship between electrical and chemical forces.

If theoretical economy led for Davy to universal explanation, the ultimate consequence of universal explanation was the creation of objectivity. Chemistry, in other words, didn't just discover the realm of fact. Instead, as Davy saw it, the role of chemistry (or, for that matter, any of the sciences) was to create the objectivity we associate with the world out there. What Davy had come to perceive was that objectivity didn't consist merely of inert, unconceptualized fact. By itself, fact was chaotic, unorganized. To put it another way, fact alone didn't lead you anywhere. To make sense of it, you had to have some means to shape it, organize it. And that meant you had to come to it with some sort of theory. Objectivity, then, would grow out of a dynamic tension between theory and fact. Rather than a static realm of fact, it would amount to a process. In his preface to *Elements,* Davy attempts to describe what that process would involve:

> The foundations of chemical philosophy are, observation, experiment, and analogy. By observation, facts are distinctly and minutely impressed on the mind. By analogy, similar facts are connected. By experiment, new facts are discovered; and, in the progression of knowledge, observation, guided by analogy, leads to experiment, and analogy confirmed by experiment, becomes scientific truth. (*CW* IV, p. 2)

Here the moral of the story might be: what begins as theory returns at the end to theory. The process starts, Davy says, by observation. By observation, facts are "distinctly and minutely impressed on the mind." But observation isn't neutral. To a large extent, as Davy himself no doubt realized, we see what we want to see. So it starts, in effect, with the mind. Which is to say: with a disposition or tendency to theory. The formative role of theory becomes even more evident in the next phrase: "By analogy, similar facts are connected." It's only natural to connect similar facts. The real question, though, is how we determine similarity. Clearly, whether two or more facts are similar or not has to depend on the perspective you take. So it comes back to the mind and, specifically, its theoretical perspective. In the last phase, Davy asserts, new facts are discovered by means of experiment. Given the need for experiment, however, the process can't just be about our perception of what's already there. After all, the "new facts" Davy speaks of can only be arrived at by experiment. In a sense, then, we might say that experiment creates or produces objectivity. But experiment itself has its source in the particular theory we want to prove. Hence theory might be described as the ultimate source of objectivity.[8]

Subsequently, Davy goes on to talk about the process by which we arrive at objectivity even more explicitly. In this version of the story, the process starts when "observation, guided by analogy, leads to experiment." Here Davy makes it more evident than before that observation doesn't operate from a neutral posture. The fact that it's guided by analogy distinctly points to a theoretical perspective. But if experiment comes about as a result of observation guided by analogy, the real source of all experimental activity must then be some form of theory. We don't engage in experimental activity, then, just to answer a question. We get into it because of a theory we already have. So the role of experiment for Davy is really to confirm or support a theory. Or, as he puts it: "analogy confirmed by experiment, becomes scientific truth." Here it's important to note that analogy confirmed by experiment doesn't just become confirmed analogy. Instead, it takes on a different kind of value. Yet the whole process is, to a large extent, a circular one: theory gets involved with factual material, but only so that at the end it can return to itself, on a higher level. And that higher level is what we mean by objectivity.

For Davy, the initial effect of all his experimental work was to foster a radical empiricism. The discovery of new elements by means of a breakdown of substances meant you couldn't rely simply on what you perceived or observed. After all, elements that couldn't normally be found in isolation had emerged as a result of experiment. Thus what you perceived no longer seemed to correspond to the way things actually were. But if what you perceived no longer gave you a reliable knowledge of how things are, the less reason to subscribe to any sort of traditional empiricism. In the quest for knowledge, experiment had clearly come to play a major role. As practiced by Davy, moreover, it was in many ways antithetical to the empiricist perspective because it was creative rather than just observational. From his standpoint, experiment led, you might say, to the creation of new elements. At the same time, experiment also frequently involved the destruction of constructs we normally use to describe substances. If substances could be broken down or made to yield previously unsuspected elements, they obviously weren't primary. In that sense, experiment gave rise to a kind of negativity. As a result, empiricism in Davy turned radical.

Yet Davy didn't remain in that posture, and the reason he didn't has to do with the emergence of theory. Here theory emerges as a consequence of negativity: the destruction of all our normal constructs for substances meant we would have to formulate a new theory to express the results of experiments. In that respect, chemistry at the outset of the nineteenth century looked like the French Revolutionary scene: once you eliminate traditional beliefs, you somehow have to fill the void you've created. For Davy, however, it all felt quite natural. From his standpoint, theory emerged ineluctably out of the very experimental data he obtained. The fact that new elements could be found by means of an electrochemical breakdown of substances pointed to a simplicity in matter itself, if not an essential sameness. And likewise for combinations of substances, where the consistency of simple proportions taught a similar simplicity in how we ought to describe chemical affinity. Without theory, moreover, you couldn't arrive at objectivity. To form a picture of the world, you had to have a mix of theory and fact. Fact alone wouldn't get you there because it couldn't explain all the lacunae created by the new experimental mode of chemistry. And so, for better or worse, chemistry found itself committed to theory.

The circumstances under which Davy turned to theory produced a need, in turn, for metatheory. As he himself promptly recognized, facts are shaped by theory. Experiments give rise to new facts, but experiments are devised by theory. Inevitably, any facts we generate by means of experiment come to exist within a matrix of theory. But if experimental fact always appears within a matrix of theory, we need to be aware of what the choices for theory are. What Davy gradually came to perceive, in other words, was the autonomy of theory. When the sciences had been more purely observational, theory was largely determined by fact. But experiment, carried out by the new instruments he now had at his disposal, gave chemistry a power it didn't have before. From now on, it could generate, by experiment, the facts necessary to support itself. If not determined by fact, however, theory now faced a need to choose what it wanted to be. And with that need to choose came the need for a basis to justify its choices. Hence the motive for metatheory. Meanwhile, metatheory would also make it possible to define the relation between the sciences. As a result of his work in electrochemistry, Davy had caught a glimpse of what that relation might be. But if each science has its own theory, he could see the need for some sort of metatheory that would embrace all the sciences. From universal explanation, then, he began to feel his way toward universal theory.

What we get from Davy, finally, is a hint of the larger picture. By means of reflexivity, he could discern the process by which theory or analogy became objectivity through experiment. But if reflexivity had shown him how theory became objectivity, what it nonetheless failed to yield was some insight into how we might arrive at theory itself. Because reflexivity could see how theory became objectivity, it could point to the need for a viewpoint above and beyond that of theory. What it couldn't give, however, was a sense of what that viewpoint ought to involve.

In that respect, theory in the sciences differed from other forms of Romantic theory.[9] For those other forms of Romantic theory, negativity and reflexivity would be sufficient to generate theory. From their standpoint, theory essentially came about through some movement of return whereby what was initially posited or asserted would come back to itself. And in the process by which it did that, it would arrive at the sort of higher awareness we call theory. The sciences, however, were different. And the reason for it lay in the role of objectivity. Because of objectivity, theory in the sciences couldn't simply return to itself. If other forms of theory were ultimately subjective in the sense that they involved a return to what they were, theory in the sciences was defined by its objectivity. Nonetheless, objectivity didn't mean that they were defined by their relation to fact. Instead, as we've seen, objectivity in the sciences was governed from the outset by theory. What objectivity meant was, rather, a tendency toward the formal. So if theory in the sciences came about from reflexivity of some kind, it would have to be a formal reflexivity.

For that, it would become necessary to incorporate the process by which we arrive at theory in general into the very form of this higher viewpoint, or metatheory. Only by means of such a move could we hope to see how the process by which we arrive at theory might determine the actual shape of theory itself. But to incorporate process into theory formally, we would need a field where theory was essentially formal. And so it would fall to a young French radical to formulate the crucial insight that would lift theory to the level of metatheory, and thereby help to create modern algebra.

CHAPTER SIX

Galois Theory

It's easy to picture the scene. The time: near dawn on May 30, 1832. The place: a field near the Glacière pond, in the Gentilly district of Paris. Two young men, accompanied by their seconds, arrive on the field at a prearranged time. They talk briefly and take up their pistols while the seconds assume their customary places. The two young men then turn their backs to each other and step off twenty-five paces. At that point, they turn and prepare to fire. But only one actually does so. The pistol of the other wasn't loaded. The one whose pistol was empty falls to the ground, shot through the stomach. Still, he doesn't die immediately. Instead, death occurs only the next day, May 31, at about 10 a.m. His name was Évariste Galois. At this point, our knowledge of the relevant circumstances comes to an end.

Everything else is conjecture. It begins virtually from the moment Galois was shot. In one account we're told he was found hours later near the edge of the road by a peasant on the way to market. Another account has him discovered by a former royal army officer. What isn't clear is why he was abandoned by the seconds as well as his opponent. Perhaps they went off to get help: while they were gone, the wounded Galois was presumably discovered. In any event, he seems to have been brought to the nearby Cochin Hospital. Informed of what had happened, his brother Alfred rushed to the hospital and was present during the final hours of the ordeal. Early in the morning of the 31st, peritonitis set in, and a priest was called. But Galois refused his services. Supposedly his last words, to Alfred, were: "Don't cry. I need all my courage to die at twenty."

From here on, the realm of conjecture widens considerably. The identity of the young man who shot Galois is a matter of some uncertainty. Although every Paris newspaper briefly reported the duel, only the Lyon paper *Le Précurseur* supplied more detail. It described the opponent of Galois as "one of his old friends, a young man like himself, like himself a member of the Society of Friends of the People, and who was known to have figured in a political trial."

The article went on to add: "It's said that love was the cause of the combat. The pistol was the chosen weapon of the adversaries, but because of their old friendship they couldn't bear to look at one another and left the decision to blind fate. At point-blank range they were each armed with a pistol and fired. Only one pistol was charged." The newspaper identified the person who shot Galois only by the initials L.D., which don't quite square with those of the two likeliest suspects. The first, Duchatelet, was definitely an old friend of Galois, but his Christian name was apparently Ernest. In his memoirs, Alexandre Dumas points to Péscheux d'Herbenville. Both Duchatelet and d'Herbenville were involved in political trials at the time.

At the level of motive, the whole affair becomes even murkier. Alfred Galois consistently maintained his brother had been murdered, the victim of a conspiracy initiated by a government anxious to suppress any hint of protest. Subsequently, the conspiracy theory gets more elaborate. We've seen that the *Précurseur* suggested love as the cause of the duel. A typical nineteenth-century scenario: two young men in love with the same woman fight on the pretext that the honor of the beloved has somehow been compromised. Over time, this element of the story finds its way into the conspiracy theory. As a result, the beloved is transformed. No longer an innocent woman whose virtue is called into question by her relationship with Galois, she now becomes an agent provocateur. Galois is lured into a situation that allows him to be challenged by a police agent, a deadly marksman supposedly concerned for the lady's honor. The whole scheme arranged by someone in the Louis-Philippe government as a way to eliminate a confirmed troublemaker. And this has been for some time the accepted explanation.

In fact, the real explanation may be even more remarkable. Recent research has shown the duel was in fact prearranged. But not by government machination or the use of a female agent provocateur. Rather, by Galois himself. At a meeting of the Friends of the People on May 7, 1832, discussion had turned on the recent return to France of the duchesse de Berry, whose son (now twelve) had increasingly come to be seen by French royalists as the true heir. The possibility of a legitimist move encouraged armed revolt by the left as a way to exploit the situation and (hopefully) overthrow Louis-Philippe. To incite the Paris masses to rise, however, required a pretext. Someone ventured to suggest a corpse to be avenged might fit the requirement. At first the suggestion made no impression. But gradually it began to be taken more seriously. Finally Galois (who had been silent) asked to speak. He explained that his own life had become pointless. All that remained was to sacrifice it for the one thing he still loved: France. He would arrange to die in a duel under suspicious circumstances. The Friends of the People would then have the necessary corpse. Everyone present began to protest, but Galois insisted so strongly that his wish finally prevailed.

We might of course dismiss his statement as mere exaggeration, prompted by enthusiasm for a cause. Still, it isn't an easy thing to die—especially with many years of life in prospect. To volunteer publicly, moreover, before friends and others who have proven their commitment shows a definite seriousness. After all, there's always the possibility you might be expected to make good on your promise. Not to do so would in turn raise questions about your own commitment. Note, further, how Galois's proposal initially provoked unanimous resistance. Understandably: no one should be allowed too quickly to sacrifice life itself merely as a means to an end. Yet somehow Galois manages to persuade a majority of those initially opposed. Apparently he convinced them of his sincerity. Finally (if we can rely on a report from many years later), Galois doesn't say his life *is* pointless but that it's become so. Which implies a narrative of some kind.

For Galois, this would presumably have included earlier political acts and their consequences. Perhaps the best-known episode was his toast at a republican banquet. On May 9, 1831, approximately 200 republicans had gathered at the restaurant *Vendanges de Bourgogne* to celebrate the acquittal of nineteen of their number previously charged with conspiracy. Toasts were drunk to the Revolutions of 1789 and 1793, to Robespierre, and to the Revolution of 1830. Then Galois, at the far end of a long table, stood up to propose a toast. Raising his glass and a knife simultaneously, he exclaimed: "To Louis-Philippe, if he betrays!" The next day he was arrested and taken to the Sainte-Pélagie prison, where he remained until June 15. Acquitted at his trial, he remained free only briefly. On July 14, armed and at the head of 600 demonstrators, he was arrested and sent to Sainte-Pélagie again. His second prison term lasted much longer (until April 1832). In his case, the judges wanted to make a point.

Prison life was hard. Poor political prisoners (like Galois) were crowded into sixty-bed dormitories. In his *Lettres sur les prisons de Paris* François-Vincent Raspail also mentions an assassination attempt on someone in the room where Galois slept. On top of that, he failed to get along with many of the other prisoners, who often forced him to get drunk. Once, in a delirium, he even attempted suicide. The strain of prison life began to tell: his sister, who visited him frequently, could see physical signs of it.

In addition, there's the hint of a failed love affair. Our information on it is somewhat scanty. It seems that when Galois was transferred from Sainte-Pélagie to the pension Sieur Faultrier in March 1832 he fell in love with a young woman named Stéphanie Dumotel, daughter of a resident physician there. Some fragments of her letters to him have survived, in transcripts by Galois himself. On May 14 she writes: "Please let's break up this affair. I don't have enough wit [esprit] to follow . . . a correspondence of this sort . . . but I will try to have enough to converse with you as I did before anything happened. . . . and don't think any more about those things which could not exist and which will never exist" (*Écrits*, p. 489). We can infer their subsequent breakup from a letter by Galois to Auguste Chevalier: "My good friend, there is a pleasure in being sad in order to be consoled; one is really happy to suffer when one has friends. Your letter, full of apostolic unction, has brought me a little calm. But how to obliterate the trace of emotions as violent as those I've felt? How to console oneself for having exhausted in one month the most beautiful source of happiness that is in man, for having exhausted it without happiness, without hope, certain as one is of having drained it for life?" (*Écrits*, p. 468).

Finally, there's the question of Galois's mathematical prospects. That he had twice failed (hence, definitively) the entrance exam for the École Polytechnique, at the time the most prestigious school for mathematics and the sciences in France, is legendary. Almost equally well known is his spotty record and ultimate expulsion from the École Normale. His attempt at private instruction (a course on algebra, held at a bookshop in the rue de la Sorbonne) had proved too unconventional in method and content, and had likewise ended in failure. Meanwhile he had tried, unsuccessfully, to obtain recognition of his now-celebrated memoir on the resolvability of equations by radicals from the Académie des Sciences. Although he made a number of last-minute additions to this and to a second memoir the night before his duel, Galois had in fact begun work on it years before. His initial efforts to interest the Academy had centered on Augustin Cauchy. Later his memoir received the attention of other members (Sylvestre-François Lacroix and Siméon-Denis Poisson), only to be at last rejected. Their report (prepared by Poisson) concludes: "it should be noted that [the theorem] does not contain, as the title would have the reader believe, the condition of solvability of equations by radicals . . . . This condition, if it exists, should have an external character that can be tested by examining the coefficients of a given equation, or, at most, by solving other equations of a lesser degree than that proposed. We have made every effort to understand M. Galois's proof. His arguments are neither sufficiently clear nor developed for us to judge their rigor, and we are not in a position to give even an idea of them in this report." Some final remarks by Poisson are not unfavorable. Yet the fact that he declined to approve the memoir meant Galois could hope for no support from the Academy. Thus all possible avenues to a future in the mathematical profession must have seemed more or less closed.[1]

Nevertheless, despite all his personal difficulties, Galois looked toward the future. He firmly believed present developments would necessitate a new mathematical style:

Les longs calculs algébriques ont d'abord été peu nécessaires au progrès des Mathématiques, les théorèmes fort simples gagnaient à peine à être traduits dans la langue de l'analyse. Ce n'est guère que depuis Euler que cette langue plus brève est devenue indispensable à la nouvelle extension que ce grand géomètre a donnée à la science. Depuis Euler les calculs sont devenus de plus en plus difficiles à mesure qu'ils s'appliquaient à des objets de science plus avancés. Dès le commencement de ce siècle, l'algorithme avait atteint un degré de complication tel que tout progrès était devenu impossible par ce moyen, sans l'élégance que les géomètres modernes ont su imprimer à leurs recherches, et au moyen de laquelle l'esprit saisit promptement et d'un seul coup un grand nombre d'opérations.

[Long algebraic calculations were at first little necessary to the progress of Mathematics, extremely simple theorems hardly gained by being translated into the language of analysis. Only since Euler has this briefer language become indispensable to the new extension that great geometer gave to science. Since Euler calculations have become more and more difficult insofar as they apply to more advanced objects of science. From the beginning of this century, the algorithm has attained such a degree of complexity that all progress would have become impossible by this means, if not for the elegance modern geometers have known how to impart to their researches, and by means of which the mind grasps promptly and at a single glance a great number of operations.] (*Écrits*, p. 9)

From what he could see, however, even Euler's simplifications would eventually reach their limit:

Or je crois que les simplifications produites par l'élégance des calculs (simplifications intellectuelles, s'entend; de matérielles il n'y en a pas) ont leurs limites; je crois que le moment arrivera où les transformations algébriques prévues par les spéculations des analystes ne trouveront plus ni le temps ni la place de se produire; à tel point qu'il faudra se contenter de les avoir prévues. Je ne veux pas dire qu'il n'y a plus rien de nouveau pour l'analyse sans ce secours: mais je crois qu'un jour sans cela tout serait épuisé.

[Thus I believe that the simplifications produced by the elegance of calculations (intellectual simplifications, understand—of the material kind there aren't any) have their limits; I believe the moment will come when the algebraic transformations foreseen by the speculations of analysts will no longer have either the time or place to produce themselves, to the point where one will have to content oneself with having foreseen them. I don't want to say there will be nothing new for analysis without this aid: but I believe that without it everything will one day be exhausted.] (*Écrits*, p. 9)

Galois then goes on to describe what he sees as necessary for further mathematical advances:

Sauter à pieds joints sur ces calculs; grouper les opérations, les classer suivant leurs difficultés et non suivant leurs formes; telle est, suivant moi, la mission des géomètres futurs; telle est la voie où je suis entré dans cet ouvrage.

[To jump with both feet over these calculations; to group operations, class them according to their difficulties and not according to their forms; such is, I believe, the mission of future geometers; such is the road on which I've embarked in this work.] (*Écrits*, p. 9)

Elsewhere, what Galois says suggests that his vision embraces more than purely formal considerations: "Nous exposerons donc . . . ce qu'il y a de plus general, de plus philosophique" [We will set forth, then . . . what is most general, most philosophical] (*Écrits*, p. 17). A remark from the "Discours préliminaire" to the first memoir is even more specific: "Il existe en effet pour ces sortes de questions un certain ordre de considérations Métaphysiques qui planent sur tous les calculs, et qui souvent les rendent inutiles" [There exists in effect for these kinds of questions a certain order of Metaphysical considerations that looms over all calculations, and frequently renders them useless] (*Écrits*, p. 41). All of this can be summed up by what Galois terms "the analysis of analysis":

ici on fait l'analyse de l'analyse: ici les calculs les plus élevés exécutés jusqu'à présent sont considérés comme des cas particuliers, qu'il a été utile, indispensable de traiter, mais qu'il serait funeste de ne pas abandonner pour des recherches plus larges. Il sera temps d'effectuer des calculs prévus par cette haute analyse et classés suivant leurs difficultés, mais non spécifiés dans leur forme, quand la spécialité d'une question les reclamera.

[Here one does the analysis of analysis: here the highest calculations carried out up to the present are considered as particular instances, which it's useful, even indispensable to treat, but which it would be fatal not to relinquish for larger researches. It will be time to perform the calculations foreseen by this high analysis and classed according to their difficulties but not specified in their form, when the speciality of a question demands these.] (*Écrits*, p. 11)

The analysis of analysis—which is to say, on a more general level, metatheory.

∼

The point of departure for what we now call Galois theory takes the form of a fairly simple question: given a polynomial equation, what can we say in advance about its solution? Or, as Galois himself puts it:

Étant donnée une équation algébrique à coefficients quelconques, numériques ou littéraux, reconnaître si les racines ne peuvent s'exprimer en radicaux, telle est la question dont nous offrons une solution complète.

Si maintenant vous me donnez une équation que vous aurez choisie à votre gré, et que vous désiriez connaître si elle est ou non résoluble par radicaux, je n'aurai rien à y faire que de vous indiquer le moyen de répondre à votre question, sans vouloir charger ni moi ni personne de la faire. En un mot les calculs sont impraticables.

[Given an algebraic equation with whatever coefficients, numerical or literal, to be able to recognize whether the roots can be expressed by radicals—that's the question to which we offer a complete solution.

If you now give me an equation chosen as you like, and about which you want to know whether or not it's solvable by radicals, I would have nothing to do except to indicate to you the means of answering your question, without wanting to charge either myself or anyone else to do it. In a word, calculations are impracticable.] (*Écrits*, p. 39)

From what Galois says here, it seems evident that the sort of treatment he has in mind doesn't involve the numerical solution of a given equation. Instead, he makes it quite clear that his treatment even precludes the use of calculations. This discrepancy between our knowledge of whether an equation is solvable and its actual solution points in turn to a distinction between the realm of specific equations and what Galois terms the "theory of equations." Clearly, then, what his proof attempts to do will pertain exclusively to the realm of theory.

For Galois, the solvability of an equation has to do with whether "the roots can be expressed by radicals." To understand what he means by that, we need to know first of all what the definition of a root is. Simply put, the roots of an equation are the values that, when substituted for the variables, make both sides equal. To solve an equation, we want to reduce each side to linear factors (i.e., factors where

the highest degree of any variable is no greater than 1: $(x - a)(x - b)(x - c), \ldots,$
for example). Nevertheless, we can't always reduce an equation to linear factors of
a particular kind (i.e., that conform to specific conditions we want to impose). Our
inability to reduce an equation to factors of that kind (even if we allow the
coefficients to exist in a "field," which generalizes our usual notion of "numbers")
forces us to try to specify various formal extensions of that "field" within which
the linear factors of the equation might be contained.

So we have to define a field, and subsequently extensions of it. But the concept
of a field takes us to that of a ring (of which it forms a somewhat specialized
example). Briefly, then, a ring has elements, commonly written a,b,c, . . . , and
two operations, commonly called $+$ and $\cdot$, which may or may not correspond to
addition and multiplication. Suppose a,b,c are in a ring R. We then have

1. $a + b$ is in R.
2. $a + b = b + a$.
3. $(a + b) + c = a + (b + c)$.
4. There is an element 0 in R such that $a + 0 = a$ (for every a in R).
5. There exists an element $-a$ in R such that $a + (-a) = 0$.
6. $a \cdot b$ is in R.
7. $a \cdot (b \cdot c) = (a \cdot b) \cdot c$.
8. $a \cdot (b + c) = a \cdot b + a \cdot c$ and $(b + c) \cdot a = b \cdot a + c \cdot a$.

A field is a ring with some additional conditions that involve multiplication.
First, it's commutative: $a \cdot b = b \cdot a$ for every a,b. Second, there is a multiplicative identity element 1 in the field, with the property that $a \cdot 1 = a$ for every a in
the field. Finally, every element of the field *except 0* has a multiplicative inverse.
In other words, if $a \neq 0$ we can find some b in the field such that $a \cdot b = 1$ (the
identity element). For obvious reasons, b would then be written as $1/a$.

To extend a field, we need more than just additional elements. Individually, in
fact, these additional elements may well have nothing to do with the original
field. But the *totality* of added elements forms a vector space, since one new
element forces others to be introduced. If we imagine a field F and a vector space
V with $\alpha, \beta \in F$ and $v, \omega \in V$, for their relationship we then have

1. $\alpha (v + \omega) = \alpha v + \alpha \omega$
2. $(\alpha + \beta)v = \alpha v + \beta v$
3. $\alpha(\beta v) = (\alpha\beta)v$
4. $1v = v$

In (1.), the $+$ operation occurs in V. In (2.), on the other hand, the $+$ operation in

$(\alpha + \beta)$ is that of the field F, while the $+$ operation in $\alpha v + \beta v$ is that of the vector space V. Thus (2.) establishes a relationship between operations of a field and those of a vector space. What we still need to know, though, is how the elements of a field and those of a vector space are related. Their relationship takes the form of a linear combination of elements. If V is a vector space over a field F where $v_1, \ldots, v_n \in V$ and a set of $\alpha_i \in F$, the combination of field and vector space will look like this: $\alpha_1 v_1 + \alpha_2 v_2 + \ldots + \alpha_n v_n$. When that vector space is finite-dimensional, we can say even more about its structure. Any finite-dimensional vector space will have a finite subset of elements the sum of whose linear combinations (i.e., its linear span) makes up that vector space. We can characterize the elements further: $v_1, \ldots, v_n \in V$ are *linearly dependent* over F if there exist elements $\lambda_1, \ldots, \lambda_n$ (not all 0) in F such that $\lambda_1 v_1 + \lambda_2 v_2 + \ldots + \lambda_n v_n = 0$. When we can't find such elements $\lambda_1, \ldots, \lambda_n$ in F, $v_1, \ldots, v_n$ are termed *linearly independent.* As a finite-dimensional vector space, V will invariably have a finite set $v_1, \ldots, v_n$ of linearly independent elements whose linear span makes up V. These linearly independent elements constitute a *basis* of V. The number of elements in a basis doesn't depend on the particular basis we choose, and gives the dimension or degree of the vector space over F.

With these definitions of a field and its possible extensions in mind, we now return to the question of solvability. For Galois, the solvability of a polynomial equation with coefficients drawn from the field F had amounted to what we could determine about the roots of that polynomial. Moreover, we know that all the roots of a polynomial frequently can't be found within F alone, which makes it necessary to extend the field. We should thereby eventually reach a point where all the roots of the polynomial become expressible in terms of linear factors (e.g., $(x - a)(x - b) \ldots (x - n)$). An extension that permits a polynomial to be so factored is termed a splitting field of that polynomial. The essence of Galois theory lies in the move to associate this splitting field with a group of automorphisms of that field. Think of a group as a collection of elements with an operation by which they can be combined. If these elements do indeed form a group, then the product that results when their elements are combined remains within the group. Furthermore, each element in a group has a unique inverse with which it can be combined to yield the identity element, which is likewise unique for the entire group. Meanwhile, an automorphism is an operation that takes elements of a field to itself with "respect" for the operations $\cdot$ and $+$. What Galois theory asserts, then, is an equivalence (not identity or equality) between a field extension that consists of elements and a group composed of algebraic operations.

But the full significance of this relationship becomes clear only when we see that it holds for subfields of the extension and subgroups of the group of auto-morphisms as well. Taken collectively, these relationships define the basic equiv-alence of Galois theory:

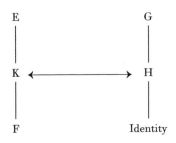

In this schema, the field F supplies coefficients for a given polynomial p(x). If all the roots of p(x) aren't in F, we suppose one or more of these to be contained in K, an extension of F and, at the same time, a subfield of E. A further extension of E, however, might include all the roots of p(x). On the other side, we begin with the identity automorphism: each element can be equated with itself. H, a subgroup of G, will have the identity automorphism and one or more others as well. Finally, G consists of all the automorphisms of a particular kind that operate on the roots of the polynomial p(x). The equivalence between E or its subfields and G or its subgroups works in either direction: we can map a given subfield of E to a specific subgroup of G or vice versa. In either case, the mapping is always one-to-one (on a historical note, we see how remarkable all this was at the time Galois proposed it if we consider that standard axioms for a group weren't adopted until late in the nineteenth century, while standard axioms for a field had to wait until the early twentieth century).

Meanwhile, the relationship between extensions of a field and a group of automorphisms needs to be defined. In Galois theory this happens via the con-cept of a fixed field. If G is a group of automorphisms that operate on an extension K, the fixed field of G will then consist of all elements a $\in$ K such that $\sigma(a) = a$ for all $\sigma \in$ G. Thus the a $\in$ K that belong to the fixed field associated with all automorphisms $\sigma \in$ G are precisely those elements that don't move (i.e., change) when the automorphisms are applied. We say they remain "fixed." These fixed elements of K give us a way to describe how the automorphisms of G act on K and, consequently, how G and K might be related.

The notion of a fixed field assumes a particular form in Galois theory. For Galois, the case in which the fixed field is exactly F has a special importance. We express this by G(K,F). It signifies the group of automorphisms of K relative to F.

In effect, it designates all automorphisms of K that leave every element of F fixed. As it turns out, the fixed field of G(K,F) frequently encompasses a great deal more than just F (which itself is infinite, since it always includes the entire set of rational numbers). Our inability to restrict the fixed field of G(K,F) to just F often results from the fact that we simply don't have enough conditions to impose. The smallest possible subgroup of G(K,F) consists of the identity automorphism, which fixes everything in K. As we get into larger subgroups, we impose more conditions on an element (which is fixed by all the automorphisms). In that way, the fixed field gets progressively smaller.

To the extent that Galois theory asserts an equivalence between extensions of F and automorphisms of G, any knowledge we obtain about those automorphisms is likely to yield information on the extensions to which they correspond and hence, ultimately, on the question of solvability (since these extensions collectively contain all the roots of the polynomial p(x)). In particular, knowledge of the size of the group of automorphisms will presumably furnish crucial data about the size of extensions of F. For that reason, it's useful to look specifically at the group of automorphisms of K relative to F (i.e., G(K,F)), where we have the concept of a fixed field to help us relate the size of the automorphism group to extensions of F. Here it turns out that if K is a finite extension of F, then G(K,F) forms a finite group whose *order* (or number of elements), o(G(K,F)), satisfies o(G(K,F)) ≤ [K:F], the number of elements in a basis for K over F. That is, there are at least as many elements in such a basis as there are automorphisms of G(K,F).

With the information we now have about the relationship between automorphisms of G and the degree by which K exceeds F, we should be able to ascertain the size of the extension itself. To do this, we need the concept of a normal extension, which restricts the fixed field of G(K,F) to F exactly. We say that K is a *normal* extension of F if K is a finite extension of F such that the fixed field of G(K,F) is exactly F. While the general notion of a fixed field points to a relationship of some kind between automorphisms and extensions, with the fixed field restricted to F we can specify the nature of that relationship much more precisely. In particular, we obtain two statements that define the correspondence between the number of automorphisms that act on an extension and its size:

If K is a normal extension of F and H a subgroup of G(K,F) where $K_H = \{x \in K \mid \sigma(x) = x \text{ for all } \sigma \in H\}$ represents the fixed field of H, we then have

1. $[K:K_H] = o(H)$
2. $H = G(K,K_H)$.

Suppose, furthermore, that H = G(K,F). Under these circumstances, F (rather than K_H) becomes the fixed field of all the automorphisms of H, since K_H (which consists of all the elements of K fixed by $\sigma \in H$) = F. So $[K:K_H]$ must be equal to $[K:F]$. Similarly, the order of H, or o(H), = o(G(K,F)), since H = G(K,F). With the appropriate substitutions in our first equality, we obtain $[K:F]$ = o(G(K,F)).

Although we now have a way to relate a group of automorphisms to extensions of a field (i.e., via the concept of a fixed field or, more precisely, G(K,F)), what remains unclear is how exactly information about those automorphisms (specifically, G(K,F)) might contribute to the solvability of a polynomial equation. Earlier, we saw that in Galois theory solvability had to do with the splitting field of a polynomial (i.e., an extension sufficient to contain all the linear factors to which the polynomial is reducible). Thus it seems natural to try to relate the concept of a normal extension to that of a splitting field. In fact, their relationship turns out to be a very simple and direct one: K is a normal extension of F if and only if K forms the splitting field of some polynomial over F.

All these considerations lead us to what's called the Fundamental Theorem of Galois theory. We begin with a number of conditions:

Let f(x) be a polynomial in F[x], K its splitting field over F, and G(K,F) its Galois group (i.e., the group of all automorphisms of K that fix every element of F). For any subfield T of K that contains F let G(K,T) = $\{\sigma \in G(K,F) \mid \sigma(t) = t$ for every $t \in T\}$ and for any subgroup H of G(K,F) let $K_H = \{x \in K \mid \sigma(x) = x$ for every $\sigma \in H\}$.

The result is a one-to-one correspondence between the set of subfields of K that contain F and the set of subgroups of G(K,F). In particular we have

1. $T = K_{G(K,T)}$.
2. $H = G(K,K_H)$.
3. $[K:T]$ = o(G(K,T)), and $[T:F]$ = the index of G(K,T) in G(K,F).
4. T is a normal extension of F if and only if G(K,T) is a normal subgroup of G(K,F).
5. If T is a normal extension of F, then G(T,F) is isomorphic to G(K,F)/G(K,T).

About (1.), we need only observe that if K is the splitting field of f(x) over F, it must also be the splitting field of f(x) over any subfield T that contains F. Moreover, our "if and only if" equivalence between splitting fields and normal extensions says that if K is the splitting field of some polynomial over T, K is then

a normal extension of T. Conversely, by the very definition of a normal extension, T must be the fixed field for G(K,T), the group of all automorphisms of K.
Which is to say: $T = K_{G(K,T)}$.

In fact, (2.) merely reiterates an earlier equality. If K is a normal extension of
F, the fixed field of K will consist of every element fixed by all the automorphisms of K (i.e., G(K,F)). The same applies to any subgroup of G(K,F): by
definition, a group or subgroup of automorphisms will have as its fixed field
every element fixed by all the automorphisms of that group or subgroup. So for
the subgroup H of G(K,F), the fixed field will consist of every element of K fixed
by the automorphisms of H, which is to say: K_H. Accordingly, $H = G(K,K_H)$, the
group of automorphisms of K that have K_H as their fixed field.

Essentially, (3.) is simply a manipulation of data already established. We
know that $o(G(K,F)) = [K:F]$. By expansion and substitution we then get

$$o(G(K,F)) = [K:F] = [K:T][T:F] = o(G(K,T))[T:F],$$

which, slightly rearranged, gives us

$$[T:F] \;=\; \frac{o(G(K,F))}{o(G(K,T))} \;=\; \text{index of } G(K,T)$$

in G(K,F).

(4.) explores a crucial aspect of what a normal extension consists of. By
definition, K amounts to a normal extension of F when K is a finite extension of
F such that the fixed field of G(K,F) is exactly F. With T, what we have is a
subfield of K. Given the general equivalence between subfields of K that contain
F and the subgroups of G(K,F), we would then expect T to be a normal extension
of F if and only if G(K,T) forms a subgroup of G(K,F). But (4.) also asserts that
G(K,T) is a *normal* subgroup of G(K,F). By this it means that G(K,T) must
satisfy the condition that $\sigma^{-1}G(K,T)\sigma = G(K,T)$. Here the link between T as a
normal extension of F and G(K,T) as a normal subgroup of G(K,F) lies in the
nature of the $\sigma(t) \in T$. These $\sigma(t) \in T$ help to make T the splitting field of a
polynomial p(x) with coefficients in F, which makes it a normal extension of F.
At the same time, the $\sigma(t)$ also allow for $\sigma^{-1}\tau\sigma(t) = t$, which in generalized form
ultimately gives $\sigma^{-1}G(K,T)\sigma = G(K,T)$, and so makes G(K,T) a normal subgroup of G(K,F).

Finally, (5.) has to do with the relationship between different groups of
automorphisms defined by Galois theory. Specifically, it tells us that the group
G(T,F) is isomorphic to G(K,F)/G(K,T), which itself is also a group. For two
groups to be isomorphic implies the existence of a special kind of homomor-

phism, a mapping from one group to the other that preserves structure (i.e., $\phi(ab) = \phi(a)\phi(b)$). In the present instance, the mapping $\sigma \rightarrow \sigma*$ from elements of G(K,F) to those of G(T,F), which takes $(\sigma\psi) \in G(K,F)$ into $\sigma*\psi* \in G(T,F)$, is a homomorphism of G(K,F) into G(T,F). To ascertain whether a homomorphism is an isomorphism (and, consequently, whether two groups are isomorphic), we need to determine its kernel. Now the kernel of a homomorphism consists of all elements that can be mapped into the identity element of the new group. If the kernel consists solely of the identity element itself, no two elements will be mapped into the same element of the new group (i.e., all mappings are one-to-one). We can then conclude that the homomorphism is an isomorphism, and the two groups are isomorphic to each other. Which is what we have here. The kernel of the homomorphism of G(K,F) to G(T,F) is exactly G(K,T), made up as it is of precisely all the automorphisms of K that fix the elements $t \in T$ (which then don't get mapped into anything else). But the homomorphism of G(K,F) into G(T,F) with G(K,T) as its kernel yields all of G(T,F). As a result, G(T,F) must be isomorphic to G(K,F)/G(K,T).[2]

~

What Galois offered Romantic theory, first of all, was a new way to look at concepts. Specifically, Galois theory attempted to describe concepts spatially. This spatial description of concepts (if we can call it that) comes out especially in the notions of a field or group. Galois himself was fully aware of the radically innovative quality of his memoir in this respect. In his "Discours préliminaire" he says: "The novelty of this material forced the use of new denominations, new characters" (*Écrits*, p. 39). Nor does he doubt that many of his readers will be annoyed by his use of what might be termed a "new language." Nevertheless, he goes on to assert, his recourse to it was prompted by a need to conform to the "necessity of the subject." In particular, he saw how a spatial description of concepts might yield a new kind of insight into various problems or questions even if you didn't know exactly what elements were involved. Precisely because you lacked that knowledge, you focused on a simple question: whether they might collectively be said to form a set of some kind. And if you could ascertain that they did, you might use that fact to relate the set they formed to others similarly defined. In this fashion, you could eventually arrive at a knowledge of the relation between different sets, even if you didn't know all their elements. And that relation, because of what it indicated about the arrangement or disposition of the different sets, could in turn convey crucial information about their content. Thus the "spatial" aspect of a relation might be made to yield a payoff on a completely different yet essential point.

The kind of spatial perspective Galois wanted to apply to concepts like that of a group comes out especially in his use of closure as an essential property. Closure, as we've seen, says that if a,b∈G, then ab∈G. It means that any element we generate by multiplication or the product from elements within the group will likewise remain enclosed within that group. So a group has the capacity to generate new elements. But the fact that they remain within the group suggests that it's defined, ultimately, by containment rather than by its elements. Otherwise we ought to be able to form an idea of the group from the actual elements it consists of. Given the potential for a large or even infinite number of elements, though, it's hard to see how we could possibly do that. Nor does a specific limit of any kind appear to be what we want. Instead, it seems more natural to suppose that the concept of a group is defined by the principle of containment itself. Containment, however, is essentially a spatial notion. As applied to a group G, the implication is that if a,b∈G, we can invariably expand G to take in any product ab∈G. At the same time, closure also conveys a condition of exclusion: whatever isn't ab∈G or any product thereof can't be in G. This combination of expansion and exclusion, in turn, is exactly what makes the concept of a group spatial: it allows G to be "filled out" by ab, but it suggests that in the process G assumes a particular form that's equally defined by what it isn't. As a result, we get precisely the sort of internal/external dynamic we associate with the spatial.

Like closure, the use of location in Galois theory is purely spatial as well. We talk about how a given root of a polynomial equation is located in a particular subfield of K. Yet we really don't have any concrete information about that root at all. Obviously, we can't specify its exact form. But what's significant here is that we can't say anything else concretely about it either. The same is equally true for automorphisms of G(K,F). Since they're based on K (i.e., they map K onto itself), our lack of concrete information about the roots that make up K is bound to preclude a concrete knowledge of any automorphisms of those roots. Nor is it just that we can't specify a particular root or automorphism from a given subfield of K or subgroup of G(K,F). In fact, we don't know any more about the other elements that make up the subfield or subgroup. But if we lack concrete information about *any* of the elements from a subfield or subgroup, our location of a given element in a particular subfield or subgroup has to be purely spatial. All we have, in other words, is the act of location itself. We say a given element can be found in a particular subfield or subgroup, and the fact that we say so establishes a relation between the element we describe and the rest of the subfield or subgroup. Yet if all we have is the relation itself, our location of the element remains purely spatial in the sense that its only property is one of inclusion (i.e., internal versus external) within a subfield or subgroup.

In a similar if slightly more complex way, the use of a spatial perspective also affects what Galois theory has to say about the dimension of vector spaces. Vector spaces, we recall, are created when we add elements to a field so as to form extensions that contain the roots of a polynomial equation (i.e., the subfields of K). For Galois, a vector space is finite-dimensional when we can find a finite set of linearly independent elements (i.e., whose sum $\neq 0$) that can be combined with elements from a field F to yield a basis of that vector space over F. Significantly, it turns out that every basis of a given vector space has exactly the same number of elements. In other words, when we try to specify a set of linearly independent elements, we invariably get the same *number* of these regardless of which we choose. So we call that number of elements the dimension of a vector space over F. It gives us, you might say, the extent of that space, shows us how far we can go before coefficients from F make the sum of vector elements no longer linearly independent. Of course, as before, we don't know what those elements are. But we care because the extent of a given vector space and hence of some extension of K over F is exactly equivalent to that of a particular subgroup of G(K,F). And so the relation of extensions or subfields of K and subgroups of G(K,F) is, like closure and location, purely spatial: it doesn't depend at all on our ability to specify the elements involved. All we need to know is a purely spatial property, the extent of subfield and subgroup.

Besides his use of a spatial perspective, Galois also introduced a new kind of abstraction into Romantic theory. Here, too, he himself was well aware of the novelty of what he had proposed. In a preface to his work he remarks: "but, my book finished, I've asked myself what will make it strange to most readers, and on reflection, I thought I observed this tendency of my mind to avoid calculations in the subjects I've treated, and what's more, I recognized an insurmountable difficulty for whoever wants to effect calculation generally in the matters I've addressed" (*Écrits*, p. 11). But it wasn't just an instinctive tendency to avoid calculation. There was a reason for it. Essentially, Galois felt algebra had to move to a higher level. As he put it: "In effect, one thinks that a mind that had the power to see at a glance not only the ensemble of Mathematical truths known to us but all the truths possible could also deduce them in a regular fashion and as if mechanically from a few principles combined by a uniform method. . . . But it isn't like that. . . . In vain the analysts want to pretend to themselves: they don't deduce, they combine, they compose: immaterial as it is, analysis isn't any more in our power than anything else; one must spy on it, sound it, solicit it" (*Écrits*, pp. 13–15). To spy, sound, or solicit what he termed analysis, however, Galois knew he would have to shift to a different viewpoint from any that had been applied before. And that meant a new kind of abstraction.

For Galois, a more abstract kind of algebra implied, first of all, a deliberate move away from specificity. From his standpoint, you didn't resort to the abstract only when you could no longer employ a specific number or quantity. Nor did he feel the need to base his use of the abstract on a massive brief of concrete instances. Instead, his strategy was to introduce the abstract *tout court*, without apology. As though he believed that if you forced the issue by recourse to the abstract without prior preparation, something fruitful might happen. So what Galois does is to ask, quite simply, what we can say about a root or roots of a polynomial equation in the absence of any specific information. What he found was that the unknown root gets treated like any known quantity within equations or formulas. At the same time, of course, it remained distinctly different in at least one respect. After all, it wasn't a specific root but a purely formal expression for *any* root (4th degree or less) of a polynomial equation. But if an unknown root could be treated like a known quantity, its behavior in equations might tell us a great deal about it, and hence about roots in general. Thus resistance to the specific led to increased knowledge at the level of generality. And the use of the abstract as if it were concrete had made it all happen.

Abstraction also meant elements could be treated *en masse* or collectively. So it wasn't just that we didn't know any of the roots for a given polynomial equation. In addition, Galois only wanted to look at the set they formed as a totality. Nevertheless, one might ask what we can possibly say about a set if we don't know any of its elements. On a purely intuitive level, it's hard to see how a set could have any properties that don't ultimately come from the elements that compose it. What Galois discovered, however, was that even if the properties of a set had to come from its elements, that didn't mean you had to know those elements in order to arrive at their properties as a set. In fact, various conditions that pertained to a set seemed to emerge only when you considered it at that level. Hence the need for concepts like those of a group or field. Of particular interest was the fact that not all subfields of K or subgroups of G(K,F) were possible. But that was a fact we learned as a result of inferences from what we knew about the conditions for groups and fields, rather than about the individual elements involved. Clearly, then, some information that pertained to individual elements could be obtained only at a higher level of generality. Thus the rationale for a treatment of those elements *en masse,* or abstractly.

Lastly, an abstract standpoint allowed Galois to relate objects that weren't of the same sort and so impossible to regard as equal under any circumstances. For Galois theory, this was crucial. It meant you could consider elements of a field K that contained the roots of a polynomial equation as equivalent in some fashion to automorphisms or functions that mapped K onto itself. And that in turn made it possible to talk about a one-to-one correspondence between the subfields of K and the subgroups of G(K,F). Obviously these weren't really equal. But by means of its abstract standpoint, Galois theory was able to go beyond simple equality to take into account other, less simple equivalences. On some level, you might say, the equivalence between subfields of K and subgroups of G(K,F) that Galois described is purely formal: it merely points out the existence of one-to-one correspondences. Yet, on another level, it's more than just that. Ultimately, its basis lay in his perception that these dissimilar elements might share a deeper relation of some kind, even if we can't articulate it completely. Intuitively, it suggested that all mathematical objects occupied, potentially, some sort of common ground. Thus Galois stretches our notion of equivalences, in the belief that if we can rise to a more abstract level a new order of perceptions might become possible.

But perhaps the easiest way to see what Galois did for Romantic theory is to consider what he says at the level of metatheory. Toward the end of his "Discours préliminaire" he remarks: "The totality of what makes for the beauty and at the same time the difficulty of this theory is that one has constantly had to indicate the march of analysis and to predict the results without ever having the power to work these out" (*Écrits*, p. 41). And if you can't actually work out the solution, all you can do is to describe what it would entail. That, however, would necessarily lead to a different notion of theory. As Galois himself put it: "A new theory is much more a quest for the truth than the expression of it" (*Écrits*, p. 19). Moreover, if we're still engaged in a quest for the truth rather than in a position to say what it is, our theory ought to reflect that. Which is to say: it ought to embody our reflection on the problems or difficulties of our quest. More broadly, it ought to convey the conditions we think a theory should satisfy, what we feel a proper theory should look like. To arrive at some sense of what that might consist of, in turn, we need to think about theory itself. So from an attempt to ascertain a mathematical result without calculation we move to reflection on the very nature of theory. Which is, I think, exactly where Galois always wanted algebra to be.

As a basis for metatheory, we might look at how Galois theory works: to arrive at a solution, generate everything else as well. So we get a lot of structure: subfields of K that extend up from F, subgroups of G(K,F) all the way up to

G(K,F) itself, and, finally, a one-to-one relation between these subfields and subgroups. In addition, we get new concepts: that of a group and a field, plus that of an automorphism, by which G(K,F) is defined. We get all this because it's all necessary to what Galois theory is after. As Galois himself pointed out, his theory could only indicate the route to a solution, not the solution itself. And that implied it couldn't give you the actual calculation on which a solution would depend. Without that, however, the only way to show how we might arrive at a solution would be to specify the totality of structure + concepts associated with a polynomial equation. Galois believed that if you could do that, the roots would turn out to be related to elements you could find out about, which would enable you in turn to form inferences about the roots. But in order to ascertain what the relation between roots and other elements really signified, you had to grasp all the relevant concepts + structure as a totality. In its effort to grasp that totality, Galois theory discovered that it had to shift to a higher, more conceptual level. Hence the motive for metatheory.

As a result of his work on polynomial equations, Galois came to realize that knowledge of whether an equation was solvable possessed a much greater value than the solution itself. Once you knew an equation could be solved, the actual process (as he remarked) was often more or less mechanical. Knowledge of whether an equation could be solved was different. Here the crucial issue was whether that knowledge could be obtained without the work required for a concrete solution. Which is to say: no specificity, no calculation. If we could ascertain solvability without the work an actual solution involved, we might then have reason to feel that the essential question about polynomial equations could be answered at a purely conceptual level. And that would mean all of algebra, potentially, could be treated very differently. Instead of an inquiry directed toward the solution of specific equations, algebra would be about the effort to find out what defined solutions to polynomial equations in general. To find out about solutions to polynomial equations in general, however, it would be necessary to reflect on the very process by which we arrived at the solution to a polynomial equation. What Galois realized was that here, as so often elsewhere, the answer is defined by the framework of the inquiry. Thus, to ascertain what a solution consists of, we need to look at the larger framework of the inquiry that produces it. In this way, then, we finally come to what Galois himself termed the analysis of analysis, whereby theory reflects on itself, and so is transformed into metatheory.

Galois always looked to the future. In a preface to a planned collection of his work, he envisioned an era when algebra would be different. At that time, he hoped, inquiry would classify problems by their difficulties rather than by their form. And even if $\sqrt{2}$ and $\sqrt{-2}$ became harder to distinguish as a result, there would be a gain in other ways. Viewed in terms of their difficulties, problems could be brought into closer rapprochement with the perspective of the inquiry itself. Given that the perspective in question is our own, we invariably come back to it, in the end. Galois also hoped for a greater open-endedness in mathematical work. In his two memoirs, he remarks, the phrase "I don't know" occurs with some frequency. Yet he yearned for a change in circumstances, so that such a confession would no longer act on readers as a turn-off. Instead, he wished others might adopt the same practice, whereby one would do everything one could, and then add: "I don't know the rest" (*Écrits*, p. 11). For him, it was all part of the process of inquiry. Considered in that light, these lacunae might even point in their own way to some of the far-off possibilities intuitively glimpsed by theory.

By his innovative perspective, Galois took Romantic theory in the sciences to a new level. If some earlier forms of theory (what we find, for instance, in Davy or Bichat) had developed by a reflexivity based on knowledge, Galois went further. As he saw it, theory ought to encompass not only knowledge but even intuition. What Galois realized was that if you relaxed the requirements of knowledge, you could extend the reach of theory. And in the end, he felt, what mattered most about concepts or elements could always be described spatially, even if you didn't know what they consisted of. Similarly, he didn't mind abstraction, because it allowed you to move away from specificity. To some extent, in fact, the less you knew about a particular case, the more freedom you had to develop metatheory. Most important, you could give your metatheory more structure. For Galois, that was where it really counted. Because the more form or structure you had in your metatheory, the bigger the scope of your theory, which always relied, in the last analysis, on spatial relationships. In that respect, the road taken by Galois and the sciences was bound to differ from that of Hegel and his predecessors. Whereas for Hegel theory had meant in some sense a return to what you already knew, theory for the sciences always looked toward what wasn't known. By means of metatheory, then, Galois could hope to extend the scope of theory, and in the process give to the unknown a more definite shape.

CHAPTER SEVEN

Toward a Definition of Reflection

It is, in many ways, the archetypal Romantic text. It begins as an anthology of extracts from Archbishop Robert Leighton, with notes by the editor. Later, the extracts are arranged systematically, so as to conform to a particular conceptual scheme. Meanwhile, the notion of a full-length commentary gradually assumes a larger role in the project. Eventually the commentary, rather than the Leighton extracts, becomes the principal feature of the work. Nor does it remain just a commentary. Instead, this commentary takes on a life of its own. It starts to talk about different fields of inquiry other than religion. Beyond that, it goes on to describe how they're related to each other. When the work finally appears in print, it no longer has the name of Archbishop Leighton as author. Now the author is S. T. Coleridge. The title of the work is *Aids to Reflection.*[1]

Timewise, *Aids to Reflection* can be placed about halfway between *Biographia Literaria* (1817) and the unfinished *Opus Maximum*, which was to occupy Coleridge increasingly in his last years. The *Biographia* had been deeply immersed in systematic philosophy, out of which it had tried to fashion a literary/critical viewpoint. At that moment, Coleridge had hoped to solve the epistemological impasse of subjective/objective, in the belief that to do so would yield a multiple payoff. By the time he began work on *Aids to Reflection,* however, his attitude toward systematic philosophy had changed. His conceptual framework, in other words, was no longer that of German idealism. In his earlier years, Coleridge had seen a resolution of the subjective/objective impasse as foundational to his entire project. Hence its title: Logosophia. By that, I take it, he meant to indicate the primacy of systematic philosophy for his work. Its viewpoint would define what his project was about, its style of argument would dictate how he went about it. In the years after *Biographia*, however, Coleridge had begun to feel his way toward a different viewpoint, one where philosophy no longer possessed the same sort of primacy. Instead, he now came to see systematic philosophy more as a field like all the rest. And if he were to try to arrive at a higher viewpoint that could be applied to any field equally, it would have to be different from that of philosophy. Specifically, it would have to be broader in scope. In this fashion, then, Coleridge comes to see the necessity for what we might call theory.

Because of his shift from philosophy to theory, it was also natural for Coleridge to see his earlier reference points differently as well. During the *Biographia* period, Schelling had clearly been uppermost in his mind: the notoriously plagiarized chapter 12 ("Requests and Premonitions") is all the evidence we need of that. But by the time of *Aids to Reflection*, Coleridge had gone back to Kant. At first glance, this might look somewhat regressive. To return to Kant more than a quarter-century after the critical philosophy had made its mark on the European intellectual scene, and after all that had happened since, might well seem hard to justify. Yet if we see Kant as primarily concerned about the process by which we arrive at knowledge or cognition, we get some sense of why he might appeal. Since Coleridge himself was now interested in metatheory, a philosophy that looked at how we arrive at knowledge in general could once more seem relevant. And since his notion of theory was based on knowledge or cognition rather than metaphysics, we can explain why he never managed to get into Hegel.

Perhaps the best description I can give of *Aids to Reflection* would be to call it a book about the way we do theory, rather than about theory itself. In that respect, you might say, it presents itself distinctly as a work of metatheory rather than one of theory. And, because of that perspective, it looks forward to where we now are. Historically, it could also look back on a quarter-century of theory work in many of the arts and sciences. Coleridge himself had witnessed the rapid rise of chemistry, thanks in part to the experimental wizardry of his friend Humphry Davy. At the same time, he was fully aware of how Kant's successors had transformed philosophy. But, precisely because of his awareness of all these advances, Coleridge could feel as the Romantic era drew toward its close that perhaps the crucial task for someone like himself wasn't to formulate theory for yet another field, but rather to think about the way we do theory. Because only then can we hope to arrive at some sense of what the consequences of theory might be. And that, as Coleridge realized, would be the most important issue for theory in years to come.

Coleridge also had a very different idea of what theory was really about. We've seen that German idealism had pursued reflexivity until it took on the more general form of a movement of return. Meanwhile the sciences had gradually come to theory by a slightly different road, one that eventually led them to incorporate the process by which we arrive at theory into the form of theory itself. For both philosophy and the sciences, nonetheless, the point of metatheory was to reveal what the form or shape of theory for any given field ought to be. Coleridge saw the matter differently. To him, theory wasn't really about answers. As he perceived it, the value of a theory didn't come from what it could tell us about a given field. No doubt a theory would try to organize knowledge within its chosen field. But for him its primary value was as a form of intellectual activity. As activity, theory meant aspiration. For Coleridge, then, all forms of theory were forms of aspiration, and all forms of aspiration expressed our quest for knowledge. To that extent, they all shared a common theme. And because they did, it was important to understand their relation to each other. That was what metatheory was for: not to answer all our questions about theory, but to show why the pursuit of theory was meaningful in terms of what it aspired to achieve. So metatheory lay beyond theory not as a higher form of theory, but for what it could tell us about that.

From a conversation recorded in *Table Talk*, we get some notion of how Coleridge perceived the role of metatheory:

> My system is the only attempt that I know of ever made to reduce all knowledges into harmony; it opposes no other system, but shows what was true in each, and how that which was true in the particular in each of them became error because it was only half the truth. I have endeavored to unite the insulated fragments of truth and frame a perfect mirror. I show to each system that I fully understand and rightfully appreciate what that system means; but then I lift up that system to a higher point of view, from which I enable it to see its former position where it was indeed, but under another light and with different relations; so that the fragment of truth is not only acknowledged, but explained. (*CC* 14: 1, 248–49)

A "system" that would attempt to "reduce all knowledges into harmony" must involve some sort of metatheoretical viewpoint. Specifically, Coleridge says, "I show to each system that I fully understand and rightfully appreciate what that system means; but then I lift up that system to a higher point of view . . . so that the fragment of truth is not only acknowledged, but explained." To lift each of these "knowledges" up to a higher point of view, however, necessitates a perspective that can talk about those "knowledges" in terms of how they analyze their material. In other words, it would have to be able to talk about them as forms of theory.

For Coleridge, to talk about "knowledges" as forms of theory meant we would need to look at exactly how thought itself worked. As he saw it, every effort we make to think about or conceptualize a given subject takes one of two forms: reason or understanding. In *Aids to Reflection* he offered this analysis of reason:

Reason is the Power of universal and necessary Convictions, the Source and Substance of Truths above Sense, and having their evidence in themselves. Its presence
is always marked by the *necessity* of the position affirmed: this necessity being
conditional, when a truth of Reason is applied to Facts of Experience, or to the rules
and maxims of the Understanding; but *absolute,* when the subject matter is itself
the growth or offspring of the Reason. (*CC* 9: 216)

Subsequently, he goes on to talk about understanding in equal detail:

The Understanding then (considered exclusively as an organ of human intelligence,) is the Faculty by which we reflect and generalize. Take, for instance, any
objects consisting of many parts, a House, or a group of Houses: and if it be
contemplated, as a Whole, *i.e.* (as many constituting a One,) it forms what in the
technical language of Psychology, is called a *total impression.* Among the various
component parts of this, we direct our attention especially to such as we recollect to
have noticed in other total impressions: the wall, the roof, the chimney, the win-
dow, the door. Then, by a voluntary Act, we withhold our attention from all the
rest . . . to reflect exclusively on these; and these we henceforward use as *common
characters,* by virtue of which several Objects are referred to one and the same sort.
They are all *Houses.* Of each alike we repeat, It is a *House.* (*CC* 9: 224–25, with
variants)

Perhaps the best way to distinguish between reason and understanding is in
terms of theoretical autonomy.[2] On this point, Coleridge clearly favors reason. To
him, reason is a "Power." Its power comes from the fact that it doesn't have to go
outside itself to generate inferences. In other words, it possesses its "evidence"
within itself. Hence the "necessity" of its inferences. The only exception is when
sensory data get involved. Under these circumstances, "necessity" is at best
conditional. A mistaken perception, or insufficient empirical knowledge, might
easily invalidate our inferences. Obviously, Coleridge is somewhat bothered by
contingency of this sort. Compared to understanding, nonetheless, reason still
displays a much greater degree of autonomy. Unlike reason, understanding has
to rely wholly on sense data. If understanding is the faculty by which we reflect
and generalize, it must be based on what we obtain from our experiences. In
contrast to reason, then, it looks solely to external sources.

His distinction between reason and understanding gives Coleridge a means to
critique the natural sciences.[3] Specifically, he feels they exhibit a bias toward
the empirical. For him, that bias has its source in the very way we apprehend
Nature itself:

The Power which we call Nature, may be thus defined: A Power subject to the Law of Continuity . . . which law the human understanding, by a necessity arising out of its own constitution, can *conceive* only under the form of Cause and Effect. That this *form* (or law) of Cause and Effect is (relatively to the World *without*, or to Things as they subsist independently of our perceptions) only a form or mode of *thinking*, that it is a law inherent in the Understanding itself . . . —this becomes evident as soon as we attempt to apply the pre-conception directly to any operation of Nature. For in this case we are forced to represent the cause as being at the same instant the effect, and vice versâ the effect as being the cause—a relation which we seek to express by the terms Action and Re-action; but for which the term Reciprocal Action or the law of Reciprocity (germanicè Wechselwirkung) would be both more accurate and more expressive. (*CC* 9: 267–68)

But if we can take in what we perceive only within a framework of cause and effect, this, as Coleridge says elsewhere in *Aids to Reflection*, will mean that every event gets "subjected to the Relations of Cause and Effect: and the cause of the existence of which, therefore, is to be sought for perpetually in something Antecedent" (*CC* 9: 251). As a result, any attempt to understand nature becomes an endless quest for prior antecedents. For Coleridge, though, the problem isn't primarily whether we can actually manage to specify these. Instead, what concerns him more is our perpetual subjection to the causal scheme, which blocks off the possibility of any other viewpoint. Because of our endless quest for antecedents, we can never rise to a higher level of analysis that might allow us to discern some broader or more general principle behind all natural activity. The real limitation, then, of cause/effect analysis lies in the way it hinders any sort of higher awareness.[4]

To counter the negative pull of cause/effect analysis, Coleridge believed the natural sciences would need to adopt a wholly different viewpoint, one that subordinated the understanding to reason. And that, in turn, would entail a different mode of inquiry for the sciences:

By a Science I here mean any Chain of Truths that are either absolutely certain, or necessarily true for the human mind from the laws and constitution of the mind itself. In neither case is our conviction derived, or capable of receiving any addition, from outward Experience, or *empirical* data—*i.e.* matters-of-fact *given* to us through the medium of the Senses—though these Data may have been the occasion, or may even be an indispensable condition, of our reflecting on the former and thereby becoming *conscious* of the same. (*CC* 9: 291)

How the natural sciences ought to deal with empirical data is really the issue here. To the extent that these sciences privilege understanding over reason, they inevitably submit to a causal framework. Since understanding can only reflect or generalize on empirical data, any scheme that favors it is bound to be subject to empirical data and hence to the causal framework it enforces. For that reason, Coleridge wants the sciences to take up a different stance toward the data they supposedly interpret. What he gives is a blueprint for the natural sciences as he thinks they ought to be, rather than as they are. Any science that consists of a "Chain of Truths" characterized by absolute necessity or necessarily true for the mind because of what it inherently is, can hardly qualify as one of the experimental sciences. Of course, Coleridge is well aware of that. Yet he seems to believe that the crucial prerequisite for any science is its capacity to arrive at inferences by itself: in other words, its autonomy as theory.

At the same time, Coleridge also wants to apply his reason/understanding distinction to religion. The result is a gloss on the myth of Original Sin:

> In the temple-language of Egypt the Serpent was the Symbol of the Understanding in its twofold function, namely, as the faculty of *means* to *proximate* or *medial* ends . . . and again, as the discursive and logical Faculty possessed individually by each Individual— . . . in distinction from the Nous, *i.e.* Intuitive Reason, the Source of Ideas and ABSOLUTE Truths, and the Principle of the Necessary and the Universal in our Affirmations and Conclusions. . . . The first human Sinner is the adequate Representative of all his Successors. And with no less truth may it be said, that it is the same Adam that falls in every man, and from the same reluctance to abandon the too dear and undivorceable Eve: and the same EVE tempted by the same serpentine and perverted Understanding which, framed originally to be the Interpreter of the Reason and the ministering Angel of the Spirit, is henceforth sentenced and bound over to the service of the Animal Nature, its needs and its cravings, dependent on the Senses for all its Materials, with the World of Sense for its appointed Sphere. (*CC* 9: 258–62)

Here, then, we have "fallenness" in the guise of an intellectual mistake. Focused on proximate or medial ends, the understanding can't see the need to defer to an ultimate end. Instead, it wants immediate gratification. The discursive/logical faculty is similarly shortsighted. Unlike the intuitive capacity of reason, it simply can't grasp the thing itself. Consequently, it produces a discourse about that thing whose only hope is to describe it approximately. What Coleridge tries to explain next is how, under these conditions, understanding manages to subordinate reason. "The first human Sinner," he says, "is the adequate Representative of all his Successors." Adequate, presumably, because he has the same faculties, not just because he happens to come first. But the notion of a "Representative" also hints that the fall of reason can't be reduced simply to a causal sequence that begins with an initial act by the "first human Sinner." Subsequently, the text reinforces this hint in a distinctly Pauline fashion: "it is the same Adam that falls in every man." For Coleridge, it all begins from "the same reluctance to abandon the too dear and undivorceable Eve." What, though, does Eve signify? Not what we might expect (i.e., the feminine nature) but (as Coleridge makes clear in a note) our tendency to think in terms of what we perceive or apprehend. We can't shake off that tendency ("too dear and undivorceable") because we're attached to the world we perceive and experience. And, because of our attachment, we fall into a particular relation to it, in which understanding becomes predominant. An understanding that the text portrays as "serpentine and perverted." Originally intended as the "Interpreter of the Reason" and the "ministering Angel of the Spirit," it was supposed to interpret the sense data we receive to the spirit. But, "sentenced and bound over to the service of the Animal Nature," it becomes "dependent on the Senses for all its Materials, with the World of Sense for its appointed Sphere." Yet we still need to explain why Eve should be "tempted" to subordinate the mind to the purely sensual. If we think of the understanding as essentially intellectual, we can imagine how it might seek to transform the purely sensory into a form of knowledge. Seduced by the empirical picture of things, however, it comes to adopt that as its own perspective.

More broadly, this gloss of Original Sin in terms of reason/understanding shows how we might look at religion. In particular, it suggests a way to elucidate religious lore by means of a conceptual perspective. Thus what looked like mere mythical narrative becomes a repository of arcane knowledge. In this fashion, we save narratives from dismissal as simple superstition. Instead, elements that reflect archaic beliefs or practices are reinterpreted. The social position of Eve vis-à-vis Adam, for instance, comes to symbolize the relation between empiricism and rationality. Or the notion of a demonic presence (i.e., the tempter) is transformed into a mental faculty. In addition, the use of a conceptual perspective on religion also significantly affects our view of historical time. Whereas myth is profoundly narrative or sequential, to see it conceptually takes away its temporal quality. When it is "the same Adam that falls in every man," what we have is no longer a causal sequence based on a single, initial act. Because the Fall is reenacted in each individual, temporality becomes cyclical. As a result, the Fall turns out to be a permanent human condition rather than one that begins at a specific historical moment.

What Coleridge says about reason/understanding can also apply equally well to a different field of inquiry: in terms of psychology, it gives us an analysis of the will.[5] In fact, one of the early sections of *Aids to Reflection* had already defined Original Sin as a malaise of the individual human will:

> I profess a deep conviction that Man was and is a *fallen* Creature, not by accidents of bodily constitution, or any other cause, which *human* Wisdom in a course of ages might be supposed capable of removing; but diseased in his *Will*, in that Will which is the true and only strict synonime of the word, I, or the intelligent Self. (*CC* 9: 139–40)

At first glance, it may seem a bit odd for Coleridge to equate the I or "intelligent Self" with the will. Since he emphasizes intelligence, one might wonder about other possible equivalents of the self. For instance, why not mind, reason, or consciousness? Elsewhere in *Aids to Reflection*, we get a definition of will that distinctly hints at some of these: "For the personal Will comprehends the *idea*, as a Reason, and it gives causative force to the Idea, as a *practical* Reason. . . . or say: —the Spirit comprehends the Moral Idea, by virtue of it's [*sic*] rationality, and it gives to the Idea causative Power, as a Will" (*CC* 9: 300). So will, as defined by Coleridge, displays an intellectual as well as volitional element. Intellectually we grasp a given idea, which, once grasped, is elevated to the level of Idea at the moment we act on it. Thus the concept of Will not only includes an intellectual element but even attempts to specify its relation to volition.

Subsequently, Coleridge comes back to Original Sin, which he can now treat more fully. He begins with a definition of will as opposed to nature:

> Herein, indeed, the will consists. This is the essential character by which WILL is *opposed* to Nature, as *Spirit*, and raised *above* Nature as *self-determining* Spirit— this, namely, that it is a power of *originating* an act or state. (*CC* 9: 268)

Will, then, is equivalent to Spirit because of its capacity to originate an act. Conversely, if Nature is opposed to Spirit, what it lacks is presumably the capacity to originate. So the essential property of Nature must be continuity. In addition, the fact that Coleridge distinguishes between "Spirit" and "self-determining Spirit" would seem to indicate that not all forms of Spirit are self-determined. Yet the text specifically says Spirit implies the capacity to originate an act or condition. But if it has such a capacity, why shouldn't it be self-determined? After all, isn't that what makes anything self-determined?

At this point, we need to look at how Coleridge connects Original Sin to the will:

> Sin is therefore spiritual Evil: but the spiritual in Man is the Will. Now when we do not refer to any particular Sins, but to that state and constitution of the Will, which is the ground, condition, and common Cause of all Sins; and when we would further express the truth, that this corrupt *Nature* of the Will must in some sense or other be considered as its own act, that the corruption must have been self-originated; —in this case and for this purpose we may, with no less propriety than force, entitle this dire spiritual evil and source of all evil, that is absolutely such, Original Sin. (*CC* 9: 273)

Now if Nature = that which can't originate its own condition or acts, a "corrupt Nature of the Will" must by definition be a will that lacks this capacity. Yet the very essence of will, as we recall, lies in its capacity to originate its own condition or acts. So when Coleridge speaks of a "corrupt Nature of the Will" he must mean a will that's *lost* its original capacity. Since the will is precisely that capacity, however, the only way it can possibly lose it must be by a self-initiated act. Thus his inference that "the corruption must have been self-originated." And so we arrive at Spirit (i.e., will) as no longer self-determined because it's lost the capacity to originate its own condition or acts. But even if this resolves the conflict posed by a will that isn't self-determined, what remains unclear is how the will could ever lose its original capacity by an act that it commits of its own volition.

Here it seems useful to turn to what Coleridge says about the particular way Original Sin acts on the dynamics of the Will/Nature relationship:

> For this is the essential attribute of a Will, and contained in the very *idea*, that whatever determines the Will acquires this power from a previous determination of the Will itself. The Will is ultimately self-determined, or it is no longer a *Will* under the law of perfect Freedom, but a *Nature* under the mechanism of Cause and Effect. And if by an act, to which it had determined itself, it has subjected itself to the determination of Nature (in the language of St. Paul, to the Law of the Flesh), it receives a nature into itself, and so far it becomes a Nature: and this is a corruption of the Will and a corrupt Nature. (*CC* 9: 285)

By means of cause and effect, then, we can finally explain how Original Sin takes away the will's capacity to originate its own acts. Unlike the will, nature works by a "mechanism" of cause and effect. Hence the lack of any self-originated acts in nature. Instead, cause and effect always occur in a purely mechanical way: cause produces effect, which in turn acts as cause to create a subsequent effect, and so on indefinitely. Thus natural activity is continuous, but never self-determined, since every act has some prior cause, itself equally necessitated. So when the will subjects itself to what Coleridge calls "the determination of Nature," it enters into the realm of cause and effect, where every act is externally determined. Imagine that the will originates an initial act (by which it subjects itself to Nature), that such an act forces a particular consequence, and that everything thereafter is determined by what precedes it. In this way, the will relinquishes its capacity to originate acts, since whatever it now does is determined by a prior act. Yet it continues to will its acts, by means of its volitional faculty. Its exercise of that faculty, however, is determined by an external agency. And so we get a will that isn't self-determined. Or, as Coleridge says, it "receives a nature into itself, and so far it becomes a Nature." Which means: it subordinates itself to some natural object and so falls under the sway of cause and effect.[6]

On a more general level, the analysis of Original Sin in terms of will shows how psychology can help to clarify religion. Specifically, psychology permits different spiritual conditions to be defined and explained. While the distinction between "fallen" and "unfallen" is probably essential to any form of belief that embodies a redemptive scheme, we might be hard pressed to say exactly what that distinction is really all about. In themselves, the terms "fallen" and "unfallen" have no content. We can't simply draw on lexicology to specify what either condition consists of. Nor is the appeal to some sort of mythic narrative terribly useful. For a mythic narrative to be useful, we would have to explain at some point how the events of that narrative affect our present condition. Typically, this gets done in one of two ways: symbolically, or causally. But if we try to interpret a mythic narrative symbolically, we end up exactly where we were before—with the need to describe our condition in other, nonmythical terms. If we interpret a mythic narrative causally, however, we find ourselves forced to ascribe historical value to a text whose historical basis is at best questionable. By contrast, psychology gives concepts like "fallenness" or "unfallenness" a specific content. Instead of a vague appeal to some mythic narrative (which itself needs to be interpreted), we now obtain a clear, distinct definition of "fallenness" and "unfallenness" in terms of the capacity of an individual to originate his or her own acts. Even more important, perhaps, the notion of a capacity in the will to originate its own acts helps to explain how the shift from an "unfallen" to a "fallen" condition might take place. If we add the notion of a sphere of activity governed by necessity (the cause/effect model), we can then see how a particular kind of act initiated by the will (pursuit of an object causally defined or determined) could compromise the capacity to originate acts, which produces the shift from an "unfallen" to "fallen" condition.

Finally, beyond any specific "knowledges" (philosophy, natural sciences, religion, psychology), we have the question of how *Aids to Reflection* sees theory in general. To some extent, this is what makes the work unique. Unlike most Romantic theorists, Coleridge doesn't favor a particular theoretical viewpoint. Instead, he simply wants to relate different fields and/or viewpoints. In fact, the absence of a single dominant viewpoint in *Aids to Reflection* is of special importance. It implies that ultimately the work isn't about either fields of inquiry or viewpoints. Throughout his life, Coleridge had consistently shown great interest in the process by which we arrive at theory. Arguably, we might even maintain that *Aids to Reflection* is more about how we arrive at theory than about any given theory. Essentially, then, the significance of the work can be found in what it has to say about the genesis of theory. For Coleridge, how we arrive at theory is more important than any actual theory insofar as it reveals, more richly and expressively than theory itself possibly could, why we should care about theory. And, to the extent that thought is dynamic rather than static, more committed to its quest for knowledge than to the forms it employs to frame its perceptions, perhaps what's most meaningful about it is the process by which it comes to be.[7]

For *Aids to Reflection*, any inquiry into the formation of thought has to begin with our experiences. But experience, as Coleridge sees it, isn't just sensory data. In fact, all of our experiences reflect a fundamental tension between internal and external, mind and world. They show the role of sense data, and of our own cognitive faculty. Obviously, sense perception has to be the basis for any kind of reflection. What isn't so clear is where to go from there. In particular, we might wonder whether reflection can ever become wholly independent of sense data. Consequently, *Aids to Reflection* is about how the mind moves from the purely sensory to thought. At the same time, Coleridge remains mindful of what happens when we rely excessively on the purely sensory. Hence his caution against an overemphasis on empirical data in the natural sciences.

What experience means as a category comes into play most fully, however, only within religion. In a prescient way, Coleridge had foreseen the difficulties that would beset any form of traditional religious belief in the modern era. His effort to rethink Original Sin in terms of a "fallen" consciousness enslaved to the external world seeks to redirect religious sensibility toward the experiential. Thus we no longer need to prove Original Sin historically (impossible anyway, given the mythic status of the Genesis narrative). Instead, we find traces of it in our own personal experiences. Much of this, of course, harks back to Augustine. Nonetheless, even a recovery of Augustine counts as a significant move given the simultaneous rapprochement with Kantian philosophy. Meanwhile, Coleridge also sought to demonstrate the need for redemption experientially. We feel "an aching hollowness in the bosom, a dark cold speck at the heart" (*CC* 9: 24). Likewise, we get a moving account of conversion as a journey: with its attendant anxiety, like that caused by shapes from our dreams that continue to haunt our consciousness after we awake, we set out on our way, somewhat uncertainly, in the morning twilight (*CC* 9: 35–38).

From another standpoint, it seems equally appropriate to describe the tendency of *Aids to Reflection* as one of aspiration. Here Coleridge himself offers the best commentary. In a discussion of various plant and animal species, he observes: "All things strive to ascend, and ascend in their striving" (*CC* 9: 118). Above all, they strive to make the spiritual prevail over the material. The opposition between reason and understanding shows what's at issue. On the one hand, you have a tendency to subordinate thought to sense data. With that comes an emphasis on external objects, and a disposition to consider only those forms of thought that either address external objects, or our thoughts about these (in short, the "school of Locke"). Not that other forms of thought are explicitly denied. But there is a definite tendency to privilege the immediate, sensory sphere. On the other hand, you have an effort to subordinate sense data to thought. In practice, it leads to modes of thought that don't depend on sense data directly, and, in some instances, not at all. Here the basic impulse is to make thought reflect on itself. Unlike the emphasis on sense data, however, reason doesn't try to deny what lies outside its sphere. Instead, it simply intellectualizes the sensory. The empirical bias of the natural sciences would subordinate thought to sense data. The opposite tendency points toward religion. How it all works becomes evident only in psychology. For Coleridge, we make the spiritual prevail over the material, or reason over understanding, only by an effort of will. Philosophy informs us what the consequences are.

In the end, all his effort to affirm the spiritual over the material has, for Coleridge, just one objective: to make reflection possible. In the Introductory Aphorisms to *Aids to Reflection,* he had already spoken of "the light which is the eye of this soul." Of it he observes: "This *seeing* light, this *enlightening* eye, is Reflection." Yet, as he goes on to say, it's more than that. Above all, we should "know too, whence it first came, and still continues to come—of what light even this light is *but* a reflection. This, too, is THOUGHT: and all thought is but unthinking that does not flow out of this, or tend towards it" (*CC* 9: 15–16). So all human thought is but a reflection of divine thought, the human mind a finite embodiment of the divine Mind. Yet if the human mind is, as Coleridge says, a reflection of the divine Mind, the activity of our minds must be, by implication, a reflection of its activity as well. But the activity of the divine Mind leads to creation. By a tradition that goes back to Augustine and to the biblical exegesis of Philo of Alexandria, and even beyond that to Plato himself, Coleridge could assert that the creation of the world takes place through divine thought. By analogy, then, reflection must create an image of the world, and so give us a notion of what creation is like. And if to imitate the divine Mind is ultimately Godlike, the effect must be to make us better than we now are. Hence the rationale for all the relationships Coleridge had sought to specify between different fields of inquiry. By means of these relationships, we obtain a conception of the whole for which each remains, in itself, but a partial explanation. And with that conception of the whole, we arrive at some sense of the world as a totality.

In many ways, *Aids to Reflection* marks a special moment both for Coleridge and for the history of Romantic theory. Special, because in this work Coleridge doesn't have a specific agenda for theory in mind. Unlike the Logosophia or *Opus Maximum* project, *Aids to Reflection* doesn't try to make a point about a given field. Instead, what it does is to step back a bit from theory, in order to look at it from a more external viewpoint. And that gives the work a special place in the history of Romantic theory. After the rise of theory in the wake of the Revolution and, subsequently, the Napoleonic era, what we have, at the end, is a tendency to question theory, to ask whether it actually delivers what it professes to give, and what its place finally ought to be. In that discussion, Coleridge plays a crucial role. To assess theory properly, he felt, you couldn't be engaged in the formation of theory within an individual field. To arrive at a theory within a given field you had to *do* theory. And if you did theory, you couldn't focus on how you did it. To do theory within a given field, you had to get into a particular mode of thought. For Coleridge, to do theory is to generalize. To become aware of how you did theory, you had to be able to see how you generalized. And that required a very different sort of perspective.

At the same time, the sort of perspective Coleridge proposed wasn't merely external to theory. For him, it also had to be on a higher level. What we get, then, is metatheory as opposed to theory. As Coleridge saw it, a theory couldn't really achieve this sort of perspective on itself. In that respect, his notion of metatheory differs in a crucial way from that of his predecessors. It didn't grow directly or naturally out of theory. In other words, you didn't simply ascend from theory to metatheory. On the contrary: theory was unenlightened about itself. And that implied, in turn, the need for a higher perspective. For Coleridge, a theory couldn't "see" itself because its formation relied less on perception than on a mode of formal development. In order to generalize, you had to think about your experiences or impressions formally. Once you began to think about these formally, however, it wasn't so easy to think about your own process of thought simultaneously. To do that, you had to have a perception. But, at the deepest level, perception wasn't formal. And that meant you couldn't express what you perceived about your own process of thought formally. To do theory, then, was precisely what made you blind to metatheory. If you wanted to think about your experiences formally, what you had to sacrifice was an awareness of your own thought processes. For other proponents of Romantic theory, its power lay in its capacity to treat our experiences formally or abstractly. And that, in turn, was how you got from theory to metatheory. For Coleridge, however, the capacity of Romantic theory for this sort of abstractness was precisely what led to trouble elsewhere.

But if theory isn't aware of the process by which it comes to be, we presumably can't expect it to understand or properly appreciate its role. For that, we need to turn to *Aids to Reflection*. And so Coleridge considers the different possibilities: explanation, knowledge, or, most interestingly, reflection. His preference for reflection shows that he didn't believe theory had to lead to knowledge. In that respect, he looks forward to where we now are: to a natural epistemology where we get, at best, explanation but not certainty. Yet the primary role of theory, for Coleridge, was as a means to reflection. Reflection, however, doesn't necessarily point to a specific end. And clearly Coleridge isn't really interested in one here. Instead, as elsewhere in his work, he shows himself to be most interested in thinking as an activity. Precisely because he didn't believe theory could ever be an end in itself, he felt we ought to define theory in terms of its use. For Coleridge, theory doesn't quite yield what we want, which is a perspective that would make our experiences meaningful. From his standpoint, we only get that by means of reflection, or metatheory. At the same time, theory led to metatheory. Through metatheory, theory appears as a form of human activity, by which we strive to impart coherence to our experiences. By what it seeks to do, then, theory becomes expressive of our spiritual quest.

CHAPTER EIGHT

The Dream of Subjectivity

It starts with a dream. In her 1831 Introduction to *Frankenstein*, Mary Shelley describes a conversation (June 17, 1816) at the Villa Diodati (near Geneva) between Byron and her husband. Her Introduction says they talked about "the nature of the principle of life, and whether there was any probability of its ever being discovered and communicated." Discussion focuses on the experiments of Erasmus Darwin, especially one where a piece of vermicelli placed under a glass case appears to display voluntary motion. But Byron and Percy remain skeptical: "Not thus, after all, would life be given. Perhaps a corpse would be re-animated; galvanism had given token of such things: perhaps the component parts of a creature might be manufactured, brought together, and endued with vital warmth." Their talk lasts late into the night. Finally the three go to bed. But Mary finds herself unable to sleep:

When I placed my head on my pillow, I did not sleep, nor could I be said to think. My imagination, unbidden, possessed and guided me, gifting the successive images that arose in my mind with a vividness far beyond the usual bounds of reverie. I saw—with shut eyes, but acute mental vision,—I saw the pale student of unhallowed arts kneeling beside the thing he had put together. I saw the hideous phantasm of a man stretched out, and then, on the working of some powerful engine, show signs of life, and stir with an uneasy, half vital motion. Frightful must it be; for supremely frightful would be the effect of any human endeavour to mock the stupendous mechanism of the Creator of the world. His success would terrify the artist; he would rush away from his odious handywork, horror-stricken. He would hope that, left to itself, the slight spark of life which he had communicated would fade; that this thing, which had received such imperfect animation, would subside into dead matter; and he might sleep in the belief that the silence of the grave would quench for ever the transient existence of the hideous corpse which he had looked upon as the cradle of life. He sleeps; but he is awakened; he opens his eyes; behold the horrid thing stands at his bedside, opening his curtains, and looking on him with yellow, watery, but speculative eyes. I opened mine in terror. The idea so possessed my mind, that a thrill of fear ran through me, and I wished to exchange the ghastly image of my fancy for the realities around. I see them still; the very room, the dark *parquet,* the closed shutters, with the moonlight struggling through, and the sense I had that the glassy lake and white high Alps were beyond. I could not so easily get rid of my hideous phantasm; still it haunted me. (*Novels* 1: 179–80)

Significantly, the passage isn't clear about whether Mary is asleep or awake. Yes, she begins: "I did not sleep." Yet she immediately qualifies that: "Nor could I be said to think." Normally, wakefulness involves some form of awareness (i.e., thought). Subsequently, we read: "my imagination, unbidden, possessed and guided me, gifting the successive images that arose in my mind with a vividness far beyond the usual bounds of reverie." Now while wakefulness implies at least some control over mental images, passivity about these points to sleep. And if we didn't know better, we might easily think that what we have here is an account of that unique moment, fraught with both pleasure and anxiety, in which we fall asleep. Note, too, the mention of "successive" images. In falling asleep, we frequently perceive a succession of images—as if the mind had lost its mental grip, and hence its capacity to fix on just one. As we relax, then, the images flow more freely. So here we have, again, a hint of passivity. For Shelley, these images merely "arose in my mind," a product of the most involuntary sort of genesis. All the same, they possess "a vividness far beyond the usual bounds of reverie." Reverie, though, can often precede sleep. Like sleep, moreover, it involves a kind of mental relaxation, whereby the mind, disengaged from both thoughts and images, gains some respite from their tyranny.

At this point, Shelley blurs the distinction between sleep and wakefulness yet further. While various traits (mental vacuity, passivity, successive images) suggest sleep, her "acute mental vision" says otherwise. Nonetheless, she does admit her eyes were shut. Nor in fact does sleep preclude acute mental vision. On the contrary: vivid dream imagery can often result from a heightened perceptual capacity. Given all that, we might wonder why Shelley insists she was awake.

One way to look at the matter might be in terms of how her wakefulness will affect the balance between subjectivity and objectivity. In sleep, we get to alter what we don't like. All the external forces that seem to pose a threat of any kind, all the pressure we just can't manage to get rid of: if we could only sleep, so we think, we might be able to dream all of these away. Sleep, then, favors pure subjectivity. Unfortunately, we can't sleep all the time. And since we can't, we need some other way to fend off the pressure we feel from objectivity or external forces. So we try to conceptualize those forces. In that way, we no longer feel their radical otherness as a threat to our own subjectivity. Once that otherness has been conceptualized, we feel our relation to it has ceased to be purely passive. Because we can conceptualize radical otherness, we believe we can somehow assimilate it into our own subjectivity. Whether we actually can or not is, of course, another question. But we need to believe in our capacity to do it. So we conceptualize external nature, in order to avoid objectivity. By means of concepts, we transform objectivity into subjectivity. Hence the appeal of theory.[1]

Like Shelley, the protagonist vacillates between sleep and wakefulness. His first response to his creation is to rush away from it in horror. Wishfully, he thinks the problem will somehow resolve itself: "He would hope that, left to itself, the slight spark of life which he had communicated would fade; that this thing, which had received such imperfect animation, would subside into dead matter." The sequel is less easy to explain: "and he might sleep in the belief that the silence of the grave would quench for ever the transient existence of the hideous corpse which he had looked upon as the cradle of life." Why sleep? If worried his creation might survive, shouldn't the protagonist go back and check on it? What if the creature were to survive and escape? Here the impersonal conditional ("and he might sleep") only highlights what's already paradoxical. Doesn't Shelley herself feel how absurd his wish is? On that point, a biographical detail from *History of a Six Weeks' Tour* seems useful. We know that their Channel crossing proved quite dangerous for the Shelleys: violent seas, quick flashes of lightning, and even a thunder squall that sent waves into their small boat. Yet Mary (who admits she was "dreadfully seasick") slept for most of the night, and woke up only as they entered Calais, despite an apparent awareness of their peril (*Novels* 8: 15). So sleep acts as a deliberate response to danger. Likewise for the protagonist: after the text suggests he *might* sleep, we're then told he *does* sleep. But if sleep is what he wants, it's also what he can't get. Instead, he's awakened by the creature itself: "behold the horrid thing stands at his bedside, opening his curtains, and looking on him with yellow, watery, but speculative eyes." Thus a protagonist intent on sleep as a way to avoid the creature he's created is roused by that same creature, determined to make the protagonist confront what he wants to avoid.

In their mutual gaze, one detail stands out particularly: the eyes of the creature are said to be "yellow, watery, but speculative." If the first two adjectives are purely physical, the third has an eerie, troubling quality. "Speculative" invariably refers to thought, of a human kind. And with that, we enter the realm of subjectivity. So the creature gazes at the protagonist with the same sort of reflective consciousness as the protagonist himself. Whatever the protagonist feels about the creature, then, could just as easily be felt by the creature about the protagonist. "Speculative": the word evokes *speculum* (lit., mirror). Taken figuratively, it might suggest the protagonist sees his own image reflected back to himself. Not exactly, of course. And yet, if we recognize an other as some form of our own subjectivity, the crucial moment for the protagonist occurs when he recognizes a similar subjectivity.

This moment of recognition duplicates itself: just as the protagonist "opens his eyes" to "behold the horrid thing" at his bedside, so Shelley, likewise: "I opened mine in terror." On a larger scale, too, the resemblances multiply. After all, both Shelley and the protagonist try some form of imaginative creation. The text hints at their relationship, with the protagonist as "the pale student of unhallowed arts." Subsequently, he's even specifically termed an "artist." And, in a complicated way, their creations also get linked explicitly. Shelley says: "I saw the hideous phantasm of a man stretched out." "Phantasm" = something dreamlike, even illusory. Similarly, the protagonist's sleep seeks to reduce the creature's existence to a dreamlike level.

Yet in one important respect, Shelley and her protagonist clearly differ. We've seen that the protagonist sleeps to avoid the creature he's created. Shelley, meanwhile, does the exact opposite: for her, it's crucial she open her eyes in order to "exchange the ghastly image of my fancy for the realities around." Nor is it insignificant that years later she can still recall what she saw vividly: "the very room, the dark *parquet*, the closed shutters, with the moonlight struggling through, and the sense I had that the glassy lake and white high Alps were beyond." Note that she doesn't actually *see* the "glassy lake," nor the "white high Alps" (despite her visual description of these). Note, too, how her own darkened bedroom matches that of her protagonist. Hence her need for a "sense" of the lake and Alps beyond: otherwise the resemblances between her own situation and his could become unbearable.[2]

Finally, we might wonder about the "terror" Shelley professes to feel. Here her earlier comment is useful: "for supremely frightful would be the effect of any human endeavour to mock the stupendous mechanism of the Creator of the world." Curiously, though, it isn't the failure to replicate what the Creator has done that's most frightful. On the contrary: "his success would terrify the artist." But why? Wouldn't it lead to a sense of Godlike capacity? To understand why that doesn't happen, we should keep in mind that what frightens the protagonist most is his ability to communicate the "spark of life" to his creation. Thus, by purely mechanical means, the protagonist can create a distinct subjectivity. And the reason this has the power to terrify is that we can't understand how a purely physical/chemical apparatus could give rise to the equivalent of a human consciousness. Hence the "terror" that seizes Shelley.

In fact, what primarily concerns Shelley isn't the creature itself. Instead, her *frisson* probably comes from the "speculative" quality of the creature's gaze, which she mentions just before she tells us how she opened her own eyes in terror. Even the way she describes it makes it uncannily suggestive. When she says, "I opened mine in terror," her use of "mine" can be understood only by reference to the previous sentence, which talks about the eyes of the creature. So the creature's subjectivity forces Shelley to recognize her own. The "ghastly image of my fancy" is ghastly precisely because of its complex relation to her own subjectivity. Were the image either similar or dissimilar exclusively, it would be easy to rationalize it. As similar and dissimilar simultaneously, it becomes uncanny.

To understand why it's so difficult to come to terms with another subjectivity, we might look at the creation episode more closely. Curiously, the 1818 text places a lot of emphasis on a detail the 1831 Introduction doesn't even mention, the dream that comes to Victor Frankenstein after he animates the creature:

> I had worked hard for nearly two years, for the sole purpose of infusing life into an inanimate body. For this I had deprived myself of rest and health. I had desired it with an ardour that far exceeded moderation; but now that I had finished, the beauty of the dream vanished, and breathless horror and disgust filled my heart. Unable to endure the aspect of the being I had created, I rushed out of the room, and continued a long time traversing my bed-chamber, unable to compose my mind to sleep. At length lassitude succeeded to the tumult I had before endured; and I threw myself on the bed in my clothes, endeavouring to seek a few moments of forgetfulness. But it was in vain: I slept indeed, but I was disturbed by the wildest dreams. I thought I saw Elizabeth, in the bloom of health, walking in the streets of Ingolstadt. Delighted and surprised, I embraced her; but as I imprinted the first kiss on her lips, they became livid with the hue of death; her features appeared to change, and I thought that I held the corpse of my dead mother in my arms; a shroud enveloped her form, and I saw the grave-worms crawling in the folds of the flannel. (*Novels* 1: 40)

Here it's important to note that the "dreams" Victor has while asleep aren't by any means the first to be mentioned. Instead, his two-year period of labor on the creature is itself a dream of some kind: "now that I had finished, the beauty of the dream vanished." While in pursuit of his goal, however, Victor "had desired it with an ardour that far exceeded moderation." Evidently, then, the "beauty" of the dream comes from the passion of his pursuit. From that standpoint, fulfillment is clearly antithetical to what the dream itself offers. Likewise, the "breathless horror and disgust" when it comes to an end only emphasize the primacy of pursuit over fulfillment.

On a more general level, we might argue for the primacy of subjectivity over objectivity. Wholly emotional in emphasis, the dream is equivalent to pure subjectivity. Conversely, the actual process of creation, as the manipulation of a wholly material element, is purely objective to Victor. As he sees it, the problem is that he can't assimilate the objective (i.e., the creature) to his own subjectivity. The fact that he "selected his [i.e., the creature's] features as beautiful" (*Novels* 1: 39) shows he wanted to make his creation conform to the beauty of his dream subjectivity. Unfortunately, it doesn't work out that way: "Beautiful! —Great God!" (*Novels* 1: 39). His exclamation points to the source of his difficulty: unless he can create *ex nihilo* like God, what he produces is bound to betray the limitations of his material. As he rushes from his workplace, "unable to endure the aspect of the being I had created," he experiences the shock of a confrontation with objectivity. Nor is it accidental that he rushes from workplace to bedroom: once his waking dream goes awry, his only wish is for the dreams that accompany sleep.

Yet even before he falls asleep, what Victor does is already indicative of his mood. Despite his efforts, he "continued a long time traversing my bed-chamber, unable to compose my mind to sleep." Clearly, sleep doesn't come without a struggle. But struggle means expenditure of energy. And so "at length lassitude succeeded to the tumult I had before endured." Simply put, he no longer has the energy to shape his dreams. Whereas earlier he had tried "to compose my mind to sleep," he now hopes at most for "a few moments of forgetfulness." In vain: "I slept indeed, but I was disturbed by the wildest dreams." Here exhaustion from his efforts to sleep produces lassitude, which is tantamount to passivity. As a result, he becomes vulnerable to whatever fears arise from his circumstances.

Perhaps the most remarkable aspect of Victor's dream is the degree to which it symbolically gives away the plot of the entire novel. The dream begins with Elizabeth, depicted as "in the bloom of health." Yet this quickly leads to an ironic reversal, so that the same Elizabeth is soon marked by "the hue of death" just as emphatically. The reversal is obviously dreamlike: it allows the narrator to alter a situation in a way rarely found in everyday life. Likewise, the very mention of

Elizabeth as an apparently aimless promeneur in a town or city like Ingolstadt renders her *disponible* to the narratorial gaze. In fact, Elizabeth never comes to Ingolstadt. Instead, the novel associates her throughout with the domestic sphere, which is based in Geneva. Ingolstadt, by contrast, is about study, far away from all domestic presences. For Elizabeth to appear *disponible* in Ingolstadt, then, points to desire symbolically.

In this novel, however, desire seems destined only to be frustrated: as soon as Victor "imprinted the first kiss on her lips," they turn "livid with the hue of death." What exactly, though, does "first kiss" mean here? If Victor and Elizabeth are in love, it's hard to believe they haven't kissed already. So perhaps "first kiss" looks forward proleptically to their subsequent wedding night. Seen in that way, the dream posits a causal relationship: Victor kisses Elizabeth, and the kiss results in her death. Or, in terms of plot, Victor decides to marry Elizabeth, which prompts the creature to murder her after Victor's refusal to create a female creature. Since the murder comes about precisely because Victor denies the creature a happiness he (Victor) seeks for himself, his marriage to Elizabeth becomes the indirect cause of her unfortunate end.

Yet if the dream episode is simply meant to expose a hidden causal relationship, we might wonder why Elizabeth should come to look like Victor's mother. As Victor himself puts it, "her features appeared to change, and I thought that I held the corpse of my dead mother in my arms." If we resist the obvious Oedipal perspective, we discover, on a more purely formal level, a whole complex of causal relationships. Elizabeth, after all, had indirectly brought about the death of Victor's mother, who catches scarlet fever from her adopted child. So we have Victor in the same relation to Elizabeth as hers vis-à-vis his mother. Clearly, loss is the dominant theme. All relationships lead to loss, in each case that of a beloved object. Brought about by causal relationships, these losses suggest in turn an external necessity of some kind.

In effect, necessity counters subjectivity. Whereas subjectivity wants to possess the beloved object, necessity works against that. When Victor tries to kiss Elizabeth, her lips take on a deathly hue. And, as if this weren't enough, her features metamorphose into those of his mother. Now, even the pleasure of the gaze is denied. Meanwhile, the beloved object also eludes him temporally: for Elizabeth to change into his mother places her agewise at a further remove. And physically as well: no longer able to kiss Elizabeth, he can only hold his mother in his arms. Yet even she becomes less accessible: "a shroud enveloped her form." Now he can't even see her. What he does see, instead, is simply frightful: "And I saw the grave-worms crawling in the folds of the flannel." So the dream is about the triumph of objectivity over subjectivity. Not only can he not possess the beloved object, but he even has to witness the process by which that object gets lost and ultimately destroyed.[3]

At the same time, the whole nightmare occurs within a distinctly subjective framework. The causal sequence that links Elizabeth's death to that of Victor's mother is based on a highly subjective portrayal of events, one that compresses and even omits relevant circumstances. Nor is there any voice other than that of the narrator. But without other voices, the dream will presumably have no awareness of its own subjectivity. So what happens when another voice speaks, and thereby breaks the spell?

To some extent, that's exactly what the creature does with his narrative. It ends with a request: "We may not part until you have promised to comply with my requisition. I am alone, and miserable; man will not associate with me; but one as deformed and horrible as myself would not deny herself to me. My companion must be of the same species, and have the same defects. This being you must create" (*Novels* 1: 107). Oddly, Victor doesn't seem to understand the request at all. His initial response shows, in effect, how hard it is for one subjectivity to recognize another. Specifically, he says: "But I was bewildered, perplexed, and unable to arrange my ideas sufficiently to understand the full extent of his proposition" (*Novels* 1: 107). Why can't he understand what the creature wants? On some level, we have to assume Victor simply can't imagine the creature with a female companion. In other words, he can't imagine why the creature would want what he himself wants. Which is to say: he can't see the creature as a subjectivity.

Significantly, what makes him grasp the request is its appeal to rights. As the creature puts it: "You must create a female for me, with whom I can live in the interchange of those sympathies necessary for my being. This you alone can do; and I demand it of you as a right which you must not refuse" (*Novels* 1: 108). Although Victor neglects to explain his anger, it presumably comes from a belief that the creature has, by his acts of violence, forfeited any claim based on the social compact. Meanwhile, the epithet "fiend" suggests a wish to deny him a place in society categorically. After all, a "fiend" is malevolent by nature, rather than merely because of circumstances. In addition, the term connotes the demonic, or some evil supernatural agency. Given the actual circumstances, however, the only plausible explanation would seem to be that Victor is genuinely biased against his own creation, and that his bias is due to his own subjectivity.

Seemingly aware of that bias, the creature establishes his "right" to a place in society by the way he demonstrates his subjectivity:

You are in the wrong . . . and, instead of threatening, I am content to reason with you. I am malicious because I am miserable; am I not shunned and hated by all mankind? You, my creator, would tear me to pieces, and triumph; remember that, and tell me why I should pity man more than he pities me? You would not call it murder, if you could precipitate me into one of those ice-rifts, and destroy my frame, the work of your own hands. Shall I respect man, when he contemns me? Let him live with me in the interchange of kindness, and, instead of injury, I would bestow every benefit upon him with tears of gratitude at his acceptance. . . . But I now indulge in dreams of bliss that cannot be realized. What I ask of you is reasonable and moderate; I demand a creature of another sex, but as hideous as myself: the gratification is small, but it is all that I can receive, and it shall content me. It is true, we shall be monsters, cut off from all the world; but on that account we shall be more attached to one another. Our lives will not be happy, but they will be harmless, and free from the misery I now feel. Oh! my creator, make me happy; let me feel gratitude towards you for one benefit! Let me see that I excite the sympathy of some existing thing; do not deny me my request! (*Novels* 1: 108–9)

The creature says, first of all, that rather than try to threaten, he wants to "reason" with his creator. Clearly, Victor himself had been totally emotional in response to the creature's request. The fact that the creature knows it is equally significant. It points to a distinct moral awareness on his part. Likewise, his description of his own act as rational displays a comparable intellectual awareness. We can only describe an act as rational if we know what rationality is. And to know that, we have to be capable of rational analysis. But a higher moral awareness + a capacity for rational analysis is more or less equivalent to subjectivity. And presumably possession of subjectivity should entitle one to ethical consideration.

Yet the creature doesn't just stop there. Instead, he also evinces an ability to perceive causal relationships: "I am malicious because I am miserable; am I not shunned and hated by all mankind?" Whereas Victor would probably contend "The creature is malicious; consequently he is shunned and hated by all mankind and hence miserable," the creature points out it would be more accurate to say: "I am malicious *because* I am miserable, and I am miserable because I am shunned and hated by all mankind." In other words, hatred and rejection by mankind have caused his malice. Here he shows a firm sense of how causal relationships work. His knowledge of causal relationships confirms, in turn, his capacity for rational analysis, and hence his subjectivity.

His perception that his "rights" argument doesn't persuade Victor moves the creature to make one last appeal. "Let him [i.e., "man"] live with me in the interchange of kindness," he says, "and, instead of injury, I would bestow every benefit upon him with tears of gratitude at his acceptance." I find this one of the most poignant moments in the text. The creature asks Victor to consider a mutual existence based on the "interchange of kindness." Yet the creature manifestly expects to give much more than he'll receive. Even so, he insists he'll shed "tears of gratitude" at the acceptance of his generosity. But why should *he* be grateful, if the balance of kindness is on his side? To some extent, "acceptance" of a benefit implies recognition of the giver. All the creature wants, then, is to be recognized as a subjectivity capable of intentionality. To recognize the subjectivity of the creature, however, would necessitate, as he himself realizes, a different conception of subjectivity. And so, finally: "But I now indulge in dreams of bliss that cannot be realized."

Precisely because he's no longer hopeful about a shared existence with humanity, the creature now makes a very different kind of request: "I demand a creature of another sex, but as hideous as myself; the gratification is small, but it is all I can receive, and it shall content me." At first glance, admittedly, his proposal might seem extravagant. After all, it involves the creation of another creature. Nevertheless, what it really points to is a drastically reduced sense of social possibility. Here we need to recall that, though physically ugly himself, the creature is fully aware of the difference between the ugly and the beautiful, and strongly inclined to the second. So when he asks for "a creature of another sex, but as hideous as myself," he appears to have in mind what might be workable rather than what he might really want. No wonder his gratification will be small. At the same time, he says: "it is all that I can receive, and it shall content me." But why so modest? Presumably any female companion Victor creates will also be endowed with the same aesthetic faculty as the creature. Were she also less ugly, it's easy to see how she might prefer another companion. In other words, the creature takes into account the subjectivity of the new creature he wants his maker to produce. His request also shows he won't impose himself on another subjectivity. Instead, he seems to hope that, exposed to the same sort of treatment he's received, she'll then turn to him as her only choice.

At that point, the creature observes, "we shall be monsters, cut off from all the world." Note that their monstrosity won't be due to their acts (if completely isolated, how can their acts possibly affect anyone?). Instead, I would argue, they become "monsters" precisely *because* they're cut off from humanity. It's their isolation, rather than their physical deformity, that's monstrous or unnatural:

their natural tendency is to associate with others. As the creature puts it: "Our lives will not be happy, but they will be harmless, and free from the misery I now feel." If a female companion won't suffice to make him happy, the real source of his present misery must presumably be his exclusion from the human sphere, its refusal to recognize him as a legitimate subjectivity. When he asks Victor to "make me happy," he says the way to do it is to "let me feel gratitude towards you for one benefit!" The fact that a single act of generosity by his creator can gratify him more than the constant companionship of a female creature points to what's at issue here. A free, voluntary act of generosity would indicate a desire for relation to him, hence an acknowledgment of his subjectivity. By contrast, if a female creature becomes attached to him, he feels it will simply be from a lack of better choices.

To some extent, we can measure the effect of the creature's appeal by the way Victor thinks about whether to create a second, female creature:

> I sat one evening in my laboratory; the sun had set, and the moon was just rising from the sea; I had not sufficient light for my employment, and I remained idle, in a pause of consideration of whether I should leave my labour for the night, or hasten its conclusion by an unremitting attention to it. As I sat, a train of reflection occurred to me, which led me to consider the effects of what I was now doing. Three years before I was engaged in the same manner, and had created a fiend whose unparalleled barbarity had desolated my heart, and filled it for ever with the bitterest remorse. I was now about to form another being, of whose dispositions I was alike ignorant; she might become ten thousand times more malignant than her mate, and delight, for its own sake, in murder and wretchedness. He had sworn to quit the neighbourhood of man, and hide himself in deserts; but she had not; and she, who in all probability was to become a thinking and reasoning animal, might refuse to comply with a compact made before her creation. They might even hate each other; the creature who already lived loathed his own deformity, and might he not conceive a greater abhorrence for it when it came before his eyes in the female form? She also might turn with disgust from him to the superior beauty of man; she might quit him, and he be again alone, exasperated by the fresh provocation of being deserted by one of his own species. (*Novels* 1: 128)

In several ways, the present scene mirrors the earlier creation scene. Both occur more or less at night. The twilight atmosphere of the present scene makes a reflective pause seem especially natural. Victor ponders "whether I should leave my labour for the night, or hasten its conclusion by an unremitting attention to it." In contrast to his earlier behavior, he now seems more aware, more disposed to consider consequences. After all, he's been there before. "Three years before I was engaged in the same manner," he says. So the present scene is, in many respects, a deliberate *reprise* of the earlier one.

On one point, nevertheless, it differs from the earlier creation episode: it begins with a distinct awareness of the problems introduced by a new subjectivity. "I was now about to form another being," reflects Victor, "of whose dispositions I was alike ignorant." He also has to be careful not to assume the new female creature will necessarily be like the male he's already created: "He [the original creature] had sworn to quit the neighbourhood of man, and hide himself in deserts; but she had not." In addition, there are the problems of intersubjectivity: "they might even hate each other." Finally, Victor considers other, less immediately foreseeable consequences: "the creature who already lived loathed his own deformity, and might he not conceive a greater abhorrence for it when it came before his eyes in the female form?" His remark that the creature "loathed his own deformity" marks a new level in his awareness of a different subjectivity. But for Victor to suppose the creature might "conceive a greater abhorrence for it [his own deformity] when it came before his eyes in the female form" displays an even greater acuteness. It ascribes to the creature some sense of what might be appropriate to a female creature. For that, the creature would need to have perceived the female (based on his experience of humanity) as inherently finer, more beautiful than the male. And that would in turn imply some sort of aesthetic faculty.

In what he says about the female creature's subjectivity, Victor displays a similar subtlety. He worries the female creature "also might turn with disgust from him [the male creature] to the superior beauty of man; she might quit him, and he be again alone." Her disgust, though, needn't be based simply on a comparative perspective. It might also involve an element of self-consciousness. After all, the original creature (as Victor points out) "loathed his own deformity." Why shouldn't the female do the same? And if she did, wouldn't the prospect of union with someone as ugly as herself intensify what she felt about her own deformity? Without self-awareness, meanwhile, she might willingly accept someone considerably less attractive than herself (whether from compassion, or some other motive). In both instances, then, Victor appears not only to recognize but even to grasp a subjectivity quite different from his own.

On a deeper level, however, Victor nonetheless constructs the subjectivity of the creature and its hypothetical companion in ways ultimately shaped by his own subjective standpoint. Thus after he admits the female creature he's about to create is one "of whose dispositions I was alike ignorant," he wonders if "she might become ten thousand times more malignant than her mate, and delight, for its own sake, in murder and wretchedness." How likely, though, is this? Clearly, the creature's narrative offers ample testimony to an *innate* disposition to kindness. With no social education, the creature feels an ardent desire to help the De Lacey family. His impulse is all the more remarkable given his previous adverse experiences. But if the original creature is so disposed, why should Victor think a female creature would be different? In fact, he even goes so far as to suppose a propensity to "delight, for its own sake, in murder and wretchedness." In other words, a fiend. Significantly, Victor's already termed the original creature a fiend. Yet nowhere does the text indicate he committed his acts of violence from a "delight, for its own sake, in murder and wretchedness." Indeed, given the hostility he's suffered, he has plenty of motive (*Novels* 1: 74). Thus his depiction as a fiend looks more like an effort to construct his subjectivity as a form of objectivity (i.e., creature as fiend, where fiend = infernal machine). In addition, it shows why Victor might interpret the female creature in the same way.

But perhaps the most extreme instance of arbitrary construction occurs as Victor considers what might happen if the female creature were to "turn with disgust from him to the superior beauty of man." At that point, Victor suggests, "she might quit him, and he be again alone, exasperated by the fresh provocation of being deserted by one of his own species." Although Victor seems to think the creature will then renew his hostility against humanity, it isn't at all clear he'll do that simply because of his failure to to win a companion. On the contrary: since the entire scheme would depend wholly on Victor's goodwill, for the creature to turn on his benefactor seems manifestly irrational. Nor does the text indicate that he ever acts irrationally. So the suspicion hardly seems justified.

Nevertheless, Victor appears to make a genuine attempt to live within another subjectivity. Otherwise it would be hard to explain how he could devote months of labor to the creation of a female creature. Note, moreover, the remorse he feels after he destroys it: "The remains of the half-finished creature, whom I had destroyed, lay scattered on the floor, and I almost felt as if I had mangled the living flesh of a human being" (*Novels* 1: 132). Yet, up to this point, he's adamantly tried to deny human status to the original creature. His apparently paradoxical behavior can be explained, I believe, by the fact that the female creature *isn't yet alive*. In other words, its subjectivity exists only in his own mind. At the same time, it's more than just another form of his own subjectivity. After all, recognition of Otherness can't be so easily explained if the other is completely transparent. Instead, it seems more natural to suppose Victor present within a subjectivity he himself has created by an imaginative act. Hence his regret after he destroys the female creature. If his existence in otherness formed part of his own subjectivity, his destruction of the female creature becomes an act of violence against himself. Meanwhile, other circumstances compel him to do it. Once animated, the female creature will obviously no longer permit the same sort of subjective possession as before. Rather, its real otherness will displace the subjective otherness imagined by its maker. To avoid the effects of that displacement, Victor has to eliminate what had previously formed a pretext for possession. His ability to brush aside any doubts about what he does points to the real motive behind his engagement in subjective otherness.[4]

Given the kind of relation Victor and his creature have, it's only appropriate for the creature to get the last word. Throughout the novel, Victor's tried to construct the subjectivity of the creature as a form of objectivity. For a brief period, nevertheless, it almost looks as if the creature might persuade his creator to recognize his subjectivity. The capstone, of course, would have been the creation of a female companion. When Victor fails to fulfill his promise, the narrative takes a critical turn. From now on, the creature can have no subjectivity other than that of Victor himself. Because of its self-awareness, no subjectivity can easily consent to become mere objectivity. Naturally, its first aim is to be recognized as a proper subjectivity. If denied that, its next move is to assimilate itself to the subjectivity by which it sought to be recognized. So when Victor destroys the female creature, he forces the original creature into a perpetual relation to himself. From now on, the creature can only haunt his creator constantly. In that way, the creature might hope to become a specter from whom Victor can never escape, and thereby merge with his creator's subjectivity. The failure of that scheme takes up the end of the novel. As the creature himself puts it:

> After the murder of Clerval, I returned to Switzerland, heart-broken and overcome. I pitied Frankenstein; my pity amounted to horror: I abhorred myself. But when I discovered that he, the author at once of my existence and of its unspeakable torments, dared to hope for happiness; that while he accumulated wretchedness and despair upon me, he sought his own enjoyment in feelings and passions from the indulgence of which I was for ever barred, then impotent envy and bitter indignation filled me with an insatiable thirst for vengeance. I recollected my threat, and resolved that it should be accomplished. I knew that I was preparing for myself a deadly torture; but I was the slave, not the master of an impulse, which I detested, yet could not disobey. Yet when she died! —nay, then I was not miserable. I had cast off all feeling, subdued all anguish to riot in the excess of my despair. Evil thenceforth became my good. Urged thus far, I had no choice but

to adapt my nature to an element which I had willingly chosen. The completion of my demoniacal design became an insatiable passion. And now it is ended. (*Novels* 1: 168)

While he seems genuinely sorry about Clerval, we might wonder why the creature should feel "heart-broken and overcome." To be "heart-broken" you have to have had a deep affection for someone now lost. Yet nowhere before does the creature display this sort of emotion for Clerval. What we do have is a warm mutual affection between Victor and Clerval. Given these circumstances, we might suppose the creature to identify with Victor and so vicariously experience what he imagines his creator must feel. And this would make sense if we assume that after his failure to get Victor to recognize his subjectivity the only recourse left to the creature is to assimilate himself completely to his creator's subjectivity. Hence his description of himself as "overcome." Normally, we depict ourselves as overcome by external forces. So Victor could describe himself, after the death of Clerval. For the creature to adopt such a posture, though, seems downright bizarre. Yet if we suppose him to identify with Victor, it all makes sense: although he commits the murder, it gives him no fulfillment subjectively. Indeed, one might even argue he commits it just so he can feel the same emotion as Victor.

In fact, his identification with Victor takes the creature to a paradoxical but logical extreme. As he himself puts it, "I pitied Frankenstein; my pity amounted to horror: I abhorred myself." Take pity, here, in the sense Aristotle seems to give it in the *Poetics:* as a strong form of empathy. A pity that amounts to horror is clearly reminiscent of the way Aristotle associates pity and fear. But if Aristotle already hints at pity as a form of catharsis, the sort of pity felt by the creature pushes that tendency to its limit. While pity focuses on some external Other, a pity that amounts to horror wants to leave its own subjectivity behind altogether. So when the creature says, "I abhorred myself," he means that subjectively he no longer has any desire to be himself. Instead, since he speaks of pity for Victor, his only desire is presumably to identify with his creator. Were he to persist, the result would be a permanent estrangement from himself. And on some level, no doubt, the creature wouldn't mind a loss of self, provided he could still exist within some other subjectivity.[5]

But for that to happen, the subjectivity to which the creature attaches himself can't form any other attachment. So when he discovers that his creator "dared to hope for happiness" and "sought his own enjoyment in feelings and passions from the indulgence of which I was for ever barred," the creature reacts: "impotent envy and bitter indignation filled me with an insatiable thirst for vengeance." At first glance, his reaction may seem hard to explain. We might wonder, for instance, why he doesn't simply feel regret or sadness. Or even a vicarious form of happiness (as for the De Laceys). To understand why neither is possible, we need to look more closely at the relationship between creature and creator. After Victor destroys the female creature, the creature murders Clerval in response. His motive, however, isn't necessarily one of revenge only. In addition, the murder serves to reduce the number of intersubjective relationships open to Victor. Progressively isolated, he might eventually be forced into an exclusive relationship to the creature.

As a demonic presence, the creature forces himself on his creator. Hence his shock and resistance to any new attachment on Victor's part. Demonic presences depend on subjective isolation: since the sense of otherness these presences convey is wholly contained within the consciousness they haunt, they constitute a creation of that consciousness. So the creature becomes a demonic presence for Victor because of his own obsession with the creature. Consequently, any attachment to an external Other (i.e., Elizabeth Lavenza) is bound to dispel that obsession. It forces subjectivity into a different kind of relationship, one not wholly contained within its own subjective element. Furthermore, since the creature's already relinquished his own subjectivity, Victor's attachment to Elizabeth would leave him without any recourse: he can't go back to himself, nor can he impose himself anymore on his creator. The result would be the extinction of his subjectivity.

The fact that the creature has to recall his earlier threat ("I will be with you on your wedding-night") is significant. It means he had forgotten all about it. But why? Presumably because when he uttered it, he had no idea Victor would want to marry. Conversely, Victor's earlier lack of interest in marriage places the threat itself in a somewhat odd light. Without any explicit engagement, the threat could easily hint at a perpetual intimacy between creature and creator. Yet the hint of perpetual intimacy with his creator needn't imply the creature plans to murder Elizabeth or anyone else at that point. And the fact that he has to "resolve" to do it suggests her murder wasn't previously anticipated. Moreover, his remark that "I knew that I was preparing for myself a deadly torture" shows he's acutely aware of how it will complicate his situation. The creature speaks of his murderous intent as "an impulse, which I detested, yet could not disobey." An irrational impulse, it points to his first loss of self-control.

Although superficially similar, the two murders (of Elizabeth and the female creature) result from very different motives. Whereas the creature desperately wants his subjectivity to be recognized by Victor, the reverse isn't at all true. On the contrary: as creator, Victor simply doesn't need to be recognized by his creation. As he sees it, the murder of his spouse looks like an attempt to reduce him to the same level as the creature. Put in another way, it challenges his subjective autonomy. Consequently, Victor wants to destroy what he perceives as a threat to his own subjectivity.

Given his reluctance to kill Elizabeth, it's odd that the creature feels no remorse after he does it. On this point, he explicitly says: "Yet when she died! — nay, then I was not miserable." His reaction differs markedly from his regret about Clerval. The reason why the creature doesn't feel anything about the death of Elizabeth is because he's already lost the capacity to experience it subjectively, after his rebuff by Victor. Now, his only option is pure activity. As he himself puts it, "I had cast off all feeling, subdued all anguish to riot in the excess of my despair." Intuitively, he realizes anguish is useless: he can't meaningfully feel for himself (after his loss of subjective autonomy), nor can he feel for Victor (who wants to marry). Hence the impulse to "riot in the excess of my despair." To riot is at least to act. "Evil thenceforth became my good," he observes (cf. Milton's Satan), presumably because evil or destruction is pure activity, whereas good requires concern for others and hence some form of intersubjectivity.

But the ultimate destructive act is to eliminate one's creator. Up to this point, the creature has acted somewhat haphazardly. Even after Elizabeth's murder, he can still say: "Urged thus far, I had no choice but to adapt my nature to an element which I had willingly chosen." Once he manages to adapt, however, a significant change occurs. What had been a series of random acts now turns into a full-blown scheme of destructive activity. Given his rational tendency, it's only natural for the creature to pursue a coherent scheme. To it, he can now devote all the emotion he had previously lavished on his efforts to be recognized as a subjectivity. Hence "the completion of my demoniacal design became an insatiable passion." Its climax is, of course, the death of Victor. Beyond that point, what happens is more or less immaterial. As the creature himself admits: "And now it is ended." His destructive scheme has become complete.

On a more general level, if the novel emphasizes how difficult it is to recognize an Other as a subjectivity, it doesn't think we can solve this problem simply by use of a gender perspective. After all, Elizabeth isn't any more concerned about the fate of Justine Moritz than Victor. Her only real concern is whether Justine's innocent. But that has more to do with her assessment of Justine than with what might happen to her. In other words, she simply wants to know whether she was right about a character judgment. Arguably, it's even worse that she apparently has no regret about what happens to Justine after she learns of her innocence. So it all comes back, in the end, to self. Gender doesn't save Elizabeth from subjectivity. From the standpoint of the novel, we all construct others objectively. And the source of our tendency to do that lies in the very way we exist. Which is to say: subjectively.[6]

Even rationality can't save us from subjective blindness. When he makes his appeal to Victor, the creature deliberately elects to frame it in a rational way. Clearly, Victor himself had made no effort to be rational when he first spoke. For that reason, the use of rational argument might seem like a good move, to get him out of his wholly subjective viewpoint. In fact, however, it turns out to be a mistake. By his recourse to rationality, the creature allows his creator to blunt the force of his request. Rationality, after all, is a kind of game. You can use it to make a particular point. But, by the same token, you can also use it to assert the contrary. Once the creature elects to put his appeal in a rational way, he gives Victor a chance to show how he can justifiably reject that appeal, in a way that appears equally rational. Because the creature restricts his appeal solely to the rational, his creator can avoid the crucial fact, which is that of another subjectivity. Instead, by his willingness to play the rational game, Victor can even pretend to himself that he's seriously considered the appeal.

For Shelley, then, the real question is why we feel compelled to objectify another subjectivity. To answer that question, we need, as she sees it, to look at our relation to the external world in general. By means of consciousness or subjectivity, we perceive the activity of external forces. From the outset, however, perception isn't neutral. Instead, we feel the urgency of it: all those external forces, by their constant activity, act on the mind, put pressure on it. So the source of our need to objectify comes from the way we feel that pressure. We objectify, in other words, as a means to avoid complete submission to external forces. Without some theory of the external, we'd simply succumb to it, through intellectual passivity. Hence the rationale for a theory of the external. In this fashion, we hope to gain some control over the chaos of external forces that act on the mind. Conversely, the absence of theory would seem to imply passivity to external forces, consequently chaos and, as a result, loss of mental stability. Thus it isn't by accident that Victor happens to be a student of the natural sciences. Only by means of the natural sciences can we possibly hope to arrive at a theory of all the external forces whose activity we perceive.

At the same time, it would be a mistake to read what happens in the novel primarily as a comment on the natural sciences.[7] Nowhere, after all, does the text go into Victor's work in any detail. The few hints we do get seem merely suggestive, at best. Nor does Victor ever really display much curiosity about natural phenomena. In fact, he himself says that his interest in the natural sciences grew out of his passion for the occult: what he read about in the works of Cornelius Agrippa, and others. Which is to say: an interest in power over nature, rather than nature. Similarly, his attempt to create a creature is defined from the start within a wholly subjective framework. For Victor, then, the natural sciences are only a means to an end. From his study of the sciences, he discovers the power of theory, its ability to dominate external nature by the way it can abstract and generalize. Ironically, though, that capacity to abstract and generalize is precisely what makes it difficult, if not impossible, for theory to appreciate nature in its specificity. Yet Victor doesn't even care about the sort of generality we get from theory. His relation to the sciences, and ultimately to theory, is simply one of use. What Victor wants is the power over nature that theory can give.

But if theory is what saves us from chaos, it also opens us up at the same time to an equally significant danger: the absence of intersubjectivity. Precisely because we formulate a theory of the external, we preclude a knowledge of what it really consists of. Ultimately, theory isn't about knowledge. When we do theory, we don't simply try to glean knowledge from our experiences. Instead, we conceptualize those experiences. Which is to say: we move from experiences to concepts. In our experiences, we take in the activity of external forces. In our concepts, we give free play to the mind only. Finally, then, theory is about the primacy of the mind over external forces. For that reason, the perfect figure for theory is the dream: in our dreams, all the pressure that external forces exert is at one remove. Meanwhile, the mind is at liberty to arrange all the stuff of our experiences freely. So Victor sleeps after his experiment, in the hope that he can dream his way back to pure subjectivity and hence to theory. And if he could do that, his dream would then be the dream of science or theory: that mind were able by itself to create the world. Yet if it were able to do that, it would only have cut itself off from a genuine knowledge of any external force or agency. And that, in turn, would mean the lack of any genuine knowledge of others, and so of any possible relationship, or intersubjectivity.

Intersubjectivity, however, is precisely what we're afraid of. As a result, the particular form of subjective/objective tension that we find between Victor and his creature isn't quite like that of Hegel (lordship/bondage) or others. As Shelley sees it, we objectify others not only from desire but also from fear. So theory, you might say, conveys the dream of subjectivity in a double sense: as a form of wish-fulfillment but also and equally by the way it tries to manage our anxiety. We do theory, in other words, in order to avoid intersubjectivity. To conceptualize or objectify the other, then, isn't about a power over some other that you can feel. Instead, we get into theory precisely so we don't have to feel the other in its otherness, its presence. Because of its abstractness, theory is different from other ways we might use to objectify. Unlike these, theory, for Shelley, is pure reflexivity: it all comes back to the self. For that reason, she repeatedly adverts to the dream as an image or motif for theory. If dreams betray anxiety, they also try to resolve it by the way they represent its sources, so that these become in effect no longer some form of otherness but rather one of pure self-reflexivity. And so, Shelley seems to say, for theory.

Beyond theory, finally, there was, for the author of *Frankenstein,* one other option. If you could somehow manage to resist the temptation to theory, you could at least speculate about what might otherwise be. And its indispensable condition would be intersubjectivity. Rather than try to draw all our experiences into a conceptual framework, we could simply take them for what they were. In that way, we might hope to give our experiences a more natural shape, without theory. For the novel, it could lead to a different kind of relationship between creature and creator, and so, perhaps, a genuine intersubjectivity. Of course, the text doesn't really show us what it would look like. It would have to take a form very different from that of the subjective dynamic that governs the narrative. Of all this, the author gives us only a glimpse, by her use of the term "sympathy." But that, as a later author says, would be another story.

CHAPTER NINE

The Limits of Theory

At some point, any inquiry into the promise or potential of theory also has to ask where its limits are. For Friedrich Hölderlin, the limits of theory are, quite simply, those of thought itself. But to arrive at the limits of thought we have to find out what thought can't conceptualize. Unlike some of those who questioned the primacy of theory in the Romantic period, Hölderlin never doubted the capacity of theory to conceptualize our experiences. He himself, after all, had been close to those who ushered in a new era for philosophy in Germany. As a result, he had seen what the new, abstract mode of theory was capable of. To some extent he had even helped to create it. He knew, then, that it didn't need to solve the epistemological impasse Kant had worried about. He had seen how the new philosophy had managed to finesse that difficulty, by means of an internal rather than external perspective. Fully aware of all the recent developments in the contemporary philosophical scene, he knew the power of theory. And because of what he had seen, he probably even believed what proponents of the new philosophy professed: that we can achieve ascendancy over anything we can conceptualize.[1]

This belief in theory was a legacy of Kant's successors. Fichte had discovered the generative capacity of thought or theory, its ability to construct an entire system out of itself. All you needed was the difference between I and not-I. Out of that dynamic, you could get everything else to emerge. Fichte, though, had staked out an internal, purely subjective viewpoint. And that meant you didn't really know whether all the stuff you were able to spin out of the I/not-I difference existed in fact only subjectively. Schelling felt the subjective/objective discrepancy that had haunted theory could be attacked more directly. His idea was that if you squarely confronted the subjective/objective dichotomy, you could demonstrate that it didn't really exist. Specifically, you'd try to show that what we regard as objective was also subjective, and vice versa. Thus at the outset of the *System of Transcendental Idealism* we find:

All knowledge is based on the coincidence of an objective with a subjective. We can speak of the intrinsic concept of everything merely *objective* in our knowledge as *nature*. The intrinsic concept of everything *subjective* is called, on the contrary, the *self*, or the *intelligence*. . . . Hence there are only two possibilities. *Either the objective is made primary, and the question is: how a subjective is added to it, which coincides with it?* . . . The problem assumes nature or the *objective* to be *primary.* Hence the problem is undoubtedly that of *natural science.* . . . The necessary tendency of all *natural science* is . . . to move from nature to intelligence. This and nothing else is at the bottom of the urge to bring *theory* into natural phenomena. —The highest consummation of natural science would be the complete spiritualization of all natural laws into laws of intuition and thought. The phenomena (the material) must wholly disappear, and only the laws (the formal) remain. Hence it is, that the more lawfulness emerges in nature itself, the more the husk disappears, the phenomena themselves become more mental, and at last disappear completely. . . . *Or the subjective is made primary, and the problem is: how an objective is added, which coincides with it?* . . . The one basic prejudice, to which all others reduce, is no other than this, *that there are things outside us:* a conviction that, because it rests neither on grounds nor on inferences . . . and yet cannot be rooted out by any proof to the contrary . . . makes claim to *immediate* certainty. . . . The contradiction, that a principle which by its nature cannot be immediately certain is yet accepted as blindly and groundlessly as one that is so, the transcendental philosopher knows not how to resolve, except on the presupposition that this principle is not just covertly and as yet uncomprehendingly connected with, but is identical, one, and the same with, an immediate certainty. . . . But . . . nothing is immediately certain except the proposition *I exist.* . . . —The proposition *There are things outside us* will therefore be certain for the transcendental philosopher only through its identity with the proposition *I exist*, and its certainty will likewise only be *equal* to the certainty of the proposition from which it borrows its own. (*Schellings Werke* 2: 339–44 / 3: 339–44)

Here what allows theory to overcome the opposition between subjective and objective is a capacity to conceptualize. Even if we start with nature or the objective, what we really have is in fact already inherently conceptual. After all, the sort of impression we receive of nature merely by perception (i.e., sense data) doesn't yield nature in its totality. To get that, we need the natural sciences. But, by the very way they look at nature, which involves an attempt at explanation, the natural sciences can only be conceptual. Or, as Schelling puts it: "the necessary tendency of all *natural science* is . . . to move from nature to intelligence."

What he then goes on to say is perhaps even more significant: "This and nothing else is at the bottom of the urge to bring *theory* into natural phenomena." We conceptualize nature, in other words, not because we want to explain it but because we want to assimilate it to intelligence or mind. Yet the reverse is equally true: we also want to posit nature as external. Here again, though, the reason we posit nature as external isn't because we perceive it that way but because we can relate our belief in external existences to our belief that we exist: the two beliefs elicit the same degree of certainty. Finally, then, the reason why we posit nature is purely conceptual: not because of the way we perceive it but because we can link it to another belief we feel certain about. Equivalently: we posit nature because we can conceptualize what we believe about it.[2]

But if Kant's successors believed in the power of theory to conceptualize the totality of our experiences, Hölderlin didn't share that perspective. For him, the question wasn't whether theory had a virtually limitless power to conceptualize but whether its power to conceptualize wasn't itself a form of limitation. Or, to put it another way, he wondered whether the conceptual mode didn't itself impose an inherent limit on theory. The kind of limit he had in mind would have arisen not because of the particular way we conceptualized, but rather from the very fact that we conceptualized at all.[3] To conceptualize was to specify formal relationships of some kind between different objects or experiences. The problem was that the particular formal relationships you were able to specify couldn't express all the complexity of what you actually perceived. Instead, it seemed to Hölderlin as if the complexity of what he perceived would inevitably transcend what he could manage to describe by means of formal or conceptual relationships. In other words, it was as if the relationships within what he perceived were of an even higher level of complexity. As a result, he began to wonder whether there might be a different kind of limit to theory.

And so we come to "Patmos." Because nowhere else does Hölderlin consider as clearly the possibility of an inherent limit to theory:

Nah ist
Und schwer zu fassen der Gott.
Wo aber Gefahr ist, wächst
Das Rettende auch.
Im Finstern wohnen
Die Adler und furchtlos gehn
Die Söhne der Alpen über den Abgrund weg
Auf leichtgebaueten Brüken.

Drum, da gehäuft sind rings

Die Gipfel der Zeit, und die Liebsten

Nah wohnen, ermattend auf

Getrenntesten Bergen,

So gieb unschuldig Wasser,

O Fittige gieb uns, treuesten Sinns

Hinüberzugehn und wiederzukehren.

[Near is

And difficult to grasp, the God.

But where danger is, grows

That which saves as well.

In darkness dwell

The eagles and fearless go

The sons of the Alps over the abyss

On lightly-built bridges.

Therefore, since round about are heaped

The summits of time, and the most loved

Live near, getting faint

On mountains most separate,

So give pure water,

O pinions give us, truest faculties

To cross over and to return.]   (*SW* 8: 682)

From the outset, Hölderlin makes it clear his poem will be about how difficult God is to conceptualize. From his standpoint, such a difficulty is a problem for theory. Since the power of theory comes from its virtually limitless capacity to conceptualize, the possibility of something beyond its scope suggests there might be a limit to theory. In his effort to find out whether this is true, he'll be led to explore a moment when the God seemed to be most human and hence most graspable: the Last Supper. To represent the Last Supper adequately, however, takes the poem beyond our normative framework of space and time. In that sense, such a scene isn't strictly representable. The fact that it isn't suggests, in turn, why the Apostles weren't able to hold on to their image of the Lord, which takes the poem into the perspective of the aftertime. From there, it's only natural for Hölderlin to ponder the consequences. As a result of his reflection, he arrives at the motif of the sower, which points toward the agricultural cycle or, more broadly, the process by which things become. But where Hegel had seen such a process precisely as what theory ought to represent, Hölderlin sees it as beyond theory. For him, the fact that we live in time renders it difficult if not impossible to grasp how events in time can form a process. Hence his sense of the need for a perspective beyond that of theory.

The initial statement of the poem, that "the God" is both "near" and "difficult to grasp," is significant. Note that the text doesn't say: "Near is / *But* difficult to grasp, the God." Instead, it explicitly connects nearness to incomprehensibility.[4]

Right away, then, we have an apparent contradiction. Normally, nearness ought to mean easier to understand. After all, close proximity lets us observe an object more fully. No doubt such a model subtly bespeaks the predominant role played by our visual faculty. Yet couldn't we apply it to immaterial objects as well? If our relation to an object is emotional, nearness becomes equivalent to intimacy. If what we want to understand is purely intellectual, nearness is tantamount to knowledge. Even for the wholly immaterial, then, the link between nearness and incomprehensibility is hard to explain.

Here it's important that we look at the first statement of the prologue more closely. In other words, we need to think about what the nearness of a God might involve. Clearly, the nearness of a God is different from other forms of nearness. Apart from mere physical proximity, even the subjective nearness or intimacy of any two individuals must have its limit: otherwise they would be identical. But the nearness of a God is different, if only because we can't assign any limits to it. Nonetheless, this needn't imply that we and the God are identical. On the contrary: if that were true, presumably the God would no longer be "difficult to grasp." Obviously, the fact that we can speak of the God suggests we must feel it in some way. But if we feel it, what we feel must be a sense of its otherness or difference. And yet, simultaneously, we also feel its nearness: this otherness we can't grasp is also very near to us, perhaps even within us, since that would be the ultimate form of nearness. What we feel, then, is an otherness we can't specify even though we know of its presence. Under these circumstances, we might even argue that it's precisely the nearness of the God, combined with its otherness, that makes it incomprehensible. To grasp it, we would have to imagine ourselves as identical to the otherness, which is impossible.

Significantly, the poem's next statement refers to danger: "But where danger is, grows / That which saves as well." Normally, when we talk about danger, our first concern is to identify its source. Curiously, the poem gives us no help on that score. Instead, it simply says "But where danger is . . . " If we turn back to the initial statement, our first temptation would probably be to equate "where" with "near": after all, these are the only terms with spatial referents. If we do that, we might infer that danger comes from the nearness of the God. Yet patristic tradition had amply affirmed the desirability of nearness to God. By itself, then, nearness to God doesn't quite suffice to explain the danger the poem speaks of. Still, it seems plausible to suppose the nature of that danger has in fact been pinpointed by the text. The third line begins: "Wo aber Gefahr ist . . . " Here the *aber* (but, however) implies qualification of a previous statement. And since our present focus is on danger, we can only assume it carries over from before. Collectively, these statements suggest that the "danger" of line 3 must consist of everything previously mentioned: that the God is near, and difficult to grasp. In other words, the combination of nearness and ungraspability is what makes the God fearsome.

Together, these conditions produce a need to represent that can't be satisfied in any obvious way. The ultimate form of nearness, as we've seen, is to be within us. So when something within us amounts to otherness or difference, it sparks a tension we instinctively seek to resolve. To resolve it, we need some way to represent that otherness or difference. Yet, precisely because of its nearness, we find the task impossible. But without a way to conceptualize what we perceive, we can't make sense of what we've experienced. The ultimate consequence would be a loss of sanity. Hence the danger that the text speaks of.

Still, the poem does hold out at least a hope. Immediately after he mentions the danger, the speaker goes on to talk about rescue. Specifically: "But where danger is, grows/That which saves as well." In fact, lines 3–4 tell us even more. Whereas danger merely exists or is, the text asserts that at the same place "*grows*/That which saves." Here the use of "grows" hints at a vital source. But if the God must by its very nature remain eternal and unchanged, what "grows" is presumably human. So the danger posed by a God who's both near and difficult to grasp can ultimately be traced to the mind itself. Because the mind can't accept the nearness of a God who's difficult to grasp and unrepresentable, it produces the danger. Less clear is how "that which saves" might come from the same source. The fact that its growth is necessary means it can't save us in any immediate way. But if "that which saves" requires time, then we who are in danger because of our inability to represent a God who's too near must learn to abide, to wait.

In addition, we need to look at "that which saves" more closely. Literally, *das Rettende* isn't quite "that which saves" but rather "the saving," or, more fully, "that which performs the act of saving." To call it *das Rettende* emphasizes the act involved, as a process or event. Unlike simpler nominatives, though, it isn't merely associated with an act. Instead, it also hints at some unnamed agency.

And if we don't know what that agency is, our only recourse is to connect it to the act by which we become aware of it.

Although we might expect the rest of the prologue to indicate how we'll be rescued, what we actually get is quite different: a depiction of the human scene in which we wait for the desired event. Since the poem's initial statement was about the mind and its inability to grasp the God, it should come as no surprise that when Hölderlin turns to the purely human sphere he focuses on subjectivity. And specifically on its problems or limits. To a mind that finds it difficult to grasp the God because of its otherness, any attempt to understand human otherness is likely to be fraught with hindrances as well. In particular, if we can't apprehend another subjectivity in its actual otherness, perhaps our only hope is to do so symbolically. From this standpoint, the symbolic image itself becomes a form of otherness. Accordingly, any effort to interpret it becomes a way to transcend our own subjectivity.[5]

Symbolically, the poem portrays what human subjectivity might still hope to achieve under difficult circumstances. "In darkness," we're told, "dwell/The eagles." Like the prologue to the Fourth Gospel, much of the poem will be about light and darkness, and that transitional interval we call twilight. But darkness is different. For the author of the Fourth Gospel, darkness and light are absolutely antithetical. Their relationship is depicted as one of struggle or agon: "a light that shines in the dark, a light that darkness could not overpower." Clearly there can be no reconciliation, no accommodation between light and darkness. From a biblical standpoint, furthermore, darkness characterizes a world where the light hasn't yet come. The same might apply to the human condition in "Patmos." Yet here subjectivity has apparently arrived at some sort of accommodation with darkness. For the eagles to "dwell" in darkness hints at a measure of duration. You don't really "dwell" in a spot if you just happen to be there briefly. But if you're in for the long haul, you have to become more tolerant to survive. Meanwhile, darkness might well typify the subjective isolation in which we dwell. In that darkness, then, the mind subsists by itself, without perception or awareness of others.

Nonetheless, the poem does yield at least limited access to the world outside oneself. Thus we get the "sons of the Alps," who "fearless go/ . . . over the abyss/On lightly-built bridges." The term "sons of the Alps" suggests they're at home in the mountainous scene. Like eagles, who typically build their nests on craggy, inaccessible cliffs, the "sons of the Alps" don't seem to mind their isolation. At the same time, they don't just stay where they are. Instead they make their way "over the abyss/On lightly-built bridges." The mention of an abyss reveals how dangerous their situation really is. If the symbolism here revolves around subjectivity, an abyss might signify the emptiness or void that lies beyond each individual consciousness. To establish a meaningful relation to others, then, we need to construct some sort of bridge over that abyss. Significantly, the text describes the bridges traversed by the "sons of the Alps" as "lightly-built" (*leicht-gebaueten*). Such a term could mean either that they're of lightweight construction or were easy to build. But it also bespeaks a definite fragility. My own belief is that these bridges consist of language. Language connects us to others. Of lightweight construction (mere sounds in air, as the text says later), easy to build (as speech acts invariably are), but fragile as well, liable to be forgotten or misconstrued. Yet we (like the sons of the Alps) take these bridges for granted, and so proceed fearlessly.

Linguistic bridges, however, don't guarantee a relation to others. In fact, Hölderlin seems to find such a relation difficult, at best: "round about are heaped/The summits of time, and the most loved/Live near, getting faint/On mountains most separate." Presumably the "most loved" should be easy to reach. Especially when they "live near." Yet even proximity doesn't suffice. Instead, we learn they're "getting faint/On mountains most separate." Here the text hints at their ultimate extinction unless they receive help soon from some external agency. Meanwhile, their location on "mountains most separate" points to the source of their plight: their extreme subjective isolation from those they love most. These mountains, in turn, look very similar to the "summits of time" (die Gipfel der Zeit). In fact, the two might even be identical. At any rate, they seem closely connected, geographically and otherwise, since the first word of the passage where they occur (*Drum* or *darum* = therefore) applies to both equally. But if summits form the highest points of a landscape, the highest points in the landscape of time are presumably those where it comes closest to eternity. Eternity, though, suggests the Godlike. What we have, then, is another expression for the nearness of a God whose presence can be felt all around, just as the "summits of time" are heaped round about. Yet the "most loved" live near, on "mountains most separate," which could easily be these self same "summits of time." But why should proximity to the "summits of time" produce subjective isolation? The simple answer is that nearness to the God can have such an effect. Yet this, too, calls for further explanation. We've seen that nearness to the God can induce a breakdown in our capacity to represent, and hence understand. But the very possibility of our relation to others is based on that capacity. Thus nearness to the God can dangerously alienate us from everyone else.[6]

The danger of subjective isolation helps to explain the kind of request the poem goes on to make. "So give pure water," it asks first of all. In fact, "unschuldig [= innocent or pure] Wasser" amounts to a sort of baptismal water, which would imply spiritual renewal. Nor is it irrelevant that for the author of the Fourth Gospel, spiritual renewal comes from metanoia, or "change of mind." At the same time, the speaker also asks for *Fittige,* or pinions, "truest faculties/To cross over and to return." If danger comes from excessive subjectivity, the only way to overcome that is by communion with others. Hence the need for pinions: given the subjective abyss around each mountain peak, our only means of access to the "most loved" who dwell on other peaks is to fly over to where they are. Yet, as the text is careful to specify, we need pinions not only to "cross over" but to "return." To do the first but not the second would cause us to get lost in pure otherness.

The second major section of the poem reflects on what the Fourth Gospel considers the central events of the Passion narrative: the Last Supper and the Crucifixion. Here, as in the prologue, Hölderlin considers the crucial role of subjectivity. But while the prologue had only hinted at a way to transcend the limits of subjectivity, the Passion reminiscence pointedly focuses on a moment when all subjective limits appear to have been overcome. This transcendence of subjectivity opens up a new perspective on how we represent what we perceive. The text displays that new perspective in the very way it arranges its material:

Gegangen mit

Dem Sohne des Höchsten, unzertrennlich, denn

Es liebte der Gewittertragende die Einfalt

Des Jüngers und es sahe der achtsame Mann

Das Angesicht des Gottes genau,

Da, beim Geheimnisse des Weinstoks, sie

Zusammensassen, zu der Stunde des Gastmals,

Und in der grossen Seele, ruhigahnend den Tod

Aussprach der Herr und die lezte Liebe, denn nie genug

Hatt'er von Güte zu sagen

Der Worte, damals, und zu erheitern, da

Ers sahe, das Zürnen der Welt.

Denn alles ist gut. Drauf starb er. Vieles wäre

Zu sagen davon. Und es sahn ihn, wie er siegend blikte

Den Freudigsten die Freunde noch zulezt. . . .

[Had gone about with

The son of the Highest, inseparable, for

The bearer of thunder loved the simplicity

Of the disciple and the attentive man saw

The face of the God exactly,

When, by the mystery of the vine, they

Sat together, at the hour of the banquet,

And in his great soul, calmly foreknowing, death

Spoke the Lord and the last love, for never enough

Words had he to say of goodness

At that time, and to brighten, where

He saw it, the wrath of the world.

For all is good. Thereupon he died. Much might

Be said about it. And they saw him, how triumphantly he looked,

The most joyful of the friends, still, at the end.   (*SW* 8: 683–84)

Perhaps what's most obvious here is the extraordinary freedom exercised by the text over its Johannine source. The commencement itself sets the tone. The first line begins in mid-sentence: "Had gone about with/The son of the Highest." In the original the sense of *in medias res* is even more pronounced, as the text literally splits the verb:

> der in seeliger Jugend war

Gegangen mit
Dem Sohne des Höchsten. . . .

Effectively, it places all the emphasis on *Gegangen* (gone or gone about), virtually the only word in the first line. Literally, it might refer to the peripatetic way Jesus performs his ministry. On a deeper level, it hints at a subjective mobility. Unlike the "most loved" of the prologue, the beloved disciple doesn't remain isolated and hence trapped on a mountain peak. Instead he moves about freely, and always in the company of his master.

Set against the prologue, however, what stands out most is the inseparability of master and disciple. What especially characterizes the disciple is his "simplicity" (*Einfalt*). That simplicity, in turn, is a form of oneness (lit., *Einfalt* or simplicity = onefold). In the prologue, we found that the isolation of the "most loved" was caused by human subjectivity, which wants to assimilate whatever is near it into a likeness to itself. To overcome our separateness from others, we need to overcome that tendency. Hence the turn to simplicity. In subjective terms, simplicity relinquishes the desire for likeness. On some level, it sees such a tendency as part of our mental disposition yet feels no need for it. Instead, what it seeks is a oneness that doesn't have to understand because it's already become subjectively identical with its object.

By itself, nonetheless, the simplicity of the disciple isn't sufficient to produce inseparability from the master. In fact, two somewhat more complex requirements have to be met. Specifically: "for/The bearer of thunder loved the simplicity/Of the disciple and the attentive man saw/The face of the God exactly." If we assume the disciple = the attentive man, the two requirements become closely linked. The first imparts agency to the "bearer of thunder," who loves the simplicity of the disciple. The second gives the disciple agency: to be inseparable from the "son of the Highest," he must see the face of the God exactly. In addition, the proximity of the two statements is suggestive.

Here we need to consider precisely how *Gewittertragende* ought to be interpreted. Instead of "bearer of thunder," for instance, we could have "bearer of the thunderstorm." Obviously the two translations point in completely different ways. From "bearer of thunder" we get divine power or omnipotence. Classical mythology had ascribed control over lightning (hence, presumably, thunder) to Zeus. A Christian equivalent might be "son of the Highest." Yet it would be equally easy to see *Gewittertragende* as "bearer of the thunderstorm" = one who suffers or endures (*tragen*) the storm/tempest. For this we get ample support later in the text. Close to the end, we find: "Still ist sein Zeichen/Am donnernden Himmel. Und Einer stehet darunter/Sein Leben lang. Denn noch lebt Christus" [Silent is his sign/In thundering heaven. And one stands beneath it/His whole life long. For Christ lives yet]. So the Christ who suffers the storm of divine wrath is as much a presence in the poem as the representative of divine omnipotence. Taken together, the two glosses seem virtually contradictory: on the one hand, omnipotence, and, on the other, complete passivity.[7]

At this point, the need for simplicity becomes apparent. Because of his simplicity, the disciple can accept both glosses simultaneously. Whereas rationality might try to force one at the expense of the other, the disciple doesn't. In other words, he makes no attempt at rational consistency. Alternatively, we might say he simply embraces what he perceives, even though he lacks the kind of rational framework necessary to sort it out. As a representative of divine omnipotence, the "bearer of thunder" is easy to make sense of. Equally easy, in a different way, is the Christ who bears or suffers, a figure with whom subjectivity can readily identify because of his likeness to itself. But while either seems feasible alone, their combination produces an extraordinary tension. To survive it, we need simplicity.

Moreover, we know any attempt to grasp the God is fraught with peril. The text clearly hints at this when it says the attentive man "saw/The face of the God exactly." The prologue to the Fourth Gospel observes that "No one has ever seen God" (John 1:18), an allusion to Exodus 33:20, where Yahweh informs Moses, "You cannot see my face, for man cannot see me and live." Note that the Exodus passage doesn't absolutely rule out our capacity to see God. Instead, it merely says we can't do so and live. Our real problem, then, lies in our inability to conceptualize what we've seen. To deny what we've seen simply because we can't conceptualize it, however, would be to call into question our entire cognitive enterprise and, consequently, the only means we have to get beyond pure subjectivity. But if we can't conceptualize what we've seen directly, maybe we can still get there indirectly. To do that, we need to ascertain precisely why we can't conceptualize what we perceive of the God.

Here the text furnishes a clue by what it has to say about the "mystery of the vine." Given the allusion, once more, to the Passion narrative of the Fourth Gospel, it seems useful to recall the original:

> I am the true vine,
> and my Father is the vinedresser. . . .
> Make your home in me, as I make mine in you.
> As a branch cannot bear fruit all by itself,
> but must remain part of the vine,
> neither can you unless you remain in me.
> I am the vine,
> you are the branches.
> Whoever remains in me, with me in him,
> bears fruit in plenty.   (John 15:1–5)

To some extent, we might describe the "mystery" of the vine as one based on the "mutual indwelling" (C. H. Dodd) of Christ and his disciples. Normally, the relation of containment or inherence is exclusive: at most, only one of two elements can be contained within the other. So when Jesus says "whoever remains in me, with me in him," the sort of relation he speaks of can only be termed a spatial impossibility. Yet that spatial impossibility is precisely what the Fourth Gospel asserts about the relationship between Christ and his disciples in the Farewell Discourses at the Last Supper. But if the Johannine narrative is spatially contradictory, the poem makes no attempt to resolve the paradox rationally. On the contrary, it actually embraces this paradox as the centerpiece of its own re-creation of the Last Supper: "When, by the mystery of the vine, they/Sat together . . . " In fact, the original (Da, beim Geheimnisse des Wein-stoks, sie/Zusammensassen) admits of many interpretive possibilities, which all depend on how we read the crucial preposition *beim* (= *bei dem*). Nevertheless, most incline to the spatial, some even emphatically (*beim* = in the presence of). The effect, I would argue, is that we see the "mystery of the vine" as almost physically present at the banquet.[8] On some level, then, we might say that for the poem the mystery of the vine is itself essentially about spatial relationships.

Ultimately, what the poem wants to get at is the connection between thought and spatial relationships. To what extent, in other words, does our capacity to think depend on whether we can spatially represent what we want to concep-tualize? We've seen that the mystery of the vine involves a spatial contradiction, one the poem makes no attempt to resolve. What it does, however, is to try to *situate* that contradiction: "by the mystery of the vine, they/Sat together, at the hour of the banquet." Here what we have is a mystery that can't be resolved rationally, but can be situated spatially. So spatial placement seems to make it possible to represent what would otherwise be unthinkable. In fact, the *absence* of any attempt to explain the spatial contradiction of the mystery rationally is just what allows the text to represent the mystery at all. And, because we can represent what we can't explain, we have to conclude that what makes thought possible, in the last analysis, isn't rationality (i.e., our ability to understand what we represent) but spatial relationships. And this in turn suggests why the divine presence is so difficult to grasp. The God is difficult to grasp because its nearness to us is spatial but not rational. Yet the mystery of the vine is precisely what the text *can* represent, spatially. Hence the need to see thought in terms that are purely spatial rather than rational.

Besides what it does to space, the Passion reminiscence of "Patmos" also alters time. Once more, its source is the Fourth Gospel itself. A prominent element of the Passion narrative is prophecy. Jesus speaks of his own end, and of a time when he'll no longer be with his disciples. Nevertheless, his tone is troubled, informed no doubt by his knowledge of Judas's imminent betrayal. In contrast, the poem displays no such anxiety. The key to its lack of anxiety lies, I believe, in the term *ruhigahnend.* To foreknow calmly or peacefully doesn't mean that knowledge of the future induces serenity. Rather, the very act of prescience itself is only possible to one who no longer lives in human time, as if all the foreseen events had already been experienced as well. And perhaps, in some way, they have. So the text would seem to suggest when it says: "in his great soul, calmly foreknowing, death/Spoke the Lord and the last love." The effect is almost one of interior monologue, as if death and the last love were spoken inwardly. In that respect, even the Godlike consciousness of Christ displays a subjectivity. From his standpoint, death and the last love exist simultaneously. That simultaneity, in turn, points to how time itself can be understood in terms of spatial relationships. Because death and the last love exist in a way in which sequence is no longer involved, their relation is, to that extent, purely spatial. Thus subjective simultaneity allows time to be defined spatially.

Of that process, the text offers at least one other significant example. As the disciple recalls the crucified Lord, he remembers "how triumphantly he looked,/The most joyful of the friends, still, at the end." Yet we know that the Fourth Gospel mentions no such detail, and that the Synoptics explicitly indicate the contrary. So how do we explain it? In a striking way, the Fourth Gospel employs the term ὑφωθῆναι to signify the crucifixion. Yet ὑφωθῆναι can mean either crucified or elevated, raised. Within the framework of the Fourth Gospel, it refers simultaneously to both crucifixion and resurrection. As a result, it manages to collapse two distinct moments into one: the event by which Christ is abased, and that by which he is glorified. The poem attempts a similar compression. The triumphant look on the face of the Lord obviously announces the resurrection. In this fashion, a framework of sequence is transformed into a framework of fulfillment.[9]

The second half of "Patmos" depicts the situation of the faithful after the death and departure of their Lord. If the Passion reminiscence takes us back to the highest moment of human consciousness, whatever comes later is clearly aftertime. As such, it pertains to modernity. Specifically, the period after Christ's departure marks a return to human time, to sequence rather than simultaneity. From now on, what we experience sequentially can no longer be arranged spatially. As a result, events within a temporal framework tend to lose the effect of presence. Perhaps the most crucial consequence, though, concerns our relation to the Christ. Even when he was alive, to "see the face of the God exactly" had required all the attentiveness of the disciple. But now that the Christ is gone, conditions are obviously no longer the same. So the poem needs to consider what its new standpoint ought to be.

Under these circumstances, it seems only natural for the text to adopt the form of a question, which it then tries to answer:

Wenn aber stirbt alsdenn
An dem am meisten
Die Schönheit hieng, dass an der Gestalt
Ein Wunder war und die Himmlischen gedeutet

Auf ihn, und wenn, ein Räthsel ewig füreinander

Sie sich nicht fassen können

Einander, die zusammenlebten

Im Gedächtniss, und nicht den Sand nur oder

Die Weiden es hinwegnimmt und die Tempel

Ergreifft, wenn die Ehre

Des Halbgotts und der Seinen

Verweht und selber sein Angesicht

Der Höchste wendet

Darob, dass nirgend ein

Unsterbliches mehr am Himmel zu sehn ist oder

Auf grüner Erde, was ist diss?

Es ist der Wurf des Säemanns, wenn er fasst

Mit der Schaufel den Waizen,

Und wirft, dem Klaren zu, ihn schwingend über die Tenne.

Ihm fällt die Schaale vor den Füssen, aber

Ans Ende kommet das Korn,

Und nicht ein Übel ists, wenn einiges

Verloren gehet und von der Rede

Verhallet der lebendige Laut,

Denn göttliches Werk auch gleichet dem unsern,

Nicht alles will der Höchste zumal.

Zwar Eisen träget der Schacht,

Und glühende Harze der Ätna,

So hätt' ich Reichtum,

Ein Bild zu bilden, und ähnlich

Zu schaun, wie er gewesen, den Christ. . . .

[But when dies thereupon

To whom most of all

Beauty adhered, that in form

A wonder was and the Heavenly had pointed

To him, and when, an enigma perpetually for one another

They could not understand

Each other, who lived together

In remembrance, and not the sand only or

The willows it takes away and the temples

Seizes, when the honor

Of the demigod and of his own

Is blown away and even his face

The Highest turns away

On that account, so that no

Immortal is to be seen any more in the heavens or

On the green earth, what is this?

It is the cast of the sower, when he takes up

With his shovel the seed,

And throws it, toward clear space, swinging it over the threshing-floor.

The husks fall at his feet, but

The grain comes to an end,

And there's no harm if some of it

Gets lost and of speech

The living sound dies away,

For the divine work too is like our own,

Not all does the Highest intend at once.

To be sure, the pit bears iron,

And Etna glowing resins,

So should I have wealth,

To form an image, and truly

To see, as he was, the Christ.]   (*SW* 8: 684–85)

Almost immediately, we get a sense of why it might prove difficult to represent the Christ. Right away, the present passage comes across as strongly subjective. Whereas the *Gewittertragende* motif had embraced both the divinity and humanity of the Christ, the present description focuses solely on his beauty. But beauty, obviously, is a very subjective category. Nor does the text try to minimize that. Instead, it explicitly invokes beauty as a category: *die Schönheit.* Furthermore, the text seems to imply a quantitative assessment of some kind. The Christ is referred to as one "To whom most of all / Beauty adhered." All of this, however, is more or less the terminology of aesthetics. For me, it bears a definite resemblance to Friedrich Schlegel's notion of *das höchste Schöne.* Yet subsequently the text goes even further, when it speaks of the Christ as one "that in form / A wonder was." Clearly, "a wonder" reflects the viewpoint of an observer. Note, too, the hint of aesthetic appreciation in the mention of form (*der Gestalt*). Altogether, what we get is that the disciple's perception of Christ has become distinctly subjective. As such, it no longer possesses its earlier exactness.

One of the principal negative consequences of increased subjectivity is an inability to understand anyone else. Or, as the text puts it: "an enigma perpetually for one another/They could not understand/Each other, who lived together/In remembrance." Here the poem refers to the gift of glossolalia, received by the disciples at Pentecost. After the departure of Jesus, the disciples continue their communal existence, united by the memory of their Lord. Assembled together on the day of Pentecost, they experience a form of inspiration symbolized by the strong wind that shakes the entire house. Inspired, they preach in different languages to various groups of foreigners gathered in Jerusalem. Earlier, the poem had rendered the event more fully: "Drum sandt' er ihnen/Den Geist, und freilich bebte/Das Haus und die Wetter Gottes rollten/Ferndonnernd über/Die ahnenden Häupter" [Therefore he sent them/The Spirit, and indeed/The house trembled and the divine storm rolled/Distantly thundering over/The foreknowing heads]. Yet the ultimate consequence of glossolalia is an inability to understand each other. Because the disciples no longer speak the same langage, they lose their capacity to communicate with each other. Significantly, the text doesn't pinpoint the exact cause. Perhaps the omission is meant to imply that glossolalia isn't a gift after all but a hindrance. A private mode of discourse, it amounts to the most extreme, most indulgent expression of individual subjectivity. Hence the inability to understand anyone else. In German, *fassen* is the term used by the prologue for our unsuccessful effort to grasp the God. Like that earlier attempt, the present one seems doomed by its excessive subjectivity.

A crucial indication of how bad things are appears just after the allusion to glossolalia at Pentecost. In its wake, we witness various disappearances: "and not the sand only or/The willows it takes away and the temples/Seizes . . . " The cause of these disappearances, however, remains unspecified. Instead, the text speaks only of a mysterious "it" by which they're brought about. Interestingly, the pronoun has no clear referent. Meanwhile, the rest of the passage offers a slight clue: "when the honor/Of the demigod and of his own/Is blown away." Here the use of *verweht* (blown away, scattered) suggests a forceful wind of some kind. A passage from Acts helps to clarify it: "When Pentecost day came round, they had all met in one room, when suddenly they heard what sounded like a powerful wind from heaven, the noise of which filled the entire house in which they were sitting; and something appeared to them that seemed like tongues of fire. . . . They were all filled with the Holy Spirit, and began to speak foreign languages" (Acts 2:1–4). Note that the wind is closely associated with the tongues of fire, and hence glossolalia. But glossolalia, as we've seen, is itself associated with excessive subjectivity. And excessive subjectivity doesn't care about the external world. As a result, our perceptions (of, say, the materiality of sand, or the beauty of the willows) no longer matter. The strong wind of subjectivity, so to speak, simply blows all of these away. By its seizure of the temples, moreover, it shakes the foundations of religion itself. To become a cult, religion has to transcend individual subjectivity. Its location somewhere other than in the mind of the individual worshipper is precisely what leads to collective worship. For radical subjectivity, however, the solidarity of a cult is irrelevant. In effect, radical subjectivity attempts to deny whatever isn't determined by subjectivity itself. Thus religion, the very source of sanctity, gets brought into question. In this fashion, the "honor/Of the demigod and of his own/Is blown away."

But if what happens to the demigod is due to excessive subjectivity, we still need to explain how we know that "even his face/The Highest turns away/On that account." After all, the ability to see the God exactly had required that we relinquish our subjective tendency. Conversely, any return to subjectivity must presumably make perception of the God difficult. We know he's turned his face away, then, only because we no longer perceive the God. Since we still yearn to do so, we infer a withdrawal on his part. Ultimately, however, we no longer perceive the God because of a change in our own subjectivity. Equivalently, we might say: we no longer perceive the God because we've lost the capacity. And we know we've lost it because we can no longer see what's temporal in terms of spatial relationships. Unable, in other words, to transcend the temporal, we fall back into the realm of sequence and hence of time.

After the first half of the passage ends on a question, the second half considers what might be possible within a temporal framework. With its figure of the sower, the passage is undoubtedly meant to recall the parable of the sower from the Synoptic Gospels. As told by John the Baptist, the parable is about separation of the wheat from the chaff (Matthew 3:12). In the version told by Jesus himself, however, it's about our reception of the word of God (Mark 4:3–9, 14–20). What "Patmos" does is to combine these in its own unique way. Here a variant from a later version of the poem proves useful: "Es ist der Wurf das eines Sinns" [It is the throw of a sense] (*SW* 8: 824). After the *parousia*, or historical appearance of Jesus, the true meaning of what he preached has become a matter of some uncertainty. As a result, our reception of the word of God is no longer just a matter of faith. Instead, interpretation is now necessary. But interpretation involves a separation of wheat from chaff. For Hölderlin, the process of interpretation can be compared to the process by which we sift grain. Hence the motif of the "throw of a sense": to throw a sense is equivalent to a toss of grain. In both instances, what we're after is a way to sift the genuine grain (i.e., the true interpretation or sense) from the chaff (i.e., non-sense).

It's all summed up by the figure of the sower. Whereas the God is difficult to grasp (*fassen*), and while the disciples can't understand (*fassen*) each other, the sower manages to seize or take up (*fassen*) the seed with his shovel. Moreover, the movement by which the sower sifts grain from husks is strongly suggestive. The text describes how the sower throws the seed upward "toward clear space." The original simply says "dem Klaren zu" (lit., toward clearness). Here the separation of genuine grain from chaff would seem to depend on clarity. Which is to say: we throw the seed or sense upward, toward the clear or open space, in an effort to force it to clarify itself. Conversely, confusion comes about because the genuine sense or seed is mixed with chaff or non-sense. But once we manage to sort these out by a perception of their differences (like the process by which we sift grain), the result should be hermeneutic clarity. Yet that clarity, as we see here, is inevitably the result of a process. Nor does the poem seem to mind that. On the contrary. Of the process by which we sift grain, it explicitly avers: "And there's no harm if some of it / Gets lost." Likewise it's also okay if "of speech / The living sound dies away." Speech, of course, is the conveyor of sense. On a deeper level, however, we can't always manage to grasp the sense of what people say right away. Like the agricultural cycle that hovers as the background for the sower, the process by which we come to understand is one for which time is profoundly necessary. And, as for the agricultural cycle, it's a process that has its own internal economy.[10]

But the notion of process doesn't just apply to human time. Subsequently, we're told: "For the divine work too is like our own, / Not all does the Highest intend at once." Here, once more, it's useful to look at the Fourth Gospel. From it we learn that on a visit to Jerusalem Jesus happens to cure a sick man at the pool of Bethzatha. Previously bedridden, the man is now able to pick up his mat and walk. His activity angers the Jews, who tell him he isn't allowed to carry his mat on the Sabbath. He answers that he was told to do it by the man who cured him. Jesus himself is then attacked. His reply is: "My Father goes on working, and so do I" (John 5:17). Influenced by Hellenistic Judaism, the Fourth Gospel had seen work as the constant, ceaseless activity of the divine energeia. In one respect, nonetheless, the acts of God are for "Patmos" like human acts: they don't always achieve their end immediately. Not, however, because of any lack of power to bring it about. On that point the text is explicit: "Not all does the Highest intend [lit., "will" = will] at once." Of course, whatever the Highest does intend should presumably happen instantly. For precisely that reason, it seems strange for God not to want it that way. The result would obviously be a form of simultaneity. Which is to say: no more time. All of which points to the divine work as a work of time, at the deepest or most profound level. And even more: that time itself is ultimately a creation of the God. To dwell in time, then, should no longer be seen as a fall from a higher mode of consciousness in which the temporal had become spatial. Instead, our existence in time is clearly a condition that was meant to be.[11]

Inevitably, the notion of time as a natural human condition leads one to ask whether, within a temporal framework, we can still see the Christ exactly. No doubt the poem wants to believe we can. After all, the notion of time as natural is related (as we've seen) to the theme of a natural economy. But a natural economy implies productivity. The land produces grain for the farmer. Similarly, "the pit bears iron,/And Etna glowing resins." And all these forms of wealth arise naturally from the productive capacity of the earth itself. The same should be true for the speaker: "So should I have wealth." For the speaker, however, wealth means creativity. Creativity, in turn, should enable one to form images. In the original we get "Ein Bild zu bilden." Specifically, the speaker wants to form an image of the Christ. By means of that image, the speaker hopes to see the Christ "as he was." But the notion that we could somehow manage to do so by means of an image is obviously a problematic one. As a visual icon, the image has no real temporal aspect. On some level, moreover, the text knows it. The term *ähnlich* (which I translate as "truly") has more to do with likeness or verisimilitude. In other words, the text doesn't pretend that an image or picture will really yield the Christ as he actually was. Nonetheless, the speaker yearns for that image. Its appeal, I would argue, comes precisely from what it *doesn't* give: the sense of time that frames any of our real perceptions. Instead, an image attempts to translate the temporal into the spatial. Despite our awareness that the divine work takes place in time, we want somehow to transcend it. For what the image ultimately gives us isn't the Christ as he actually was, but a representation. So it comes back, in the end, to our need to represent the God in its nearness.

The final section of the poem, by contrast, looks at what it might be like to submit to the nearness of a God we can't represent:

Und wenn die Himmlischen jezt
So, wie ich glaube, mich lieben,
Wie viel mehr dich,
Denn Eines weiss ich,

Dass nemlich der Wille

Des ewigen Vaters viel

Dir gilt. Still ist sein Zeichen

Am donnernden Himmel. Und Einer stehet darunter

Sein Leben lang. Denn noch lebt Christus.

Es sind aber die Helden, seine Söhne

Gekommen all und heilige Schriften

Von ihm und den Bliz erklären

Die Thaten der Erde bis izt,

Ein Wettlauf unaufhaltsam. Er ist aber dabei. Denn seine Werke sind

Ihm alle bewusst von jeher.

[And if the Heavenly now

So, as I believe, love me

How much more [must they love] you,

For one thing I know,

That namely the will

Of the eternal Father is of much value

To you. Silent is his sign

In thundering heaven. And one stands beneath it

His whole life long. For Christ lives yet.

But the heroes, his sons,

Have all come and holy scriptures

About him and lightning are explained by

The deeds of the earth up to now,

A race that cannot be stopped. He is however near. For his works are

All known to him from the beginning.]   (*SW* 8: 686)

Right away, subjectivity becomes apparent. The initial statement starts off with a conditional: "And if the Heavenly now / . . . love me." This, moreover, is itself qualified by "as I believe." Subsequently, the initial statement is further qualified in other ways: "And if the Heavenly *now* / *So* . . . love me." The temporal modifier "now" restricts any love by the Heavenly to the present. Instead of the timeless love of God for the Son ("because you loved me before the foundation of the world," John 17:24), the speaker can only vouch for the present moment. Similarly, "so" points to a particular kind of love, rather than the unqualified variety of the Farewell Discourses in the Fourth Gospel. Clearly, then, his purely subjective viewpoint doesn't take the speaker very far.

The sequel is equally characterized by uncertainty. After the conditional premise "And if the Heavenly now/So, as I believe, love me," the speaker goes on: "how much more you." I give the line as literally written. A fuller version would be: "how much more [must they love] you." In the original, the objective case of *Dich* (you) means the verb (love) must be directed toward "you." Significantly, the poem can't quite bring itself to say so explicitly. The premise that the speaker is loved by the Heavenly had elicited, as we've seen, a similar hesitancy. But what holds for the premise must presumably apply equally to the conclusion. While not so explicitly qualified as the premise, the inability of the text to actually say the Heavenly loves "you" would seem even more indicative of hesitancy.

Given his general uncertainty, it isn't clear why the speaker should insist that the Heavenly do indeed love the "you" whom he addresses even more than himself. By way of preface, he observes: "For one thing I know . . ." His preliminary comment is reminiscent of the Cartesian formula for which the only indubitable fact is that of self-consciousness. Yet what the speaker says next appears at first to promise a distinctly more objective form of knowledge: "That namely the will/Of the eternal Father is of much value/To you." Initially, the original seemed poised to assert even more: "Dass nemlich der Wille/Des ewigen Vaters viel." Here we expect the rest of the passage to say what the will of the Father is about to make happen. And that should decisively demonstrate how much the "you" is loved by the Heavenly. Instead, the poem suddenly veers into the subjective: "Dir gilt." Which means: is of value to you. So, rather than a statement about visible evidences of the divine will, we get a statement about subjective viewpoint. In other words, we know the "you" is loved by the Heavenly not because of any sign from the Heavenly itself but because of what it means to the putative recipient of that love. But if all we know about divine love comes from what we feel, the very basis of our relationship to the God never gets beyond subjectivity.

In fact, the only objective statement we get about the God points to his absence: "Silent is his sign/In thundering heaven." Not a word about love, or even concern. On the contrary: here, silence looks curiously like indifference. In the original, the word for silent is "still." Which naturally suggests stillness. Silences can be intervals between what gets spoken, hence meaningful in their own way. Stillness, however, hints at absence. Not only, then, do we not get any sign from the God, but we can even feel we shouldn't expect any. At the same time, the abode of the God isn't exactly silent. "Thundering heaven" is a reminder of Pentecost, when the divine storm rolled "distantly thundering" overhead while the house of the disciples shook freely. The fact that it was visibly shaken would appear to indicate a latent destructive force. And yet, despite the threat posed by its nearness, the God gives us no sign. So we have no reason to construe its nearness favorably. Even as it threatens us by its nearness, then, the God doesn't communicate in any way.

Nonetheless, we still have one last resource. From a theoretical standpoint, we don't know quite how to address the nearness of a God we can't represent. Given that fact, our only hope is to try to learn from someone who's managed to avoid the problems caused by that nearness. The text distinctly has a person in mind: "And one stands beneath it/His whole life long." Clearly, that person makes no attempt to avoid the danger posed by the nearness of the God. Instead, his lifetime endurance of it suggests an effort to live with it. Hence the use of the term "stands" (*stehet*). To "stand" is to endure, but also to exist. By his choice merely to "stand" he teaches a crucial lesson: that it's possible to live under such circumstances.

What the poem offers next is a comment on this example of how we might live. In its terse assessment, the text simply says: "For Christ lives yet." Here, the use of present tense seems a bit odd. After all, if the "one" is supposed to be identical to the historical Christ, the only appropriate verb tense would have to be the past. Furthermore, the poem employs the phrase "his whole life long." But a life that can be so described must presumably have come to an end. Since the next line begins with a logical connective, the fact that Christ stands beneath a thundering heaven for his entire lifetime would seem to be related to the assertion that he lives yet. Specifically, I would argue that his endurance of the threat of divine nearness serves to perpetuate his example in human memory. In other words, the perpetual significance of his act of endurance from a human standpoint makes his accomplishment relevant to the present rather than just to the past. This transformation of past into present is similar to the rearrangement of time we encountered earlier in the Passion reminiscence. But the transformation that now takes place is very much a work of collective memory. As such, it pertains distinctly to the aftertime.[12]

In addition, the current transformation of past into present differs from the Passion reminiscence in another way as well. The text observes that "the heroes, his sons,/Have all come." Earlier, in its description of Pentecost, the poem had spoken of the *Todeshelden* (heroes of death, or death-heroes), assembled after the death of Jesus, who await the advent of the Spirit: a clear reference, it would seem, to the Apostles. Yet even here, the text displays a trace of irony. For, in their fearful, anxious frame of mind after the death of their Lord, the Apostles can hardly be considered heroic. That, in effect, comes later, in the Acts of the

Apostles. Both the disciples (as "sons") and "holy scriptures" (i.e., Acts) can be said to emanate from the Christ in some way. The same is true for lightning: different in kind, it also attests to the God. All of these, the poem goes on to say, are "explained by/The deeds of the earth up to now,/A race that cannot be stopped." To some extent, as we've often heard, the significance of any event emerges as a result of subsequent events. In its description of these, however, the poem betrays a slightly negative tone. As if to imply the Christ himself has inadvertently been forgotten in a process of elucidation that's focused excessively on the emanations. Thus, perhaps, the comment: "a race that cannot be stopped." We live, in other words, in an aftertime marked by an endless succession of events that provide explanation or commentary. In the process, we've somehow managed to lose sight of the source from which they all come.

Nonetheless, even the forgetfulness of the aftertime can lead us back to the theme that formed our point of departure: the nearness of the God. For, as the text points out: "He is however near." Near, though, with a difference. In the original, the term is *dabei* (lit., thereby, or, more idiomatically, nigh or nearby). Which isn't quite the same as the nearness of the God in the prologue: "Near is/And difficult to grasp, the God" [Nah ist/Und schwer zu fassen der Gott]. Whereas the earlier nearness of the God had been too close, and so impossible to conceptualize, the present nearness of the Christ has a somewhat different quality. We might describe it as the sort of nearness that allows one to render aid or assistance. Given the problem posed by the nearness or presence of the God, however, it's crucial that the text specify how it knows about the nearness of the Christ. And so it says: "For his works are/All known to him from the beginning." From a divine standpoint, knowledge is equivalent to presence. In order to know his works (i.e., his emanations or manifestations), the Christ has to be present at the scene of their occurrence. But if his "works" are "known" to him from the very outset of time, his "knowledge" must then involve the same sort of temporal rearrangement we found earlier in the Passion reminiscence. In that respect, you might say, he fills all of time. Consequently, any knowledge we obtain in human time must be distinctly informed by an awareness of his presence. As the presence of the God, it's obviously beyond our capacity to conceive. All the same, we can apprehend it, like the seasonal cycle of the sower, by means of its relation to time.

If we retrace our steps all the way back to the prologue, we can now see in what sense "Patmos" is essentially about the limits of theory. The nearness of the God forced us to become aware of our inability to conceptualize particular experiences. Specifically, the poem seemed to imply that in the case of the God we couldn't conceptualize what we perceived precisely because of its nearness. Here, then, was the blind spot of theory: if you got too close to it, it could no longer see you clearly. Instead, we conceptualize only what we manage to place at a distance. So the abstract tendency of theory had an inherent weakness: it couldn't deal with anything that impinged on it too closely. Put in another way, we might say it couldn't deal with presences. If theory emerges out of our own subjectivity, what we can't conceptually frame is the proximity of another subjectivity. For theory, then, the nearness of the God might just be the nearness of another subjectivity. At the same time, it could just as easily be the nearness of thought itself. What the text doesn't say, but seems to hint at as a possibility, is that the nearness of the God might come from the similarity between its element and that of thought. In other words, what theory can't conceptualize is thought itself.

Perhaps what prompted Hölderlin to introduce the Passion narrative was a sense of how it might afford some way to transcend concepts. From Kant he knew space and time were merely concepts, part of the framework by which we perceive. But if space and time were no more than that, it ought to be possible in principle to get beyond these. Equivalently, we ought to be able to apprehend what we perceive more immediately, without the mediation of that framework. Hence the motive for his version of the Passion narrative. It offers, in effect, a conceptual equivalent of what Rimbaud would later call the "dérèglement de tous les sens." Moments of the narrative that we perceived sequentially before now come to be seen simultaneously. And what had before been expressed only abstractly is now treated spatially. For Hölderlin, the Passion narrative within "Patmos" marks an attempt to break down our tendency toward a conceptual framework. What he hoped to achieve by means of that breakdown was an immediate apprehension of what we perceive that would be closer to the way things really are. The nearness of the God, as it were, without the danger it only seemed to pose because of our fear of what might happen if we abandoned concepts.

Finally, however, Hölderlin knew he also had to think about the aftertime, about what might happen if the mind couldn't sustain those epiphanic moments of consciousness at which all of our conceptual framework broke down in face of the fullness of what we perceived. Yet even here, he felt, was another way we might go beyond the limits of theory. It had to do with the process by which things come to be, become what they are. Hence his use of the motif of the sower. That sort of process couldn't really be expressed by means of concepts. And yet, at the deepest level, he felt that it defined what we are. To talk about it, then, theory would have to look beyond itself, beyond what could be expressed by means of theory. Ultimately, the reason why theory couldn't really think about this sort of process by means of concepts was that they, too, were subject to that same process, by which they came to be. In other words, theory couldn't think about the process by which things came to be because it, too, came to be in the process of its reflection on that process. But if thought or theory itself came to be, perhaps to think about the process of its own genesis would somehow enable it to transcend the limits of theory.

Conclusion

At the end, we come back to history. For a study like the present one, that would imply a look at Romantic theory in terms of its relation to the Romantic period. Certainly, Romantic theory itself had from the outset an awareness of its historical moment. In his Preface to the *Phenomenology*, Hegel observes that "ours is a time of birth and of transition to a new era." But if Romantic theory was fully aware of its historical moment, it could hardly fail to be aware of itself historically. In fact, its historical self-awareness is crucial. Because of that, we can say that all its activity, all its movement or development was informed by a perception of its period. So historical consciousness is equivalent to self-consciousness: in order for Romantic theory to know itself, it had to be equally aware of its historical or temporal position, of where it was in terms of historical time, and of how it was defined by that very fact. And so, by means of a historical perspective that focuses on the position of Romantic theory in relation to its historical moment, we might hope to get some sense of how it saw its own enterprise, and thus, ultimately, of what Romantic theory was really all about.

In order to grasp the position of Romantic theory historically, however, we need to consider first of all how it came to be. Once again, Hegel seems useful: "Spirit has broken with the former world of its existence and its representing, and is of a mind to submerge it in the past, and in the labor of its own transformation." And, subsequently: "the gradual crumbling that doesn't change the physiognomy of the whole will be cut short by a flash of lightning that in one instant will reveal the shape of the new world." Out of the ruins of the present, then, a new world of theory was about to emerge. And that new theoretical consciousness, as Hegel saw it, would submerge the present in the past. Yet its motive wasn't just iconoclastic. Instead, such a move seemed to constitute a necessary preliminary to the creation of theory. Thus Hegel speaks of how Spirit, or the force that produces theory, would assimilate the present not only to the past but to "the labor of its own transformation." Here, then, we arrive at a sense of how theory perceived its position historically. Face to face with its own historical condition, the theoretical consciousness would internalize all of history into itself, and in that process theory would come to be.

But before it could transform the historical moment, Romantic theory had to immerse itself completely in external, material circumstances. In that respect, what the Romantic era produced wasn't armchair theory. On the contrary, Romantic theory embraced the sheer materiality of its stuff. Recall Bichat's final year, the 600 cadavers supposedly dissected, not to speak of the countless animals sacrificed earlier in an effort to identify the source of life from a physiological standpoint. Nor, apparently, were these careful experiments, designed to elicit the answer to some well-formulated question. Rather, Bichat seems to have worked almost haphazardly, without any preconceived plan. As if he believed a theory of vitality would somehow emerge merely from his engagement with the material itself. Nevertheless, it must have been essentially no different at the Hôtel-Dieu or any other Paris hospital. Here the brutal reality was that doctors often simply watched their patients die. As patients died, observations were collected of how they had gradually slipped out of life: a massive record of the minutiae of vitality, from which the new medical researchers expected to formulate a theory of the *élan vital.* What all of this betrays is the extent to which Romantic theory could become absorbed in pure materiality. Unlike its late eighteenth-century counterpart, it brought no theoretical preconceptions to its inquiry. Perhaps that was the Revolutionary legacy. Thus theory would go back to square one.

The fact that such a commencement didn't cause any notable anxiety might well be due to the mixture of subjectivity and objectivity in the genesis of Romantic theory. Yes, in one respect Romantic theory looks as if it sprang from pure materiality. But, in another way, it never really did exactly that. Because from the outset there was always an element of subjectivity. It comes out most clearly, I think, in Friedrich Schlegel. *Das höchste Schöne* is complete objectivity. Yet objectivity of this kind isn't incompatible with subjectivity. In fact, it turns out to have been produced by subjectivity. And if objectivity can be produced by subjectivity, the two aren't really antithetical. At a stretch, we might even say that for Friedrich Schlegel and others objectivity is just a form of subjectivity. As Schlegel saw it, Greek culture created objectivity, the highest form of the beautiful, out of its desire for an objective embodiment of subjectivity. Its ability to do so meant in turn that objectivity was just a cultural viewpoint like any other, and that all of these, ultimately, were permeated by subjectivity. More broadly, it translated into a belief that materiality could always be transformed by the creative ferment of subjectivity. Or, on another level, that materiality would inevitably yield to the formative impulse of theory.

But even if the force that produced Romantic theory had transformed materiality, it still lacked a crucial element: the concept of theory. Romantic theory, in other words, wasn't really Romantic theory until it arrived at this concept. From a Romantic standpoint, the concept of theory is the flash of lightning "that in one instant will reveal the shape of the new world." And that new world was theory. What the concept of theory meant to the Romantic period was theoretical autonomy. Hegel's quip ("If a theory doesn't fit the facts, so much the worse for the facts") is well known. But it does convey a point. By any measure, Romantic theory lavished plenty of attention on facts. But its attitude toward these was radically different from that of late eighteenth-century theory. Unlike earlier approaches, its primary relation wasn't just to fact. That didn't imply, *pace* Hegel, a disregard for it. What it did mean was that theory could no longer think of itself merely as an analysis of fact. For Romantic theory, it had become equally important to think about theory itself. In that respect, theory was no longer simply about the relation of concepts to external existences. Instead, what Romantic theory had finally realized was that its relation to fact would ultimately depend not on any sort of external necessity but rather on whatever use it opted to make of its own inner resources.

In retrospect, we might say that what the Romantic period really witnessed was the triumph of theory. We think of the period, of course, as defined by the Revolution. But much of what the Revolution sought to achieve was to be retracted by Napoleon, who represents, as he himself put it, the end of the Revolution and the Revolution itself. We could just as easily survey the period from a Napoleonic perspective. Yet even here we find much of what it tried to do erased by what followed: the Congress of Vienna, the Restoration, the Regency. What couldn't be undone or retracted, however, was the revolution in theory. As Hegel had foreseen, Romantic theory marked the advent of a new era. And the reason its revolution couldn't be reversed was that it brought theory to a new level of self-awareness. But what the Romantic era experienced from the standpoint of theory wasn't just a revolution. What began as revolution would finally prove to be the triumph of theory. From marginal observer, theory now moved to center stage, as the new mode of discourse for all the arts and sciences. Yet it was more than just their lingua franca. In the last analysis, theory becomes for the arts and sciences the language of thought itself.

One clear indication of the ascendency theory acquired in the Romantic period appears in the way we find culture interpreted by theory. Unlike some forms of intellectual activity, culture didn't need a lingua franca. On the contrary: the fact that it was culture implied its capacity to talk about itself. For that very reason, to see culture described not by itself but by theory marked a radical shift. Most of all, perhaps, in the field of classical philology. Antiquity, the precious repository of tradition, ought to be discussed only by a form of discourse authenticated by the nearly equal extent of its own antiquity. Hence the sensation caused by Friedrich Wolf when he brought a new kind of historical method to the study of Homer. Here Goethe comes to mind: the secret auditor, who supposedly hid behind a curtain to hear Wolf lecture. The image seems apt: Goethe, as representative of culture, afraid to offer homage publicly to the new philology, yet irresistibly drawn by a sort of *Schadenfreude* to the usurpation of his own field. What fascinated Goethe was theory. He could look skeptical when it came in the guise of Hegel and the attempt by philosophy to legislate the future development of all the other arts and sciences. But the kind of theory Wolf brought to classical philology was different. Because it came out of classical philology itself, theory about the development of the Homeric text couldn't be so easily resisted. And that itself might indicate, as well as any other testimony, the degree of ascendency attained by theory.

For the Romantic period, theory was equally preeminent as universal theory. In fact, the possibility of universal theory had already been explored to some extent by a number of eighteenth-century sources. From an eighteenth-century perspective, however, universal theory simply meant an effort to explain theoretically all the different fields of human inquiry. At most, then, explanations of one or another field might be related in some way. What these sources could hardly have imagined was that a given theory might apply to all fields universally. Yet that was precisely what Romantic theory offered. Its proposal amounted to a very different form of universal theory. Its ascendency grew from the insight that a theory able to explain phenomena in one field possessed a distinct advantage when it turned to a new field over a theory that lacked such a capacity. And, by implication, a theory that could potentially explain phenomena in *any* field would have primacy over all other attempts at theory. Similarly, if you could explain, as Coleridge did, the relation between theory as defined for different fields of inquiry, that, too, would presumably have primacy over a theory that pertained to one field only. Thus the ascendency of Romantic theory didn't necessarily imply its capacity to present a better explanation for a specific field. It came, rather, from what it could say about all of these collectively.

But perhaps the clearest indication of the ascendency of theory in the Romantic period lay in the fact that thought itself had come to be defined by theory.

Theory, then, replaces philosophy as the paradigm by which thought is defined. And that in turn meant rationality was no longer the paramount concern. For thought, the shift from philosophy to theory is crucial. Philosophy had never pretended to speak for thought in its entirety. Rationality only delineated a particular mode of intellectual inquiry. Theory, on the other hand, wanted to embrace all of it. When the *Phenomenology of Spirit* undertook to describe the movement from Substance to Subject, what it really had in mind was the very movement of thought itself. For Hegel, the movement he traced wasn't simply that of thought applied to a given field. Instead, what he hoped to specify was the kind of movement thought enacted regardless of field. Thus instead of the rational viewpoint demanded by earlier philosophy, the *Phenomenology* opted for a more holistic perspective. Through its effort to grasp thought as a totality, it hoped to arrive at perceptions that would be true for all fields of inquiry. Here, then, was the ultimate source of the ascendency of theory: by its use of a holistic perspective, it attempted to move beyond inferences about specific topics to a higher level of generality, one that earlier forms of thought hadn't even been aware of.

Finally, we come to the question of what theory meant to the Romantic period, and, more broadly, why its existence mattered. In many ways, it grew directly out of concrete, material circumstances. Despite the difficulties that beset its genesis, it rose to a position of ascendency within the period. All in all, the history of Romantic theory suggests that for those who developed it, and even for many who simply witnessed its development, theory was more than just the work of the dispassionate observer, that for those who formulated it, theory was meant to play a more vital role. Certainly its connection to its time was in many respects immediate and fraught with consequences. To those who cared for the sick at the Hôtel-Dieu and other Paris hospitals, to those who held responsibility for the lives of the patients there, what they came to know about the nature of vitality mattered. Similarly, for those who believed that new advances in chemical knowledge might make possible a radical improvement of human life, the relation of electrical to chemical forces and, more largely, the whole chemical theory of elemental substances mattered. What the Revolution brought was a sense of how the years that followed might prove the dawn of a new era. And, in the process by which that era gradually emerged, those engaged in the development of theory could see its capacity to shape the form that era assumed.

For the Romantic period, we might say that what theory meant, first of all, was the dream of a power over things. In his Introductory Discourse on chemistry from 1802, Humphry Davy announced the new ambition of the sciences. From now on, chemistry would no longer be simply a disinterested inquiry into the combination of elements or substances. Instead, Davy hoped that a knowledge of how different substances combined would enable chemistry to transform human life. It would lead to the perfection of various chemical and technical processes, the invention of new instruments, the improvement of conditions of labor. And these in turn would promote the birth of a new era. In the formation of that era, chemistry, he felt, had a significant function to fulfill. It would give humanity a new kind of power over things, greater than any it had known before. The key to its power would be its knowledge of what lay behind the chemical activity of different substances. Its knowledge would allow it to explain the inner dynamics of combustion or fire, the formation of new substances, the breakdown of others. But that knowledge, Davy argued, would become possible only by means of "an acquaintance with the fundamental and general chemical principles." Which is to say: theory. Theory, then, would give its possessor a power over things. By means of theory, we could aspire to know what went on at the very heart of external nature. And once we knew its innermost secrets, we might hope to harness the energy of its basic processes. As a result, substances that had been inert or even resistant to our projects would take on a new plastic quality. And that, in turn, would make it possible to transform the conditions of human life.

In addition to whatever power it might convey over things, theory for the Romantic period is equally about creation. Perhaps the last place where we might think to look for it would be in the sphere of military tactics. For many, the battlefield epitomized the rule of necessity. Yet even here, a creative impulse can be felt. Napoleon once said that every engagement was like a theatrical piece, with a distinct beginning, middle, and end. And the sole aim of his tactics was to make its drama possible. His success over his opponents came from their lack of awareness of how they participated in that drama. All the elements of Napoleonic tactics could be found, more or less, in eighteenth-century sources. Nor were his opponents unaware of the theory of war. Some, like Jomini, had even served under him. Others, like Clausewitz, had fought against him in the field. What they failed to recognize, however, was the creative aspect of his tactical arrangements. From their standpoint, theory meant analysis: a calculation of the weight of numbers, cavalry, and artillery. To Napoleon, by contrast, theory meant creation: a fusion of all the elements of eighteenth-century strategy to form an original synthesis. In this way, we arrive at one of the basic insights of Romantic theory: that the essence of theory, in the end, isn't really analysis at all but rather intellectual creativity.

Finally, what Romantic theory exemplified most of all, perhaps, was a sense of possibility. It hovers, so to speak, just on the threshold of our awareness. We find it beautifully figured in "The Triumph of Life," as the "shape all light" that is the ultimate image at the heart of the poet's obsessive dream sequence, the symbolic object of his quest. But we also find the sense of possibility that looms over the Romantic consciousness equally manifest in Galois theory. It was the great insight of the first memoir on the resolvability of equations by radicals that what we didn't know could be formally expressed as if we knew it, and that by means of our treatment of its formal expression we could actually bring what was unknown closer to knowability. For Galois, that insight suggested a new perspective on the sciences in general. It amounted, for him, to a belief that if we could only manage to situate what we wanted to know within a framework of inquiry, that framework itself might then become a means to knowledge and hence an index of possibility for theory. Beyond what he has to say about a purely formal kind of solvability, however, Galois seemed to feel that any form of theory endowed with the capacity to think about what was possible would always be able to raise itself to a higher level. And from his standpoint, our ability to think about the possible is invariably connected to the creativity of theory. In that respect, his work might be said to reiterate that of an earlier Romantic author, who had written:

> Our destiny, our nature, and our home
> Is with infinitude, and only there;
> With hope it is, hope that can never die,
> Effort, and expectation, and desire,
> And something evermore about to be.

For Romantic theory, perhaps it is this promise of "something evermore about to be" that best expresses its sense of possibility.

Epilogue

From history it's only natural we should turn to the present. Which is to say: from Romantic theory in its own time to its relation to contemporary theory. And rather than give what would at best amount to a brief, inadequate survey, it seemed to me better to treat the topic very selectively. Specifically, I want to look at how a few contemporary theorists have chosen to respond to Hegel. If Hegel was in many ways exemplary of what Romantic theory tried to be, his presence in the contemporary theory scene might shed suggestive light on the larger issue. My sense was that if we traced the response of contemporary theory to Hegel over the past thirty years, we'd find it has a story to tell. Briefly, the story would be about an attempt to undermine the Hegelian system, followed by an impulse to question it, and finally by a move to return to it. And the moral of this story, I suggest, is that Hegel (and by implication Romantic theory) isn't just our past but, more important, a possibility for our future.

I want to begin with the work of Jacques Derrida. Although we could go back even earlier, Derrida seems especially appropriate because of the way he framed the whole question of theory. In particular, he was perhaps the first to ask whether theory could really be adequately expressed in terms of some metalevel discourse such as philosophy, and whether we could ever hope to arrive at a full awareness of our own thought processes by means of theory. And even if he wasn't the first to posit a lack of such self-awareness (Heidegger's *Nietzsche* comes to mind here), he was perhaps the first to suggest we might want to rethink our relation to theory, on a level other than that of theory itself.

Given his impulse to question theory in a radical way, it was easy to see that at some point Derrida would most likely wish to confront the figure who, of all his predecessors, had made the largest claims for theoretical self-awareness: Hegel. Hence the rationale for *Glas*, which we might describe as an attempt to sound the final knell for philosophy, by means of a commentary on Hegel. *Glas* presents itself, quite simply and succinctly, as a discourse on the law of the family. Specifically, it wants to be a discussion of Hegel's family, of the family in Hegel, and of the concept of family according to Hegel (p. 4). Here we apparently have an upward progression or ascent toward conceptual awareness, which is exactly what you'd expect in a commentary on Hegel or, more broadly, German idealism. So we might find it normal to begin with the biographical circumstances of Hegel's family. From there we'd move on to the family in Hegel, a kind of middle ground where those biographical circumstances get assimilated into a consciousness of family, a sense of the family as a theme in Hegel. And from there we'd finally arrive at a concept of the family, as the point where all our efforts to impose a kind of structure on family achieve their highest form of theoretical awareness.

Ironically, what we get in *Glas* turns out to be exactly the reverse: from the concept of family according to Hegel, Derrida wants to work outward to the much larger sphere of all the ways family might be conceptually structured in Hegel, and from there onto the even larger sphere occupied by Hegel's actual family, whose complex relationships go far beyond what we can apprehend by means of theory. Or, as Derrida himself puts it: "If the living relation of father to son is life as a nonconceptual unity, every conceptual unity presupposes that relation, implies that nonconcept as the concept's production, the concept's non-conceptual conception" (p. 80). For Derrida, then, the commentary on Hegel is a way to trace his concept of the family to the larger conceptual matrix out of which it presumably arose. But if *Glas* is thus about the conceptual matrix to which we can trace the Hegelian concept of the family, the point isn't simply to give a history of its genesis but rather to expose the "displacements or the disimplications of which it will be the object," displacements that "would not know how to have a simply local character" (p. 5) because of the deep significance of this family concept for the whole Hegelian project. In other words, displacements that would ultimately destabilize the entire Hegelian system.

For Derrida, I would argue, the point at which such displacement or destabilization comes about can be found in the story of Hegel's family, which we glean from the letters that pass between Hegel and those of his intimate circle. Nor is it an accident, I suspect, that immediately after it reproduces some of these letters *Glas* goes on to say: "And what if what cannot be assimilated, the absolute indigestible, played a fundamental role in the system, an abyssal role rather, the abyss playing an almost transcendental role and allowing to be formed above it, as a kind of effluvium, a dream of appeasement? Isn't there always an element excluded from the system that assures the system's space of possibility? The transcendental has always been, strictly, a transcategorial, what could be received, formed, terminated in none of the categories intrinsic to the system. . . . And what if the sister, the brother/sister relation represented here the transcendental position, ex-position?" (pp. 151, 162). Because it's based on sexual difference without desire, the brother/sister relation is the only one that doesn't fit into the Hegelian concept of the family. And yet, as Hegel's letters attest, it's part of his own family. So we get a displacement of the Hegelian family concept by the one element it can't really assimilate, but can't reject.

But if what Derrida hoped to achieve in *Glas* was an extension of the Hegelian text until it ran into contradiction and ultimately into spaces it couldn't cover (such as the real), that hope was bound to fail. And the reason it was bound to fail lay in the inherent capacity of the Hegelian system for endless reflexivity. Clearly the aim of *Glas* was to begin with the Hegelian text and, by a proliferation of commentary that attempted to reproduce the thought-mode of the text, to bring about an expansion or development of the Hegelian system that would eventually produce gaps or lacunae, places where it couldn't properly connect to itself. The existence of such places would point in turn to the *unrepresentability* of some circumstances by Hegelian theory, or by any form of theory. And that would suggest that what was unrepresentable might in fact form the base or ground of theory, the condition of its possibility. What Derrida failed to take into account, however, was the way Hegelian theory could absorb all these gaps or lacunae, and even any supposedly unrepresentable actuality, by acts of reflexivity in which it would simply subsume these into the process of its own formation. Because it wasn't the kind of system whose concepts are all at the same level, it could just take what couldn't be represented at one level to the next higher level, through a Romantic reflexivity by which it simply rethought or redefined its own concept of itself. As a result, the Derridean maneuver would not only fail to dislodge or displace Hegelian theory but could, arguably, be easily subsumed into it.

More than a decade later, we get a different kind of take on Hegel from Judith Butler. Unlike Derrida, she didn't try to undermine the Hegelian system. Instead, she merely questioned it. Specifically, *Subjects of Desire* put forward a critique of the Hegelian subject. From Julia Kristeva, Butler adopted a notion of the body as a heterogeneous assemblage of drives. Like Kristeva, Butler urged we should replace the Hegelian subject by the body. And from Michel Foucault, Butler took over the argument that instead of an analysis of desire we should have a history of bodies, one that would investigate how the desiring subject was produced. For Butler, this critique of the Hegelian subject and the proposal to replace it by a history of bodies offers "a major conceptual reorientation which, if successful, would signal the definitive closure of Hegel's narrative of desire" (p. 235). As Foucault saw it, the way to arrive at that history was by a gene-alogical inquiry into how subjects of desire emerge out of power relations at a given moment. From his perspective, genealogical inquiry would reveal that the "truth" of desire as the essence of the subject was in fact a fiction, produced by other forces. What exposed it as fiction was the fact that both the "self" and its "truth" were "immanently locatable within the reflexive circle of thinking." As a result, Butler can ask: "What if Foucault were right, that the conceit of an immanently philosophical desire grounded the further conceits of the subject and its truth? Then Hegel's narrative would have entered fully the domain of the fantastic, and the phenomenology would require a genealogical account of the hidden historical conditions of its own structure" (p. 236).

Nonetheless, questions arise for Butler about the Foucauldian genealogy, that have to do with its tendency to simplify historically. For example, she notices the way Foucault will from time to time rely on a naturalistic vocabulary (e.g., the strength versus weakness of an instinct). The upshot is that the body "is always the occasion for a play of dominations and regulations" (p. 236). From that Butler goes on to say: "Here we can see that Foucault has elevated the scene of bodily conflict to an invariant feature of historical change, and it makes sense to ask whether war itself has not become romanticized and reified through this theoretical move" (p. 237). Finally, then, Butler has to question Foucault: "Why does Foucault appear to eschew the analysis of concrete bodies in complex historical situations in favor of a single history in which all culture requires the subjection of the body?"

Perhaps the most important consequence of Butler's impulse to question Foucault is that the Hegelian narrative reappears, as a way to enhance the story we get from Foucault. Because Foucault doesn't really specify how abstraction from the body occurs within a concrete social scene, we need on that point to look elsewhere. Hence the reappearance of Hegel, since for Butler "it is Hegel's account of lordship and bondage that . . . appears a more promising framework within which to answer such a question" (p. 238). If Foucault is all about how a "subject" is generated, what he can't say is which subjects get generated, and at whose expense. And the reason he can't say, Butler seems to suggest, is because he isn't able to give an account of relationships that can offer a rationale for two of their indispensable aspects: reflexivity and intersubjectivity. To explain either of these, we need, obviously, a theory of some kind, and since both involve process, that theory will have to take the form of narrative. Thus Butler has to conclude: "If the history of desire must be told in terms of a history of bodies . . .

and if it is not a hermeneutics of the self that is required, then perhaps it is the narrative of a certain philosophically instructive comedy of errors" (p. 238). So, at the end, we return to Hegel.

If we now turn to Slavoj Žižek on *Tarrying with the Negative*, almost twenty years after *Glas*, we can see how much the relation of contemporary theory to Romantic theory has changed. Derrida had felt the best way to think about theory ought to involve an analysis of Hegel that would focus on the places where his system couldn't connect to itself, places that would in turn lead to a displacement of the entire system by what it couldn't represent, by the reality that in fact formed its base. In this fashion, he hoped to raise the question of whether theory could ever arrive at an adequate awareness of itself. For Žižek, such a question no longer seems to have the same urgency. Instead, we might say that for him theory is the only way we can hope to arrive at an adequate self-awareness. Nor does he even have the same sense of how we ought to define theory. To Derrida, theory presupposed some sort of consistency. In order to produce a displacement of the Hegelian system, he had to be able to expose its inconsistency on some level. By contrast, Žižek doesn't see inconsistency as a big issue. From his perspective, different forms of theory can even come together in a fruitful way. His eclecticism marks what we might term a late phase in the development of theory. But for precisely that reason it's all the more remarkable that what he should advocate is a *return* to Kant and Hegel.

Likewise, I find it equally significant that at the outset of his discussion of Hegel, Žižek urges us to go back to Kant. Specifically, Žižek says we need to forget all the standard textbook stuff on Hegelian idealism, by which the Concept manages to generate all its content out of itself and so is able to dispense with any external agency. Instead, Žižek avers we should "return to the Kantian duality of the transcendental network of categories and of Things-in-themselves" (p. 19). If we do that, we then discover exactly what Kant discovered: that the sum total of all the affects we experience isn't enough to give us access to the things-in-themselves or noumena. But here's where Hegel comes in: as Žižek sees it, what Hegel's critique of Kant points out isn't the insufficiency of the affects we receive but rather the abstract character of thought itself. In other words, our very need for affects becomes an index of the insufficiency of thought. From there, Žižek can go on to propose a new way to see the Hegelian process of Substance $\Rightarrow$ Subject. For Žižek, this is a process that never quite becomes complete: for him, the subjectivization of substance remains incomplete. And the remainder or leftover is what we might call the real, the very being of the subject.

The fact that we never quite get to the real produces in turn a situation where we become very dependent on any epistemic markers we can come by. Hence in his treatment of Hegel on identity Žižek is careful to emphasize the crucial role played by differences. From an epistemological perspective, if we try to grasp a thing irrespective of its relationship to everything else or as it is "in itself," we find we don't get anywhere. As Žižek puts it, *"identity hinges upon what makes a difference"* (p. 130). Yet if differences are in fact crucial from an epistemological perspective, what's perhaps equally significant here is the move by which Žižek attempts to pass from the epistemological to the ontological. Epistemologically, a subject is bound to be empty or void in itself, given that we can't ascertain what it is without some differences to act as epistemic markers. Žižek, however, wants to maintain it's empty or void in an ontological sense as well. To make his claim, he has to assert that the subject in Hegel is purely empty or void in itself, that it exists only from the standpoint of what it is "for others." Yet Hegel himself, in a passage quoted by Žižek, had said "The father also has an existence of his own apart from the son-relationship" so that opposites are either "negatively related to one another or *sublate each other* and are *indifferent* to one another" (p. 131). But to be indifferent to another, a subject clearly has to exist in itself.

What Žižek has to say about the void of the subject "in itself" displays its radical consequences when he comes to his discussion of the Hegelian movement from "in-itself" to "for-itself." For Žižek, there simply isn't any such movement: we don't go from "in-itself" to "for-itself" because the two perspectives are in fact one and the same. They're the same because "in-itself" in opposition to "for-itself" means (1) what exists only potentially, as an inner possibility, versus the actual, and (2) actuality itself in the sense of an external, immediate objectivity that hasn't yet been internalized and so hasn't yet arrived at its Concept or Notion (p. 141). For Žižek, then, the two conditions exist simultaneously: in-itself potentiality is only possible if we have the external perspective of the actual for which it hasn't yet fully realized itself, and vice versa. On that basis, Žižek can say: "We can see, now, why Hegel is as far as possible from the evolutionist notion of the progressive development of in-itself into for-itself: the category of 'in itself' is strictly correlative to 'for us,' i.e., for some consciousness external to the thing-in-itself" (p. 142). Yet Hegel himself, as we've seen, had affirmed in his *Phenomenology* Preface that "this being-in-and-for-itself is at first only for us, or *in itself*. . . . It must also be this *for itself*." Contrary to Žižek, then, there appears to be a development of some kind after all.

By his resistance to any movement from "in-itself" to "for-itself" in Hegel, Žižek offers a clue to the current impasse in theory. Ultimately, I would argue, his refusal to accept such a move is based on his belief that to understand Hegel we need to go back to Kant. In other words, our perspective on theory finally has to be epistemological. Because that, in the last analysis, was what Kant was all about: the notion that we don't in the end have access to things as they are, and that the task for theory must then be how best to make sense of our epistemological situation. Yet for Hegel and others who helped to define what I've described as Romantic theory, there had been another option: instead of an epistemological framework in which we never quite manage to resolve the issues that matter most, we might try to address these from a radically different perspective, that of pure theory. By that I mean a perspective by which we try to reframe questions we can't answer at a level where we can think more abstractly about what their solution would have to involve. Which is to say: that we move from theory to metatheory.

~

In recent years, theory seems to have entered a kind of twilight phase. For the past decade, at least, no new forms of theory have emerged. Thus, what began more than thirty years ago with the advent of structuralism appears to have come to an end. But if the era of theory is in fact over, it seems only natural to ask what brought about its demise. Of course, questions about the end or demise of theory inevitably lead to questions about its origin. Specifically, we wonder whether the way a movement will end can invariably be discerned from the way it began. But the question of how theory began is obviously a complicated one. Because it isn't just a matter of when it took shape explicitly. Instead, the real moment of origin for every theory lies in its premises. Yet in most instances those premises don't originate from that theory itself. Thus, to pinpoint its real origin, we need to go back to its sources. As I thought about all this in the course of my work on the Romantic period, I couldn't help but feel how relevant Romantic theory really was to the current theory scene. After all, most of the present forms of theory could easily be traced back to the Romantic era. And that in turn suggested that a study of Romantic theory might shed some light on the fate of contemporary theory.

At the same time, I had to acknowledge the distance between present-day theory and that of the Romantic period. Obviously, we don't do theory in quite the same way anymore. But maybe it wasn't just a question of style. Heidegger says somewhere that metaphysics has never been the same since the death of Hegel in 1831. For me, such a remark carried a sort of poignancy. I knew that Heidegger himself had frequently lectured on Hegel. In addition, his published oeuvre offered a careful, detailed commentary on the Introduction to Hegel's *Phenomenology*. And I knew he considered *Identity and Difference*, in which a commentary on Hegel's *Logic* plays a crucial role, the most important work of his own later period. To him, then, the history of theory wasn't simply a story of continuous advancement. Evidently there were losses as well. Moreover, some of these even seemed to outweigh any advances. What all this pointed to was that our advances were inextricably connected to our losses. Because we had gotten committed to particular forms of theory believed to mark advances of some kind, we had unavoidably sacrificed other advantages we weren't fully aware of, inherent in earlier forms of theory. Thus the advances defined by forms of post-Romantic theory to which we adhered were precisely what had brought theory to its present position.

But even if all that were true, I wondered whether an effort to revisit Romantic theory might not allow us to recover some of those sources of possibility we had apparently lost. No doubt a few aspects of Romantic theory pertained largely to its particular period. This seemed especially true of some forms of theory in the sciences, several of which were then still in their infancy. In other ways, nevertheless, Romantic theory distinctly looked beyond its own era. As I studied the forms theory assumed in the period, I became increasingly aware of how many of these had come to think not only about the particular field they sought to understand but about theory itself. Here, then, was the crucial insight of Romantic theory, the ultimate source of all its possibility: the perception that in order to arrive at a meaningful analysis of theory, you couldn't just think about it in relation to a particular field. Instead, you had to think about theory on a more general level, regardless of field, so as to be able to say what would hold true for any given form of theory. Of course, the Romantic period had applied this insight primarily to those forms of theory that dominated its own era. Nonetheless, an awareness of the larger scope of its insight was constantly present. Its relevance to contemporary theory becomes apparent if we look at the Romantic position on theory in terms of what it had to say about theory itself, rather than theory in a particular field.

Significantly, many forms of Romantic theory resisted anything that resembled an elaborate formal definition of their concepts. On that point, their posture was clearly minimalist. In the sciences, researchers like Davy and Bichat preferred to immerse concepts in pure materiality: Bichat's vital properties reflect a strictly observational perspective, while Davy chose to think in terms of chemical elements rather than concepts based on the nature of substances. In other fields, meanwhile, Romantic theory showed itself equally resistant to any formal definition of concepts. Fichte, for example, left the basic concepts of his *Wissenschaftslehre* completely undefined. To a slightly lesser extent, so did Hegel in the

Phenomenology. Or, at best, a concept is defined only to have its definition overturned by a subsequent one that contradicts the first. From a Romantic standpoint, excessive emphasis on the definition of concepts only made a system or theory top-heavy. For Romantic theory, definition implied fixation: once defined, a concept no longer offered the same kind of latitude as before. In that respect, you might say, Romantic theory inclined to distinctly different criteria from those of contemporary theory: above all, it looked for lightness, flexibility. Specifically, Romantic theorists felt concepts ought to be as lightly defined as possible, so as to allow for maximal flexibility in their use. What mattered most to Romantic theory was what you did with your concepts. For that reason, it was never impressed merely by the way concepts got defined. To its eye, all definition was just preliminary. Invariably, it looked to what lay beyond that.

What Romantic theory came to realize as it worked out its position on concepts was that theory is all about trade-offs. What you give to one, you take from somewhere else. And that meant you had to decide where you wanted the thought content of theory to be. Faced with a number of choices, Romantic theory refused to put all its stuff into concepts. It knew that when you did that, they became increasingly difficult to apply. In effect, the more you put into a concept, the more you had to worry about it. After all, concepts could be raided, by the equivalent of a corporate takeover. Consequently, they had to be rendered foolproof against appropriation by others. But that necessitated more and more specificity. Ultimately, the quest for specificity takes on a life of its own. Against rival approaches, it seems clear that the one most elaborately defined (and hence most resistant to appropriation) will win out. As a result, conceptual specificity itself becomes the goal. People start to worry about the limits of a definition, about how much you can pack into a concept. From now on, the most sophisticated form of theory is the one that hasn't left anything out. The only problem with all this is that, precisely because of their own extreme specificity, concepts so defined become almost impossible to apply. Because of their specificity, they possess the same sort of uniqueness as any other individual existences. And that wasn't at all what Romantic theory wanted. What it wanted, as Hegel said of Napoleon, was to reach out over the world and master it. For that, however, it would need a different kind of theory.

What made Romantic theory essentially different from other approaches to theory was the primacy it gave to development over concepts. On some level, it seems to have felt that the very fact that theory produces concepts is more important than any individual concepts it produces. Because the work of theory invariably goes on. We supersede our present concepts by the creation of new concepts. Inevitably, since that's precisely what theory is all about. But if our concepts are necessarily transient, it seems only natural to suppose theory should put its commitment elsewhere. What remains inescapable is the development of concepts, the fact that they come to be. Hence the rationale for the Romantic belief that development itself, rather than what it produces, should define theory. As a result, the form theory takes in the Romantic period is simply that of pure development. Development pointed to the notion of a larger whole, a totality. Yes, concepts might enable the mind to fix some vital perception or insight. But any insight, no matter how good in itself, became more meaningful only in the context of a larger totality. At the same time, development also hinted at the possibility of a narrative. Unlike any concept or set of concepts, a narrative allowed us to make sense of an entire field, whose story we could then tell. But if concepts became meaningful by the role they played within a narrative, pure development clearly offered the most comprehensive framework.

By means of a framework of development, Romantic theory hoped to find a way to talk about the process by which we come to be. The ultimate task for any theory, of course, is to be able to talk about our human condition. But our condition isn't a static one. That was what the Romantic era discovered. The advent of the life sciences especially had made this very apparent. Collectively, they showed that the most important fact about our condition is that we don't simply exist: rather, we become what we are. So the existential or ontological perspective has to be assimilated into one of development. What we perceive as existential/ontological, in other words, is simply a photographic still from a film reel: the glimpse of a moment without its temporal quality. If even the existential/ontological is just an aspect of development, however, any theory that wanted to explore our condition fully would have to acknowledge how basic its temporal element really is. Hence the argument for a framework of development. Development can assimilate the existential/ontological without any problem about its relation to the process by which we come to be. And the reason it can do that is because the process of our development is the same as that of theory itself. To understand what was essential about our condition, then, all theory had to do was to think about how it had come to be.

Because its framework was one of development rather than reason, Romantic theory could look at rationality from a new perspective. The crucial requirement for any theory is this: that its thought movement have about it an element of necessity. Rationality tried to get there by means of logical inferences. From its standpoint, the move from particular premises to particular conclusions seemed logically irrefutable. Through a sequence of such moves, it hoped to construct a theory for a given field. Unlike rationality, Romantic theory didn't care about inferences. More broadly, it wasn't rational in terms of its thought movement because it knew it didn't have to be. Essentially, Romantic theory didn't worry about whether it was logical or not because it felt it could always count on a deeper, more basic kind of necessity. This deeper necessity was that by which persons or objects came to be. For Romantic theory, the necessity by which something came to be was of a different kind: since it existed, you simply couldn't deny its genesis. But the same sort of necessity applied equally to thought: like people or objects, thought, too, came to be. Thus, if you could trace the movement by which thought had come to be, you would presumably have arrived at the ultimate goal of theory: the discovery of that to which we could ascribe the quality of absolute necessity.

For Romantic theory, the perception of development, or how something came to be, necessitated reflexivity. Every theory has to have some source or ground, some principle that has the capacity to generate theory. In Romantic theory, reflexivity plays that role. People and objects come to be. We perceive a necessity in the fact that they do so. But our perception of that necessity doesn't grow out of our knowledge of either people or objects. It grows out of our perception of the simple fact that they come to be. The reason we recognize an element of necessity here is that we've seen it elsewhere: in the genesis of thought. Our perception of necessity in the genesis of thought is based, in turn, on reflexivity, or the capacity of thought for awareness of its own movement. Because we feel our own capacity for thought, where thought follows our will or desire to think, we find in the movement of thought a kind of necessity that comes from a perception of its source in our own capacity. But the way we arrive at that perception is by means of reflexivity. Thus reflexivity is the way we come to a perception of necessity. And if this description is in fact true, it points to how reflexivity could function for Romantic theory as the source of theory, which began as an effort to explain what lay behind that necessity. Yet if reflexivity could help Romantic theory to explain how we perceive necessity in the way thought comes to be, it could also shed light on a great deal more. As it turned its focus on the very movement of thought, it introduced the possibility of an analysis of theory. In that way, it offered Romantic theory its first glimpse of metatheory.

By its use of a spatial perspective in the analysis of concepts, Romantic theory opened up a whole new world. In effect, the use of a spatial perspective in the analysis of concepts showed that there was another dimension to theory, one that had absolutely no relation to the content of concepts. You might compare it to a formal compositional principle that looms over the structure of some musical work, completely unaffected by the expressive value of that work. Of course, it's possible to listen to the work without any awareness of the principle by which its structure is determined. Likewise, one might study theory without any sense of how it possessed another dimension. And yet, on some level, that unseen dimension dictated the form assumed by theory. Thus the fact that a concept gets externalized because of a need to posit itself meant for Hegel that there had to be at some point a movement of return. To infer the necessity for a movement of return, however, didn't require any knowledge of the particular concept involved. Instead, the logic was purely spatial: if the concept had in its effort to posit itself become external to what it originally was, it would have to return to itself. But that implied we could know all we wanted about any concept within a theory solely from its spatial aspect. Even now, to some extent, we still haven't fully appreciated what this might mean for theory. Simply put, it seems to say that an aspect of metatheory can tell us all we want to know about the conceptual elements of any given theory.

Besides its use of spatial perspective, Romantic theory also introduced a new kind of abstraction into theory. Earlier forms of theory had of course been familiar with the sort of abstraction that involved external objects. But the kind of abstraction Romantic theory introduced was different. Rather than objects, it abstracted from concepts. As a result, concepts could be treated in a purely formal way. The consequence of all this was to reveal a great deal of structure no one had previously even suspected. Normally, we associate generality with a loss of structure: as a field comes under survey at a higher level of generality, it tends to lose structure. What Romantic theory showed, however, was that, contrary to expectation, an increase in generality actually led to a greater amount of structure for theory. And since the forms of theory I speak of had abstracted from the specificity of particular concepts, all this structure had to be inherent in theory itself. Here Galois theory comes especially to mind, with its multiple levels of generality (subfields that embrace other subfields of an extension K, subgroups that include subgroups of the automorphism group $G(K,F)$). Yet it would be just as easy to cite other, equally relevant instances. What it all meant was that any move to a higher level of generality would offer a glimpse of the inherent structure of theory, and so reveal how any given form of theory was ultimately determined.

In a sense, what every theory wants is to be the final word on theory. Ever since Kant, with his *Prolegomena to Any Future Metaphysics*, the ambition of each new attempt at theory had been to create the framework by which all its successors would be defined. But the dawn of the Romantic era had seen the ante raised to an even higher level. From now on, it no longer seemed enough just to supersede all previous forms of theory. To be the final or definitive word, theory now had to meet a new requirement: rather than just expose the inadequacy of earlier efforts, it had to show how all its predecessors had figured in a development that culminated in itself. To be the definitive form of theory, in other words, you couldn't simply critique all earlier forms of theory. Instead, you had to explain everybody else, demonstrate that you had fully understood what they wanted to achieve and why they had fallen short of their goal. Only then could a theory qualify as the final word, by which the history of theory comes to an end. So Hegel had implied in his *Phenomenology*. But if the final word on theory had to explain all earlier forms of theory, the only form of theory able to do that would have to involve metatheory, or theory about theory. By means of metatheory, theory might hope to show why a form of theory whose subject is theory rather than any external field has to be the last word about theory. And its explanation would suggest that if theory, as the Romantic period believed, possesses a distinct autonomy, its ultimate goal should then be to arrive at some insight into the nature of theory itself.

One • The Triumph of Theory

1. For a description of Rousseau's tomb at Ermenonville and its cult, see Simon Schama, *Citizens* (New York: Knopf, 1989), pp. 156–62. In *The Great Cat Massacre and Other Episodes in French Cultural History* (New York: Basic Books, 1984), Robert Darnton talks about Rousseau's readership (pp. 215–56 and, for readers' reactions specifically, pp. 242–49).

2. On the genesis of *La Nouvelle Héloise*, see Lester Crocker, *Jean-Jacques Rousseau: The Prophetic Voice* (New York: Macmillan, 1973), pp. 52–57.

Of the Rousseau commentators, Jean Starobinski, *Jean-Jacques Rousseau: La transparence et l'obstacle*, 2nd ed. (Paris: Gallimard, 1971), is still probably the most influential. Paul de Man, *Allegories of Reading* (New Haven: Yale UP, 1979), devotes a large amount of space to Rousseau. My own take on *La Nouvelle Héloise* is closer to that of Starobinski than that of de Man because of my emphasis on the psychological over figuration, but I see the psychological in Rousseau as more dynamic than experiential (i.e., passion rather than consciousness). In *Metaromanticism* (Chicago: U of Chicago P, 2003) Paul Hamilton discusses Rousseau in interesting ways. See, for example, his remarks on Rousseau's tendency to write retroactively rather than retrospectively (p. 53) and on Rousseau's belief that we derive pleasure from reverie by writing or reading it (pp. 57–58), both of which bear on my analysis of the pleasure of emotion in Rousseau.

The celebrated *scène du lac* has attracted considerable attention. Christie McDonald Vance, *The Extravagant Shepherd*, in *Studies on Voltaire and the Eighteenth Century*, vol. 105 (Banbury, Oxfordshire: The Voltaire Foundation, 1973), pp. 157–60, focuses primarily on landscape, while Starobinski, "Les Descriptions de journées dans *La Nouvelle Héloise*," in *Reappraisals of Rousseau*, ed. Simon Harvey et al. (Manchester: Manchester UP, 1980), pp. 46–62, stresses time rather than space. Laurence Mall, *Origines et retraites dans* La Nouvelle Héloise (New York: Peter Lang, 1997), pp. 73–76, looks at different forms of nostalgia and how they interact. The most detailed analysis is by Felicity Baker, "La scène du lac dans *La Nouvelle Héloise*," in *Le Préromantisme: hypothèque ou hypothèse? Actes et Colloques* 18 (Paris: Klincksieck, 1975), pp. 129–52. Baker interprets what happens between the lovers from a positive, ethical perspective, but neglects the signs of trouble that emerge in the scene (that Julie has to warn Saint-Preux not to speak anymore about what they feel for each other, or her effort to conceal the fact that she's wept). The most incisive commentary, however, remains that of Bernard Guyon in the Pléiade edition. Guyon points out that whereas Saint-Preux grieves for a passion he can no longer feel, Julie appears disturbed by the fact that hers isn't dead (pp. 1639–40). Yet even Guyon treats the pleasure of tears merely as part of a hypnotic spell whose other elements are reverie, night, and harmonious cadences (p. 1641).

3. While Gregory Dart, *Rousseau, Robespierre and English Romanticism* (Cambridge: Cambridge UP, 1999), hardly mentions Shelley, there is ample coverage of Rousseau and Shelley in Edward Duffy, *Rousseau in England* (Berkeley: U of California P, 1979), pp. 86–105. Specifically, Duffy stresses the pivotal role of Shelley's reading of *Julie* in 1816 (pp. 86–89).

4. Donald Reiman, *Shelley's "The Triumph of Life": A Critical Study* (Urbana: U of Illinois P, 1965), was one of the first to look closely at the role played by Rousseau (pp. 42–43, 45, 48–50, 59–60, 73–76, 79–82), but doesn't consider the possibility Shelley might have changed his mind about Rousseau by 1822 (especially given the failure of his own Rousseauistic experiment with Mary). Later Reiman puts forward a somewhat contradictory view of the "shape all light," as a symbol of the human imagination (pp. 62–64) yet with a tendency to blot out the narrator's thoughts (pp. 65–66). Since Reiman goes on to describe the "shape" as a *beau idéal* for Shelley (pp. 69–73), he presumably sees the imaginative faculty as inimical to the rational. For Shelley, that seems unlikely. Nonetheless, Reiman on "The Triumph of Life" remains one of the two or three major assessments, in part because of its careful, detailed work on the Bodleian manuscript.

To some extent, Kenneth Cameron on "The Triumph of Life," in *Shelley: The Golden Years* (Cambridge: Harvard UP, 1974), reflects his general interest in Shelley's politics. Cameron considers the poem as primarily about life in a social sense (pp. 451–53), and focuses on Rousseau as a political figure (pp. 460–62, 468–70).

Edward Duffy (*Rousseau in England*) is of course also interested in Rousseau, but more from a cultural/historical viewpoint. His argument is that Rousseau succumbed to a desire for Enlightenment clarity over the imaginative faculty (pp. 122–32). The result: the failed outcome of the French Revolution (pp. 113–16). By itself, such an argument can seem unnecessarily reductive, but much of Duffy's other commentary is highly apt.

5. In *Shelley's Mythmaking* (New Haven: Yale UP, 1959) Harold Bloom insists that we treat the poem as vision rather than allegory (pp. 242–43). His remarks on many figures and motifs pursue their symbolic resonances.

6. On Shelleyan negativity as deconstructive, see Paul de Man, "Shelley Disfigured" (orig. 1979, rpt. in *The Rhetoric of Romanticism* [New York: Columbia UP, 1984]). Specifically, de Man observes: "The structure of the text is not one of question and answer, but of a question whose meaning, as question, is effaced from the moment it is asked. The answer to the question is another question, asking what and why one asked, and thus receding even further from the original query" (p. 98). In effect, de Man wants to make a case for Shelleyan negativity based on his characterization of thought's self-erasure in the poem as an endless process (pp. 118–20). But this perpetual self-erasure is to some extent blocked by the fact that the "shape all light" isn't completely obliterated by its successor. Instead, we encounter it again in the next section—as if to imply its *ne plus ultra* quality. For de Man, moreover, the "shape all light" acts as a figure for the figurality of disfiguration (p. 116). Yet even at the figural level, the net result of any "disfiguration" has to be an iteration or assertion of the figural that gets disfigured. For a more extensive critique of de Man, see Orrin Wang, *Fantastic Modernity: Dialectical Readings in Romanticism and Theory* (Baltimore: Johns Hopkins UP, 1996), pp. 46–68. Here the tacit theoretical premise is that the Shelley and de Man texts can fruitfully talk to each other, since both are informed by theory. On a larger scale, however, we might ask whether the relation of Romanticism to postmodern theory doesn't necessitate a theoretical standpoint independent of either, one that would allow us to think their relation historically. Wang also offers a fresh take on the negativity of the poem with his suggestion that the poem is less concerned about the right answer than about the impossibility of asking the right question (p. 53).

Despite obvious resemblances, J. Hillis Miller's "Shelley" chapter in *The Linguistic Moment* (Princeton: Princeton UP, 1985) tells the deconstructive story a bit differently, with more stress on pattern and less on sequence. Yet even Miller has to admit that self-erasure can never be complete (pp. 165–67).

Obviously influenced by de Man, Stuart Sperry, *Shelley's Major Verse* (Cambridge: Harvard UP, 1988), glosses a progression from the "shape all light" to the dusky "shape" in the chariot of life as merely a movement toward death (pp. 187–90, 193). But I find such a gloss hard to accept, given the sense of disclosure embodied in the vision-within-a-vision sequence.

Meanwhile Earl Schulze, "Allegory Against Allegory: 'The Triumph of Life,' " *Studies in Romanticism* 27 (Spring 1988): 31–62, offers a useful corrective to de Man by his insistence on how the self-reflexivity of Shelley's allegory might lead to knowledge through awareness of its own limits. Take that self-reflexivity one step further, and you then have the structure or framework necessary for knowledge actually embedded within the text.

Several recent accounts are less theoretical. Angela Leighton, *Shelley and the Sublime* (Cambridge: Cambridge UP, 1984), addresses crucial thematic ambivalences (pp. 168–70, 171–73); Michael O'Neill, *The Human Mind's Imaginings: Conflict and Achievement in Shelley's Poetry* (Oxford: Clarendon, 1989), glances at "Triumph" only briefly; and Timothy Clark, *Embodying Revolution: The Figure of the Poet in Shelley* (Oxford: Clarendon, 1989), is suggestive on the "shape all light" (pp. 242–45) and the wolf/deer motif (pp. 253–56) but elsewhere treats the allegory too literally.

7. In *Shelley's Process* (New York: Oxford UP, 1988) Jerrold Hogle tries to characterize the movement in Shelley's texts as one of process or transference. But I find the notion of transference awkward for "Triumph," if not all of Shelley: it misses the sense of disclosure or insight that de Man held out. Thus for Hogle the upshot of the movement sponsored by the "shape all light" is merely a choice between different ways of reading (p. 336).

With William Ulmer, *Shelleyan Eros* (Princeton: Princeton UP, 1990), we get a similar nonprogressive concept of movement: repetition (pp. 161–64). And Ross Woodman, "Figuring Disfiguration: Reading Shelley after De Man," *Studies in Romanticism* 40 (Summer 2001): 253–88, offers an even more reductive version of de Man.

But I detect a significant shift within poststructuralist work in Tilottama Rajan, *The Supplement of Reading* (Ithaca: Cornell UP, 1990). Like Hogle (*Shelley's Process*, p. 337), Rajan points out that it's possible to challenge de Man's reading since it describes a process on the referential level (pp. 326–28). And subsequent remarks hint at the possibility of a positive viewpoint (pp. 331, 338–40).

Finally, Stuart Peterfreund in *Shelley Among Others* (Baltimore: Johns Hopkins UP, 2002) puts forward a suggestive idea about the "shape all light": that because of the identity dynamics in Shelley, what the shade of Rousseau sees isn't what the "shape" perceives but merely his own vision (pp. 305–6). Peterfreund goes on to propose that in the Jane Williams poems the speaker approaches her as a variant of the "shape," but less reductively (p. 314). Nonetheless, I can't help but feel that even in "Triumph" the radiance of the "shape" points to the possibility that what the speaker's perception of it offers is a capacity for insight that would take him beyond himself.

Two • Forms of Nostalgia

1. On Hadrian's villa the standard work is William L. MacDonald and John A. Pinto, *Hadrian's Villa and Its Legacy* (New Haven: Yale UP, 1995). MacDonald and Pinto discuss the villa sculpture on pp. 141–51.

2. For a survey of the image in classical antiquity, see Hans Belting, *Likeness and Presence: A History of the Image Before the Era of Art*, tr. Edmund Jephcott (Chicago: U of Chicago P, 1994).

3. My information about temple idols comes from Ramsay MacMullen, *Paganism in the Roman Empire* (New Haven: Yale UP, 1981), pp. 44–45.

4. All Basil citations from the Loeb edition of St. Basil, *The Letters*, ed. Roy J. Deferrari, 4 vols. (Cambridge: Harvard UP, 1926–34). Basil to Maximus the philosopher in vol. 1, p. 93.

5. For Libanius I use the Loeb edition: Libanius, *Autobiography and Selected Letters*, ed. A. F. Norman, 2 vols. (Cambridge: Harvard UP, 1992). My material on Libanius's hero-worship of Aelius Aristeides is from vol. 2, pp. 295–97.

6. Basil to Peter, bishop of Alexandria, in Basil, *Letters*, vol. 2, p. 303.

7. For Wolf biography, see the recent but brief Hermann Funke, "F. A. Wolf," in *Classical Scholarship: A Biographical Encyclopedia*, ed. Ward W. Briggs and William M. Calder III (New York: Garland, 1990), pp. 523–28. The early but still attractive biography by Mark Pattison in *Essays by the late Mark Pattison*, vol. I (Oxford: Clarendon, 1889), pp. 337–414 has more detail, especially on topics like Wolf's programme for classical studies (pp. 364–66) and Wolf's relation to Humboldt (pp. 398–99, 404–7). Bertrand Hemmerdinger, "Philologues de Jadis," *Belfagor* 32 (1977): 485–522, has questioned some of the details in Pattison and other early sources.

8. For my discussion of Wolf, I cite from F. A. Wolf, *Prolegomena to Homer, 1795*, tr. Anthony Grafton, Glenn Most, and James Zetzel (Princeton: Princeton

UP, 1995). Unfortunately, this translation suffers from a number of errors: see William M. Calder III, *American Historical Review* 92 (1987): 121–22; M. D. Reeve, *Journal of Hellenic Studies* 108 (1988): 219–21; and E. J. Kenney, *The Classical Review* 37 (1987): 89–91, all with corrigenda. Where relevant, I've incorporated these.

9. For Wolf bibliography the most helpful source is *Prolegomena to Homer,* ed. Grafton et al. Its bibliographical essays (pp. 249–54) cover material up to 1985. Arnaldo Momigliano, *New Paths of Classicism in the Nineteenth Century* (*History and Theory* Beiheft 21 [1982]), gives a good survey of nineteenth-century German classical scholarship. Unfortunately, no treatment of Wolf, but many of the issues discussed are relevant to his work. If history offers one perspective on Wolf, another might be that of classical philology. For general background, see E. J. Kenney, *The Classical Text* (Berkeley: U of California P, 1974); and Sebastiano Timpanaro, *La genesi del metodo del Lachmann* (German translation: *Die Entstehung der Lachmannsche Methode,* tr. Dieter Irmer [Hamburg: Helmut Buske, 1971]). Kenney briefly mentions Wolf (pp. 97–98) but focuses primarily on works whose origin is written rather than oral. The "Homeric question" receives a helpful summary from E. R. Dodds in *Fifty Years (and Twelve) of Classical Scholarship,* ed. Maurice Platnauer (Oxford: Blackwell, 1968), pp. 1–17, 31–35, 38–42. Dodds explains the controversy between "Analysts" (Homeric epics as collective effort) and "Unitarians" (attribution to single author). Obviously Wolf favors the first.

10. On Wolf's critical viewpoint, Manfred Fuhrmann, "Friedrich August Wolf," *Deutsche Vierteljahrsschrift für Literaturwissenschaft und Geistesgeschichte* 33 (1959): 187–236, is excellent. Fuhrmann looks at Wolf's predecessors in some detail (pp. 207–16) before he goes on to Wolf's own delicate balance between an idealized Greece and objectivity (pp. 229–31, 231–34). In addition, Fuhrmann points out that Wolf's use of the life-cycle concept is conservative, yet distinct from that of Herder or Winckelmann in its historical/research perspective (pp. 234–36).

In English, the most extensive analysis is by Anthony Grafton, "Prolegomena to Friedrich August Wolf," *Journal of the Warburg and Courtauld Institutes* 44 (1981): 101–29. Grafton is especially useful on Wolf in relation to his sources (pp. 103–9, 109–11, 115–19) and biblical textual scholarship (pp. 119–26). At the same time, Grafton also discusses Wolf's originality (pp. 111–15, 126–29). Michael Murrin, *The Allegorical Epic* (Chicago: U of Chicago P, 1980), pp. 189–96, places Wolf in the context of Vico and others.

11. Unfortunately, the "Studium" essay hasn't gotten much notice so far. To

date, the most detailed treatment is in Peter Szondi, *Poetik und Geschichts-philosophie* I, ed. Senta Metz and Hans-Hagen Hildebrandt (Frankfurt am Main: Suhrkamp, 1974), pp. 99–148, from lecture texts published posthumously. Szondi offers an insightful analysis of Schlegel's "organic" concept of Greek antiquity as part of a cultural cycle (pp. 105–13). Later, he specifically places Schlegel close to the Herder/Winckelmann notion of the organic or Nature (pp. 124–26), which means we ought to see Greek literature as natural history (i.e., Nature, teleology) rather than history (pp. 135–37, 144–45).

The "Studium" essay is also discussed by Ernst Behler, whose work on the *Kritische Friedrich-Schlegel-Ausgabe* has significantly helped to increase aware-ness of Schlegel's critical stature. In his *German Romantic Literary Theory* (Cambridge: Cambridge UP, 1993) Behler portrays the classical/modern conflict in the "Studium" essay as one of interaction/oscillation (pp. 102–8). His sugges-tion that Condorcet's notion of perfectibility might have influenced Schlegel's theory of artistic development (pp. 106–7) is also of interest. Behler's introduc-tion to vol. 1 of the *Kritische Ausgabe* furthers our knowledge of the context of the "Studium" essay by an account of its compositional circumstances (pp. clxi–clxiv) and its three versions (pp. clxv–clxvii).

A recent translation by Stuart Barnett, *On the Study of Greek Poetry* (Albany: SUNY P, 2001), gives additional references to other Schlegel commentary.

12. In *Metaromanticism* (Chicago: U of Chicago P, 2003) Paul Hamilton puts forward a suggestive comparison between Schiller and Friedrich Schlegel based on deferred versus present access to experience of the ideal (pp. 28–29).

13. Klaus Behrens, *Friedrich Schlegels Geschichtsphilosophie* (Tübingen: Nie-meyer, 1984) faults Schlegel for failure to apply general critical/historical princi-ples to his study of Greek culture (p. 60), but doesn't seem to see how their very "universality" might make them suspect.

14. On the development of a Romantic or modern self in Schlegel, see Gerald Izenberg, *Impossible Individuality: Romanticism, Revolution, and the Origins of Modern Selfhood* (Princeton: Princeton UP, 1992), pp. 54–138. Although Izen-berg stresses the political (pp. 98–100), much of what he says qualifies that by a look at other forms of theory in Schlegel (pp. 64–67, 93–96, 134–38).

15. David A. Campbell, *Greek Lyric,* vol. 2 (Cambridge: Harvard UP, 1988), pp. 93, 57.

16. Here René Wellek, *A History of Modern Criticism: 1750–1950,* vol. 2 (New Haven: Yale UP, 1955), is still quite useful, especially on Schlegel's treatment of the organic/natural cycle of Greek art in relation to genre theory (pp. 6–8).

17. For theory in Friedrich Schlegel, see, first of all, Werner Hamacher,

Premises, tr. Peter Fenves (Cambridge: Harvard UP, 1996), which focuses on various kinds of performativity from Fichte's I = I (pp. 230–37) to the "I" as project, parekbasis, poetry/prose, and assertion *ex nihilo* in Schlegel (pp. 238–44, 248–50, 250–54, 255–60). Meanwhile, Manfred Frank, *Einführung in die frühromantische Ästhetik* (Frankfurt am Main: Suhrkamp, 1989), talks about various forms of opposition in Schlegel—finite/infinite, allegory, wit, and irony—and how they're overcome (pp. 291–92, 292–94, 294–95, 301–4). But perhaps the best treatment of theory in Schlegel remains that of Philippe Lacoue-Labarthe and Jean-Luc Nancy, *The Literary Absolute,* tr. Philip Barnard and Cheryl Lester (Albany: SUNY P, 1988). Lacoue-Labarthe and Nancy see literature in Schlegel as a kind of autoproduction best exemplified by the Romantic fragment (pp. 39–58). Although they take excessive liberties with the concept, their own enactment of it gives their work an authentic feel absent from other treatments of Schlegel.

18. See Laurie Johnson, *The Art of Recollection in Jena Romanticism* (Tübingen: Niemeyer, 2002), for much of suggestive value on remembrance as a creative act and on the unknowability of the past for Friedrich Schlegel (esp. pp. 142–43, 145–46, 152, 166–67).

Three • The Movement of Return

1. For my account of what happened at Jena, I rely primarily on three sources: F. Loraine Petre, *Napoleon's Conquest of Prussia* (London: The Bodley Head, 1907); F. N. Maude, *The Jena Campaign 1806* (New York: Macmillan, 1909); and David Chandler, *The Campaigns of Napoleon* (New York: Macmillan, 1966). Petre covers the Prussian war in its entirety and so has less detail on Jena specifically. Based on a careful study of the actual battlefield and other relevant circumstances, Maude is often the most vivid of these sources. In his account, Hohenlohe's "dangerous frame of mind" (i.e., inability to act) and the massacre of Prussian infantry at Vierzehnheiligen are memorably rendered (pp. 148–49, 155–56). Although criticized by some for his failure to go back to primary sources, Chandler remains the standard work on Napoleon's military career. My Jena narrative is based largely on Chandler, but I draw equally on his discussion of Napoleonic strategy and tactics (pp. 479–88 on Jena, 133–91 on strategy/tactics). Chandler is especially good on the *manoeuvre sur les derrières,* or advance of envelopment (pp. 163–70).

2. In *Strategy* (London: Faber & Faber, 1967) B. H. Liddell Hart discusses Napoleon's early use and later neglect of the indirect approach (pp. 107–8). As Hart sees it, Jena marks one of the last great instances of its use. To some extent,

The Ghost of Napoleon (London: Faber & Faber, 1933) is even more relevant because of its detailed yet elegant treatment of what Napoleon learned from his predecessors: mobility and pursuit after victory from de Saxe (pp. 31, 33, 38–48), strategic concentration from Bourcet (pp. 53–57), and the maneuver to attack an enemy flank or rear from Guibert (pp. 81–86). J.F.C. Fuller has also discussed Napoleonic strategy in various places. Like Clausewitz, Fuller places more stress on the relation of military strategy to political and economic objectives than on tactics per se. In *A Military History of the Western World* (New York: Funk & Wagnalls, 1954–57), vol. II, chap. 13, Fuller looks at Jena/Auerstädt specifically, and in *The Conduct of War, 1789–1961* (New Brunswick: Rutgers UP, 1961), Napoleonic warfare more broadly.

3. For a purely theoretical perspective on tactics we have Azar Gat, *The Origins of Military Thought from the Enlightenment to Clausewitz* (Oxford: Clarendon, 1989). Gat doesn't treat Napoleon directly, but puts Jomini forward as his representative. Despite useful remarks on "geometrical" versus "spatial" military theory, however, Gat never really adequately answers Hart's critique of Jomini as an interpreter of Napoleon (*The Ghost of Napoleon*, pp. 110–17).

The best recent book on Napoleonic tactics is Brent Nosworthy, *Battle Tactics of Napoleon and His Enemies* (London: Constable, 1995), which covers its subject in great detail. Not as much, unfortunately, as one might want on grand tactics, but the remarks on tactics versus grand tactics (pp. 25–26, 457–58), the French "impulse" system (pp. 93–102, 127–31), and grand tactics as conceptual (pp. 460–61) are all worth study.

4. By his concern with a tactical "physics" Napoleon displayed awareness of the importance of the actual battlefield experience, a subject of great interest in recent years. Here the indispensable work is John Keegan, *The Face of Battle* (New York: Viking, 1976). Keegan does Waterloo rather than Jena, but obviously many of the same conditions apply. Keegan's influence is evident in Rory Muir, *Tactics and the Experience of Battle in the Age of Napoleon* (New Haven: Yale UP, 1998). *Pace* his title, Muir has more on Wellington than Napoleon, and more on the battlefield experience than tactics. An earlier study by Gunther Rothenberg, *The Art of Warfare in the Age of Napoleon* (Bloomington: Indiana UP, 1978), covers multiple aspects of Napoleonic warfare more fully, with a wealth of data on formations, artillery, and army organization, all of which shaped Napoleonic tactics in crucial ways.

5. In my transition from Napoleon to Hegel, I rely on David Chandler, *The Campaigns of Napoleon*, for all material about Napoleon. Hegel's circumstances at the time are briefly recounted in a new biography: Terry Pinkard, *Hegel*

(Cambridge: Cambridge UP, 2000), pp. 221–30. The text of Hegel's letter to Niethammer is from G.W.F. Hegel, *Briefe von und an Hegel*, ed. Johannes Hoffmeister and Friedhelm Nicolin. I've consulted the English versions in G.W.F. Hegel, *Hegel: The Letters*, tr. Clark Butler and Christiane Seiler (Bloomington: Indiana UP, 1984); and Walter Kaufmann, *Hegel: Reinterpretation, Texts, and Commentary* (New York: Doubleday, 1965), but the translation given here is my own. The same applies to what I quote from the Preface to the *Phenomenology of Spirit*. I use the text of G.W.F. Hegel, *Gesammelte Werke*, ed. Nordrhein-Westfälische Akademie der Wissenschaften, vol. 9. I incorporate Hegel's revisions from the 1832 edition. Relevant English versions of the Preface appear in G.W.F. Hegel, *Phenomenology of Spirit*, tr. A. V. Miller (Oxford: Clarendon, 1977); Walter Kaufmann, *Hegel: Reinterpretation, Texts, and Commentary;* and Yirmiyahu Yovel, *Hegel's Preface to the* Phenomenology of Spirit (Princeton: Princeton UP, 2005). Finally, although I came to it late and my own treatment is somewhat different, Alan Liu, *Wordsworth: The Sense of History* (Stanford: Stanford UP, 1989), pp. 401–7, on Hegel and Napoleon is noteworthy as part of an impressive study. In his juxtaposition of Napoleon and Hegel, Liu was anticipated to some extent by the commentary of Alexandre Kojève, *Introduction to the Reading of Hegel*, assembled by Raymond Queneau, ed. Allan Bloom, tr. James H. Nichols, Jr. (New York: Basic Books, 1969), esp. pp. 34–35.

6. Even a summary as brief as what I've given here is already to some extent interpretive. Nor can anyone who looks at the secondary sources on Hegel fail to notice how widely different they are. As Charles Taylor puts it, one can either be clear about Hegel at the risk of distortion, or faithful but impenetrable. In addition, there's the issue of how best to describe the Hegelian enterprise (i.e., as a sort of metaphysics, phenomenology, epistemology, or theory). Hence the diversity of approaches.

Despite its relatively early date, Martin Heidegger, *Hegel's Phenomenology of Spirit*, tr. Parvis Emad and Kenneth Maly (Bloomington: Indiana UP, 1988), based on a lecture course from 1930–31, remains of great interest. It benefits, obviously, from Heidegger's unique perspective but equally from its careful attention to detail. Its main fault is that it tends to identify Hegelian "science" with knowledge, and so short-circuits negativity or development, the process by which we arrive at knowledge, which gives Spirit its content.

A similar perspective informs Hans-Georg Gadamer, *Hegel's Dialectic*, tr. P. Christopher Smith (New Haven: Yale UP, 1976). For Gadamer, self-consciousness is the motive of Hegelian movement (pp. 11–12). But the otherness that consciousness seeks to understand isn't merely similar by analogy (Gadamer), but its own otherness. The difference between Hegel and Gadamer is that Gadamer wants to see consciousness as the real ground or basis of Hegel's scheme (i.e., a phenomenology), whereas for Hegel it's only a formal category.

Of those sources that take consciousness rather than some form of metatheory as their framework, Jean Hyppolite, *Genesis and Structure of Hegel's* Phenomenology of Spirit, tr. Samuel Cherniak and John Heckman (Evanston: Northwestern UP, 1974), remains in many ways the best. Unlike Heidegger or Gadamer, Hyppolite doesn't have an agenda (language, phenomenology). At the same time, he's attentive to the whole question of development. The only weakness of his work lies in its effort to see the *Phenomenology* as a concrete history of consciousness, which makes the generation of concepts difficult.

Unlike earlier continental commentators, Charles Taylor, *Hegel* (Cambridge: Cambridge UP, 1975), is less exegetical. Instead, Taylor opts for restatement. Essentially, he places Hegel within an expressivist framework: the task of philosophy is to overcome oppositions that arise from the breakup of an original expressive unity with nature (p. 76). The problem with this expressivist picture of Hegel is that it doesn't leave any work to analysis. Whereas, for Hegel, development takes place largely by an analysis of moments of consciousness. Nor is it accidental that Taylor sees Hegelian negativity purely as opposition (p. 110) rather than as analytical.

From M. J. Inwood, *Hegel* (London: Routledge & Kegan Paul, 1983), we get an even more radical restatement. Whereas Taylor discusses works, Inwood focuses on problems or topics. The effect is to force one to rethink Hegel's position on various questions. But what Hegel says about any given topic makes sense to some extent only within the context of his entire enterprise.

Robert C. Solomon, *In the Spirit of Hegel* (New York: Oxford UP, 1983), marks a turn in Anglo-American Hegel studies toward the exegetical. On occasion Solomon can seem way off. But his commentary is often suggestive, even if one doesn't buy his argument that beginning and end aren't the same for Hegel, or that Hegel plays fast and loose with "in itself" and "for itself" (pp. 258, 262–63). Likewise, it isn't clear why teleology shouldn't be a metaphysical principle for Hegel. But the notion of "speculative" as thinking from the standpoint of the whole is elegantly defined (pp. 270–71).

In a vein similar to Solomon, but more deeply grounded in the cultural/historical (as well as more detailed exegetically) is H. S. Harris, *Hegel's Ladder*, 2 vols. (Indianapolis: Hackett, 1997), a massive commentary on the *Phenomenology* based on a lifetime of work on Hegel. The introduction to vol. 1 (esp. pp. 1–9) elegantly summarizes the conclusions Harris reached in his two earlier books on

Hegel's development. Subsequently (pp. 9–18) Harris considers the relation of the *Phenomenology* to Hegel's larger philosophical project. His particular thesis is that "the unifying topic of the *Phenomenology* is 'how eternity is comprehended in time'" (p. 15), which has to do with the relation between the development of Spirit and the viewpoint of religion. But the way Harris treats the crucial section of the Preface (pp. 54–64 in vol. I) suggests that (like Hyppolite) he sees the development of Spirit primarily in terms of human consciousness. What his treatment doesn't address is the question of whether Hegel saw that development as based on one at the ontological level, and hence as a result of ontological (rather than human) necessity.

The most recent comprehensive commentary on the *Phenomenology* is Michael Forster, *Hegel's Idea of a* Phenomenology of Spirit (Chicago: U of Chicago P, 1998). Most relevant is what Forster has to say about the movement in Hegel from Substance to Subject (pp. 194–95). But Forster's notion that the Absolute should be seen essentially as a self or person (or human subject, p. 196) is unpersuasive. Given the kind of development by which we arrive at it, the Absolute seems distinctly closer to thought than to consciousness.

In *Hegel's Preface to the* Phenomenology of Spirit, Yirmiyahu Yovel offers a detailed commentary on the Preface only. Like other recent exegetical work on Hegel (e.g., Harris), Yovel tries to get as close as possible to the Hegelian project. But the discussion of Substance and Subject (pp. 16–19) seems to me slightly vitiated by Yovel's insistence that they obey "different ontical logics" (p. 29). So we miss the necessity for the movement from one to the other. And in the treatment of negativity (pp. 19–20), where Yovel stresses the link between negation and the subject or consciousness, I miss a sense of negativity as the necessary activity of thought. But there is helpful commentary on textual and conceptual matters throughout.

Four • The House of Life

1. My description of the Hôtel-Dieu comes largely from two sources: Phyllis Richmond, "The Hôtel-Dieu of Paris on the Eve of the Revolution," *Journal of the History of Medicine and Allied Sciences* 16 (1961): 335–53; and Charles Coulston Gillispie, *Science and Polity in France at the End of the Old Regime* (Princeton: Princeton UP, 1980), pp. 244–56. Richmond gives detailed information on the physical layout of the hospital, while Gillispie discusses the late eighteenth-century Paris hospital reform movement. His description of patient conditions at the Hôtel-Dieu is from Jacques Tenon's celebrated memoir, para-

phrased by the Academy of Science for its report. For more general background on the public hospital in France at the outset of the Revolution, see Dora Weiner, *The Citizen-Patient in Revolutionary and Imperial Paris* (Baltimore: Johns Hopkins UP, 1993), chap. 2.

2. For Bichat biography, Maurice Genty, "Xavier Bichat," in *Biographies médicales et scientifiques: XVIIIᵉ siècle*, ed. Pierre Huard (Paris: Dacosta, 1972), pp. 181–276, is the best source. Of particular interest: his association with Desault (pp. 218–21), his efforts (mostly unsuccessful) to find a place in the French medical establishment (pp. 243–45, 257–60), and the circumstances of his final year (pp. 272–76).

3. On the rise of surgery in eighteenth-century France, Toby Gelfand, *Professionalizing Modern Medicine* (Westport, CT: Greenwood, 1980), is authoritative. Gelfand focuses on the conflict between medicine (largely theoretical) and surgery (stress on clinical work and observation). The ultimate outcome was the takeover of the Paris medical faculty by the surgical group (pp. 173–76), which defined the French medical scene at the time Bichat entered it. For Desault's hospital routine and its influence on Bichat, see John Lesch, *Science and Medicine in France: The Emergence of Experimental Physiology, 1790–1855* (Cambridge: Harvard UP, 1984), pp. 52–54.

4. On the primacy of observation in early nineteenth-century French medicine, see Erwin Ackerknecht, *Medicine at the Paris Hospital 1794–1848* (Baltimore: Johns Hopkins P, 1967). In addition to a detailed assessment of Paris hospitals in the Revolutionary era (pp. 15–22) and some discussion of Bichat (pp. 51–58), Ackerknecht is especially good on the skeptical, expectant posture of French medicine (pp. 128–38).

5. The question of where to locate vitality is crucial for both Bichat and his predecessors. On Bichat's eighteenth-century sources, see Elizabeth Haigh, *Xavier Bichat and the Medical Theory of the Eighteenth Century* (London: Wellcome Institute for the History of Medicine, 1984). Haigh comments extensively on Bichat's predecessors, especially the Montpellier school (pp. 31–42) and the late eighteenth-century French intellectual scene (pp. 56–85). Later she tries to connect Bichat's vitalism to tissue theory (pp. 110–20), despite Bichat's own admission that we can't finally identify tissue properties with vital properties. Michael Gross, "The Lessened Locus of Feelings: A Transformation in French Physiology in the Early Nineteenth Century," *Journal of the History of Biology* 12 (1979): 231–71, also tries to link Bichat to late eighteenth-century medical theory. Gross claims early nineteenth-century French physiological theorists located sensation exclusively in the neuromuscular system and a few organs,

while for late eighteenth-century theory and Bichat, the whole body was sentient (pp. 232–38). Michel Foucault has a chapter on Bichat in *The Birth of the Clinic* (New York: Pantheon, 1973)—frankly, one of his weaker performances. Foucault traces a thematics of the gaze that emphasizes tissue surfaces (pp. 128–29). No mention of pathological anatomy, nor any hint of the link between tissue and vitality.

A recent revisionist account, Othmar Keel, *L'Avènement de la médecine clinique en Europe, 1750–1815* (Montreal: Les Presses de l'Université de Montréal, 2002), is highly critical of Bichat's originality. As Keel sees it, Bichat merely reproduces the concept of tissues and of pathological anatomy formulated earlier by John Hunter, Haller, Pinel and others (see esp. pp. 255–60, 265–67, 273–76, 299–306, 311–18). The attack comes to a climax in "Bichat: la généalogie d'un mythe" (pp. 360–73). Later, Keel argues Bichat and the Paris school eclipsed Hunter and the Scottish school largely because Hunter and his group didn't fit the professional politics of nineteenth-century medicine (pp. 428–30).

Philippe Huneman, *Bichat, la vie et la mort* (Paris: Presses Universitaires de France, 1998), offers an elegant answer to Keel. Huneman freely acknowledges Bichat's debt to Hunter, Pinel et al. (pp. 28–40, 42–44), then goes on to comment that the section on life in the *Recherches physiologiques* harks back to eighteenth-century sources (Cabanis et al.), while the section on death, with its emphasis on experiment, looks forward to Magendie and Claude Bernard (pp. 62–67). Huneman avers that because of the variability of vitality, Bichat discovers he has to rely on experiment to establish an invariant link: in death, only the *sequence* of decease (i.e., for different organs) is invariant (pp. 72–73). Hence the extensive experimentation by Bichat on the cause of death in laboratory animals, as a way to ascertain the source of vitality. What we get from Huneman is that the theoretical element of a work isn't restricted to what it can specify: in Bichat, experimentation is meant to engender a future development of theory.

The brief treatment of Bichat (pp. 663–67) in Charles Coulston Gillispie, *Science and Polity in France: The Revolutionary and Napoleonic Years* (Princeton: Princeton UP, 2004), echoes Huneman. As Gillispie puts it: "Bichat's originality was in the architecture of his work, not in its details" (p. 666).

6. On Bichat and pathology, see Russell Maulitz, *Morbid Appearances: The Anatomy of Pathology in the Early Nineteenth Century* (Cambridge: Cambridge UP, 1987). Maulitz has a suggestive meditation on Bichat as outsider who becomes insider through his creation of a new research programme based on tissue pathology (pp. 1–6, 52–59). But most of the discussion is about Bichat's career

within the context of the early nineteenth-century Paris medical school (pp. 25–27, 36–52).

7. How important a role experiment plays in Bichat is crucial to two of the best Bichat studies. William Albury, "Experiment and Explanation in the Physiology of Bichat and Magendie," *Studies in History of Biology* 1 (1977): 47–131, argues for observation over experiment, which doesn't give enough overview (pp. 67–70). For Bichat and the Montpellier school, observation yields key concepts, whereas for Magendie these come from experiments (pp. 70–73).

By contrast, John Lesch is distinctly critical of observation over experiment (*Science and Medicine in France,* esp. pp. 122–24). Instead, Lesch posits two physiologies for Bichat: (1) classificatory (eighteenth-century vitalism) and (2) one based on surgery + experiment (p. 51). On a more theoretical level, Lesch sees the *Recherches physiologiques* as marked by duality between a "physiology of reasoning" about life and experimental inquiry into death (pp. 61–66). For Lesch, the conflict between Bichat's two physiologies dissolves once we accept this duality (pp. 76–79). Throughout, however, Lesch portrays Bichat's work from a standpoint of method rather than content.

Two other studies try to situate Bichat somewhere in the middle between vitalism and experimental science. Geoffrey Sutton, "The Physical and Chemical Path to Vitalism: Xavier Bichat's *Physiological Researches on Life and Death,*" *Bulletin of the History of Medicine* 58 (1984): 53–71, asserts that Bichat forges a new vitalism precisely in response to recent developments in the physical sciences. Meanwhile Roselyne Rey, "Bichat au carrefour des vitalismes," in *Vitalisms from Haller to the Cell Theory,* ed. Guido Cimino and François Duchesneau (Florence: Olschki, 1997), pp. 175–203, surveys Bichat's work as an attempt to formulate a vitalist position that can mediate between inside/outside as well as mix life and death processes.

Five • Beyond Radical Empiricism

1. Most of our biographical data on Humphry Davy comes from two sources: John Ayrton Paris, *The Life of Sir Humphry Davy,* 2 vols. (London: Colburn & Bentley, 1831); and John Davy, *Memoirs of the Life of Sir Humphry Davy,* 2 vols. (London: Longman et al., 1836), later shortened to vol. I of Davy's *Collected Works.* For a list of Davy biographies, see June Z. Fullmer, *Sir Humphry Davy's Published Works* (Cambridge: Harvard UP, 1969), p. 17; and, for an evaluation, "Davy's Biographers: Notes on Scientific Biography," *Science* 155 (1967): 285–91. Fuller has also collected other relevant material not found elsewhere: "Davy's

Sketches of His Contemporaries," *Chymia* 12 (1967): 127–50, candid personal assessments of fellow scientists; and "Humphry Davy's Adversaries," *Chymia* 8 (1962): 147–64, which has accounts of his lectures at the Royal Institution (esp. pp. 156–58). More recently, we have her *Young Humphry Davy* (Philadelphia: American Philosophical Society, 2000), vol. I of a biography she unfortunately wasn't able to complete.

Of course, any biography is bound to raise questions of reliability. Although unreliable in detail, Paris can be useful when corroborated by other sources. I draw on him for my account of Davy as lecturer (Paris, vol. I, pp. 134–49). On many points, John Davy offers a corrective to Paris. His description of Davy as lecturer at the Royal Institution (*CW* I: 88–89, 91–96) complements Paris, and he is equally informative about his brother's scientific practices (*CW* I: 53–55, 120–22, 156–57). The most recent biography (apart from Fullmer's) is David Knight, *Humphry Davy: Science and Power* (Oxford: Blackwell, 1992). Knight points out Davy's resistance to particular forms of theory (pp. 58–60, 68–69, 75–87) and offers some perspective on Davy's achievement vis-à-vis that of Berzelius or Faraday (pp. 71–72, 122–24, 130–37).

2. Here we have the background for what Linda Colley refers to as the "cultural reconstruction of an élite," the process by which the British aristocracy refashioned itself during years of war with Napoleon. See her *Britons* (New Haven: Yale UP, 1992), pp. 164–77.

3. See Morris Berman, *Social Change and Scientific Organization: The Royal Institution, 1799–1844* (Ithaca: Cornell UP, 1978), for a rich, detailed history of the institution where Davy spent his most fruitful years (pp. 20–29). Berman offers much valuable information on the social/economic interests behind the Royal Institution (pp. 14–17, 32–45), and how these largely dictated Davy's research choices (pp. 49–65). He concludes that Davy's failure to do significant theoretical work was caused by the Royal Institution agenda of practical science (pp. 71–74).

4. The political/social context of Davy and British chemistry is ably explored by Jan Golinski, *Science as Public Culture: Chemistry and Enlightenment in Britain, 1760–1820* (Cambridge: Cambridge UP, 1992). Golinski sets Davy squarely against the Enlightenment tradition of audience involvement developed by Joseph Priestley and others (pp. 9–10). By the use of new and powerful instruments, Golinski avers, Davy induced audience passivity and so forged a middle-/upper-class constituency at the Royal Institution (pp. 190–203), which then became a means of support in the chlorine controversy (pp. 223–35). But this sort of perspective ignores the fact that the scene of debate isn't just Brit-

ain but Europe, which presumably means Davy can't rely solely on popular audiences.

5. On the phlogiston controversy, see Joshua Gregory, *The Scientific Achievement of Sir Humphry Davy* (London: Oxford UP, 1930). Its exposition of the controversy (pp. 10–15) is a model of clarity. In several instances, Gregory also tries to trace the process by which Davy arrived at a particular theory (e.g., pp. 67–72, 73–81). For a more general survey of the phlogiston controversy from a historical perspective, see Maurice Crosland, "Chemistry and the Chemical Revolution," in *The Ferment of Knowledge: Studies in the Historiography of Eighteenth-Century Science*, ed. G. S. Rousseau and Roy Porter (Cambridge: Cambridge UP, 1980), pp. 389–416 (esp. pp. 405–11). Crosland points out that "in terms of explaining combustion the oxygen-caloric theory was merely an alternative to phlogiston and it can even be argued that when Lavoisier said caloric was given off he was merely describing phlogiston under a new name" (p. 408).

6. On qualitative versus quantitative approaches, see Sir Harold Hartley, *Humphry Davy* (London: Thomas Nelson, 1966), esp. pp. 2–8, 30–34. For Hartley, Davy's acceptance of the (quantitative) theory of definite proportions in 1809 marks a decisive turn in the conflict between these two approaches (pp. 69–70, 74–78). Nonetheless, Hartley thinks Davy was really at his best in qualitative chemistry (pp. 78–82).

7. For Davy's electrochemistry, Colin Russell, "The Electrochemical Theory of Sir Humphry Davy," *Annals of Science* 15 (1959): 1–13, 15–25, and 19 (1963): 255–71, is exceptional. Russell offers a detailed account of Davy's initial hypothesis that chemical affinities = electrical forces, the difficulties it raised, and Davy's modified notion of a common cause for electrical and chemical phenomena (pp. 17–19). At a more general level, Russell is equally good on Davy's complex relation to theory (pp. 257–60, 266, 270).

8. On Davy's theoretical outlook we have Trevor Levere, *Affinity and Matter: Elements of Chemical Philosophy 1800–1865* (Oxford: Clarendon, 1971). As Levere sees it, a unitary theory of forces represents the main theme of all Davy's work (p. 27). Later, Levere looks at Davy's quest for theoretical simplicity (pp. 46–53), which he believes Davy reaches by an inclusion of opposites, synthesis, and unity (pp. 54–55).

9. See *Romanticism and the Sciences*, ed. Andrew Cunningham and Nicholas Jardine (Cambridge: Cambridge UP, 1990), especially the essays by Christopher Lawrence, David Knight, Simon Schaffer, and Trevor Levere. Also *Romantic Science*, ed. Noah Heringman (Albany: SUNY P, 2003), especially Catherine Ross

on Wordsworth and Davy, and *Studies in Romanticism* 43 (Spring 2004), a special issue on Romanticism and the Sciences of Life.

Six • Galois Theory

1. For Galois biography, most of the relevant documents can be found in the best edition of his work: *Écrits et mémoires mathématiques*, ed. Robert Bourgne and J.-P. Azra (Paris: Gauthier-Villars, 1962). Bourgne and Azra reproduce the manuscripts verbatim, even when fragmentary, and I do the same in my translation.

Two recent biographical studies, based on material previously neglected or distorted, supersede virtually all predecessors: Tony Rothman, *Science à la Mode: Physical Fashions and Fictions* (Princeton: Princeton UP, 1989), chap. 6; and Laura Toti Rigatelli, *Evariste Galois 1811–1832*, tr. John Denton (Basel: Birkhäuser, 1996). Rothman sets out to demystify the Galois legend. He shows Galois wasn't simply persecuted or misunderstood by his teachers, that he probably received encouragement from Augustin Cauchy at the Academy of Science, and that Siméon-Denis Poisson (who rejected his memoir for the Academy) read his work carefully (pp. 152–54, 158–60, 174–76). We then get an extensive inquiry into Galois's duel, and evidence that Galois didn't just work out his celebrated proof the night before he was shot (pp. 176–88). Rigatelli covers much of the material similarly, but is richer in detail. Of particular interest is her description of his unsuccessful advanced private course in algebra, too unconventional to be easily followed (pp. 79–80). Unlike Rothman, however, Rigatelli places more stress on the political: Victor Cousin's instrumental role in Galois's expulsion from the École Normale (pp. 68, 70, 71–75), and Galois's own political activity (pp. 82, 85–88, 92–94). What happens at the end, though, is a surprise: from autobiographical accounts by police personnel (especially police chief H. J. Gisquet and Lucien de la Hodde, a police spy) Rigatelli manages to demonstrate that Galois prearranged his own death as a sacrifice for the Republican cause (pp. 107–14). I follow Rigatelli rather than Rothman in my narration of this episode.

2. For Galois theory I rely mostly on I. N. Herstein, *Topics in Algebra* (New York: Wiley, 1964/1975). I differ from Herstein, however, in the order or sequence of my presentation and in the omission of proofs. I've also found some of the diagrams in Richard Dean, *Classical Abstract Algebra* (New York: Harper & Row, 1990), quite useful. All modern texts owe a great debt to Emil Artin, *Galois Theory* (Notre Dame: Notre Dame UP, 1942/1944; rpt. New York: Dover, 1998).

Artin was the first to develop much that was only implied in Galois's highly elliptical memoir.

Recent years have witnessed efforts to work out Galois theory solely by means of what was available to Galois himself. See, for instance, Joseph Rotman, *Galois Theory* (New York: Springer, 1998), pp. 138–50; and for more detail, Harold Edwards, *Galois Theory* (New York: Springer, 1984); and Jean-Pierre Tignol, *Galois's Theory of Algebraic Equations* (New York: Wiley, 1988). The fact that Galois himself was highly intuitive and formally simple, however, can help justify a more modern treatment.

Seven • *Toward a Definition of Reflection*

1. On the genesis of *Aids to Reflection*, see the introduction by John Beer to his edition (1993) for *The Collected Works of Samuel Taylor Coleridge*. Beer provides a wealth of detail on compositional circumstances (pp. xlii–lxxi), far more than Richard Holmes in his *Coleridge: Darker Reflections* (New York: Pantheon, 1998).

2. The basic problem for any assessment of *Aids to Reflection* and, more generally, the larger project that occupied Coleridge throughout his later years, was aptly summed up by René Wellek over half a century ago: "If we look into the workshop of Coleridge's mind, we must admit a fundamental flaw in Coleridge which never allowed him to integrate his thought into an organic, individual, Coleridgean whole. . . . Coleridge has little insight into the incompatibility of different trends of thought. . . . Coleridge's structure has here a storey from Kant, there a part of a room from Schelling, there a roof from Anglican theology and so on. The architect did not feel the clash of the styles, the subtle and irreconcilable differences between the Kantian first floor and the Anglican roof" (*Immanuel Kant in England* [Princeton: Princeton UP, 1931], pp. 66–68). Wellek went on to make his point in detail: he showed how Coleridge had combined Kantian concepts and terminology with a viewpoint that essentially echoed early Schelling (see esp. pp. 80–81, 95–102, and 124–32 on *Aids to Reflection*). Almost four decades later, Wellek would get ample support from G.N.G. Orsini, *Coleridge and German Idealism* (Carbondale: Southern Illinois UP, 1969). Like Wellek, Orsini was critical of the originality and consistency of Coleridge's work *qua* philosophy (pp. 144–48, 216–21, 263–68). Orsini points out that the Reason/Understanding distinction in Coleridge is inconsistent because the concept of Understanding is based on Kant whereas that of Reason isn't (pp. 140–42). But Orsini treats the Kant/Coleridge relation in much fuller detail. In addition, he offers a close,

careful analysis of the Coleridge/Schelling relationship (especially in the *Biographia* period), and an explanation of why it subsequently drops off (pp. 209–15). And even John Beer in the introduction to his edition of *Aids to Reflection* has to admit a lack of rational proof for some of its central tenets in religion (pp. lxxiv–lxxvi, lxxxiv–lxxxviii). Beer is also helpful on reason/understanding (pp. lxxix–lxxxiv) and "reflection" (pp. lxxxviii–xcvi).

More recently, two studies advance our knowledge of the context and sources of Coleridge's thought, yet fail to address the Wellek/Orsini charge of inconsistency. Mary Anne Perkins, *Coleridge's Philosophy* (Oxford: Clarendon, 1994), makes abundant use of notebook and manuscript material from Coleridge's late years, but often appears insufficiently critical. For instance, she takes Coleridge at his word on how he differs from Schelling (pp. 192–95), and so misses the larger point: that both thinkers propose will as their ontological ground. On a more general level, the problem of conceptual inconsistency is never really considered (see esp. pp. 168–70, 267–68). By contrast, Douglas Hedley, *Coleridge, Philosophy and Religion* (Cambridge: Cambridge UP, 2000), is quite aware of the problem and promises to refute Wellek et al. (pp. 18–19). On the positive side, Hedley gives the fullest, most detailed treatment of *Aids to Reflection* to date, with a wealth of material on sources and context, especially from the Christian Platonic tradition and German idealism. Frequently, however, Hedley simply downplays the influence of German idealism in favor of Cambridge Platonism without proof (e.g., pp. 150–52, 195). Nor, despite assertions of how Coleridge creatively transforms his sources (pp. 12–13), does Hedley ever show how Coleridge manages to avoid inconsistency in his fusion of Platonic and German idealistic material. In addition, Hedley gives far too little space to the theoretical perspective of *Aids to Reflection,* despite the emphasis Coleridge himself places on theory throughout the work.

Finally, Seamus Perry, *Coleridge and the Uses of Division* (Oxford: Clarendon, 1999), though it doesn't discuss *Aids to Reflection* in detail, points to a way around the Coleridgean problem of conceptual inconsistency. For Perry, Coleridge's "double-mindedness," his inability to conclude, can be perceived as instrumental. My own position would be that we can accept conceptual inconsistency in Coleridge if we take it as indicative of his quest for a system, where the quest (rather than its fulfillment) has primacy.

3. On Coleridge and science, see Trevor Levere, *Poetry Realized in Nature: Samuel Taylor Coleridge and Early Nineteenth-Century Science* (Cambridge: Cambridge UP, 1981). A detailed look at Coleridge and Davy (pp. 20–34) is of particular interest, but in his effort to show the importance of science for Cole-

ridge, Levere stretches some points too far (e.g., science as secondary reason, pp. 54–57). We do, however, get a useful discussion of Coleridge on metascience, where polarity plays a crucial role (pp. 112–21).

4. In "Metaphysics of Culture: Kant and Coleridge's *Aids to Reflection,*" *Journal of the History of Ideas* 31 (1970): 199–218, Elinor Schaffer tries to link Coleridge on causality to Kant's *Religion within the Limits of Reason Alone,* but somewhat unpersuasively, since Kant hardly discusses causality in this text.

5. Despite its title, David Vallins, *Coleridge and the Psychology of Romanticism* (New York: St. Martin's, 2000), addresses only some aspects of Coleridgean psychology. And the definition of thought Vallins gives reflects a materialist bias hardly consonant with that of Coleridge himself. But the commentary on what Coleridge has to say about the experience of thought (pp. 143–52) is suggestive.

6. For another large account of the Coleridgean self in relation to external others, see Graham Davidson, *Coleridge's Career* (New York: St. Martin's, 1990), perhaps the most significant attempt in the last twenty years to think about the overall shape of Coleridge's development. As Davidson sees it, the essential model for Coleridge is one whereby we arrive at a knowledge of self through love of another person (pp. 173–78). What we really love, though, isn't that other person in his or her specificity but as an idea (pp. 137–51). To construe Coleridge's intellectual development in this way, however, can be slightly reductive: even if we believe a career to be shaped by the same concerns throughout, we still have to allow for the possibility that these concerns might lead someone to try different viewpoints at various moments of his or her development. Nonetheless, Davidson does make a cogent case for the relevance of disparate Coleridge texts to a larger enterprise.

7. On the significance of Coleridge's enterprise, see Thomas McFarland, *Coleridge and the Pantheist Tradition* (Oxford: Clarendon, 1969). McFarland even openly confesses the lack of what he terms a "reticulating characteristic of mind" in Coleridge (p. 49). But perhaps his best move is to assert that "Coleridge's endeavour was always toward system" (p. 110) and what he terms a "sense of *relevance*" (p. 112). A later study by McFarland, *Romanticism and the Forms of Ruin* (Princeton: Princeton UP, 1981), discusses Coleridge's doctrine of polarity and some parallel instances in German Romanticism (pp. 290–306, 309–13, 319–24). McFarland is especially good on Coleridge's *magnum opus* (pp. 342–44, 348–63), but the search for parallels occasionally leads to excessive generality (e.g., pp. 333–36 on Marx or pp. 375–81 on the modern condition). While McFarland tries to defend Coleridge by a show of nineteenth-century parallels and contexts, Owen Barfield, *What Coleridge Thought* (Middletown, CT: Wes-

leyan UP, 1971), makes a case for his modernity. Although Barfield relies excessively on a contemporary analytical framework, he can be excellent on a topic
like *natura naturans,* a fine example of historical recovery (pp. 22–25).

Eight • The Dream of Subjectivity

1. On Mary Shelley's account of her dream in the 1831 Introduction to *Frankenstein,* see James O'Rourke, "The 1831 Introduction and Revisions to *Frankenstein:* Mary Shelley Dictates Her Legacy," *Studies in Romanticism* 38 (Fall 1999):
365–85 (esp. pp. 372–73 on the dream itself). O'Rourke has doubts about the
reliability of the account, and points out that the narrative perspective silently
passes from that of Mary Shelley herself to that of the creature's creator. From
my standpoint, this is all the better: it suggests we can't define the boundary
between her dream and the story she goes on to tell, which is precisely the way it
should be for a novel that's all about the problem of subjectivity and otherness.
For further comment on the Introduction, see James Rieger's edition of *Frankenstein* (Indianapolis: Bobbs-Merrill, 1974), pp. xvi–xix. Although Rieger doesn't
question Mary Shelley's account of her dream, he does point out (like O'Rourke)
a number of other discrepancies. Altogether, we can perhaps best take the dream
narrative in the way O'Rourke suggests: as a literary performance. It allows Mary
Shelley to break down the subjective boundary between us (the readers) and
herself.

2. These resemblances have led some early commentators to stress the biographical element in *Frankenstein.* See Ellen Moers, "Female Gothic," and U. C.
Knoepflmacher, "Thoughts on the Aggression of Daughters," in *The Endurance
of Frankenstein,* ed. George Levine and U. C. Knoepflmacher (Berkeley: U of
California P, 1979). William Veeder, *Mary Shelley and Frankenstein: The Fate of
Androgyny* (Chicago: U of Chicago P, 1986), also stresses biography, in a study
that sees the novel as an appeal for interdependency between the sexes.

3. The fact that many of these losses involve women offers ground for a
feminist critique. See first of all Sandra Gilbert and Susan Gubar, *The Madwo-
man in the Attic* (New Haven: Yale UP, 1979). But Gilbert and Gubar aren't at
their best on Mary Shelley, partly because of her own resistance to involvement,
partly from their disregard of plot development. Subsequently Barbara Johnson,
"My Monster/My Self" (rpt. in *A World of Difference* [Baltimore: Johns Hopkins
UP, 1987]) and Margaret Homans, chap. 5 of *Bearing the Word* (Chicago: U of
Chicago P, 1986) focus on the link between creation and the maternal. Both note

the deaths of mothers in the text, and how creation = self-love, but Homans has a bit more on Frankenstein's attempt to circumvent the maternal.

4. In *The Proper Lady and the Woman Writer* (Chicago: U of Chicago P, 1984) Mary Poovey avers that *Frankenstein* wants to question artistic self-assertion because of its impulse to project itself into the natural world and to find objects to conquer and consume (pp. 122–26). Its particular victims, Poovey claims, are the creature and women (pp. 128–29, 138–39). But this sort of objectifying tendency is everywhere in the text (e.g., the De Lacey family, or even Elizabeth Lavenza on Justine Moritz).

5. On the role of sympathy in the novel, see David Marshall, *The Surprising Effects of Sympathy* (Chicago: U of Chicago, 1988), chap. 6. Marshall offers the most detailed look at Mary Shelley and Rousseau (pp. 182–95, 228–33), but is especially good on the novel as an appeal for sympathy (pp. 195–208), which we find strongly amplified elsewhere in Shelley. He only neglects to discuss Romantic subjectivity in the novel as the obverse of sympathy. Somewhat more traditional is Paul Cantor, *Creature and Creator: Myth-Making and English Romanticism* (Cambridge: Cambridge UP, 1984), chap. 4. Although Cantor glances at the context of Romantic idealism (pp. 108–9, 115–17) and Rousseau (pp. 119–22, 125–27), his critique of the creature as one who should make a better life for himself (pp. 124–25, 130–32) is unpersuasive. Other useful studies on *Frankenstein* from an eighteenth-century perspective are Frances Ferguson, *Solitude and the Sublime* (New York: Routledge, 1992), pp. 105–13, on the tension between Victor's desire for solitude and the creature's for companionship; Mary Favret, *Romantic Correspondence: Women, Politics, and the Fiction of Letters* (Cambridge: Cambridge UP, 1993), chap. 6, on *Frankenstein* as an epistolary novel composed of multiple voices; and Elizabeth Bohls, *Women Travel Writers and the Language of Aesthetics, 1716–1818* (Cambridge: Cambridge UP, 1995), chap. 8, on the use of aesthetics as a means to exclude other forms of subjectivity.

6. For more on this theme, see Anne K. Mellor, *Mary Shelley: Her Life, Her Fiction, Her Monsters* (New York: Routledge, 1988). Like Poovey, Mellor treats *Frankenstein* as a critique of Romantic ideology (pp. 70–77) and a feminist critique of science (pp. 89–114). But the real question is whether we can separate Romantic ideology or science from other, similar forms of subjectivity that implicate women in the novel as well. Later, Mellor focuses on what she terms "problems of perception" in the novel (pp. 127–31, 134–36), which usefully points to the wider scope of subjectivity.

7. A recent trend has been to connect *Frankenstein* to the sciences. In her

introduction to the Oxford World's Classics *Frankenstein* (Oxford: Oxford UP, 1994.) Marilyn Butler argues for the influence of William Lawrence, a political radical, proponent of materialist vitalism, and friend of the Shelleys (pp. xvii–xxi, xli–li). Yet Shelley herself writes to Sir Richard Phillips: "I am not well read enough in such questions to comment on your theory; I own I have a great respect for that faculty we carry about us called *Mind*—and I fear that no Frankenstein can so arrange the gases as to be able to make any combination of them produce thought or even life" (*Letters* I: 401). Alan Rauch, "The Monstrous Body of Knowledge in Mary Shelley's *Frankenstein*," *Studies in Romanticism* 34 (Summer 1995): 227–53, considers science in the novel from a more social perspective. His claim is that Victor makes no attempt to contribute to collective knowledge, the goal of all proper science. But given Victor's sources (Cornelius Agrippa et al.) we might ask whether his enterprise is even scientific at all. Maureen McLane, *Romanticism and the Human Sciences* (Cambridge: Cambridge UP, 2000), chap. 3, treats subjectivity in Shelley's novel from the standpoint of what it means to be human, but doesn't show why it has to be so exclusively. Most recently, Stuart Peterfreund, "Composing What May Not Be 'Sad Trash': A Reconsideration of Mary Shelley's Use of Paracelsus in *Frankenstein*," *Studies in Romanticism* 43 (Spring 2004): 79–98, argues for Paracelsus as a way to remedy the deficiency of science or theory by his humanistic perspective.

In a related vein, publication of *The* Frankenstein *Notebooks*, ed. Charles Robinson (New York: Garland, 1996) in two volumes has opened up a whole new angle on the novel. Specifically, it shows that the novel's critique of Victor's enterprise was much stronger before Percy Shelley's intervention. See the review by Susan Wolfson, "Reconstructing *Frankenstein*," *Review* 20 (1998): 1–15.

Nine • The Limits of Theory

1. From the outset, Hölderlin's poetry has always been associated with a philosophical or theoretical framework of some kind. The real issue, then, is to determine which of these is the most appropriate. In his *Ends of the Lyric* (Baltimore: Johns Hopkins UP, 1996) Timothy Bahti offers a useful summary of Hölderlin scholarship (pp. 97–102).

2. On Hölderlin and German idealism, the work of Dieter Henrich, especially *The Course of Remembrance and Other Essays on Hölderlin*, ed. Eckart Förster (Stanford: Stanford UP, 1997), is central. For Henrich, the centerpiece of Hölderlin's engagement with philosophy is a short fragment entitled "Urteil und Sein" or "Sein/Urteil/Möglichkeit" (see esp. pp. 25–30, 74–76, 85–89). To my

mind, Henrich makes far too much of it. From his standpoint, the metaphilosophy of the fragment lies in its argument against the possibility of a first, foundational principle (Fichte): since Being isn't propositional, it's impossible to derive consequences from it (pp. 104–8). Such an argument, however, amounts to no more than a move in a much larger game. Yet it does point to the bigger issue of a conceptual framework for subjectivity, which is crucial both for "Patmos" and for any attempt to think about Hölderlin on theory. Frederick Beiser, *German Idealism: The Struggle against Subjectivism, 1781–1801* (Cambridge: Harvard UP, 2002), glosses the "Urteil/Sein/Möglichkeit" fragment somewhat differently. To Beiser, its gist is that the absolute can't be subjective because self-consciousness involves a distinction between subject and object, which contradicts the subject-object identity of the absolute (pp. 386–91). Like Henrich, Beiser sees Hölderlin as part of a movement away from Kant, toward absolute idealism. Hölderlin's critical move is to affirm the aesthetic sense as that which gives us an intellectual intuition and hence knowledge of the absolute, a knowledge we can't otherwise obtain (pp. 391–97). The problem with this story is that neither Henrich nor Beiser goes beyond 1799. My own belief is that the late poems (like "Patmos") offer further theoretical developments not described anywhere in Hölderlin's prose.

3. Some of the early twentieth-century work on Hölderlin had a tendency to favor other modes of awareness over philosophy/theory. See, for instance, the biographical/critical essay on Hölderlin by Wilhelm Dilthey in his *Poetry and Experience*, ed. Rudolf Makkreel and Frithjof Rodi (Princeton: Princeton UP, 1985), pp. 303–83. After Dilthey, the most influential figure in Hölderlin interpretation was undoubtedly Martin Heidegger. *Erläuterungen zu Hölderlins Dichtung* (Frankfurt am Main: Klostermann, 1971) gathers a number of his pieces. Of these, "Hölderlin und das Wesen der Dichtung" (particularly pp. 36–38) is especially relevant to "Patmos." Because his terminology takes over Hölderlin's own, much of what Heidegger says has a unique resonance. The only fault (as with Dilthey) is to stress concepts like *aletheia* or *Erlebnis* over Hölderlin's own *topoi*.

4. On the dynamic of near versus far, see Karlheinz Stierle, "Dichtung und Auftrag: Hölderlins Patmos-Hymne," *Hölderlin-Jahrbuch* 22 (1980–81): 47–68. Stierle portrays the near/far tension of strophes 1–9 as resolved in strophes 10ff. by an affirmation of the immediacy of song as the mission of poetry, rather than representation.

5. On expressivity versus nonexpressivity in Hölderlin imagery, see Timothy Bahti, *Ends of the Lyric*, pp. 114–27.

6. In '*Kubla Khan*' and The Fall of Jerusalem: *The Mythological School in Biblical Criticism and Secular Literature 1770–1880* (Cambridge: Cambridge UP, 1975), Elinor Shaffer argues for the poem's initial scene as a displaced Edenic landscape, and the Last Supper narrative as a visionary re-creation similar to that of early Hegel (pp. 157, 167–71). More broadly, she traces the roots of "Patmos" back to biblical Higher Criticism in eighteenth-century Germany. But the second half of her explication departs from a more literal early Christian framework without explanation of why a more general mythological standpoint is necessary.

7. On the difficulty of reconciling Greek gods with Christ in Hölderlin, see Peter Szondi, *Hölderlin-Studien* (Frankfurt am Main: Insel, 1967), pp. 66–70. Szondi also discusses religious syncretism (pp. 62–64) and signs/names of the God (pp. 71–73).

8. On the detachment of images from narrative in the Last Supper sequence of "Patmos" as a deliberate strategy, see Eric Santner, *Friedrich Hölderlin* (New Brunswick: Rutgers UP, 1986), pp. 106–10, 114–19.

9. Not surprisingly, work on "Patmos" has been especially favorable to *Heilsgeschichte,* or sacred history scholarship. Much of the preliminary labor was done by Wolfgang Binder, "Hölderlins Patmos-Hymne," in his *Hölderlin-Aufsätze* (Frankfurt am Main: Insel, 1970), pp. 362–402. In addition to identification and elucidation of many of the poem's scriptural references, Binder stresses several ways in which "Patmos" differs from orthodox religious belief: (1) Christ without the doctrine of Atonement, which the poem sees as unnecessary; (2) Christ not as Revelation (spoken Word) but in his *historical* appearance; and (3) the naming of God as the goal of the poem, with the poem itself as a process toward that end (see esp. pp. 363–68).

10. On the figure of the sower, see Andrzej Warminski, " 'Patmos': The Senses of Interpretation," in his *Readings in Interpretation: Hölderlin, Hegel, Heidegger* (Minneapolis: U of Minnesota P, 1987), esp. pp. 80–82. I find Warminski highly persuasive on this motif, and have incorporated much of his material into my own discussion.

11. On progressive revelation and the divine economy, see P. H. Gaskill, "Meaning in History: 'Chiliasm' in Hölderlin's 'Patmos,'" *Colloquia Germanica* 11 (1978): 19–52 (esp. pp. 26–36). Gaskill is particularly good on these topics, which he traces to the influence of German Pietism and specifically Johann Albrecht Bengel (pp. 19–26). His later remarks on the dangerous nearness of the God and the need for Scripture (pp. 36–45) are less open to the radical risks the poem appears to take.

12. For an interpretation that focuses on the aftertime as the crucial section of the poem, see Jochen Schmidt, *Hölderlins geschichtsphilosophische Hymnen* (Darmstadt: Wissenschaftliche Buchgesellschaft, 1990), pp. 185–288. The fullest, most detailed discussion of "Patmos" to date, Schmidt takes up many of the insights in Gaskill and Binder, but places more stress on the theological development of Hölderlin and those closest to him (Hegel, Schelling) in the Tübingen *Stift*. For Schmidt, "Patmos" is about the process by which the *pneuma* or *Geist*, the Spirit, gets expressed in history (pp. 197–98, 233–34). As Schmidt sees it, God is difficult to grasp because of historical separations, but the Spirit acts as a unifier both in general and in the Last Supper sequence specifically (pp. 201–4, 220–24). Afterward, it becomes necessary for the Apostles and their successors to get away from a desire for the image of Christ, his literal presence. The high point of the poem, for Schmidt, comes with the perception of Christ as the imageless sign, the consummation of history brought about by the *Gemeingeist*, or unity in Spirit (pp. 249–50). But if Schmidt and his predecessors in the *Heilsgeschichte* perspective on Hölderlin point toward a historical process of some kind, what they don't explain is why the poet should see it as fraught with difficulty. For that, I would argue, we need to think about Hölderlin vis-à-vis German idealism and, more broadly, theory.

Although my book focuses mostly on forms of theory in the Romantic period, it's perhaps only natural for any study of this kind to be construed (to some extent) as an attempt to propose a new paradigm for Romantic studies. With that in mind, I begin with some earlier efforts to define the field conceptually.

In his well-known position piece "On the Discrimination of Romanticisms" (rpt. in Lovejoy, *Essays on the History of Ideas* [Baltimore: Johns Hopkins P, 1948], pp. 228–53), A. O. Lovejoy questioned the feasibility of such a project. His challenge produced an equally well-known rejoinder by René Wellek, "The Concept of Romanticism in Literary History" (rpt. in Wellek, *Concepts of Criticism*, ed. Stephen Nichols [New Haven: Yale UP, 1963], pp. 128–98). Unlike Geoffrey Hartman, I don't see the debate as a standoff (see *The Fate of Reading* [Chicago: U of Chicago P, 1975], p. 277). Instead, I would argue that what Wellek demonstrated was the possibility of a conceptual link between different national literatures in the Romantic period. He also showed that if you viewed some of the internal conflicts within the period (e.g., between Weimar Classicism and Jena Romanticism) at a higher level of generality, you could achieve conceptual definition in a meaningful way.

Before deconstruction began to have an impact on Romantic studies, the most influential attempt at a conceptual synthesis was clearly that of M. H. Abrams, in his *Natural Supernaturalism* (New York: Norton, 1971). Once considered the standard account of the period, it has in recent years been criticized for a variety of weaknesses: (1) that it wasn't sufficiently open to Romantic indeterminacy or irony and its capacity to destabilize or undermine any sort of Romantic ideal; (2) that it failed to recognize the importance of noncanonical authors, and especially of gender as an issue in Romantic literature; and (3) that its exclusively literary perspective blocked any perception of how Romantic literature might be determined by economic and/or other material forces. Yet these claims, even if true, didn't suffice to justify the negative assessment of the critique. Nor did they entirely invalidate his considerable achievement. After all, the kind of Romantic idealism Abrams described had the capacity to absorb Romantic irony, and the omissions his work displayed didn't necessarily nullify the value of what he discussed but only limited it. Other problems, however, seem more significant, because more internal. First, Abrams deliberately restricted the scope of his study to Romantic literature and philosophy. And because he didn't look at any other forms of cultural activity, he couldn't really make the larger claims necessary for a conceptual synthesis of the entire period. Thus his attempt at a synthesis ultimately rested on an insufficient base. Second, and perhaps more important, his analysis of Romantic concepts wasn't sufficiently theoretical. By that I mean he didn't take them to a higher level of generality, which would have allowed them to range over any given field. As a result, they were deprived of explanatory force. Instead, his treatment of German philosophy reduced it to a purely thematic level (e.g., Hegel's *Phenomenology* as a narrative of the circuitous journey). To some extent, moreover, these two problems reinforced each other: because he didn't consider other forms of cultural activity, he lacked the incentive for a higher level of generality. And because he opted to avoid that higher level, he lacked the appropriate framework for a broader cultural assessment.

At roughly the same time, two important position papers pointed to a felt need for more emphasis on reflexivity within Romantic texts. In "Romanticism and Anti-Self-Consciousness" (rpt. in *Beyond Formalism* [New Haven: Yale UP, 1970], pp. 298–310), Geoffrey Hartman approached the issue from a perspective largely shaped by phenomenological criticism and especially the Geneva *critique de conscience* of Georges Poulet and others. Meanwhile, Harold Bloom in "The Internalization of Quest Romance" (rpt. in *The Ringers in the Tower* [Chicago: U of Chicago P, 1971], pp. 12–35) came at reflexivity from a background of myth criticism, derived from Northrop Frye, and psychoanalysis. Inevitably, both papers now seem slightly dated as the perspectives they rested on have passed into the history of criticism in the later twentieth century. Moreover, neither *mythos* nor consciousness could quite explain why the reflexive turn occurred: why self-consciousness led to anti-self-consciousness, or why the quest romance had to be internalized. As theoretical constructs, in other words, *mythos* and consciousness weren't sufficiently analytical. And that placed a limit on their critical usefulness. Nonetheless, the emphasis on reflexivity in these papers helped highlight a crucial aspect of Romantic literature, and especially Romantic theory.

A similar lack of explanation could be said to characterize *The Literary*

Absolute of Philippe Lacoue-Labarthe and Jean-Luc Nancy, which appeared a few years later (1974, English translation by Philip Barnard and Cheryl Lester [Albany: SUNY P, 1988]). But here we seem to get closer to one: the notion of a Romantic literary absolute as defined by autoproduction (pp. 11–12) at least gives us a generative principle for Romantic art. And the idea of criticism as necessary to the formation of a work of art, of the formation of Form as the essence of Romantic art, linked the generative principle to a mode of self-consciousness or reflexivity (pp. 104–6, 110–12). What Lacoue-Labarthe and Nancy didn't explain, however, was how reflexivity or criticism could act as a generative principle for art.

If *The Literary Absolute*, based on Friedrich Schlegel and Jena Romanticism, tried to characterize the Romantic period solely by means of theory, other studies such as Marilyn Butler's *Romantics, Rebels, and Reactionaries* (Oxford: Oxford UP, 1981) are by contrast purely historical. The advantage of a purely historical perspective is greater width or scope: Butler manages to incorporate women writers of the 1790s like Ann Radcliffe and Maria Edgeworth (pp. 94–97), conservatives like Austen and Scott (pp. 97–109, 109–12), James Gillray and caricature (pp. 53–57), and the professional intellectual as a type in both England and Germany (pp. 69–77). The disadvantage of such a perspective is that it becomes hard to discern any differences that aren't merely local. To put it another way: without larger differences, we miss a sense of structure.

Even before, the impact of deconstruction had already begun to make itself felt. In *English Romantic Irony* (Cambridge: Harvard UP, 1980) Anne Mellor taxed *Natural Supernaturalism* for its failure to discuss Romantic texts that were "open-ended and inconclusive" (p. 6). As an alternative model, she proposed Romantic irony, with explicit acknowledgment of its link to Paul de Man and deconstruction (pp. 4–5). Unfortunately, Friedrich Schlegel (from whom she derived her notion of irony) is too narrow a base: if irony is to be our point of departure, we need a larger *rapprochement* between English and German Romanticism (Tieck, Hoffmann, et al.). Nor does Mellor mention how close Schlegelian irony is to Hegelian negativity, which perpetually undoes itself. And that would make Romantic irony closer to the "circuitous journey" motif of *Natural Supernaturalism* than she allows for. A later example of the same ironic perspective is L. J. Swingle, *The Obstinate Questionings of English Romanticism* (Baton Rouge: Louisiana State UP, 1987). Unlike Mellor, Swingle doesn't think it's a good idea to start with either eighteenth- or nineteenth-century philosophical tradition. Instead, he opts for a "somewhat less formal, more literary model of the intellectual situation that induces Romantic questioning" (pp. 11–12). As a result, he surrenders the possibility of a link to German or European Romanticism. At the same time, by this loss of historicity, his book risks the repetitiveness of a deconstructive exercise: if the aim of Romantic questioning is just to free up an "open space of creative opportunity" (p. 77), what isn't clear is why we need to go through the process repeatedly.

The introduction of previously neglected women writers into the Romantic canon marked a major change in Romantic studies. Although the work was begun by Marlon Ross in *The Contours of Masculine Desire* (New York: Oxford UP, 1989), I want to focus on Anne Mellor's *Romanticism and Gender* (New York: Routledge, 1993) because it discusses other genres besides poetry and so widens the field considerably. The addition of so many new authors across a broad range of genres proved immensely beneficial. And because of the tendency of women's writing in the Romantic period to reflect one or another tradition, any recovery project concerned with this material naturally had inherent historical value. Several significant issues, however, remain to be addressed: (1) Confusion at the terminological and even at the conceptual level. Gender is always tricky to talk about. But when both male and female writers display traits of the other gender (Emily Brontë and John Keats in part III, for example, or the male poets' "takeover" of female traits described on pp. 23–24), the usefulness of any characterization in terms of gender must obviously come into question. (2) Ideological ambivalence. If Mary Wollstonecraft and a number of other women writers are progressive, many (Felicia Hemans, Letitia Landon, et al.) clearly aren't. The imbalance makes for an awkward situation. Ideally you don't want to back a lot of conservative authors. Yet in her conclusion Mellor has to admit: "the ideological investments of most of the women writing between 1780 and 1830 in England have more in common both with their eighteenth-century forebears . . . and with their Victorian descendants" (p. 210). Still, Mellor obviously wants to try to make a case for the entire group. Subsequently she says: "Indeed, from a late twentieth-century perspective, we might see Victorian literature as a *regression* from the more liberated stance of feminine Romanticism" (p. 212). But if most women writers in the Romantic period are in fact conservative, how do we justify her characterization of the "liberated stance of feminine Romanticism"? (3) Lack of relation to Romantic theory. While many women writers have now begun to be explored, we still lack a way to connect their work to theory in the period. Without that, we can't quite arrive at an overall picture of the Romantic scene.

Another significant trend of the past decade has been toward the study of nationalism and nation-formation. In *Romanticism, Nationalism, and the Revolt Against Theory* (Chicago: U of Chicago P, 1993), David Simpson brought it to bear in a fruitful way on the Romantic period. His argument that an attitude toward theory marked a national tendency made it possible to see the cultural work of the entire period as a product of the interplay between different national forces. Its only weakness was that it didn't sufficiently sort out different pro-theory stances that are ideologically fairly close but that differ on the proper direction for theory (German idealism, for example, or versions of rationalism in England). By contrast, Katie Trumpener, *Bardic Nationalism* (Princeton: Princeton UP, 1997), is much less interested in theory. Nor do we get the international perspective of Simpson. Moreover, the focus has narrowed to a single genre (the Romantic novel). The advantage is that we now get to observe the process of nation-formation much more closely. For Trumpener, nationalism is intimately linked to the work of cultural recovery. The implication is that a way of life that characterizes a particular region can itself be a repository of value. So we find Scottish or Irish nationalism set against British imperialism. But one might ask whether such a perspective doesn't tacitly subscribe to a form of cultural essentialism (the region, with its way of life, intrinsically has value: all we have to do is affirm it). Nor is it proof against the kind of national relativism espoused by E. J. Hobsbawm in *Nations and Nationalism Since 1780* (Cambridge: Cambridge UP, 1992) (see esp. pp. 180–92).

Perhaps the most sophisticated example of New Historicist work on the Romantic period to date is James Chandler's *England in 1819* (Chicago: U of Chicago P, 1998). Unlike Trumpener, Chandler offers a lot of theoretical framework for his analysis of the period. In fact, you might even say his point has as much to do with historiographical self-consciousness as it does with historical consciousness: that the first is our only means of access to the second. The deftest move of Chandler's work was to embed the historical moment of 1819 within a framework formed by our own historiographical perspective (see esp. pp. xiii–xvi, 3–7, 31–39, 105–14, 135–51, 169–85). But its silence on most of the theoretical work produced by the Romantic period itself meant that the kind of analysis it advanced would have to be theoretical rather than metatheoretical. And that left it open to the possibility of an end-around move, a counter-analysis by theoretical forces within the period. In other words, its refusal to subsume Romantic theory into its own story left open the possibility that Romantic theory might tell a different story. On some level, we can see such an omission as dictated by the Marxist assumption that a period can't possess a full theoretical awareness of its own activity, that it's the privilege of historical hindsight to have a monopoly on theory. Yet the limit of any theoretical monopoly must inevitably lie in those forms of theory that remain beyond its control.

A number of recent developments show promise. In his *Romanticism at the End of History* (Baltimore: Johns Hopkins UP, 2000), Jerome Christensen has suggestively proposed 1798/ 1802/1815 as a way to think about the structure of the Romantic period (pp. 3–8). But perhaps the most noteworthy new development is to be found in Paul Hamilton, *Metaromanticism* (Chicago: U of Chicago P, 2003). Unlike Chandler, Hamilton sees the Romantic project as inclusive of self-critique (pp. 1–4). Specifically, it produces its self-critique by creative discourse in another sphere, and so acts as Romanticism and metaromanticism simultaneously (pp. 17–18). In this fashion, Romantic theory looks toward the development of metatheory.

~

Any attempt to think about Romantic theory in its historical context has to think about its relation to what's clearly the most important event of the period: the French Revolution. Here I draw first of all on the works of Georges Lefebvre, particularly some of his late surveys: *The French Revolution from Its Origins to 1793*, tr. Elizabeth Moss Evanson (New York: Columbia UP, 1962); and *The French Revolution from 1793 to 1799*, tr. John Hall Stewart and James Friguglietti (New York: Columbia UP, 1964). Although the revisionist critique first advanced by Alfred Cobban in *The Social Interpretation of the French Revolution* (Cambridge: Cambridge UP, 1964) and later more fully developed by François Furet in *Interpreting the French Revolution*, tr. Elborg Forster (Cambridge: Cambridge UP, 1981) and elsewhere did much to erode the Marxist explanation established by Lefebvre and his predecessors, it didn't affect his analysis of the radical reformist tendency of the Terror. What Lefebvre discovered was a particular kind of logic in the legislative work of the Terror, one that might help to explain what Simon Schama characterized in *Citizens* as its almost unnatural efficiency. I see the same extremist rigor at the base of French clinical reform in the hospital and hence as the background to my discussion of Bichat and the French medical scene.

In the wake of revisionist work on the Revolution, it's become increasingly clear that any attempt to grasp the processes involved will have to survey these at the micro-level. Of exemplary value here are the works of Richard Cobb, especially *The People's Armies*, tr. Marianne Elliott (New Haven: Yale UP, 1987); *The Police and the People* (London: Oxford UP, 1970); and *Death in Paris* (Oxford: Oxford UP, 1978). Equally important, in other ways, are George Rudé, *The Crowd in the French Revolution* (Oxford: Clarendon, 1959); and Colin Lucas, *The Structure of the Terror* (London: Oxford UP, 1973). Nor should I fail to mention their model predecessor: Georges Lefebvre, *The Great Fear of 1789*, tr. Joan

White (New York: Pantheon, 1973). What Cobb, Rudé, and Lucas showed in impressive detail was how the Revolutionary impulse managed to make itself felt in everyday life, in both Paris and the provinces: the creation of a gendarmerie as a popular force, the formation and role played by the crowd in Paris, and the structure and transmission of provincial Revolutionary authority. In their work we get a sense not only of which forms the Revolutionary impulse took, but also of those subtler ways in which the Revolutionary fervor of the *menu peuple* transformed the emotional life and above all the outlook of a nation. From studies like these, we become aware of how causality in the French Revolution typically takes the form of a stage-by-stage progression: from spontaneous mass movements that initially express an impulse we move to institutional arrangements that embody it, and finally to their activity and its consequences for a wider sphere. Hence in my study of Bichat and the French hospital scene I move from the physical circumstances of the Hôtel-Dieu in Paris to the institutional circumstances of Revolutionary medicine and finally to its ideological circumstances, as a prelude to vitalist theory.

Because they open up the possibility of eighteenth-century cultural influences on theory, works on the origin of the Revolution are also useful: for example, Georges Lefebvre, *The Coming of the French Revolution*, tr. R. R. Palmer (Princeton: Princeton UP, 1947); and its revisionist counterpart, William Doyle, *Origins of the French Revolution* (New York: Oxford UP, 1980/1988). A considerable amount has also been done on the cultural sources of the Revolution itself (e.g., Robert Darnton, Lynn Hunt, Roger Chartier). Nonetheless, what isn't clear is whether any of the pre-Revolutionary cultural sources can actually be said to exert any kind of direct effect on the Revolution. And this is a problem that goes all the way back to the work done by Daniel Mornet. For that reason, I haven't tried to impose Rousseau or any of the other pre-Revolutionary sources on actual Revolutionary circumstances, but have instead treated these separately (chap. 1).

For any study of the Romantic period as a whole, a crucial question has to be how to define the exact relationship between the Revolution and the Empire. On that issue, the best treatment to date is probably D.M.G. Sutherland, *France 1789–1815: Revolution and Counter-Revolution* (New York: Oxford UP, 1986). Here the continuity between Revolution and Empire is to some extent one of necessary sequence: any action produces an equal and opposite reaction = revolution by a well-placed urban population produces a counter-revolution by disaffected agrarian masses. The counter-revolution alone is the subject of Jacques Godechot, *The Counter-Revolution: Doctrine and Action 1789–1804*, tr. Salvator

Attanasio (New York: Howard Fertig, 1971). We get a slightly different perspective from Louis Bergeron, *France under Napoleon*, tr. R. R. Palmer (Princeton: Princeton UP, 1981). For Bergeron, Napoleon is both the preserver of the Revolution and an Enlightenment sovereign. I see this combination of development + rationality as a key to how the Napoleonic regime could affect Romantic theory, which is largely a product of the Empire period. In Wolf, Friedrich Schlegel, and Hegel we find the same mix of development + rationality. Nor should the decisive effect of Napoleon on Germany come as a surprise: in *Germany from Napoleon to Bismarck,* tr. Daniel Nolan (Dublin: Gill & Macmillan, 1996) Thomas Nipperdey asserts that even German resistance and reform are determined by Napoleon's conquest and administration of Germany. The same point was already borne out by Friedrich Meinecke in *The Age of German Liberation, 1795–1815,* tr. Peter Paret (Berkeley: U of California P, 1977).

∿

Besides the French Revolution, I've also found it necessary to think about several sources of theory from a historical perspective: (1) preromanticism, (2) the sciences, and (3) German idealism.

For the first, my point of departure (as my use of the iconography of Rousseau's tomb will have made evident) is that a turn to the visual is crucial for preromanticism. Here I draw on John Barrell, whose argument in *The Dark Side of the Landscape* (Cambridge: Cambridge UP, 1980) has to do with the unrepresentability of the rural poor as they actually are within the English landscape tradition from Gainsborough to Constable. Since the period Barrell covers (1730–1840) encompasses the transition from preromantic eighteenth century to Romanticism, his analysis can help to uncover what preromanticism was all about.

But if we take the primacy of the visual as constitutive for preromanticism, it tacitly sets up the possibility of a link between the visual and the verbal that can be read in at least two ways. One way would be to see the visual as a substitute for the verbal: the language of the picture says what we can't say verbally. Thus Ronald Paulson in *Literary Landscape: Turner and Constable* (New Haven: Yale UP, 1982). For Paulson, the literary landscape involves the use of landscape as a backdrop for human activity. Under these circumstances, the landscape offers a commentary on the human condition and so acts as a substitute for what we might say about it verbally. But Turner and Constable, as Paulson sees it, go beyond any verbal formulation. In the process, they perfect and ultimately transcend the literary landscape genre. Another way to see the visual-verbal link would be to trace a tendency toward the visual within the verbal medium itself.

This was the route Paul van Tieghem took, in *Le Sentiment de la Nature dans le Préromantisme Européen* (Paris: Nizet, 1960). For van Tieghem, the dominant mode of much preromantic literature was essentially descriptive. By various means, literature worked to paint or render nature mimetically. Its efforts focused on particular aspects of nature (the countryside, mountains, the sea). And that led to the expression of sentiment or emotion, especially in the form of reverie.

In one respect, however, the two ways of looking at the visual-verbal link that I've described share a basic similarity: both posit a split between the visual image and what can be expressed verbally. And that, to my mind, is precisely what made preromanticism possible: the absence of an exact verbal equivalent to the visual image engenders emotion around the visual, which produces the kind of sensibility we associate with preromanticism.

Two recent explorations of preromanticism treat the subject somewhat differently. In his *Preromanticism* (Stanford: Stanford UP, 1991), Marshall Brown stresses such *topoi* as self-consciousness, space, time, articulation, and form, while Isaiah Berlin, in lectures issued as *The Roots of Romanticism*, ed. Henry Hardy (Princeton: Princeton UP, 1999), considers preromanticism a kind of outlook that doesn't believe in either rationality or solvability or compatibility but that does believe in self-affirmation and creativity. Neither, then, lays any particular stress on the visual or its link to the verbal.

In my chapters on the sciences in the Revolutionary or Romantic era, I try to take account of several major shifts in historiography on the period.

Much of the best early work adopted an approach similar to the prosopography practiced by Ronald Syme and others on the Roman Empire: it looked at the careers of prominent men in French science during the Romantic era and their links to each other, especially through Napoleon. Thus Maurice Crosland, *The Society of Arcueil* (Cambridge: Harvard UP, 1967). Despite reservations voiced by recent scholarship, the approach worked to some extent: lines of filiation are useful in the sciences when it comes to influence or thought transmission, and I make use of a similar tactic in my presentation of Bichat via his mentor Desault.

Meanwhile, other scholarship employed a very different strategy, one that attempted to conceptualize the sciences. Not, however, by means of concepts produced by the period itself, but rather by larger theoretical constructs loosely based on the material. So we have Georges Canguilhem, *La Connaissance de la vie* (Paris: Vrin, 1965) and *Études d'histoire et de philosophie des sciences* (Paris: Vrin, 1968). This approach was subsequently historicized and given even wider scope by Michel Foucault in *Les mots et les choses* (*The Order of Things*)

(New York: Random House, 1970). Here Foucault traced the emergence of the human sciences back to what he called the Classical episteme, a seventeenth-/eighteenth-century moment defined by belief in a correspondence between things and their verbal representation. But while such an approach offered the advantages of an overview or higher perspective, it couldn't explain either how exactly a theory arose, or why it was later abandoned. In other words, it couldn't explain historically. Hence in my treatment of theory in the Romantic sciences I've largely preferred to stick to the concepts they produced, in the belief that these afford a better access to the formation and development of any given theory.

More recently, the trend has been toward institutional history: witness Charles C. Gillispie, *Science and Polity in France at the End of the Old Regime* (Princeton: Princeton UP, 1980) with its sequel, *Science and Polity in France: The Revolutionary and Napoleonic Years* (Princeton: Princeton UP, 2004); and Nicole and Jean Dhombres, *Naissance d'un nouveau pouvoir: sciences et savants (1793–1824)* (Paris: Payot, 1989). Both rely heavily on an institutional matrix: the Academy of Science, the Museum of Natural History, the Institute, the Egyptian expedition, the École Polytechnique. Since all of these tend to organize scientific activity, and since they play a particularly important role in the history of the sciences in France, the advantages of such a perspective are evident. Hence my use of the Revolutionary hospital as a framework for Bichat. It doesn't always work, however: the radical or revolutionary makeover of higher algebra by Galois (which I discuss in chap. 6) is a case in point.

For scholarship on the history of German idealism, the main question in recent years has been whether to emphasize the exact process by which idealism emerged after Kant, or to focus instead on the link between idealism and early Romanticism. What's at stake here is the payoff from idealism: those who emphasize the exact process by which it arose seem to believe it can contribute to current epistemology, while those who stress its link to early Romanticism feel its main value might be in its contribution to aesthetic theory.

Representative of the belief in idealism *qua* epistemology are Dieter Henrich, especially *Between Kant and Hegel*, ed. David Pacini (Cambridge: Harvard UP, 2003); and Frederick Beiser, *German Idealism: The Struggle Against Subjectivism, 1781–1801* (Cambridge: Harvard UP, 2002). As Henrich sees it, the motive behind German idealism is the desire to arrive at a coherent theory of self-consciousness that can resolve the problems raised but not solved by Kant, problems that continue to be crucial for current epistemology. Here Fichte has primacy.

In support of the idealism/early Romanticism link, meanwhile, we have Manfred Frank, *Einführung in die frühromantische Ästhetik* (Frankfurt am Main: Suhrkamp, 1989); and Andrew Bowie, *Aesthetics and Subjectivity: From Kant to Nietzsche,* 2nd ed. (Manchester: Manchester UP, 2003) and *From Romanticism to Critical Theory* (London: Routledge, 1997). From the standpoint of Frank and Bowie, the kind of foundational theory of self-consciousness envisioned by German idealism isn't an achievable goal. As Bowie puts it, "What we can consciously know of ourselves does not exhaust what we are" (*Aesthetics and Subjectivity,* p. 63). Instead, they opt for aesthetics as the best way to link the theoretical to the sensuous world and so give our experiences value. Hence their emphasis on Friedrich Schlegel and the Jena circle. The notion of aesthetics as a replacement for a theory of self-consciousness is problematic, simply because it doesn't have the same foundational quality. But so far a theory of self-consciousness via a modified form of Fichte hasn't proved persuasive either.

My own take is that the move in German idealism from Fichte to Hegel involves a radical shift not recognized by either Henrich/Beiser or Frank/Bowie, from epistemology to metatheory. Likewise, I would argue, the move from Kant to Fichte required, in effect, an equally radical shift from classical epistemology to meta-level criteria (Reinhold's programme) for epistemology. Unlike Henrich or Beiser, then, I don't treat Hegel as the last attempt in German idealism to work out a foundational theory of consciousness but rather as the first full-fledged instance of pure philosophical metatheory. At the same time, I concur with Henrich when he asserts that we need to recover the total situation of an individual (life circumstances and all) in order to grasp the philosophy that is the result. Hence my attempt to evoke the circumstances associated with Napoleon and the battle of Jena.

Bichat, Xavier. *Anatomie générale, appliquée à la physiologie et à la médecine*. 2 vols. Paris: Brosson, 1801.

———. *Recherches physiologiques sur la vie et la mort*. Paris: Brosson, 1800.

Butler, Judith. *Subjects of Desire: Hegelian Reflections in Twentieth-Century France*. New York: Columbia UP, 1987.

Coleridge, Samuel Taylor. *Collected Letters of Samuel Taylor Coleridge*, ed. Earl Leslie Griggs. 6 vols. Oxford and New York: Oxford UP, 1956–71.

———. *The Collected Works of Samuel Taylor Coleridge*. Kathleen Coburn, general editor. 16 vols. Princeton and London: Princeton UP and Routledge & Kegan Paul, 1969–2002. Abbreviated as *CC*.

———. *The Notebooks of Samuel Taylor Coleridge*, ed. Kathleen Coburn. 5 vols. New York, Princeton, and London: Bollingen, Princeton UP, and Routledge & Kegan Paul, 1957–2002. Abbreviated as *CN*.

Davy, Humphry. *The Collected Works of Sir Humphry Davy*, ed. John Davy. 9 vols. London: Smith, Elder, 1839–40. Abbreviated as *CW*.

Derrida, Jacques. *Glas*, tr. John P. Leavey Jr. and Richard Rand. Lincoln: U of Nebraska P, 1986.

Galois, Évariste. *Écrits et mémoires mathématiques d'Évariste Galois*, ed. Robert Bourgne and J.-P. Azra. Paris: Gauthier-Villars, 1962.

Hegel, G.W.F. *Briefe von und an Hegel*, ed. Johannes Hoffmeister and Friedhelm Nicolin. 4 vols. Hamburg: Felix Meiner, 1952–81.

———. *Gesammelte Werke*, ed. Nordrhein-Westfälische Akademie der Wissenschaften. Hamburg: Felix Meiner, 1968ff. I use vol. 9: *Phänomenologie des Geistes* for all references to the *Phenomenology*, cited by page and line number only.

Hölderlin, Friedrich. *Sämtliche Werke*, ed. D. E. Sattler. Frankfurt: Stroemfeld/Roter Stern, 1976ff. Abbreviated as *SW*. I use vol. 8: *Gesänge II* for all references to "Patmos."

Rousseau, Jean-Jacques. *Oeuvres complètes*, ed. Bernard Gagnebin and Marcel Raymond. Paris: Gallimard, 1959ff. [Bibliothèque de la Pléiade]. I use vol. 2 for *La Nouvelle Héloise*.

Schelling, F.W.J. *Schellings Werke*. After the original edition in new arrangement, ed. Manfred Schröter. 13 vols. Munich: Beck and Oldenbourg, 1927–59. I cite vol. 2 for the *System des transscendentalen Idealismus*, page number in vol. 2 followed by vol. and page number in the original edition.

Schiller, Friedrich. *Schillers Werke*, ed. Julius Petersen et al. Weimar: Böhlau, 1943ff. I cite vol. 20 for "Über naive und sentimentalische Dichtung."

Schlegel, Friedrich. *Kritische Friedrich-Schlegel-Ausgabe*, ed. Ernst Behler et al. Munich, Paderborn, and Vienna: Schöningh, 1958ff. Abbreviated as *KA*.

Shelley, Mary. *The Journals of Mary Shelley 1814–1844*, ed. Paula Feldman and Diana Scott-Kilvert. 2 vols. Oxford: Clarendon, 1987.

———. *The Letters of Mary Wollstonecraft Shelley*, ed. Betty Bennett. 2 vols. Baltimore: Johns Hopkins UP, 1980–83.

———. *The Novels and Selected Works of Mary Shelley*, ed. Nora Crook et al. 8 vols. London: Pickering, 1996. Cited by volume and page number.

Shelley, Percy Bysshe. *Shelley's Poetry and Prose*, ed. Donald Reiman and Neil Fraistat. 2nd ed. New York: Norton, 2002. Cited for the text of all Shelley poems.

Wolf, Friedrich August. *Prolegomena to Homer, 1795*, ed. Anthony Grafton, Glenn W. Most, and James E. G. Zetzel. Princeton: Princeton UP, 1985.

Žižek, Slavoj. *Tarrying with the Negative: Kant, Hegel, and the Critique of Ideology*. Durham: Duke UP, 1993.